Hall

R.Welland

R.Welland

R.Nene

Peterborough

Peterborough Milton

Oundle

Oundle

erby

R.Nene

Kettering

Thrapston

Kettering
Wellingborough

Raunds

Embankment

llingborough

Rushden

Rushden

John White

St Andrews Hospital

Kingsthorpe

Delapre Park

Collingtree Park

Kingfisher

tlebury Park

GOLF IN NORTHAMPTONSHIRE

1876-2008

A PERSONAL EVALUATION OF GOLF IN THE COUNTY
INCLUDING A DESCRIPTION OF OUR CONNECTIONS
TO THE REGIONAL AND NATIONAL ELEMENTS
OF THE GAME

MARTIN JOHN IZZARD

PREFACE

THIS book describes the evolution of golf in Northamptonshire over the last one hundred and thirty years; this includes the history of male, female and professional elements of the game together with any notable incidents, which have occurred during this period. My focus has been on the county, however, the book also includes a slightly wider view of how golf is played nationally. My challenge being to take a snapshot in time (1876-2008) and provide an accurate description of the past, present and possible future positions of the Clubs and Organisations in the County.

This is inevitably a personal view gathered during my lifetime as a golfer born in the county town in 1955; however, I have also attempted to give the reader a balanced description.

This book would not have been possible without the help, encouragement and assistance from Richard Aitken N.G.U. past President for proof reading the first manuscript, the late Ray Baldwin for permission to use material about the Midland Golf Union from his "Midland History" book, Brian Barron for his N.G.U. sponsored research on the history of golf in Northamptonshire in 1999, Andrews Blows Secretary of the Cambridgeshire Union for his compilation of the Anglian League results and information concerning the formation of the league, *Chronicle and Echo* for results and permission to use material from its website, David Croxton N.G.U. Past President for Chapter 12, Malcolm Evans, Richard Halliday, Angela Howe from The Royal & Ancient Golf Club of St Andrews for clarification and permission to use material from their website, Liz Izzard "The Wife" for emotional support during some dark times and for proof reading some of my "turgid" sentences!, Gillian Kirkwood for permission to use the history of the L.G.U. from their website, Mike Lewis head of Geography at Northamptonshire Grammar School for details on Geology of the County, Harry Lovell for his local knowledge of Boughton and the history of the Whyte Melville public house, Richard Lobb for Chapter 9, Ian Marshall, Peter McKay Archivist at Castle Ashby House, the late Mike McMahon, Brian Mudge for help with the Northants P.G.A.Chapter and information on Staverton Park G.C., Stuart Tipplestone for the excellent aerial photographs from www.tippleston.com, Jane Towler a life long friend at Unilever Research for assistance and care in scanning some faded historical documents during her lunch breaks, Jennifer Prentice and Market Harborough G.C. for permission to use material from their 1998 centenary book, Judy Ray for the history of the N.C.L.G.A. and for co-ordinating many elements of the Ladies contribution, Tony Warren for information on the Society of Northamptonshire Golf Captains, Tom Ward E.G.U. photographer, Eve Wilkins for the Cecil Leitch results, the late Brian Woodcock N.G.U. Past President & his wife Mary for encouragement me to complete this major project.

Also to those golfing and non golfing friends I have chatted to over the last six years too numerous to mention individually who have provided information and encouragement for my many long winter nights spent in front of the computer.

DEDICATIONS

THIS BOOK IS DEDICATED TO

NORTHAMPTONSHIRE'S GOLFERS,

WHO HAVE, LOVED AND DEVELOPED THIS GREAT

GAME TO ITS CURRENT POSITION AND TO THOSE IN

THE FUTURE WE TRUST WILL CARRY ON THE

TRADITIONS AND DEVELOPMENTS OF GOLF IN

OUR COUNTY OF SPIRES AND SQUIRES.

MARTIN JOHN IZZARD

JUNE 2008

Published by the Northamptonshire Golf Union

ISBN 978-0-9520291-3-7

Printed in a limited edition of 1000

Printed in the EU by L.P.P.S. Ltd.
Northampton Road, Wellingborough, Northants NN8 3PJ

CONTENTS

Abbreviations used in this book

A.G.M.	Annual General Meeting
CONGU	Council of National Golf Unions
C.S.S.	Competition Standard Scratch
E.G.U.	English Golf Union
E.G.T.F.	European Golf Teachers Federation
E.L.G.A.	English Ladies Golf Association
E.W.G.A.	English Womens Golf Association
E.S.G.A.	English Schools Golf Association
G.C.	Golf Club
G.B&I	Great Britain and Ireland
L.G.C.	Ladies Golf Club
L.G.U.	Ladies Golf Union
M.G.U.	Midland Golf Union
N.G.U.	Northamptonshire Golf Union
N.L.C.G.A.	Northants Ladies County Golf Association
N.N.R.	National Nature Reserve
N.P.G.A.	Northamptonshire Professional Golf Association
P.G.A.	Professional Golf Association
R&A	The Royal and Ancient Golf Club of St Andrews
S.N.G.C.	Society of Northamptonshire Golf Captains
S.S.S.	Standard Scratch Score
U.S.G.A.	United States Golf Association

INTRODUCTION

A S I sat in my study on the evening of Sunday the 23rd July 2002 reflecting on the Open Championship won by the friendly relaxed South African Ernie Els, I contemplated tackling a bigger project than my first attempt as an author describing Golf at Northampton Golf Club[1]. My first appearance in this relatively arty area by a scientist appears to have been quite well received by a relatively small population of the county's golfers.

During this self-analytical time my eyes happened to fall on the 1930 Flora of Northamptonshire by Claridge Druce[2]. My mind focussed on what he might have been thinking, as he lay awake at night prior to embarking upon his difficult journey to catalogue where each species of plant could be seen in our County. Claridge Druce's efforts acted as an inspiration for me, since if he was able to complete such a monumental task as describing where all the plants were in Northamptonshire in 1930, it should not be too difficult a task to describe the past, present and future of golf in our County.

In the 1970-1990s it was a nice trend that boys & girls were trying out this great game in local schools, driving ranges, local Clubs and with their friends under the supervision of teachers, Club Professionals and people with a passion for the game and subsequently joining golf clubs. Golf is a very traditional game which has a simple code of honesty and trust, many other sports have experienced a deterioration in their standards, the game of golf will not go down this route although it is realised the need to balance the traditions of over six hundred years golf with recent commercially motivated trends. In 2008 there are fewer people taking the game up and we need to find routes to welcome everyone to participate in this physical and mental trial which can bring so much fun and fresh air. This is part of the Sport England Plan which the Northamptonshire County Partnership is supporting as England's leading county, so the spotlight is on Northamptonshire.

It is indeed a pleasure to describe the history of golf in our county and its evolution to the present day with the many organisations and Clubs which have developed and contributed to the game in Northamptonshire. The men's amateur, men's professional and ladies amateur organisations together with results of the respective major competitions are described in their own chapters.

This book also describes some of the history of golf in Britain to illustrate where Northamptonshire's golf is situated administratively within the game. This includes the interaction with the Royal and Ancient Golf Club of St Andrews, the English Ladies Golf Association, the English Golf Union, the Ladies Golf Union and the Midland Golf Union. I hope that readers will find this diversion from Northamptonshire's golf of interest from a wider golf and historical point of view.

My aim was to bring together a significant amount of the information available on the game in

Northamptonshire in one volume. This is therefore a personal impression of this great, almost unequalled time-less game we play here in "the county of spires and squires". I hope that this book might stimulate debate around the Clubs, where Northamptonshire golfers analyse their recent performance, discuss the state of the course and the possibility of playing below their handicap the following day with some new found friends.

If after reading this book you have further information available, I look forward to hearing from you with material for the archive and to receiving any comments on the quality of this publication.

I apologise for any errors that might upset the reader.

Enjoy the read.

CHAPTER 1

THE HISTORY OF GOLF IN NORTHAMPTONSHIRE

1876-2008

"Risk and reward travel side by side. Avoid one, and the other will also pass you by."

ANON

GOLF in Northamptonshire, as we know it today was started by a Scotsman Dr John Allison at Kettering in 1891; he became famous in the town and area. Prior to this date there is positive evidence to indicate that Great Harrowden Hall was probably the first place in the county where golf was formally played. The Hall, part of the estate of Earl Fitzwilliam was used by the Great Harrowden School for Daughters of Gentlemen between 1876-1895 for ladies entertainment, which included golf[3]. This location, currently the home of Wellingborough G.C. very likely, had a course lain out in the grounds and a single Gutty Ball has been found there by Wellingborough's late Past Captain Ken Ellson. A photograph of this ball, which was found in the woods to the right of the ninth fairway, is reproduced here on page 2.

During my research for this book, I have not found a date prior to 1876 linking golf and Northamptonshire. We are therefore left with a slight dilemma in terms of the true start date of golf in the county; factually it is not later than 1891 but could have been as early as 1876. It was certainly after 1848 since the Gutty or to be strictly correct the solid gutta percha ball was first introduced around 1848. Kettering's golf course survives to this date in 2008; Great Harrowden School disappeared over a century ago. Consequently it is my personal judgement that 1891 is the true factual start date, however those of a more romantic disposition might consider it to have been earlier in 1876.

Dr John Allison arrived from Scotland in 1889 aged twenty-six to take up a post in Kettering as a doctor. As a result of his drive and enthusiasm for the game Kettering G.C. was founded two years later in 1891 and golf in the county was established. The first hole at Kettering is named Allison's.

The oldest golf artefact in Northamptonshire. The gutty ball found in the grounds of Harrowden Hall by Wellingborough's late Past Captain Ken Ellson.

He originated from Coldstream in Berwickshire and qualified in Edinburgh, over time and his abilities as a surgeon he became the senior practitioner in Kettering until he retired in 1930. His father was a schoolmaster. Dr Allison persuaded "Old" Tom Morris from St Andrews to set out the Club's original nine-hole course on farmland owed by the Duke of Buccleugh and subsequently became the first Captain of the Club. His enthusiasm for the game was demonstrated on the course when he would personally think nothing of mowing the greens in the morning and trimming up the greens with the sharpened edge of a tobacco tin. The local newspaper reported at the time *"About sixty acres of Mr Grundy's land (the local tenant farmer) have been secured for the links. The course (probably nine holes) will be about a mile and a half in extent. Tom Morris, the custodian at St Andrew's*

links, has already been invited to lay out the course. There are already about thirty members."

The *Golfing Annual* of 1893/94 lists the entrance fee as one guinea and the annual subscription as £1 11s 6d. It also stated that "The town is within easy distance of the meets of four packs of hounds, including the famous Pytchley, and there is good accommodation for visitors, who are always welcome".

A clubhouse was built in 1893 and the top player that year was Norman Dawson who was also one of the founder members of Northampton G.C. One year later the nine-hole course was extended to 18 holes when the first ever professional match to be played in the county marked the occasion. This match was contested by John Henry Taylor one of The Great Triumvirate who in the future became the five times Open Champion (1894, 95, 1900, 09, 13) and Hugh Kirkcaldy, professional at Oxford University.

The following year "JHT" returned to Kettering G.C. to play Alexander "Sandy" Herd for a "purse of gold". Alex Herd became The Open Champion in 1902 and was runner–up four times.

Kettering G.C. also helped to launch the Ryder Cup since the Club contributed £2 towards the fund of £3000 set up by the magazine *Golf Illustrated* in 1927 towards the costs of sending the British professionals for the first ever match between Great Britain and the United States of America. Other Clubs contributed a much lower sum; their contribution of £2 was at the time, a significant amount.

In the county town Northampton, golf was first played in 1892/3, although Northampton golf clubs first site and exact location is almost unknown [4]. Over the last one hundred and ten or so years, Northampton G.C. has moved location twice and is now established at Upper Harlestone close to Althorp House, the seat of the Spencer Family. The Club has, like Kettering G.C. been a strong backbone for Northamptonshire's golf and produced many players and officials who have made an impact on the county's golf scene.

At Northampton G.C. the names of Norman **Daw**son (Captain 1895) and John Havi**land** (1st Club Captain 1894) are remembered in the **Dawland** Trophy. G.A.T.Vials Captain in 1926 was the first secretary of the Northamptonshire Golf Union between 1921-26 and was immediately followed by Frank (F.C.) Wild (Club Captain 1933) between 1926-38.

In 1933 the Club welcomed the flamboyant Walter Hagen to Northampton. As was usual he arrived late, downed two large whiskies and headed to the first tee. Between 1934-1960 Charles Catlow won the County Championship an almost unbeatable eleven times, whilst a member of Rushden (1), Northampton (3) and Northants County (7).

Golf in Northamptonshire

During the 1930s Frank (F.C.) Roe was a prolific winner of titles at the Club and was a member of the County side for 25 years and also Chairman of the Greens Committee for a staggering 20 years. During the 1940s, the club's and some county trophies were stored for safety by the Club's Secretary at his place of employment, the United Bus Company (see page 49).

On the 16th June 1940 Henry Cotton the former Open Champion played an exhibition match at the Club. The three times Open Champion was partnered by the former County Club's professional Len Holland against the 1937 Open Champion Alf Padgham and Northampton professional Jimmy Jones. The four figure total of spectators, were to quote the local press, "spellbound at the quality of the play". On the day several fund raising events took place including the sale of player's golf attire and clubs. Two of Henry Cotton's irons raised 17 guineas.

In 2006 I was contacted by a Rushden gentleman Mr Stevenson now in his eighties who was looking for photographs of the now defunct Kettering Road course and by sheer coincidence caddied at this event. He described it to me as though it was yesterday with great enthusiasm "The crowds were huge and Henry Cotton was powerful even with wooden clubs. The event was called Red Cross day to raise money and I caddied for Mr Holland who was a Northampton member. Henry Cotton easily cut the corner on the eighteenth hole and was only a few score of yards from the green. We caddies had a marvellous time being so close however we were not paid, we were given no tea, no nothing". Later that year, I took him some photographs for his records and we enjoyed reminiscing together, this was the first course I had played, aged fourteen with my Cherry Orchard school friend Michael Luck.

In 1959, Richard G. Halliday became Northampton Golf Club's County Champion and was soon followed by Richard G. Aitken who won the trophy a total of 8 times including five victories as a member of Northampton G.C. before transferring to Northants County G.C. Both Richard's are unique in the fact that they are the only golfers in Northamptonshire to have won the Boys under 21 (at the time a Nett competition, Braid's Driver) Men's and Seniors Championships and are justifiably proud of such achievements. Until about 1970, the Braid's Driver was for the best scratch score in the County Championship by a player under 30 years of age and later changed to under 21.

Richard G. Aitken played in 40 consecutive County Championship; Richard G. Halliday played in the County Championship in six decades starting in the 1950s but did not compete in every year. They were both were presented with a bottle of champagne each to mark these fine achievements at the millennium County Championship held at Northants County (see photograph on page 183).

A further exhibition match took place in 1962 in June when Peter Allis, Bernard Hunt, Dai Rees and Dave Thomas played the old Kettering Road "links". Allis narrowly missing setting a new course record following a missed short putt on the 18th green. During the round he recorded an eagle at the 305 yards second hole having driven the green.

Dave Thomas appeared anxious to impress the gallery, opening his shoulders on the eighteenth tee he put his tee shot some forty yards along Elmhurst Avenue, close to the house once occupied by one of the Clubs Past Captains Glynn Coles. Also during 1962 since the death of Earl Spencer early in the century the post of Club President had not been renewed and moves were afoot to remedy this situation.

At a general Club meeting in 1962 John Arthur Eyton-Jones proposed to those present that the post be recreated and awarded to Bill Hollingsworth "for his work for our Club and for golf" this was warmly approved. Bill Hollingsworth played golf in to his nineties and even had a lesson with Alf Lovelady during his eighties, The Hollingsworth Trophy is the major team trophy played for by almost every Club in the county in 2008. Bill's home Club have recorded eight victories to date, four behind leaders our long term rivals and friends from Kingsthorpe.

Bill Hollingsworth died in 1981 and the position of President was taken over by Harold Shenfield from 1982-1990. Harold's good friend John Arthur Eyton –Jones became Club President in 1991. All three gentlemen were elected life members of the club.

I remember all of them fondly as elderly stalwarts who guided the Club through some major changes. I played no golf with Bill Hollingsworth or Harold Shenfield but was taken aback when I first played against John Eyton-Jones in the late 1970s in my mid twenties. The normal match rates were negotiated and for my first time in my life we were also played for Nett birdies worth two new pence! I also received a great deal of ribbing back in the clubhouse as the young Cherokee (my Kettering Road nickname in view of my long hair) was out driven by a gentlemen in his sixties on the 13th hole, unlucky for some especially the author!

During the 1970s/80s a move to a new location was in the front of most members and the committee's minds which eventually resulted in the Club moving to its current location at Harlestone in 1990.

In 1893 Oundle and Wellingborough Golf Clubs were also formed. Oundle G.C. is still on its original site on Benefield Road which is located west from the beautiful stone town towards the famous remains of Lyveden new Bield. This distinctive lofty partial ruin was built by Sir Thomas Tresham of Rushton (1545-1605) as a lodge or summer-house in the shape of a cross to demonstrate his "stubborn adherence to the Old Catholic Faith". Thomas's son Francis became involved in the Gunpowder plot of 1605 and although only on the edge of the plot was arrested and died in the Tower months after succeeding to the estate. Heavy fines were imposed on the family which resulted in the building work at Lyveden being discontinued as the family were deep in debt and the estate was sold in 1614, after the death of Sir William Tresham in 1634 the family died out[21].

The site of the course was originally an old stone quarry formerly known as Bailey Hills and was a favourite picnic site for the town's folk. Some evidence for excavation can still be seen, notably the shapes of the land around and beside the current eighteenth green. It is unknown who the architect was, players used to change in a small hut before a small pavilion was erected on the site of the old ninth green. The whole course was used as grazing land and the greens were mown "occasionally" by a single greenkeeper who came in one day a week until 1907 when their first full time grounds-man was appointed. He was R. Falconer, a noted cricketer of the time, from Norfolk.

The course reverted to agriculture during the First World War and it was not until 1920 that attempts were made to resurrect the golf course. The course was radically redesigned with only the sixth and eight holes escaping reconstruction. The members accepted all the changes except for one hole, the second which had to be played over a group of beech trees. Northants County professional the well-respected Len Holland was bought in as arbiter. He played the course with his assistant and set a new professional course record of 66 and duly proclaimed the whole course to be to his satisfaction including the second hole. He further declared that the second hole was one of the best short holes in the county.

During the Second World War there was no repeat of the shutdown of 1914-1920. One innovation brought in was to allow students from the Finishing School for Young Ladies at Biggin Hill to join en bloc for an agreed subscription, the scheme attracting 20 members. At the end of the war, Club membership was just 12 although the Club had £132 in the bank.

P. G. Cotton Secretary during the war years was made a life member in 1950 in view of his sterling service under great difficulties and in 1961 was elected President of the Northamptonshire Golf Union, the Club's one and only N.G.U. president to date. Past Club Secretary Gordon Brooks became N.G.U. Secretary in 2001 and served the Union until 2004.

Wellingborough G.C. was founded in 1893 and has used three sites as described in detail in chapter 6. The Club was originally in the town on Nest lane and laid out by Old Tom Morris before moving to the waterworks site in 1923. The current location (1975-present) is a parkland course in the grounds of Harrowden Hall a grade 1 listed building and a superb venue for golf, weddings and corporate events. It was acquired together with 25 extra acres, staff cottages and outbuildings for £125,000 in 1974. The building dates back as far as 1511 when Henry VIII was entertained there by Sir Nicholas Vaux. The Hall featured in the gunpowder plot of 1605 since Lord Vaux is said to have hidden some of the prominent conspirators there. The current building was built to its current form in 1719 as the date is scribed on to two water heads on the south wing, within its walls lies at least one of the late-sixteenth-century hiding places. This is in the former stable block, at one stage the caterers flat, somewhere behind a thick wall at the top of a short staircase.

The location of the hiding places in the main house is not recorded after the building was refurbished in the 1970s. When the Club's excellent Centenary book by Ralph Grey-Jones was produced in 1992[3] there were two or possibly three members who had actually played golf at all three of the Club's venues. One of these gentlemen was Peter James who joined the Club in 1921 and became Club Captain in 1977 and President of the N.G.U. in 1982-83. The Club has over the years produced many quality players and officials for both the men's and ladies game including County Champions J (John).E. Saxby 1965, J.C. (Chris) Hodgson 1974, Duncan.K. Ellson (1988) & Matchplay (1987) and greenkeeper Ian Marshall Matchplay (1990). The Wellingborough Ladies are represented by County Captains Mrs H.Castel 1979-80, Mrs Glenda Abbott 1983-4 and Veterans Captains Mrs.E.Gilbert 1976-77 and Mrs.D.Redden 1992-3. Carol Gibbs, now a member of Wellingborough has won the Ladies County Championship seven times over three decades between 1989-2004 and Roseann Youngman was victorious in 2005.

The three Clubs formed in 1893 played a three-corner celebration competition during their centenary year at all three golf clubs, which became an annual event in the Club's calendars. The author holed in one at Wellingborough's 11th hole during this inaugural event which produced much discussion concerning the purchase of a round of drinks in three clubhouses, drinks at Wellingborough was sufficient for the author's pocket! Rumours around Northampton suggest that Kingsthorpe G.C. came into being through a fit of pique. The Club was founded in 1908 by a group of employees of the old Union Bank now part of the National Westminster in the Drapery, Northampton, after a friend of the manager was apparently refused membership at Northants County G.C. as he was considered to be "trade". This spirit of defiance is still slightly present in some elements of the Club almost a century later, although the story doesn't stand up to too much scrutiny since Kingsthorpe was actually formed a year before Northants County opened!

The original site of the Club was a nine-hole affair off the Harborough Road near to the cemetery but in 1912 land was acquired in what was known as Gypsy Lane and two years later an eighteen-hole course opened. At that time it was on the outskirts of the town but has subsequently been engulfed by council and private housing, making the course the subject of much speculation for a move to a new location over the years.

In 1962 the *Chronicle and Echo* reported that builders Atkins & Shaw were on the verge of the biggest deal in Northampton's history by acquiring Kingsthorpe's 75 acres for houses and building a new course "within two miles of the present site". The plan thought to be on land near Boughton Hall failed to materialise as did a proposed move in the 1980s to land on what is now Brampton Heath GC. Charles Allison secretary at Stoke Poges G.C. laid out the original 18 holes and in the 1930s it was re-designed and enlarged by the famous golf course architect Harry Colt who also laid out Northants County. A press report at the time of Kingsthorpe's opening stated that "its sandy soil and contour of the land will lend itself to making a really sporting course".

In 1914 the Club engaged Ernest Hanton as professional which turned out to be an inspired choice as he stayed until he retired in 1952; he won the German Open during his time at Kingsthorpe G.C. although the records do not confirm this. Members bought hickory shafted clubs constructed by him and on his departure and with steel shafts coming in to fashion Kingsthorpe had a big bonfire to make space for the new style, a scene no doubt repeated over the whole country. With hickory shafted clubs now fetching considerable amounts of money in the memorabilia market one can only speculate how much money went up in smoke!

The competitive nature of the Club is borne out by the Club's record number (12 up to 2007) of Hollingsworth victories and the six County Champions produced over the years. Their first Champion was Egerton Speakman in 1926 who had to give the game up a year later after a coronary thrombosis. He was followed by Mike Haddon in 1981 at Staverton Park in atrocious conditions followed by Steve MacDonald in 1982 (Kingsthorpe) and 1991 at Kettering, Darren Jones in 1987 at Northampton and Neil Goodman in 1989 on his home course. Steve MacDonald has made a significant contribution to the local golf scene and is certainly a well-known character who holds the course record of 63, which has stood since 1985, and in his prime, had one of the best short games around.

He also once beat our mentor and past County B Team Captain Barry Highfield 10 & 8 in a Scratch League match around Kingsthorpe however Barry still managed to find something amusing about it as he recounted the story with a typical laugh "Every time I got a par Steve got a birdie and every time I got a bogey Steve got a par and that was that after an hour and ten minutes". This "fun in adversity" and level of camaraderie undoubtedly arose from the team spirit that was generated on many Anglian League away matches that we played in together during the late 1970s and 1980s and finally won the B league in 1980 under Barry's leadership.

Another very special member who is remembered fondly by so many was Alex Good, who started the *Chronicle & Echo* Team Tournament after moving down from Scotland, where in his youth he trained along side Olympic Champion Eric Liddell, immortalised in the film *Chariots of Fire* for winning the 400 metres in Paris in 1924. The *Chronicle & Echo* tournament became extremely popular and the winners are given in Chapter 6, sadly in 2003 the competition was discontinued. Alex was N.G.U. President in 1977-8 adding his name to the half a dozen or so Presidents that the Club has produced for the N.G.U.

The latest one would have been John Crouch in 2006-2008 however pressure from "other areas" brought about his untimely resignation as Vice President in 2005 after a good period of service to the N.G.U. A new purpose built clubhouse was completed in 2004 with the assistance of many members who are involved in the construction industry; the building is quite spacious and provides good views of the first and eighteenth holes. The opening ceremony took place on the 14th May 2004 and was followed by the Captain's drive-in the following morning.

An explosion of interest in golf at the start of the twentieth century lead a number of the county's dignitaries to convene a meeting at the County Hall on the 14 January 1909 under the chairmanship of Edward Algernon Fitzroy to discuss the possibility of building a course in the Brampton area. Fifteen months later Northamptonshire County G.C. officially opened on the 4 April 1910. Even more remarkably the course was designed in two days by the famous golf architect Harry S Colt, the budget for designing and laying out the course was £1500 pounds. The Club's captain for the first eight years was not surprisingly Edward Algernon Fitzroy. Brampton, as it quickly became known, was founded by landed gentry and their friends, so it was hardly surprising that it came to regarded as the "snobs" Club. This sobriquet was further enhanced in 1932 when a future King of Britain took over the captaincy. The Duke of York was a fourteen handicapper and it turned out to be a purely figurehead appointment as the Duke did not attend any meetings. He did however mark his captaincy by donating a cup (The Duke of York Cup) first won by R.A. ("Peter") Palmer in 1932.

Peter Palmer made a huge contribution to the local golf scene and I would personally describe him as a man with great vision, he was President of the N.G.U. in 1952 and started the Captain's Society in 1965. His parents were founder members of Northants County. The original committee were authorised to approach 170 men and 70 women to become members under the following terms Men's subscription £3 1s. 5d entrance fee £4 2s. 0d; Ladies Subscription £1 0s. 5d: entrance fee £2 6s. 3d. He was given an O.B.E. in 1972 for his work as a Justice of the Peace. In 2006 Peter is 93 years of age and still has a great deal of energy, he regularly attends Sunday worship at St Botolphs in Church Brampton. He is the oldest N.G.U. President and even now sends apologies for annual council meetings and A.G.M. which I am sure he would attend if able.

The route to play the 18 hole course has changed several times over the years (see Appendix by Charles Catlow in reference 5). It is widely regarded as the best course in the county and as a result has hosted many regional and national events. On a national level many golfers have heard of Church Brampton and have no idea that Northampton and Brampton Heath are within a couple of miles from "Brampton". In recent times visitors to the area often arrive at the wrong Club. Most recently (2004) a further three magnificent tree lined holes have been added. There are now many routes to play quick nine holes or the full eighteen although there is obviously an allowed route to prevent congestion.

When the Northamptonshire Golf Union was formed in 1921 it was a Brampton man, Fredrick Bostock who became the first president and his son Lancelot was the first county champion to collect the trophy presented to the union by his father the following May at Brampton. The Bostocks were linked by marriage to another great sporting Northamptonshire name, the Mobbs, and between them between 1910 and 1988 the two families had claimed an amazing 69 Brampton titles. The Club has produced many quality golfers and officials such as Charles Catlow who won the county championship a record eleven times between 1934 and 1960, his son-in law Richard Aitken also won the title eight times taking on the mantle between 1962 and 1977. Brampton men have been President of the N.G.U. for 25 of its 85-year history and have produced a record 34 County Champions.

The Club also has the only two Honorary Life Members of the N.G.U. in Richard Catlow and Richard Halliday who were both given this prestigious award for their excellent service to golf in the county over several decades. The County Champion (2004) was sixteen-year-old Stuart Ashwood who scored 74+71 over his home course to become the youngest ever County Champion. Stuart achieved a clean sweep that day by not only becoming County Champion but also won the Parsons Cup for the best handicap score and the Braid's Driver for the best performance from a player under 22 years of age. Also that year he became the Boys Champion and winner of the N.G.U. Order of Merit to add to a wonderful season where he played in the England School's team against Wales and Scotland as Vice Captain. He is currently studying at the University of Louisville Kentucky USA and enjoying the challenge of intercollegiate league matches. Stuart also became County Champion in 2008.

Rushden G.C. was started around 1908 by a group of well-heeled boot and shoe owners at a site close to near-by Stanwick. A horse and cart used to trot around the town picking up players and transporting them the mile or so to the course believed to have consisted of six holes. The land was used for grazing in the Great War and when hostilities ceased the Rushden and District Club found a new home at Kimbolton Road on the outskirts of Higham Ferrers, which opened in 1919. The Club badge which is proudly worn by many members shows a sheep to denote their farming past, a leather bucket, symbolic of the leather trade, the heraldic lion depicting Duchy of Lancaster ownership and wavy lines to represent the ridge and furrow farming style carried out on the original land.

The Club dropped it's "& District" part of its title in 1986 is still on Kimbolton Road and uniquely consists of only 10 holes on its 78 acres. For sixty years between 1919-1979, Rushden had the normal quota of nine holes, sharing the course with a flock of sheep owned by the Duchy of Lancaster's tenant farmer Harry Robinson. It was described as an uneasy alliance since Robinson was a keen Shire horse breeder but was none too keen on golfers. When Robinson died Rushden acquired 10 more acres and a great more control over their own destiny. However, the land was still owned by the Queen. A new par three hole was added, which represents the fifth and 14th today, which is played from two different tees to the green and named after the Club's most accomplished member, the late Charles Catlow.

The 11 times, County Champion, designed the hole and the club reciprocated by naming it "The Catlows". The subtle mound on the right and dell to the left affect many tee shots. Unusually, for a nine hole course, the Club had four county players in the 1950s – Charles Catlow, Hugh Denton, Jimmy Sharpe and Ray Kilsby. Jimmy Sharpe was chauffeur to the giant of the shoe industry John White, was a superb player and one of the best anecdotes of bygone days relates to the day he was playing with the junior member. At the 133 yard par three third hole, the youngster inquired which club Sharpe had used. "An eight iron" came the reply from the old-timer. "I used the wedge", beamed the young upstart. "But you're not on the green", said Jimmy who then proceeded to take every club out of his bag including the driver and put a succession of balls on the putting green. The old ones are the best! For the record the rest of the round was played in silence. This particular hole was Charles Catlow's pride and joy. Prior to changes to the course in 1979, it used to be the fifth and the tee was adjacent to the sixth tee. Members used to drive at both holes before finishing off the fifth, a course of action which required special dispensation from the R&A Rules committee. The 243 yards par four hole currently the twelfth (Little Field) was aced by Ian Dickerson some time in the 1980s with a three iron, his first albatross.

Being at the centre of the original shoe trade, Rushden had regular visits from celebrity customers, among them golfing legend, Bobby Locke, the South African who won The Open Championship four times between 1949 and 1957. Bobby Locke always played the course, often to break in a new pair of shoes and was made an honorary member. A faded photograph taken in 1963 of Bobby Locke with three club members (J.A. Sharpe, R. Mackellar and R.W. Kilsby) still hangs in the clubhouse. In 2008 there are about 300 members of which 80 regularly play competitions. Anymore and there would be chaos on the course. There are now some ambitious plans to extend the course to 18 holes.

Daventry and District G.C. is similarly still a nine hole course after 100 years of its existence. Attempts have been many to expand to an 18 hole course only to be thwarted by those seeking to preserve a dim and distant past. As tenants of Christ Church College, Oxford, they have nothing to sell off for housing development in order to relocate so it would appear they are destined to remain a hilly nine hole "Borough Hill" course. The course features the famous second hole which is just 100 yards long straight uphill. I remember in particular in 1976, making my good friend the late Barry Highfield collapse with laughter, when my tee shot which pitched 1 yard short of the green finished out of bounds behind me!

Daventry G.C. started in 1907 but not in its present site. At that time it was very primitive stuff, men in carts sticking flags in the ground. Now one knows where that was, but N.G.U. Past President, Peter Meacock, whose family connection with the course go back decades think it could be Long March fields, which is now part of Southbrook housing estate. The Club moved to its present location in 1911 on land rented from Oxford University, Club records which go back to 1922 have confirmed their Centenary year as 2007.

The location on the edge of Borough Hill is on the site of two Iron Age forts and the Roman encampment. The remains of a Roman villa are beneath the sixth fairway, which is a significant handicap when it comes to developing the course.

When the BBC closed down their transmitters on adjacent Borough Hill 23 years ago there was a window of opportunity for the golf club to expand. The Club attempted to buy 70 to 200 acres which would have given nine flat holes to go with the nine hilly holes. Sadly English Heritage opposed the idea and ultimately won the day when it came before Daventry councillors. Daventry District Council now own the land and it is used only for grazing sheep and the people walking their dogs, although from an ornithological point of view it is quite an important area since it attracts many migrating birds. Overall however it still feels like a wasted opportunity. Christ Church College also refused to budge when it came to the Club attempting to buy the existing site as this was on the basis of since they have owned it for 400 years why sell? The Club has a tenancy agreement which is renewable every 21 years on "generous terms".

In golfing terms Daventry area has been swallowed up during the last 35 years by Farthingstone, Staverton Park and Hellidon Lakes. The Club has suffered slightly and maintains a membership of over 300. The two best players from the Club were probably Jim Punch, (NGU President 1980-1) who was secretary of Danetre Hospital from around 1949, who went on to become a county player as did Barry Highfield, Anglian League second team captain for a record eight years and captain of the 1980 winning team and N.G.U. President 1985-6.

John White G.C. which started as one hole stuck in the corner of a sports field is now a thriving, go-ahead nine hole course that is being eyed up for the par three national competitions. Originally the site was the John White Shoe Company Sports and Social Club sports field, which catered for tennis, rugby, cricket, football and bowls. All except the bar walls have now gone, as has the shoe manufacturing company, once the largest employer in the town. It was a former managing director, George McWatters who had the first hole made and although the Club would not actually admit it, the golf eventually took over from the other sports. Employees played free, members of the public naturally had to pay. When the Ward-White group sold out to Boots the chemist, the pharmaceutical giant discovered it also had a sports ground that it did not want. The members made what was described as a derisory offer and for five years negotiations dragged on. With the help of a £83,074 Sport England grant, the members paid £126,974 +VAT to buy their Club and a watering system in 1997 from the Boots Company, having raised the difference themselves.

At that time the members were in control of their own destiny and the golf club dramatically modernised its facilities, which included knocking down the original clubhouse that dated to around 1930 and building a new one with a professional shop. This was run at the time by chirpy Trevor Eaton, who also ran a golf shop in the town. The Sports England grant was obtained largely by the persistence of Club secretary John Macdonald who sadly passed away in March 2004; the Club were one of the first in England to receive such monies.

Peterborough Milton, opened in 1938 and is the only 18 hole course to be built in Northamptonshire between the two World Wars. The five times Open Champion James Braid designed the course and was the first to play it, when it opened on the 14th of July on land owned by the sixth Earl Fitzwilliam. It took James Braid, golf tutor of Winston Churchill, David Lloyd George and W. G. Grace, all of one day to plan out the course. A walk around the site equipped with stakes a mallet and a few clubs, was all the great man needed to produce some of the finest courses in Britain. The Earl had built a nine hole course a decade earlier, but with Peterborough rapidly expanding decided to extend it in order to avoid any compulsory or unwanted developments close to his stately pile, Milton Hall. He invited two nine hole clubs in the area to amalgamate and form one super club and captain of the new club H.B. Hartley hit the opening tee shot which triggered off a scramble for the ball as a souvenir. The race was won by his chauffeur! Acknowledging the troubled times of the period, Mr Hartley commented in his inaugural address: "If the dictators and the rest who are piling up arms could only establish golf courses for the public instead of upsetting the world, they would perform a better service to humanity".

At the outbreak of war, Milton was kept open. Professional, Archie Thorburn, joined the RAF as a Sergeant Air Gunner, while his father John, a retired professional from Peebles, took over his duties. In April 1942, Archie Thorburn was killed in a flying accident just six months after his father died, after a spell of poor health. The course was turned over to sheep grazing, but that did not stop four major events being held to help war charities. Professional players, among them Henry Cotton, raised over £1,500. 1944 Captain, J.E.G. Hassall, reported at the 1945 A.G.M. on "several outstanding features during my year as captain, the foremost of which is the restoration of peace in this country which has brought with it relief from the mental and physical strain". Bob Gill, one of two surviving founder members 83 years old (in the year 2000) recalled that members paid a guinea a year to retain their membership during the war. James Braid's course design remains largely intact, including the famous 10th hole known as Cotton's Fancy so-called because Henry Cotton eulogised about it in a golf magazine article. The narrow two tier green is extremely difficult to hit especially with a three iron in one's hand.

In the 1990s the installation of an automatic watering system has led to a significant addition to the course, Lake Temptation serves as both a water storage facility and a dominant feature on the 1st and 18th holes. Recently the off course facilities have been upgraded with a half a million pounds extension to the clubhouse. The Club continues to produce many good players at all levels and regularly has players in the county's squads. Somewhat surprisingly the Club has only produced four men's county champions, although at senior level Richard (Old King) Cole won the 2002 Championship at Stoke Albany playing off a handicap of one with a gross score of 73. This was a vintage year for the club when young Matt Peacock also won the men's Championship at Kettering G.C. with a pair of 71s to win by a shot over his County foursomes partner Neil Presto. The finishing holes starting at the fourteenth with views of Milton Hall are some of the most demanding in the county. I am sure that many a good medal card has been ruined over this demanding stretch.

The origins of the nine hole course at St Andrews Hospital are lost in the mists of time, the founding date is nominally stated at 1960. The Secretary can trace nothing further back than 1960, although the hospital has been in Billing Road Northampton since 1844. Much of the course was once used to grow fruit and vegetables to feed patients and staff. When the course dries out in the summer, the layout of the old cress beds can still be seen. The needs of the hospital have always made the golf course vulnerable to expansion, which resulted in the loss of the original starting hole a par three at the start of the 1990s. The course has 18 tees and following the acquisition of Lime Tree Cottage facilities for washing, toiletries, a lounge kitchen and office are now available in this Clubhouse. It also generated a new starting hole (the old 13th) which is an attractive par four which cuts through the heart of the golf course. St Andrews appeals to golfers on both ends of the experience scale. Some players cut their golfing teeth before moving on to a more challenging course, whilst others who find the longer courses too taxing to enjoy the gentle terrain of St Andrews. The Club currently has around 400 male members supplemented by some 60 ladies 60 staff and 14 juniors, mostly from neighbouring Northampton School for Boys.

Golf in the county owes a great debt to the advent of the municipal course which enables all and sundry to try their hand at the game, those who get the bug then move on to play at private clubs. In Northamptonshire the first one of these courses was at Corby. It is entirely appropriate that Corby provided the first golf course for the masses, considering its strong links with Scotland. Corby Council gave the go ahead for the project in February 1961, four years after their first efforts failed because the designated site was needed for industrial development. Their attention was drawn to the Priors Hall quarry site, which was certainly large enough for a course but where no provision had been made for the reinstatement of top soil after opencast working for iron ore. The course, a natural crescent shape allowed designers, Hawtree and Son to create two nines on the horns of the crescent.

A high mound had been left halfway along the outer perimeter of the crescent, which was deemed the ideal spot for a clubhouse whilst full advantage was taken of various features such as permanent hillocks, ponds and areas for future woodland. In the summer of 1961, 50,000 cubic yards of topsoil was spread and levelled on the fairways. At the same time tees and greens were shaped and following a recommendation from the Sports Turf Research Institute it was decided to import top soil for these critical areas which was obtained from a local gravel company.

The summer of 1962 was, apparently, a good one for grass growing which was just as well as 8 tonnes of seed had been sown. The following summer over two miles of underground pipe was laid to create an irrigation system, but as the soil settled the greens were constantly changing their slopes. Whatever the teething problems were, the course opened in May 1965 with temporary wooden buildings where green fees could be payed. The cost of the course (plus car park and drinking water main), less than £19,000 grant received from the ironstone restoration fund came to £34,500 while another £50,000 was spent on building the clubhouse and furnishing it. The course is a very good test of golf and anyone equalling par figures should be proud of themselves.

The course was officially opened on Sunday July the 23rd 1967 with a celebrity fourball which consisted of Dick Kemp the first professional of Priors Hall, Stuart Murray (Northants County), Scottish Ryder Cup star Eric Brown and up-and-coming youngster, Tony Jacklin from nearby Lincolnshire. Dick Kemp used his local knowledge to record a one under par gross score of 71 which comfortably beat Tony Jacklin (77), Eric Brown (78), and Stuart Murray (80). Priors Hall has produced some outstanding county players most notably Malcolm Scott and Ronnie McIlwain (County Champions1984&6 and 1993 respectively) and the Club are still the only Club to win the Hollingsworth Trophy three years in a row (1973-5).

Three private courses opened up in five years during the 1970s when farmers turned land over to recreational purposes and golf for the masses came in at Woodlands, Cold Ashby, Staverton Park and Delapre. Business groups, specifically aimed at the leisure market, began to spring up, although the first course to be opened during the boom period Woodlands (now Farthingstone) in 1974 owed its creation to the enterprise of farmer Don Donaldson. The original construction used up just over 100 acres of land for the golf course which is located next to a famous old piece of ancient woodland, Mantles Heath. In 1989 the course was called Woodlands Vale. Over the years the Club have spent a considerable amount of money on drainage systems and arguably have the finest sprinkler system in the county. The course has some extremely demanding holes notably the 198 yard par three 11th (Gallagher's Lakes) which is across water to an extremely narrow green. The 213 yard par three 13th hole (Knightly Way) with out of bounds close to the green is similarly very demanding.

During the early years of the course's evolution Don had a real battle to be recognised by the N.G.U. and the two sides frequently did not see eye to eye. Nowadays the relationship has improved somewhat as a result of better communication and possibly the appointment of a N.G.U. President from the Club Mike Taylor 2004-6. The original name of Woodlands springs from Wood Farm though nowadays the Club is known as Farthingstone Hotel and Golf Course. The facilities include a 16 room hotel which overlooks the 18th fairway and a restaurant capable of seating 60. The Club is still run by Don Donaldson who is quite proud of what he has achieved.

Also that year Cold Ashby G.C. was greeted with lukewarm interest from the hierarchy of the time. It was surely destined to become a golf course as it is built on land originally known as Bunkers Hill farm. It nestles on the western slopes of a piece of land known as Honey Hill. Four generations of the Lill family have been associated with Bunkers Hill, and Mick Lill who originally applied for planning permission back in 1972, is still very much part of the Club. Bunkers Hill got its name from the fact that some old farm buildings apparently bore some resemblance to some early American fortifications at the Battle of Bunker's from the US Civil War!

Mike Lill applied to convert 130 acres of undulating farmland into a golf course without actually telling his father, John. When he eventually plucked up the courage to do so Mick was greatly relieved with his dad's reaction that it sounded like a "good idea". Alphagreen, who owned five golf courses, took over the lease and John Day an amateur golfer, won the commission to design Cold Ashby. The course opened in June 1974, just four years into their leasehold, Alphagreen wanted out and much to his surprise, a package put together by the then vice captain, David Croxton to become proprietor was accepted. David who later became Cold Ashby's first N.G.U. President (1998-2000) took over as vice-captain on December 12 1978 and the following year became Club captain. In 1983 the course was lengthened and to mark the occasion, David invited the young Welshman Ian Woosnam to play Club professional Simon Ward in an exhibition match. Woosie, then virtually unknown brought along a young South African, David Frost to play in the match, both players going on to become greats of the game. Woosie's 67 set a course record for professionals, David Frost shot 69 and Simon Ward 70. David Croxton showed flair and imagination for golf course management, building up the facilities before turning his attention to the course and expansion to ease the increasing congestion.

Land known as Elkington Hollows where Cromwell's army had set up camp in the Civil War, was after a lengthy planning battle allowed to be developed. On the Captain's Day in July 1995 the 27th hole course was officially opened heralding the dawn of a new era at Cold Ashby. The new nine holes have matured somewhat and a composite 18-hole layout from the three nines was used for the 1999 N.G.U. County Championship won by Nick Soto who showed some considerable stamina for 36 holes up and down the hills. When the golf clubs are put away because of snow most courses close, but Cold Ashby transforms into a winter fun park. The two portable ski lifts are set up and the rolling terrain is used to full advantage. You can sometimes forget that you're not in the Alps! Lift passes, boot and Ski hire are available. Recent mild winters have unfortunately reduced this element of the Cold Ashby year.

Staverton Park is now a marvellous success story, but it has been the downfall of its originator. David Green was a local landowner in the 1970s and followed the trends set at Farthingstone and Cold Ashby on the golf trail. Staverton Park was established in 1977 and is a fine undulating parkland course with good bracing views. Unfortunately he ran into trouble when he built a hotel overlooking the 18th green. He finished up millions of pounds in debt and in the bankruptcy courts. It was said at the time that if every one of his 52 rooms was occupied every day of the year, he still would not be able to pay the mortgage on it. It was bought from the receivers by Style Conferences in 1993, who have made a fantastic success of the site. It has been sold on initially to Rentokil, and is now run by De Vere Venues. The course hosts Regional, County and Midland P.G.A. events each year. The hotel now has more than 200 rooms and has been a major conference centre for Barclays Bank, and the complex has grown enormously. During its darkest days, the golf club suffered as membership plummeted and the group of golfers made a vain attempt to purchase the course. Recently a separate smaller clubhouse was constructed largely for the golf club members and to house the Club professional and repair shop. Built on the old practise ground the building also has a swimming pool and leisure facilities.

In the early days David Green staged a series of top level pro-ams to raise money for Northamptonshire County Cricket Club and the likes of Dennis Thatcher, David Gower and Henry Cooper have all played the course. The Club's first professional (for five years) was a certain David Leadbetter, remembered as a rather aloof sort, now famous as a coaching guru notably for his work with Nick Faldo. I had a lesson with him once and it did not make me an Open or Masters Champion, perhaps I was not in tune with his teaching methods, swinging a golf club with a medicine ball stuck between my knees felt rather alien and very uncomfortable!

In 2000 a familiar face at the Club was top European women's player Sofia Gronberg-Whitmore who lived in the county with her husband and two children. In 1999 Sofia won two European tour events and narrowly missed out on a place in the 2000 Solheim Cup team.

She also played for the European tour team in their annual match with the Seniors, being one of only two women to remain unbeaten including a half with men's captain Tommy Horton. In that event her caddie was Club assistant Andy Garth.

The Embankment G.C. near to Wellingborough has similar origins to that of John White, the land was originally part of the Morris Motors sports ground in Wellingborough, and started off life with one hole. This has subsequently evolved into a nine hole course with seven par threes and two par fours. The longest hole on the course is 352 yards long. The subsequent holes were laid out by the late Harry Neale, groundsman of Wellingborough School, who rent the land from the Co-operative Society as an addition to its playing fields. Many rugby posts and cricket squares come into play on the course, "you get a free drop if your ball lands on a cricket square, but rugby posts are treated as trees and have to be negotiated" said secretary John Andrew in 2000. This has subsequently been changed. The holes meander through the school's playing fields and there is much out of bounds to the golfers left.

After some debate they decided to join the N.G.U. so that members could get an official handicap. "In 1999 Rob Price is in single figures and their players are more than able to play to their handicap on other courses" said John. Also in 1999, the Club signed an agreement with the School that gave them a five-year tenancy, the first one to be negotiated in the club's 25-year history, which was subsequently renewed. "This has brought an element of security and the course provides a challenge for golfers starting out or for those at the other end of the playing spectrum who don't want to trek around the much bigger golf course at Wellingborough anymore" said John, himself a former Cold Ashby member.

Since joining the N.G.U. they have become active in many of the golf competitions and social functions and we wish them success in their search for their first ever golf trophy.

Delapre Golf Complex "call it a complex and not a course" stressed golf director John Corby, back in 1976 as it became a major sporting landmark in Northampton. The complex consists of a massive 500 acre site in the grounds of Delapre Abbey and the complex's message was simple "golf for the masses". The course was designed by John Corby and his more famous partner, John Jacobs the Ryder Cup Captain, teacher and broadcaster. "We've passed the time when golf was a sport with a social advantage" was the Jacob's theme 30 years ago." "Hopefully we'll bring the game to a lot of new people. We all know the thousands who watch it on television but golf isn't the sort of game when you can go and knock on the door of the nearest club and say "I want to play"

You certainly can now thanks to the likes of Delapre and all the pay-and-play courses which have sprung up during the last 30 years. Delapre started with an 18 hole course, is played back to front now from the original design, a par three course, a pitch and putt course, a driving range and a significant welcoming clubhouse. It was one of the most advanced golf arrangements in Europe. Since that time the Hardingstone nine has been added on the opposite side of Nene Valley Way in the shadow of Hardingstone village and the second par three course. For most of Delapre's 30 year life, the course has been run by John Corby's management team with a string of fine teaching professionals, including John Cuddihy a former Scottish Boys Champion. Teaching has always been high on the agenda of Delapre's priorities, and from the outset the approach was to target businesses and schools. The lights of the driving range, piercing the cold winter night sky have become a familiar sight. North-east facing away from the prevailing winds the driving range has been the starting point for many aspiring golfers young and old. A nearby lake is used to irrigate the course which in drought summers, has stood up remarkably well a real testament to the work of the green staff. John Corby retired in 2002 having made a very notable contribution to the local golfing scene and we will miss his gentlemanly approach and sense of humour. Recently in 2004 the council owned course has been sold on to the Jack Barker Golf Company and is now known as Delapre Golf Centre. Unfortunately in recent years there have been many problems with motor cycles and burnt out cars on the course, this has attracted a significant amount of feeling in the local press and town hall on the problem and a solution has been implemented. Golf however still goes on in relative tranquillity as it rightly should.

Cherwell Edge is something of a rarity, starting off life as a municipal course now privately run after being sold off in the early 1990s initially to a consortium headed by Richard Clark and recently to Jim Gallant. Originally built as a nine hole course in 1981 on an old chalk mine, Cherwell Edge became an 18 hole course in the mid 1980s when land was developed on the other side of the Chacombe to Middleton Cheney Road. In some ways it was a strange decision by Cherwell district Council to sell because the course was doing a roaring business. The asking price was over £1 million, and at one stage a group of members tried to put together a purchase package, although they got the backing of the banks the membership hesitated and the chance was lost.

The membership then within the municipal course was around 400, but that has now swelled to well over 500 in 2007. Cherwell Edge G.C. features some challenging holes but is definitely user-friendly both on and off the course. The last years of the old century proved pretty sensational for promising youngster Gary Boyd, in 1998 when 12 years old became the English Handicap Golfer of the Year over two rounds at the home of English golf Woodhall Spa and Club Champion in 1999. On top of that, five-year-old Matthew Draper entered the Guinness book of records by becoming the youngest player to sink a hole in one on the 122 yard fourth hole using a cut

down four wood made the national press. Between 2000-2006 the Club had seen some considerable changes as described in Chapter 6. Gary Boyd has matured to an England International and was first reserve in the 2007 Walker Cup team at the beautiful Royal County Down course in Northern Ireland.

After quiet period in the 1980s a second golf boom took place in the last decade of the 20th century in Northamptonshire and England. Collingtree Park G.C. brought glamour to the area with the cream of Europe playing on the Johnny Miller designed course. Together with Collingtree Park, Brampton Heath, Hellidon Lakes, Kingfisher, Overstone Park, Silverstone, Stoke Albany and Whittlebury Park all took off as County courses during the 1990s. I also include here for completeness the little known course Elton Furze G.C. close to Peterborough which opened in 1993 since the ladies section (and not the men's) are affiliated to Northamptonshire.

At Collingtree the Property Company of London, whose directors included former professional Warren Humphries showed they meant business when they hired the 1973 US Open Champion Johnny Miller to design the course. Johnny Miller

A young Gary Boyd, Cherwell Edge G.C. with N.G.U. President in 1998.

personally inspected the site on several occasions and with luxury homes dotted around the course it was suggested that this was Northampton's answer to Wentworth. The course opened in May 1990 with TV personality and comedy script writer, Barry Took, as its first captain to continue the glitzy theme. It was not initially a great financial success and plans to build a hotel to go with the upmarket homes and nursing homes were initially shelved. In stepped the PGA European Tour and IMG group to buy the course. By 1995 they had acquired four, two in England one in Germany and one in Sweden. This led to a major coup for the town when the British Masters was played at Collingtree Park in 1995. The event attracted a star studded field including nine of Europe's 12 Ryder Cup players who flew out to America a week later to record a famous victory at Oak Hill, New York.

Nick Faldo, José Maria Olazabal and Bernard Langer were missing, however golf fans from the area still had to pinch themselves to realise that the likes of Seve Ballesteros, Ian Woosnam and Colin Montgomerie were actually playing on a Northamptonshire course, the biggest thing to happen in more than 100 years of golf in the county.

The N.G.U. was invited to assist with the organisation of the tournament and it was not difficult to recruit volunteers from the Clubs to act as marshals, scorers, bunker rakers etc. Although Monty was favourite, it was another Scot, cigarette smoking Sam Torrence in the best form of his life who took the title from New Zealander Michael Campbell. Watching the young New Zealander at the time one could see that he was a fine ball striker with a slightly fiery temperament, one would have paid more attention to him if we had known that he was to become the US Open Champion in 2005. The British Masters returned to the course a year later but problems with the greens meant the kiss of death for the club's relationship with the Masters tournament. I remember in particular Monty storming into the tournament office to make his views known.

On a personal note playing in the Pro-Am with another future US Open Champion Retief Goosen (2001 & 4) was special for myself, the late Brian Woodcock and Angus McLeod. I have never seen a ball struck more sweetly with such power by such a quiet gentle man. Retief had a level of calmness and confidence perfectly suited to the emotional game we play, and quite different to Michael Campbell's approach. I wished on that day I could emulate his attributes, which were in reality light years away from my slower ageing golf swing!

In 1989 the famous 1966 World Cup winning footballer Bobby Charlton drove his golf ball into the Holy Lake to mark the official launch of Hellidon Lakes G.C. on the Northants/Warwickshire border. Since that time thousands of balls have also ended up in the lake as players have attempted to carry the 200 yards to the fairway by the 18th green rather than skirting the perimeter of the water until the course changes in 2004. The former England and Manchester United star made a spectacular helicopter entrance, the final leg of his journey along the 18th fairway as course owner Stuart Nichol introduced his pride and joy to the media. The course consists of 220 acres of hillside terrain with seventeen man made lakes etched into the natural ridges and valleys.

The course was designed by English professional David Snell and built from the profits of a low cost satellite marine electronic navigation system, pioneered by Mr Nicoll. He sold his company to Polytechnic Electronics of Daventry for several millions of pounds and originally bought the land as a secluded spot to walk his retriever dogs. With an imposing hotel overlooking the 18th green with restaurants, bars, gymnasium and tennis courts, Hellidon Lakes is very much a modern day golf and country club concept. It has also added another 9 holes, known as the Holywell course in 2000. Nowadays the club is part of the Marston Hotels group and is a popular venue for company away days and conferences.

Whittlebury Park Golf and Country Club opened in 1991 and was originally known as West Park G.C. The site is situated on what was the Royal Whittlewood Forest, which used to cover many miles of the surrounding area; it is thought that some of the large oak trees, which are a characteristic feature of the course, have stood for more than a thousand years. A private nine hole course existed at the end of the 19th century, this was lost at the beginning of the first World War as the landowners grew much needed crops for the war effort. Details of the original course were uncovered in the library in St. Andrews, and subsequently a modern reconstruction of the original nine hole layout gives the course its name of "1905" in memory of times gone by. There are three loops of nine holes the Royal Whittlewood, the Grand Prix and the Wedgewood which stand next to the 1905 course and within the oak parkland. The architect was Northants County member Cameron Sinclair, who has rapidly developed a reputation as "one skilled in the art" and has produced 36 holes of championship quality. All the nines are quite challenging especially when the wind blows across the parkland and has some of the finest greens in the county for such a young layout.

Silverstone Golf Club was established in 1992, and has recently been taken over by the owners of Cherwell Edge Golf Club so could be described as its sister course. During the last few years the course has undergone extensive improvements. The par 72 course is challenging for the beginner and experienced player at a length of 6472 yards of the white blocks and in 2004 held the N.G.U. County family Foursomes Championship. The Club was originally affiliated to the Berks, Bucks & Oxon golf union but jumped over the fence in to Northamptonshire in 2001.

Elton Furze opened in 1993 around some 200 acres of mature woodland largely in Furze Wood. The course is 6279 yards in length and a par of 71. The men in the county have little contact with the Club's gentlemen since they are affiliated to the Cambridgeshire Area Golf Union. The ladies of the county play some matches there however since their ladies are affiliated to the N.L.C.G.A. This must be quite a unique scenario and I wonder what happens with mixed golf?

One of the jewels in the nineties crown it could be argued is Overstone Park G.C. which was opened in 1994 by the Huntingdon based Watermark Club plc. Built on what was described as "poor farmland" the Donald Steel design course has some demanding holes and etched into the landscape are Scandinavian style timber lodges, some of which are occupied as permanent homes. The land has excellent drainage as one of its main features which allows the course to stay open whilst many others are forced to close.

Apart from golf, the complex offers leisure facilities including a 20-metre pool, spa pool, steam room, sauna, fitness and aerobics studio and an 80 seater restaurant. There is also fishing in the lakes, tennis courts and the bowling green. Many local sporting celebrities used the facilities, including the Northampton Saints rugby squad and some of the County Cricketers for example Allan Lamb. Just three years after opening, the Overstone Park golf and leisure club was put up for sale with a reputed £4 million price tag by developers JPI group. Covering 167 acres Overstone had 122 lodges dotted around the course at the time of the sale. Out on the course, the par three fourth hole and the short par four fifth are very demanding holes though not for some players. For example at the fifth hole the powerful Lincolnshire player Steve Dixon and former Club professional Brian Mudge have both recorded albatrosses, I also witnessed Northampton's Glenn Keates lip out for an albatross during practise for an Anglian League match. The course has now become a significant challenge with a par of 72 following the addition of more trees and bunkers. In the millennium year a splendid innovation was to invite members to sponsor 20 mature trees, these are now dotted around the course with plaques along side them denoting the sponsor's name.

Brampton Heath G.C. has come a long way since it opened in 1995 as a pay and play course. Originally offered to Kingsthorpe golf club as an alternative site, a decision was taken to plough ahead with a golf course after Kingsthorpe decided to stay put. The opening ceremony included a buffet reception in a marquee followed by a trick shot golf show by the famous ex European tour professional Noel Hunt. The initial concept was to make it as easy as possible so that the rookie golfer would be welcomed. In the year 2000 there was a change of mood in the air which generated a five-year plan to make the course more challenging and to improve the drainage at the same time. The fairways have been shaped and tightened new bunkers have appeared together with an abundance of trees and gorse. Off the white tees the course has been extended to 6533 yards significantly longer than the original design. All of this has helped to enhance Brampton Heath's reputation. The course is now attracting lower handicap golfers as members and has a thriving junior section. Brampton Heath is also proud of its short course which has been used for two Midland qualifiers of the British Championships. Top quality greens have been laid and the facilities have been kindly made available to County players for their short game practice. The Midland Golf Union also uses the facilities for their regional coaching. The 18 bay driving range is quite popular especially on winter evenings. In the clubhouse a second floor has been added and was officially opened in the spring of the millennium year. The new story can accommodate up to 150 people for a function or sectioned off for smaller groups. They plan to attract businesses for seminars and conferences.

One of the problems golfers face when they come to this area is to arrive at the correct golf club. With Brampton Heath, Northants County (Church or Chapel Brampton) and Northampton Golf Clubs all within a three-mile radius some confusion often occurs. At Northampton when a car pulls into the car park and asks to be directed to Brampton golf club the driver often looks bemused when confronted with the question which one? A sign of the club's development is that they have managed to produce the 2005 County Champion young Dan Wood who also lifted the County Scratch Foursomes Trophy with partner Matt Bird of Northants County.

Stoke Albany opened in 1994, and although the postal address is in Leicestershire the club is affiliated to the Northants Golf Union. The clubhouse is sympathetically designed to blend in with the surrounding countryside using reclaimed timbers and specially made of bricks give it a rustic feel while the landscape is planted with native British trees. There are several lakes and ponds all man made dotted around the course. A significant number of their members originate from Priors Hall G.C. The golfers of Stoke Albany have quickly establish themselves by winning N.G.U. Scratch League Division four in 1998 and consolidating their status in 1999 as competitors division three. The club have built up a good junior section and have competed in the semi-finals of the N.G.U. Inter-Club leagues and knockout competitions. Over the last few years the course has been extended with the introduction of new medal tees on certain holes, the land drains extremely well allowing play throughout the winter months on normal greens.

Adrian Clifford, the Midland P.G.A. Golfer of the year (2000/1) is the Club professional. He successfully fought a battle against cancer, and raised £1200 for research purposes by running a half marathon in his hometown of Bristol. As a director of the Big Red Golf Schools he has built up a reputation for being an outstanding teacher and devotes some considerable time coaching youngsters not only from the club but also from the surrounding area.

Kingfisher Hotel Golf and Country Club is a charming nine hole course serving the Milton Keynes area near to Deanshanger in the south of the county. In 2000 it was under the same ownership as Overstone Park and the course opened in 1995. In 1999 a hotel was constructed. It is a picturesque course though quite demanding with six holes being influenced by water in the shape of lakes, ponds and ditches. A more unwelcome feature to influence play is the nearby Great Ouse River a quarter of a mile from the fourth and fifth fairways. Unfortunately the Ouse has been known to flood its banks and saturate the course, when this occurs for more than three days the members are offered courtesy facilities at Overstone. The hotel has 28 double rooms for golfers and potentially fishermen.

To complete the picture, since 1995 only one more Club has been formed bringing Northamptonshire's total to 27. Pytchley Lodge near Kettering was established in 1995 initially as a driving range with a tiny cosy clubhouse which could seat fifteen at a push. A warm cup of soup or something a little stronger served by the enthusiastic Scot John McFarland were very welcome to me and my son Alex after hitting a few balls on a cold winters night. The Club has gone from strength to strength with a new course, clubhouse and professional shop and is always quite busy. They recorded their first N.G.U. trophy win in 2003 (The Izzard Club Team Trophy) at Northampton G.C. and became the first team to retain the trophy when they successfully defended it the following year at Cold Ashby G.C.

In 2007 Northamptonshire the number of male club members is about 10,000 the ladies total is about 1500.

Millennium Golf Ball

Northamptonshire Golf

Saturday 15th January, 2000

Wicksteed Park
Kettering

Northamptonshire Golf Union
Northamptonshire Ladies County Golf Association

President: David Croxton
Captain: Mrs Carol Gibbs

Dinner Menu for Northamptonshire Golfers Millennium celebration.

CHAPTER 2

THE HISTORY OF THE GAME,
THE ROYAL AND ANCIENT GOLF CLUB OF
ST ANDREWS AND THE LADIES GOLF UNION

"When good friends walk beside us
On the trials that we must keep
Our burdens seem less heavy
And the hills are not so steep
The weary miles pass swiftly
Taken in a joyous stride
And all the world seems brighter
When friends walk by our side"

I HAVE included this short chapter to give an impression of where Northamptonshire's golfers are positioned within the wider elements of the game. As the governing body for the game their stewardship over Rules and player's handicaps is felt by all of our golfers. As we play the game locally on the 27 county courses we feel quite at home which is one of the beauties of the game. I would encourage anyone interested in the game to make the pilgrimage up to St Andrews at least once in their lifetime. To soak up St Andrews unique atmosphere is an experience not to be missed at "The Home of Golf". There are now seven golf courses to be savoured which have varying degrees of difficulty to suit the tastes of all golfers, some very nice restaurants and airy walks to be found under big skies on a mile long sandy beach. Once you have been to St Andrews I am sure you will return, the spirit of the place gets in to your soul.

My friends tell me that when I arrive at such places as Links Hotel, 1 Golf Place[26] an aura of inner calmness comes over me, possibly as a result of the sea air and the feelings of being "back home". This hotel is about a seven iron from the Old Course and is one of the places caddies and students still assemble to mingle with visitors from around the globe. The hotel was established in 1827 when the street was built, prior to this date the first

The Home of Golf

ever "Golf Inn" was in Bruntsfield (Edinburgh) in 1717. The Old Links bar was first frequented by caddies around 1920 and between 1960-2000 was the place where Arnold Palmer's "famous" caddy for 35 years Tip Anderson could often be found. A colourful personality, he had golf in his blood and his father was a well-known caddie before him at St Andrews. The bars in the hotel are filled with golfing memorabilia and in the evening talk of the days play resonates around the building in many accents particularly American, Japanese and Scottish. The figure below demonstrates Northamptonshire's links to the wider golf scene:-

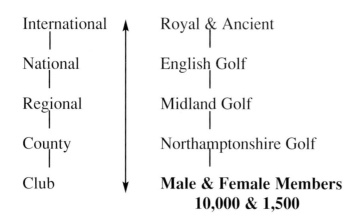

International   Royal & Ancient

National   English Golf

Regional   Midland Golf

County   Northamptonshire Golf

Club   **Male & Female Members**
10,000 & 1,500

It is strongly believed by many historians that Golf, as we know it, was started by gentlemen in Scotland, the first Club being formed at Leith rather than St Andrews and this was where golf was first played in Great Britain. Some authorities trace golf back to a Roman game called paganica. The Romans, who occupied most of the island of Great Britain from the A.D. 40s to the early 400s, played paganica in the streets with a bent stick and a leather ball stuffed with feathers. Other historians trace golf to a Dutch game called het kolven, a French and Belgian game called chole, a French game called jeu de mail, and an English game called cambuca. However while these games and countless others are stick and ball games, they are missing that vital ingredient that is unique to golf – the hole.

Having previously laid dubious claims to being the birthplace of football and the Japanese martial art of judo, the Chinese have now added golf to their list of inventions. Scotland has always been considered as the traditional home of golf since the 15th century but now, according to *The Scotsman* (11 January 2006), a Chinese academic has claimed that golf was played among the noble classes in China some 500 years earlier. According to Professor Ling, golf only arrived in Scotland after it was exported to Europe by Mongolian travellers during the late Middle Ages.

Professor Ling Hongling of Lanzhou University claims to have uncovered evidence in a book called the Dongxuan Records that proves golf was played in China in AD 945. The book, written during the Song Dynasty from AD 960 to AD 1279, claims the game was called chuiwan and was played with ten different jewel-encrusted clubs, including a cuanbang equivalent to a modern-day driver, a pubang, a brassie or two-wood, and a shaobang the ancient three-wood. The term chui actually means 'to hit' while wan is the term for a ball. Scotland's acceptance as the home of golf rests on a resolution dated March 6, 1457, when King James II of Scotland banned football and 'ye golf'.

The sport's traditional home, St Andrews, is first mentioned as a golf venue in Archbishop Hamilton's Charter of 1552 in which the people of Fife are reserved the right to use the links land – the land where golf is played at St Andrews – 'for golff, futball, schuting and all gamis' and for grazing livestock – golf, football, shooting and all games for those who do not speak Ye Olde Englysh.

Scots have long acknowledged that other stick and ball games existed but their assertion is that they were the first to use holes rather than targets. Professor Ling's findings would even appear to dispute that as he claims a reference in the Dongxuan Records sees a prominent Chinese magistrate of the Nantang Dynasty (AD 937-975) instructing his daughter "to dig holes in the ground so that he might drive a ball into them with a purposely crafted stick."

His claims are certain to add fuel to fierce international controversy about which country invented the sport, now played by 50 million people around the world. China has a history of making audacious claims to having invented sports. The R&A were characteristically diplomatic in there response stating "Stick and ball games have been around for many centuries, but golf as we know it today, played over 18 holes, clearly originated in Scotland."

The ancient city of St Andrews was also the country's religious capital and had been a place of pilgrimage for centuries. Legend claims that the bones of St Andrew were brought from Patras in Greece by a monk called Regulus in about AD 390. Historical evidence tends to lean more heavily towards the relics arriving in the possession of a bishop fleeing from England almost 400 years later. Their presence in the city which took his name brought pilgrims from all parts of the known world. Unfortunately the reformation destroyed its religious significance. Following this tragedy the under-funded university was in danger of being moved to Perth and the huge cathedral once attended by Robert the Bruce lay in ruins.

The history of The Royal and Ancient Golf Club of St Andrews began on the 14th May 1754, when 22 noblemen and gentlemen of Fife presented a Silver Club to be played for annually over the Links of St Andrews. The winner became "Captain of the Golf". The Society of St Andrews Golfers, as the Club was originally known, soon evolved from this competition and a revised set of rules were written in 1766.These rules stipulated that members were to meet "once every fortnight by eleven of the clock…and to play a round on the links. To dine together at Bailie Glass's and to pay each a shilling for his dinner, the absent as well as present".

They were motivated by two themes involving friendship and reputation in order to enjoy the sport and the conviviality which always followed, and also by staging an annual contest for a significant trophy.
The challenge for the Silver Club was played for between 1754-1764 and the rules show that competitors played a total of twenty two holes, eleven out and eleven back. A minute dated 4th October 1764 records a significant change." The Captain and Gentlemen golfers present are of the opinion that it would be for the improvement of the links that the four first holes should be converted into two, they therefore have agreed that for the future they will be played as two holes". Despite a round of eighteen holes being established at St Andrews, it was another 100 years before it became the pattern for golf elsewhere.

In 1834, King William IV agreed to become the Patron of the Club and the Society of St Andrews Golfers became known as The Royal and Ancient Golf Club of St Andrews. Like many early golf clubs, it still did not possess its own headquarters. The following year, Club member Major Hugh Lyon Playfair formed the Union Club. Its premises, known as the Union Parlour, provided clubhouse facilities for golfers and archers. Unsurprisingly, the majority of Union Club members were also members of The Royal and Ancient Golf Club. In 1853, the Union Club financed the construction of a new clubhouse, situated behind the first tee of the Old Course. Completed in 1854, The Royal and Ancient clubhouse is a familiar image to golfing enthusiasts around the world. The founding stone was laid by John Whyte Melville on the 13th July 1853. The event was marked as a ceremonial occasion and John Whyte Melville, as a long standing R&A member and senior Freemason, was invited to perform the task. It was done with full Masonic honours, starting with a procession from Madras College accompanied by a band. Many St Andreans residents watched as Whyte Melville struck the foundation stone with a mallet and called for "the Great Architect of the Universe to shower down his blessings upon the work" (see later in this chapter for the Northamptonshire–Whyte Melville connection).

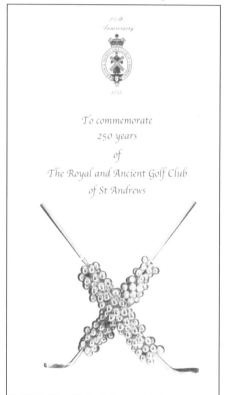

It continued to be known as the Union Clubhouse until the The Royal and Ancient and Union Clubs formally merged in 1877. Each of the four elevations presents a different image and each has a different story to tell; for the building, so familiar to modern golfers, is not as it appeared when it was first unveiled. Over the years, the clubhouse has expanded to meet the needs of the growing number of Royal and Ancient members, yet none of the original structure has been destroyed; rather, it exists within the framework of today's building. For further details of this magnificent building which is such a significant feature of the St Andrews landscape visit The Royal & Ancient website[6].

The relationship between The Royal and Ancient Golf Club and the Old Course is one that has often been misunderstood. The Club does not own the Old or indeed any of the St Andrews courses. The courses are actually managed by the St Andrews Links Trust.

As the The Royal and Ancient Golf Club celebrated its 250th anniversary in 2004, it devolved responsibility for the administration of the Rules of Golf, the running of The Open Championship and other key

The front cover of the menu to celebrate the 250th Anniversary of The Royal and Ancient Golf Club of St Andrews, attended by kind invitation to 2004-6 N.G.U. President Mike Taylor and his wife Jean, who represented Northamptonshire together with N.C.L.G.A. President Pam Giles.

The Home of Golf

golfing events, and the development of the game in existing and emerging golfing nations, to a newly formed group of companies collectively known as The R&A. Today, in 2007, The R&A's priorities at all times are to engage in activities that are for the benefit of the game. It operates with the consent of more than 125 national and international, amateur and professional organisations, from over 110 countries and on behalf of an estimated 28 million golfers in Europe, Africa, Asia-Pacific and the Americas (outside the USA and Mexico).The United States Golf Association (U.S.G.A.) is the governing body in the United States and Mexico.

The R&A does not impose the Rules of Golf, but governs by consent, so that anyone who wants to play the true game of golf plays by the rules. Although The Open Championship is the obvious public focal point in The R&A's annual golfing calendar, in reality it is only one of 11 championships and international matches which come under the its administrative umbrella.

As a separate entity, The Royal and Ancient Golf Club of St Andrews remains as a private golf club with a worldwide membership of almost 2,400. As a members' golf club, it aims to provide first class golfing facilities. Twice yearly, in spring and autumn, the members meet to compete in competitions, which include the Spring and Autumn Medals. In Northamptonshire we have two R&A members, both from Northants County Golf Club; the well respected golf course architect Cameron Sinclair and Malcolm (J.M.) Peel. They are both Past Captains of the Club.

In 1857, The Royal and Ancient Golf Club of St Andrews organised the first Grand National Tournament after consulting other leading golf clubs. It was to be a team event with one pair of players representing each club in a knock-out matchplay competition over 30 holes (one round plus six holes out and back), with opponents being drawn by lot for each round. This was the first attempt at holding a national golf championship. Such was the popularity of the 1857 Tournament that it was decided to hold another the next year at St Andrews, but with a major difference. Instead of being a team competition, it was to be a championship "open to all amateur gentlemen players, members of any established golf club". Twenty-eight competitors took part. Another Grand National Tournament was held at St Andrews in 1859, but it proved to be the last.

R&A Connections to Northamptonshire, The Family Whyte Melville

John Whyte Melville of Bennochy and Strathkinness Fifeshire (1797-1883) stands out as one of the foremost figures in the history of the Union, Club and the R&A. He became a member of the latter in 1816, when it was still known as the Society of St Andrews Golfers and in 1823, he served as Captain. A dedicated if not very accomplished golfer, his skills lay more in the administrative side of Club affairs. For six decades, he worked tirelessly as a committee man for both the Union Club and the R&A. When they formally merged in 1877, he took the chair of the new management committee of the amalgamated clubs. It was indeed a mark of the esteem in which he was held that he was given the honour of laying the foundation stone of the R&A clubhouse when building work began in 1853.

When the Prince of Wales (later Edward VII) was elected to serve as captain in 1863, it was John Whyte Melville who stepped in as acting captain in the Prince's absence, to drive the ball from the first tee. He was first elected Captain in 1823 at the age of twenty-six and for a second time sixty years later in 1883, a rare occurrence, but died before he could take office. As a mark of respect, the office was left vacant for 1883. The artist who painted the famous portrait *(see opposite page)* was Sir Francis Grant (1803-1878), also an R&A member and a friend of John Whyte Melville. Francis Grant himself had been elected a member in 1823. Grant trained as a lawyer, but gave up his studies to concentrate on painting. The portrait of John Whyte Melville was commissioned in 1874; it has hung in the Big Room of the R&A since it was completed that same year.

John Whyte Melville was a noted "waggler" when addressing the ball. His red coat was seen as the first official uniform of the R&A, golfers wore these bright red coats so that they could be seen by the locals who used the same links land for strolling, doing the laundry and picnicking. Honourable gentlemen golfers in the 18th

Reproduction of the famous Whyte Melville picture which hangs in the big room at The Royal & Ancient Golf Club of St Andrews

century wore these red coats because most of them had served as grunts in the British army. Red government-issued field jackets were the only coats they owned.

This practice soon spread to places such as Blackheath and Royal Wimbledon Golf Clubs. In order to protect the public from being hit by the hard ball, a bye-law was passed by the London County Council stating, "no male person shall play golf on the men's course after 10 a.m. without wearing a red coat or some other exterior garment coloured red". In the Midlands many courses also started out on common land so red coats became an important safety feature at courses such as Sutton Coldfield, where the players were instructed to dress" scarlet coat with grey collar and with brass buttons with SCGC thereon; the coat to be without cuffs" The trend was continued at Northampton Golf Club, in the Ladies section! An extract from the 1908 L.G.U. yearbook states[4p23] for Northampton L.G.C. that Club Colours are "Red coats, green collars and cuffs" the annual subscription was £1 10p.

Returning to John Whyte Melville, he gave the Silver Putter to the R&A as a result of a wager in 1820 with Sir David Moncreiffe on who would live longer. The survivor was to present a Silver Club with the arms of both men engraved upon it. The task fell to John Whyte Melville who outlived his friend by fifty years; Moncreiffe died in 1830.On the first day of the 1833 Autumn Meeting John Whyte Melville honoured his bet by presenting the Silver Putter. At the age of eighty-three, he was still playing thirty six holes a day in a December gale and was a member of the R&A for 67 years. John Whyte Melville had a massive public profile as "in some respects the most public man in Fife" as described by the St Andrews Citizen.

In the Scottish Episcopal Church located at Queens Gardens St Andrews, there is a stained glass window presented to the church by John Whyte Melville in memory of his wife Lady Catherine. A plaque just below the window which was virtually unreadable due to the dust on it bore the inscription" This window is the gift of John Whyte Melville Esq of Bennochy and Strathkinness in memory of his dear wife The Right honourable Lady Catherine Whyte Melville youngest daughter of Francis Godolphin 5th Duke of Leeds Died 23rd December 1878". The plaque is much cleaner now after my visit to photograph the window in 2007.That was a very special and emotional trip for me. Standing quietly, reflecting on my life in a church at the home of golf generated many timeless personal and golf connections. It is quite a beautiful church and well worth a look the next time you are in St Andrews. Their son George was to become a far more prominent figure nationally[22].

Captain George John Whyte Melville (1821-1878), he was born on the nineteen of June in 1821. On his mother's side, he was the grandson of the fifth Duke of Leeds. He was educated at Eton and entered the Army in 1939 serving in the Crimean war with the 93rd Highland regiment. After transferring to the Coldstream Guards he became Captain in 1846 and retired in 1849. He married Charlotte Hanbury the daughter of the first Lord Bateman of Kelmarsh Hall, Northamptonshire and they made their home in what is now known as the Whyte Melville Arms in the Northamptonshire village of Boughton. Boughton was a thriving farming community and its situation led it to be a meeting place of one of the largest fairs. At this time, Boughton used to hold a three-day horse fair, which attracted many highwaymen who were rife in the area at the time. The last to be caught-Captain Slash- was hanged at Whitehills Northampton on Gallows Hill in 1826.

The marriage produced one child Florence who was born on the 26 August 1848. The family moved to London and finally to The Bartons, Tetbury, Gloucestershire. Florence married the 11th Viscount Massereene in 1870 and had six children by 1878! In 1928, after the sale by Sir Richard Howard-Vyse of the Boughton Estate, the old village inn (The Griffin) closed and the license was transferred to the present spacious property and named the "Whyte Melville Arms" after its most famous occupier. He was made Captain of the Royal & Ancient in 1851. He made frequent trips to St Andrews for golf and family visits but the novels he wrote from the perspective of an Englishman rather than a Scotsman. He became best known as a popular novelist and developed a great interest in fox hunting. He was the laureate of fox hunting. Many of the twenty-four novels he wrote, including "Holmby (Holdenby) House 1860" and "Market Harborough", were written during his years at Boughton and featured fox hunting and the Northamptonshire countryside.

As a rich man in his own right, the monies he made from his books he generously donated for the provision of rest rooms and libraries for stableboys and groom's living quarters. In 1865, he donated the proceeds of one of his books to build the Whyte Melville Working Men's Club in St Giles Street, Northampton, which caused a furore amongst Northampton's inhabitants.

After moving to Gloucestershire, he became the hero of many a stiff ride. Whilst hunting with the "Vale of the White Horse" foxhounds he was thrown from his horse and killed on the 5th December in 1878 whilst galloping quietly over an ordinary ploughed field near Malmesbury. The fall broke his neck and he died minutes later without regaining consciousness. When the first edition of the "Horse & Hounds" was published the following year in 1884, the following inscription appeared on its front cover largely as a tribute to George John Whyte Melville's persona "I freely admit that the best of my fun, I owe to the Horse & Hound". Each subsequent edition has this included on or near the front cover.

Northamptonshire connections were maintained after his death when on the 30 May 1879, *The Times* reported on the annual meeting of the Hunt Servant's Benefit Society, which was presided over by the Duke of Buccleuch. Anstruther Thompson took the

The Whyte Melville Public House at Boughton near Northampton

opportunity to announce that proposals were underway to erect a monument over the grave in Tetbury and also a drinking fountain in St Andrews. The article states, "already without speaking to the public, £350 had been contributed to the subscription list, which had been opened. The Duke of Buccleuch said there could only be one feeling as to the memorial to the late Major Melville among the persons who had been acquainted with him. All who knew him and recollected his superiority as a sportsman would be glad to testify their admiration for the man both as a friend and as a sportsman"

   Such was the fame and reputation of George John Whyte Melville, the massive fountain in Market Street at the home of golf is one of three monuments erected in his memory, the second at his burial place in Tetbury and the third memorial within the Guard's Chapel in London, was destroyed during a bombing raid in 1944.
The current Whyte Melville Arms at Boughton has a warm and welcoming atmosphere. I strongly encourage the reader to enjoy a drink there and slowly savour the atmosphere of historical golf and countryside connections.

THE ORIGINAL SET OF RULES ADOPTED BY THE SOCIETY OF ST ANDREWS GOLFERS WHEN FOUNDED IN 1754

ARTICLES & LAWS in playing the Golf

1. You Must Tee your Ball within a Club-length of the hole.

2. Your Tee must be upon the ground.

3. You are not to Change the Ball which you Strike off the tee.

*4. You are not to remove Stones, Bones or any Break Club for the
sake of playing your Ball Except upon the fair Green,
and that only within a Club length of your Ball.*

*5. If your Ball come among Water, or any Watery filth, you are at
Liberty to take out your Ball, and throw it behind the
hazard,6 yards at least, you may play it with any Club and
allow your Adversury a Stroke, for so getting out your Ball.*

*6. If your Balls be found anywhere touching one another, you are to lift the first Ball,
till you play the last.*

*7. At holing, you are to play your Ball honestly for the hole, and
not to play upon your Adversury's Ball, not lying in your way to the hole.*

8. *If you should lose your Ball,by its being taken up,or any otherway*
you are to go back to the Spot, where you struck last,and drop another Ball and allow
your Adversury a stroke for the misfortune.

9. *No Man at Holeing his Ball, is to be Allowed to Mark his way*
to the Hole with his Club or any thing else.

10. *If a Ball be Stop'd by any Person,Horse,Dog, or any thing else, the*
Ball so Stop'd must be played where it lyes.

11. *If you draw your Club in order to Strike, and proceed so far in thee Stroke*
as to be bringing doun your Club; if then your Club Shall
break, in any way, it is to be Accounted a Stroke.

12. *He, Whose Ball lyes furthest from the Hole is Obliged to play first.*

13. *Neither Trench, Ditch, or Dyke made for the preservation of the*
Links, nor the Scholars holes or the Soldiers Lines Shall be Accounted a Hazard, But
the Ball is to be taken out Teed and played with any Iron Club.

This first set of rules have stood the test of time very well and stand as a great tribute to the gentlemen of the Society of St Andrews Golfers.

Club Terminology

19th Century	20th Century
Driver	Driver
Brassie	2 or 3 Wood
Spoons	3, 4 or 5 Woods
Iron	1 Iron
Driving Cleek	2 or 3 Iron
Mid- Iron	4 Iron
Mid-Mashie	5 Iron
Mashie Iron	6 or 7 Iron
Mashie	6 or 7 Iron
Spade Mashie	7 Iron
Mashie Niblick	7 or 8 Iron
Pitching Niblick	7 or 8 Iron
Niblick	8 or 9 Iron
Putter	Putter

Autumn afternoon shadows across the 18th green at The Home of Golf, with the Valley of Sin and the St Andrews Links Trust Clubhouse

The Open Championship

The first Open Championship was not in fact an open competition; it was for professionals only and it was by invitation. Organised by the members of Prestwick Golf Club, it was played on 17 October 1860 at Prestwick at the end of their Autumn Meeting. A total of eight players played three rounds of the 12 hole course. The rules were changed in 1861 so that amateur players could compete. No prize money for The Open was awarded until 1863; the winner simply received the Belt for a year. In 1863 it was decided to give money prizes to those finishing second, third and fourth but the winner still only received the Belt. The following year, 1864, the winner received £6. The average field in the 1860s was 12 players.

The original rules of the competition in 1860 had stated that the Belt "becomes the property of the winner by being won three years in succession". In 1870, Tom Morris Junior won the Belt for the third year in a row and took possession of it. He won £6 for his efforts out of a total prize fund of £12. No championship was held in 1871 whilst the Prestwick Club entered into discussions with the Royal and Ancient Golf Club and the Honourable Company of Edinburgh Golfers over the future direction of the event.

One of the key turning points in the history of The Open took place at the Spring Meeting of the Prestwick Club in April 1871. At that meeting, it was proposed that "in contemplation of St Andrews, Musselburgh and other clubs joining in the purchase of a Belt to be played for over four or more greens, it is not expedient for the Club to provide a Belt to be played solely for at Prestwick". This was countered with an amendment that Prestwick should provide a new Belt and continue to be the host of the event. The amendment was defeated and from that date onwards, The Open ceased to be under the sole control of the Prestwick Golf Club.

The Championship was played again under this new agreement in 1872 and from 1873, the new trophy was the now world famous Claret Jug. Until 1891, the host club remained responsible for all arrangements regarding the Championship, which was played over 36 holes in one day. In 1892, the Honourable Company of Edinburgh Golfers took four radical steps to transform The Open Championship. It expanded the Championship to 72 holes over two days instead of 36 in a single day and imposed an entrance charge on all competitors. A new green at Muirfield was the venue for that year's championship. The total prize fund was increased from £28/10s to an advertised £100. These actions were all taken unilaterally by the club, with the increased purse to counter a rival tournament held at Musselburgh.

A meeting was held between the three host clubs on 9 June 1893, for the purpose of "placing the competition for The Open Championship on a basis more commensurate with its importance than had hitherto existed". Three resolutions were agreed. Two English clubs, St George's, Sandwich and Royal Liverpool would be invited to stage the Championship and join the rota, now consisting of five clubs. Four rounds of 18 holes would be played over two days. The second resolution was that each of the five clubs would contribute £15 annually to the cost of staging the Championship, and the balance of expenses would come from an entry fee for all competitors. The prize money would total £100, with £30 for the winner, plus £10 for the cost of the medal and decreasing prizes down to twelfth place. The third resolution was that the date of each year's Championship would be set by the host club, which would also bear any additional necessary expenses. The representatives of the five clubs became known as the Delegates of the Associated Clubs. The 1893 Championship was played under these conditions.

The increasing number of entrants caused a cut to be introduced after two rounds in 1898. The Championship was played over three days between 1904 and 1906. It then reverted to two days in 1907 with the introduction of qualifying rounds. The entire field had to qualify and there were no exemptions. The total prize money was raised to £125 in 1900 and £135 in 1910. On 24 January 1920, the Delegates of the Associated Clubs for The Open asked the R&A to take over "the management of the (Open) Championship and the custody of the Challenge Cup" and the Club agreed this on 21 February. The new Championship Committee was responsible for running both The Open and Amateur Championships. In 1922, the Championship Committee decided that

The Open should only be played over links courses. The venues included in today's circuit are: Carnoustie, Muirfield, Royal Birkdale, Royal Liverpool, Royal Lytham & St Anne's, Royal St George's, Royal Troon, St Andrews and Turnberry.

The last time Prestwick, birth place of the Open, played host to the Championship was 1925. In total The Open was played at Prestwick 24 times, starting with the first in 1860. Other courses that have been used in the past but no longer host the Open are: Musselburgh (1874, 1877, 1880, 1883, 1886, 1889), Royal Cinque Ports, Deal (1909, 1920), Princes, Sandwich (1932) and Royal Portrush (1951).

The Open was played regularly over three days starting in 1926, with a round on each of the first two days and two rounds on the final day, which from 1927 onwards was a Friday. The total prize money had reached £500 by 1939. The prize money was increased to £1,000 in 1946 and reached £5,000 in 1959. As the Open went into its second century in the 1960s, it grew tremendously both as a Championship and a spectator event. In 1963 exemptions from pre-qualifying were introduced for the leading players. Then in 1966, play was extended to four days, with the Championship finishing with a single round on the Saturday. Two years later, in 1968, a second cut after 54 holes was introduced to further reduce the field on the final day. This stayed in effect until 1985.

Throughout the 1960s much emphasis was placed on improving spectator facilities. Grandstands were first introduced at the 1960 Open and they became a standard feature from 1963 onwards. First tried as an experiment in 1926, Regional Qualifying was introduced in 1977. Some players were exempt from that but had to take part in final qualifying, whilst others were exempt from both Regional and Final Qualifying. Since 1980, the Championship has been scheduled to end on a Sunday instead of a Saturday. In the event of a tie for first place, playoffs took place over 36 holes up until 1963. The next year, the playoff was reduced to 18 holes and then in 1985 to 4 holes.

The Open Championship was first televised in 1955 and was shown on the BBC. The first live broadcast of The Open to America was in 1966 and was shown on ABC. In 1958, the television coverage lasted for a total of three hours, one and half hours on each of the final two days. In 2006, The Open was broadcast for 2051 hours worldwide. Admission charges to watch The Open were introduced in 1926. Paid admissions went over 50,000 for the first time in 1968 at Carnoustie and over 100,000 for the first time at St Andrews in 1978. The 200,000 attendance figure was reached for the first time at St Andrews in 1990. A new record was set at the Home of Golf in 2000 when 238,787 watched the Millennium Open.

The growth of prize by decade has been as follows:

Year	Total Prize Money	First Prize
1860	£0	£0
1863	£10	£0
1866	£11	£6
1876	£27	£10
1886	£20	£8
1896	£90	£30
1906	£115	£50
1914	£125	£50
1926	£200	£75
1936	£500	£100
1946	£1000	£150
1956	£3,750	£1,000
1966	£15,000	£2,100

Year	Total Prize Money	First Prize
1976	£75,000	£7,500
1986	£634,000	£70,000
1996	£1,400,000	£200,000
2006	£4,000,000	£720,000

Harry Vardon has had the most victories in the Open Championship. He won it six times between 1896 and 1914. J.H. Taylor, James Braid, Peter Thomson and Tom Watson have all won the Open five times each. Between 1860 and 1889, all the Open winners were Scottish. John Ball Junior became the first Englishman and the first amateur to win the Open in 1890.

Arnaud Massy from France was the first continental player to win the Open in 1907 at Hoylake. One of Northamptonshire's connections to the Open are through Richard Aitken who knew his daughter who was named in celebration of the fine course up on the Wirral, Margo *Hoylake* Edgar was also a member at Prestonfield G.C., Richard's Club in Edinburgh.

Four players have completed a hat trick of Open wins:
Tom Morris Junior 1868, 1869 & 1870
Jamie Anderson 1877, 1878 & 1879
Bob Ferguson 1880, 1881 & 1882
Peter Thomson 1954, 1955 & 1956

The Open has been won by an amateur six times - John Ball in 1890, Harold Hilton in 1892 and 1897 and Bobby Jones in 1926, 1927 and 1930. Walter Hagen was the first native-born American to win the Open when he triumphed in 1922. Jock Hutchison, who had won the previous year, was resident in America at the time of his victory but was born in St Andrews.

Open Champions –Almost

The closest Northamptonshire have been to having a "The Champion Golfer of the Year" was Len Holland Professional from the Northants County Golf Club who finished in fifth place over the links at Deal in 1920. Despite his small and slight stature Holland possessed a fluid and powerful swing. He also finished 16th in 1921 at St Andrews, 13th in 1922 at Royal St Georges and 6th in 1924 at Royal Liverpool Golf Club (Hoylake). He was the first professional at the County Club and served from 1910-1924. He was noted for his iron play and exhibition shots and was featured as one of the country's 30 prominent golfers on Churchman cigarette cards, which were first published in 1931.

Len Holland Northants County professional at The Open Championship

Year	Venue	1st round	2nd round	3rd round	4th round	Total	Placing
1920	Deal	80	78	71	79	308	5th
1921	St Andrews	78	78	76	74	306	16th
1922	St Georges	79	81	74	76	310	13th
1924	Hoylake	74	78	78	78	308	6th

Our neighbouring counties of Warwickshire and Lincolnshire have produced one Champion Golfer each, Jack Burns in 1888 and Tony Jacklin in 1969 respectively. Jack Burns originated from St Andrews and was at that time greenkeeper and professional to the Warwickshire golf club. Jack Burns scored 86, 85 over the St Andrews links beating David Anderson Jr and Ben Sayers of North Berwick by one shot. With sixteen names already on the Claret Jug the hand engraver was forced into relegating Jack Burns's name to the underside of the spout. Tony Jacklin's four under par total of 280 over Royal Lytham and St Annes beat runner up Bob Charles by two shots. Jacklin originates from Scunthorpe and played many times for the Lincolnshire team against Northamptonshire in the Anglian League before turning professional in 1962 having served as a 17-year-old assistant pro to Bill Shankland at Potters Bar, Hertfordshire in 1961.

Having won at Royal Lytham and St Annes in 1969, he was not out of the top ten until 1974. He followed this Open Championship victory with the US Open in 1970, making him, aged 26, the first Britain to hold both titles for 70 years. He never won another major: 'those that the Gods seek to destroy, they first drive mad', in Jacklin's case by pairing him with Lee Trevino. With the Open Championship of 1972 within Jacklin's grasp, at the 17th at Muirfield, Trevino holed a casually struck chip and Jacklin three putted. He dropped another shot at 18, lost the championship and, perhaps, his golfing career.

He is widely recognized as the man who helped re-establish European competitiveness in the Ryder Cup Matches. In 1987, he again led the European team to a surprise win at Muirfield Village, Ohio, a first victory on American soil on the same day that the Hollingsworth Trophy was being won in Northamptonshire. Suitable celebration ensued on both sides of the Atlantic!

For Tony Jacklin, there is a feeling in golf that the Ryder Cup victories in 1985, 1987 and the tie in 1989 have partially mending the mental wounds inflicted by Trevino's cruel chip in.

It was never meant to be a fair game.

LGU

Founded in 1893, the Ladies' Golf Union (L.G.U.) is the governing body for Ladies' amateur golf in Great Britain and Ireland. This union consists of the National Organisations (English Ladies' Golf Association, Irish Ladies' Golf Union, Scottish Ladies' Golfing Association and the Welsh Ladies' Golf Union) who represent lady members from all those clubs within Great Britain and Ireland.

There are currently ca 220,000 lady members from ca 2,750 golf clubs. The Union also consists of are a number of overseas unions, associations and overseas clubs affiliated to the L.G.U. The Union is administered by an elected Council representing England E.L.G.A., Ireland I.L.G.U., Scotland S.L.G.A. and Wales W.L.G.U. There are eight elected members, two from each of the four Home Countries with a Chairman, elected annually from the Council members, a President and an Honorary Treasurer. Upholding the rules of the game is the primary objective of the Ladies' Golf Union together with advancing and safeguarding the interests of ladies' golf. Most of the Union's income is generated by membership subscription, this is a small annual fee incorporated within each lady golfer's golf club membership fee. This income provides the Union with the resources to manage the affairs of the Union for the benefit of the members.

L.G.U. History

1893 – The L.G.U. was formed

1893 – The first Ladies' British Amateur Championship was played over Royal Lytham & St Anne's. This was won by Lady Margaret Scott who defeated Miss Issette Pearson by 7 & 6. The Amateur Trophy is currently on display in the British Golf Museum, St Andrews. The original trophy is still played for today. Details of the winners of this Championship from its inception can be found in the Lady Golfers' Handbook.

1895 – The first Home International Match (England v Ireland) won by England at Royal Portrush G.C.

1919 – First Girls' Open Golf Championship (GOGC) held at Stoke Poges. Won in 1933 by Jessie Anderson (now Valentine).

1931 – The first Vagliano Trophy Match played against only France. It is now played against a European Team.

1932 – The first Curtis Cup match took place against the USA at Wentworth.

1949 – The first British Girls' Championship was played at Beaconsfield Golf Club.

1949 – The first Girls' International Matches. The Stroyan Cup won by England.

1969 – The first British Ladies' Stroke Play Championship was played at Northumberland Golf Club.

1976 – The first Women's British Open.

1981 – The first British Seniors Ladies' Championship was played at Formby Ladies' GC.

2002 – Inaugural British Mid-Amateur Championship was played at the Berkshire Golf Club in memory of the late Angela Uzielli.

2003 – The first Senior International Matches was played at Whittington Heath G.C

The L.G.U. offices are currently located in St Andrew a wedge up the road from the R&A Clubhouse at The Scores, Fife, KY16 9AT. The building has a flat close by which is available for rent to lady members and has a vast collection of old books and photographs housed in its library. The upper floor flat has lovely views across the sands of St Andrews Bay; it can be a peaceful spot in the old grey town especially when the wind and rain are gone surrounded by solid local stone buildings which are steeped in local and golf history.

In Northamptonshire, Northampton G.C. Lady Member Dilys Tyrrell supplied one of the earliest summaries of the Ladies golf year from the 1908 L.G.U. Year Book to my good friend the late Gil Sibley for the Club's 1993 Centenary publication[4]. Gil was a schoolteacher at Weston Favell and a long-standing member at Northampton G.C. Dilys was made a Life Member of the Club in 2007 in view of her outstanding service over fifty years to the Club.

I reproduce the text here without shame since both these books are largely inaccessible to the majority of readers. It is interesting to note the addresses of the Lady members, the scores recorded at the time and that a gentleman looked after their finances. Most notably to me, is a lady playing off scratch and winning the monthly medal with a nett 85, the presence of Lady Delia Spencer and the Club's unbeaten performance in Inter Club matches. I do not understand what $\frac{1}{4}$ in a match result means. Can anyone help?

Extract from 1908 L.G.U. Year Book

Northampton Ladies Golf Club

Founded 1893

—— ○○○ ——

President: EARL SPENCER

Captain and Hon. Secretary: Mrs CHARLES W. PHIPPS, Cliftonville, Northampton

Hon.Treasurer: Mr A.C. Pearson, County Hall, Northampton

Committee: Mrs CHARLES W. PHIPPS, Mrs LOBBETT, Mrs PHILLIPS, Miss Norman, Miss G.Hughes

List of Members

L.G.U. Hcp	Club Hcp	
15	16	Mrs F. Bostock, Cliftonville
9	12	Mrs E.R. Bull, Duston House
8	6	Mrs W.H. Hope, Wellingborough
15	16	Miss G. Hughes, Hardingstone
4	4	Mrs E.H. Lancester, Abington Street
12	14	Mrs A.R. Lobbett, Kingswear
20	19	Mrs C.L. Mason, East Park Parade
7	9	Miss Norman, Cheyne Walk
scr.	scr.	Miss Phillips, Towerfield
11	11	Mrs C.W. Phipps, Cliftonville

Miss Atherton, Miss Balten, Miss Beasley, Miss Bouverie, Mrs Briggs, Mrs Brindle, Miss Busyard, Miss Church, Miss Crockett, Mrs Dulley, Mrs Horton, Miss Lobbett, Miss Horries Jones, The Misses Manning, Mrs Norman, Miss Pearson, Miss Randall, Miss Rawlins, Mrs Saville, Hon.Delia Spencer, Mrs Stanton, Miss Stanton, Miss Thursby, Mrs Walker Mrs Wright.

MONTHLY MEDAL WINNERS, 1907

					On Par of 74 Gross	Hcp.	Net
January	... Mrs Phillips	...	...	...	85	scr.	85
February	... Mrs Bostock	...	...	...	97	18	79
March	... Mrs Lobbett	...	...	...	104	17	87
April	... Mrs Bostock	...	...	...	94	18	76
					On Par of 84		
May	... Mrs Phillips	...	...	...	89	scr.	89
June	... Mrs Lankester	...	...	...	98	6	92
July	... Miss Mason	...	...	...	116	19	97
August	... Miss Hughes	...	...	...	104	25	79
September	... Miss Lobbett	...	...	...	102	16	86
October	... Miss Lobbett	...	...	...	103	16	87
November	... Miss Hughes	...	...	...	109	18	91
December	... Miss Hughes	...	...	...	115	18	97

Golf in Northamptonshire

WINNERS OF PRINCIPAL PRIZES, 1907

Spring Meeting.

April 16th, "Goodyear" Challenge Bowl, won by Miss Lobbett, 100-17=83.
Silver Challenge Tray, 36 holes Bogey, won by Miss G. Hughes, all square.
Silver Challenge Salver, won four times in succession by Mrs Lobbett.

INTER CLUB MATCHES

December 11th, 1906, at Rugby v. Rugby, won by $5^3/_4$ matches to $^1/_4$.
January 28th, 1907 at Leicestershire, v. Leicester, won by $3^1/_2$ to $^1/_2$.
April 10th, at Birstall v. Birstall, won by 5 matches to 2.
May 3rd, at Coventry v. Coventry, won by 4 matches to 2.
Nov. 12th, at Northampton, v. Birstall, won by $7^1/_4$ matches to $2^1/_2$.
Dec.3rd, at Northampton, v. Leicester, won by 4 matches to 1.
Dec.9th, at Northampton, v. Bedford, won by $4^1/_4$ matches to 2.

Length of Holes

1st hole	... 264 yards	6th hole	...	248 yards
2nd ,, ...	... 107 ,,	7th ,, ...	...	303 ,,
3rd ,, ...	... 326 ,,	8th ,, ...	...	260 ,,
4th ,, ...	... 340 ,,	9th ,, ...	...	220 ,,
5th ,, ...	... 360 ,,			

Total 2428 yards

Par of Green, 34. L.G.U. & Club.

Fixtures: Medal days, 1st Wednesday in every month. L.G.U. scores Every Tuesday

Club Colours: Red coats, green colours and cuffs.

Entrance Fee and Subscription: Entrance Fee, £1, 10s. Subscription, £1, 10s.

Club Telephone: 0483.

Station: London & N.W. and Midland

Hotel: Grand Hotel

"The growth of the Ladies Golf Union is nothing less than a romance. In 1893 twelve clubs belonged to the Union; now the affiliated number seven hundred."
Cecil Leitch 1922

Historic Events in Golf from 1754-2007

1744 First written code of rules. Rule 1 stated: "You must tee your ball within a club's length of the hole."

1850 With the introduction of the gutta percha ball a new rule provided that if a ball broke up in flight another ball could be dropped without penalty where the largest piece was found

1897 Formation of the R&A Rules of Golf Committee.

1904 Time allowed in searching for a ball reduced from 10 to five minutes.

1909 Limits on the form and make of clubs applied for the first time.

1922 Restrictions on the size and weight of golf balls imposed in an effort to limit the distance they would travel.

1929 Steel shafts became legal for the first time.

1939 Only 14 clubs to be carried from this date.

1949 To stop the spread of slow play, committees were empowered to disqualify players who unduly delayed others. Modified in 1952 to loss of hole or two-stroke penalty, with disqualification for repeated offences.

1952 First world code agreed between R&A and USGA. Stymie abolished - players no longer forced to chip over an opponent's ball coming to rest between their ball and the hole in match play.

1960 Distance measuring devices banned.

1984 Ball no longer dropped over the player's shoulder, but at arm's length and at shoulder height.

1990 The 1.68-inch ball becomes the only legal ball, marking the demise of the 1.62 British ball.

2004 The Royal and Ancient Golf Club of StAndrews celebrated its 250th year. Northamptonshire were in attendance and represented by N.G.U. President Mike Taylor and N.C.L.G.A. President Pam Giles. The largest marquee ever assembled at St Andrews was the venue for several dinners hosted by Club Captain HRH The Duke of York KCVO, ADC.

2006 Distance measuring devices now allowed under a local rule.

—— ooo ——

The following lines by Allan Junior describe St Andrews perfectly; you must go there once in your life, I am sure that like me you will be enchanted with the place & return.

There is no where in the world quite like it.

> *"O glory of a dying day*
> *Reflected on St Andrews Bay*
> *O music of the surging foam*
> *Upon the windswept shores of home*
> *O grey old city by the sea*
> *You are the whole wide world to me"*

CHAPTER 3

THE NORTHAMPTONSHIRE GOLF UNION

"Never grip it hard boy, hold it like a little bird"

Sam Snead 1912-2002

I N THIS chapter, I aim to give a flavour of the administration of the Union together with a description and results of the major competitions that individuals and teams participate in. The administration section contains many minutes taken from Council meetings and A.G.M.s and whilst a little lengthy and detailed describes how the N.G.U. has evolved from 1921-2008. In the early days of the Union detailed minutes of every meeting were lovingly hand written in minute books by the County Secretary and this practice lasted up until 1971. This produced three lengthy tomes which are stored for safekeeping in the N.G.U. office. After 1971 minutes have been typed or word processed by the County Secretary and are available if necessary. I have used my own records and those of other administrators from 1971-2008 to complete the picture.

The Clubs initially formed the Northamptonshire Association of Golf Clubs in 1921 and changed title to the Northamptonshire Golf Union in 1929. I would respectfully suggest to the reader that this section is consumed in a bite sized chunks.

During the last eighty six years many dedicated officials and volunteers have assisted in the day to day running of the Union's affairs, a list of the County Officials can be obtained from our annual yearbook[7] or from our website[8]. In 2008 all the competitions and events are managed and a run by the Executive Committee and there are half a dozen or so sub-committees in place to assist the elected officers. Many people give up their spare time to help the running of Northamptonshire's golf; we formally thank them here together with many unsung workers whose contribution is invaluable.

The major events that individuals and teams participate in are described after the administration section. In view of space considerations I have restricted the list; further details of the winners of all competitions may be obtained from the two sources described above.

N.G.U. Administration 1921-1971

The first preliminary meeting took place on the 12th of October 1921 at 18 Market Square Northampton. Those present were Mr A. J. Fraser (in chair) & Major J. C. Lewis (Northamptonshire G.C.), W.P. Cross, C.Wright, W.Kew and G.A.T.Vials (Northampton GC) E.V.Stuckey, E.Speakman (Kingsthorpe G.C.) A.E.Bryan, W. J.Thomson & E. Franklin-Smith (Kettering G.C.)

Mr Vials explained that the meeting had been called to consider the desirability of forming a County Golf Association in Northamptonshire with the main objects of promoting and guarding the interests of the game generally in the county and playing county matches and organising county meetings. A full discussion took place and it was eventually proposed by Major Lewis seconded by Mr Cross and carried unanimously that an association be formed. A discussion as to the representation of Clubs on the Council of the Association led the proposition which was unanimously carried that each affiliated Club have two representatives on the council.

It was resolved that a subscription to the Association by each affiliated Club should be £1-1-0 for every hundred male members or part of a hundred. It was resolved that the President of the Association be elected to hold office for one year and who should not be eligible for re-election until the expiration of one year from the termination of his period of office. It was unanimously resolved that Mr F. Bostock be invited to become the first President.

Mr Vials was elected Hon Secretary and Treasurer. Various expressions of opinion were made as to the form in which the Association Rules should be prepared and a sub-committee consisting of Messrs Lewis, Brian, Speakman and Vials was appointed to prepare draft rules for submission to the next meeting.

The minutes were signed by Fred Bostock.

The First true meeting of the Council was held at The Northampton Club on Tuesday 29th of November 1921 with Mr F. Bostock in the chair. The minutes of the first preliminary meeting were passed as read. The secretary reported that the following Clubs had now affiliated:- Northampton G.C. (Kettering Road), Northamptonshire G.C. (Church Brampton), Kingsthorpe G.C., Kettering G.C., Wellingborough G.C., Market Harborough G.C., Rushden and District G.C., whilst Oundle G.C. had written declining to affiliate.

The rules sub-committee submitted draft rules which they had prepared and a full discussion took place and the rules of the Association settled. It was the opinion of the majority that the word "Association" in the title was more appropriate than the word "Union". Mr G.P.M.Skae was invited to become Competition Secretary. Mr Frazer said he was able to offer the Church Brampton course for the first County match and the first County meeting. The offer was unanimously accepted and the Competition Secretary was authorised to make arrangements at once for the holding of a meeting in the spring.

The First Annual General Meeting was held at The Clubhouse Church Brampton on Thursday 12th of January 1922 at 12 noon. During the proceedings a discussion took place as to the first meeting when the Brampton course was available. The Secretary reported that he had been promised a Cup by Mr T.Higgs to be placed at the discretion of the Council. Mr Bostock and Mr W. P. Cross kindly offered to give cups and the thanks of the meeting were accorded them.

At the next (2nd) Council meeting held at The Northampton Club on Wednesday 22nd of March 1922 Mr Frazer reported that he had attended the general meeting of the Midlands Association when a lengthy discussion had taken place as to the desirability of fixing par and scratch scores for all courses with a view to arriving at uniformity in handicapping, the Midlands had decided to support the St. Andrews scheme. Mr Skae reported that he had arranged a match with Warwickshire for 25th October 1922 in Warwickshire and was authorised to arrange a fixture with Worcestershire at Stourbridge on the 20th of May 1922 (This was the first Match). The match played against Leicestershire on the 7 Sept 1922 was lost 3-5 and has become Northamptonshire's longest standing fixture 1922-2008. Details of the many matches between the two counties can be seen on the Leicestershire & Rutland G.U. website.

The First Annual Meeting was fixed for the 11th & 13th of May 1922 at Northamptonshire County G.C., Lancelot Bostock from the home Club became the first County Champion with a score of 81 gross and received the Scratch Challenge Cup from The President his father Fred Bostock. Northants County also won the Inter-Club Competition (Today's Scratch League Division 1 Trophy) with a 3 man total of 250. (The format and results from the first meeting are shown on pages 40-44) All arrangements were left in the hands of the Hon Competition Secretary and Hon Secretary although on the days of the Meeting a Committee from Northants County supervised the arrangements. In modern times, this event is now known as the County Championship and is held on a Saturday in June over 36 holes.

Regular Council Meetings were held up until the Second World War and notable highlights included:

21 November 1922

The Secretary was instructed to write to all clubs to make a return on their par and scratch scores. The Secretary presented some accounts for payment and these were passed but it was decided that entertaining expenses in future must not exceed 3/6 per head for visiting teams. The Second Annual Meeting was fixed for 25th January 1923 at The Clubhouse Church Brampton at 12 noon. At this meeting it was decided to arrange a match with the Professionals. Dr John Allison (See Chapter 1) was in the chair.

April 15th 1924 at 18 Market Square Northampton

The Secretary read further letters with regards to the recent formation of the English Golf Union, and it was decided that this Association should join the Union when funds permitted. The exact date of affiliation is unknown, but was certainly prior to 1929.

Fourth Annual Meeting was held at Kingsthorpe GC 6 May 1926.

The Secretary submitted the accounts of the Association as audited by Mr P.Scott and these were passed. A vote of thanks to the Club for the use of the course was proposed.

The first meeting of the "NGU"

Northamptonshire Association of Golf Clubs.

FIRST ANNUAL MEETING

TO BE HELD AT

Northamptonshire County Golf Club, Church Brampton,

(By the kind invitation of the Committee)

On Thursday, May 11th and Saturday, May 13th, 1922.

Open to members of all Clubs affiliated to the Northamptonshire Association.

THURSDAY. MAY 11TH.

Morning.—**Bogey Competition.** 18 Holes under handicap. First Prize value £2:2:0; Second Prize value £1:1:0.

Afternoon.—**Medal Competition.** 18 Holes under handicap. First Prize value £2:2:0; Second Prize value £1:1:0.

A Cup presented by T. Higgs, Esq. will be held for one year by the Club of which the winner of this competition is a member.

Limit of handicap for the above competitions, 20.

Entrance Fee 2/6 each player in each competition.

SATURDAY. MAY 13TH.

Morning.—**Inter-Club Competition.** Medal Round 18 holes (Scratch) for Cup presented by W. P. Cross, Esq.

Teams to consist of 3 representatives from each Club.

Entrance Fee 10/- per team.

Afternoon.—**Foursome Competition.** Medal Round 18 holes under handicap. First Prize value £4:4:0; Second Prize value £2:2:0.

Limit of handicap, 20.

Entrance Fee 2/6 each player.

SCRATCH CHALLENGE CUP.

The above Cup presented by the President (F. Bostock, Esq.) will be held for one year by the Club to which the player belongs who returns the best scratch score for 18 holes during the meeting.

G. A. T. VIALS, *Hon. Sec.*

REGULATIONS.

A Committee appointed by the Northamptonshire County Golf Club will supervise the arrangements on the days of the meeting.

All cards will be issued by this Committee only, and when returned must be placed in the box provided.

Competitors must arrange for their own partners and opponents excepting in the Inter-Club Competition, when opponents will be drawn by the Committee.

All points arising shall be settled by the Committee whose ruling shall be final.

There will be an optional sweepstake of 2/6 on each event.

All entries together with Entrance Fees and name of Club must reach the Hon. Competition Secretary, **G. P. M. SKAE, 19, Bradshaw Street, Northampton,** not later than Thursday, May 4th, 1922.

LUNCHEONS & TEAS PROVIDED AT THE CLUB HOUSE.

Xpres Printers, Ltd., 36, St. Mary's Street, Northampton.

THE

NORTHAMPTONSHIRE ASSOCIATION OF GOLF CLUBS.

HON. COMPETITION SECRETARY'S OFFICE:—

G. P. M. Skae,

19 Bradshaw Street,

Northampton.

TELEGRAMS:
"SKAE, NORTHAMPTON."

TELEPHONE 977.

FIRST ANNUAL MEETING of the Association, held at The Northamptonshire County Golf Club, Church Brampton, Northampton, on Thursday MAY 11th and Saturday MAY 13th 1922.

Thursday MAY 11th - MORNING.

BOGEY COMPETITION - 18 holes under handicap.

R E S U L T S

Name of Competitor.	Name of Club.	Handicap.	Score.
E SPEAKMAN	Kingsthorpe G C	8	1 Up
		Winner of FIRST PRIZE value £2-2-0	
G P M SKAE	N'ton County G C	7	1 Down
		Winner of SECOND PRIZE value £1-1-0	

OTHER SCORES

F F IRONSIDE	N'ton G C	9	2 down
L BOSTOCK	N'ton County G C	2	3 "
A E GREEN	do	15	3 "
R WEST	N'ton G C	20	5 "
E G ELLIOTT	N'ton County G C	20	5 "
A H BRYAN	Kettering G C	10	5 "
W P CROSS	N'ton County G C	11	5 "
R W KILSBY	Rushden G C	12	6 "
A C HULETT	Kettering G C	18	7 "
R W DAVIES	Rushden G C	18	7 "
G A T VIALS	N'ton G C	13	9 "

NORTHAMPTONSHIRE ASSOCIATION OF GOLF CLUBS (Cont'd)

Thursday MAY 11th - AFTERNOON.

MEDAL COMPETITION - 18 holes under handicap.

R E S U L T S

Name of Kompetitor.	Name of Club.	Cross.	Hdcp.	Nett.
G A T VIALS	N'ton G C	89	13	76

Winner of FIRST PRIZE
value £2-2-0 and CUP
presented by T Higgs Esq

W A S TALBOT	N'ton County G C	86	9	77
E SPEAKMAN	Kingsthorpe G C	85	8	77

Tie for SECOND PRIZE
value £1-1-0

L BOSTOCK	N'ton County G C	81		

81 - Winner of CUP
presented by F BOSTOCK ESQ
for the BEST SCRATCH SCORE

OTHER SCORES

J F STOPS	N'ton County G C	86	8	78
S COOPER	N'ton County G C	88	7	81
L C BALLION/	N'ton County G C	94	13	81
C TRETHEWY	Daventry G C	90	9	81
R W KILSBY	Rushden G C	93	12	81
A H BRYAN	Kettering	93	10	83
H A MILLINGTON	N'ton County G C	99	15	84
W P CROSS	N'ton County G C	95	11	84
H G JELLEY	Kingsthorpe G C	104	19	85
R WEST	N'ton G C	106	20	86
F F IRONSIDE	N'ton G C	95	9	86
A C HULETT	Kettering G C	98	12	86

NORTHAMPTONSHIRE ASSOCIATION OF GOLF CLUBS (Cont'd)

Saturday MAY 13th - MORNING.

INTER-CLUB COMPETITION.   Medal Round 18 holes (Scratch)
                            for CUP presented by W P CROSS Esq.

                            Teams of 3 from each Club.

R E S U L T S

Name of Club	Competitors	Cross Scores.	TOTAL.
NORTHAMPTON COUNTY	L BOSTOCK N BOSTOCK S COOPER	84 85 81	250
	Winners of CUP.		

OTHER SCORES

Name of Club	Competitors	Cross Scores.	TOTAL.
NORTHAMPTON G C	P D RIDDELL F F IRONSIDE H H C DAWES	85 95 95	275
KETTERING G C	A J WRIGHT J BAKER W J THOMPSON	89 91 88	278
KINGSTHORPE G C	O HANWELL E SPEAKMAN W J WATKINS	96 92 92	280
DAVENTRY G C	Dr HARRISON C TRETHEWY Rev FITZGERALD	94 100 109	303

NORTHAMPTONSHIRE ASSOCIATION OF GOLF CLUBS (Cont'd)

Saturday MAY 13th - AFTERNOON.

FOURSOMES COMPETITION   Medal Round 18 holes under handicap.

R E S U L T S

Names of Competitors.	Gross Scores.	Hdcp.	Nett
G P M SKAE and W J WATKINS	86	8	78

Winners of FIRST PRIZE
value £4-4-0

L C BALLION and A L VELLACOTT	93	13½	79½

Winners of SECOND PRIZE
value £2-2-0

OTHER SCORES

F BRITTEN and O HANWELL	92	11½	80½
F T ALLAN and H B JUDKINS	92	11	81
G A T VIALS and W TYRRELL	96	13½	82½
W J THOMPSON and A H BRYAN	91	8	83
G C HULL and A J WRIGHT	87	4	83
A JONES and E SPEAKMAN	96	11½	84½
F W PANTHER and W P CROSS	100	15	85
L BOSTOCK and Dr HARRISSON	92	6½	85½
A J FRASER and N F BOSTOCK	93	7½	85½
J H C DAWES and A D FAIRE	97	11	86
F F IRONSIDE and P D RIDDELL	93	6	87
J BAKER and A C HULLETT	96	8	88
Rev FITZGERALD and C TRETHEWY	104	12½	91½

Pages 41-44 show the Results of the First "NGU" Meeting

NORTHAMPTONSHIRE ASSOCIATION OF GOLF CLUBS.

HON. COMPETITION SECRETARY'S OFFICE:—

G. P. M. Skae,

19 Bradshaw Street,

Northampton.

TELEGRAMS:
"SKAE. NORTHAMPTON."

—

TELEPHONE 977.

—

FRIDAY.
SEPT 8/22

RESULT of MATCH

NORTHAMPTONSHIRE V LEICESTERSHIRE

Played at Northampton County Golf Club,
CHURCH BRAMPTON, on THURSDAY SEPT 7/22

NORTHAMPTONSHIRE		LEICESTERSHIRE	
A J WRIGHT	0	H KING	1 (7-6)
G P M SKAE	0	J MORTON	1 (1 up)
H C OLDREY	0	G M STUART	1 (1 up)
G W BUCHANAN	1 (4-3)	F C BOLTON	0
G B G HULL	1 (19th)	M E WHITEHEAD	0
N H MOHUN	0	W A THOMPSON	1 (3-2)
W J THOMPSON	1 (3-1)	C RUSSELL	0
W J WATKINS	0	J HAMILTON	1 (4-3)
	3		5

LEICESTERSHIRE WON by 5 points to 3.
Two of the matches finished on the last green, and one
finished on the 19th.   Neither side had their strongest
team in the field.
The Course was in excellent condition and the weather ideal.

The first match against Leicestershire in 1922

Golf in Northamptonshire

THE
NORTHAMPTONSHIRE ASSOCIATION OF GOLF CLUBS.

HON. COMPETITION SECRETARY'S OFFICE:—
G. P. M. Skae,
19 Bradshaw Street,
Northampton.

TELEGRAMS:
"SKAE, NORTHAMPTON."

TELEPHONE 977.

NORTHAMPTONSHIRE V WORCESTERSHIRE

Match played at BRAND HALL COURSE, QUINTON
Near Birmingham, on Saturday MAY 20th 1922.

RESULT

WORCESTERSHIRE.	Hdcp.	SCORE.	NORTHAMPTONSHIRE.	Hdcp.	SCORE
No 1 S C CRAVEN	Plus 2	0	L BOSTOCK	2	1 (4-2)
2. E SOMERS-SMITH	" 1	0	A J WRIGHT	2	1 (2 up
3. W PEARSON	Scratch	0	P D RIDDELL	3	1 (7-6)
4. R C AUSTIN	"	0	H C OLDREY	7	1 (1 up
5. F STUART-KING	"	1 (4-3)	B G HULL	6	0
6. E F HARRIS	1	1 (4-3)	G W BUCHANAN	7	0
7. C REECE	1	1 (2 up)	G P M SKAE	7	0
8. C WHEELER	4	1 (4-2)	E SPEAKMAN	8	0
9. H WHEELER	6	1 (1 up)	F M McKELLEN	10	0
TOTAL............		5			4

One of Northamptonshire's earliest matches versus Worcestershire in 1922.

46

April 17 1929 Council Meeting of the Northamptonshire Association of Golf Clubs.

A discussion of the title Northamptonshire Golf Union arose for submission to the general meeting.

The Seventh A.G.M., April 27th 1929

Mr Albert Jones, President was in the chair. After some discussion it was proposed and seconded by Mr J.H.C.Dawes that the title of the Northamptonshire Association of Golf Clubs should be changed immediately to the Northamptonshire Golf Union, this was carried unanimously in view of the fact that the majority of the other counties had adopted this manner of describing their affiliation to the English Golf Union.

April 8, 1931 Council Meeting 31 Market Square Northampton

It was proposed and carried that a report for the year 1931 should be issued by the Hon Secretary & Treasurer similar to that issued in 1930 showing a balance sheet.

24 Feb 1932, 31 Market Square Northampton

The card of fixtures for summer competitions was submitted and approved, an alteration of entrance fee from1/6 to 1/9 (3d for greenkeepers) was confirmed. It was proposed by Mr Timson and seconded by Mr Ford that £75 be invested in the Town and Country Building Society and resolved. Regarding Handicapping and Scratch Scores this matter was reviewed and it was pointed out that the scratch scores of many clubs contained too many allowances for course difficulty. (Note by author, the same is still true at some courses in 2008! In 2008, the meeting rooms used by the N.G.U 31 Market Square is the address of the Peacock Place Shopping Centre Northampton)

31 Market Square Northampton Feb 12th 1933

A letter was read from Mr Bond, Treasurer of the English Golf Union suggesting that Peterborough, Burleigh and any new Clubs should be approached with regard to being affiliated within the Union.

January 23, 1934 31 Market Square Northampton

Mr F.C.Roe proposed and Mr Jillian seconded that the Club's subscription to the county union should be raised from 21 shillings to 25 shillings per 100 members, carried.

May 15, 1935 at 6 p.m.

It was decided that a sub-committee should be formed to consider the proposition of County Team matches and County Team competitions, the sub-committee to be Messrs Roe, Kilsby, Passmore, Catlow and the Hon Secretary.

The 13th A.G.M. June 6, 1935 Mr A.G.Seward (President) in the chair

It was decided to hold a mixed Foursome Competition as soon after the play-off as possible in September, on a date convenient to the County Golf Committee and on the Brampton course if possible.

March 11, 1936

Mr Catlow the Match Secretary reported that he had arranged County fixtures against Leicester at Brampton on June 13th and against Bedford at Dunstable Downs on July 19th.

14th A.G.M. Northampton Golf Club June 11, 1936

It was proposed by Mr F.C. Wild and seconded by Mr Collier that the Club subscriptions should be increased to 30 shillings from 20 shillings per 100 members. This had become necessary as the E.G.U. had been compelled to double their subscriptions per Club in order to carry out the necessary engagements of providing a salary for a paid Secretary as it was impossible to carry on with a Hon Secretary as in the past. At this time the telephone number of Northants County was Chapel Brampton 313.

September 16th 1936

It was agreed the fee of 10 shillings each County Match should be given to the Greenkeeper at all the County Matches played away. It was also decided that more evening competitions should be played in June and if necessary each Thursday in that month to avoid meetings being held during the Summer Holidays when so many competitors would be away.

Feb 3rd 1937

It was proposed that Mr Catlow be invited to make a calendar of golf events in the Northampton County for the whole year and print it on a good paper.

September 29, 1937

It was agreed that the Council is strongly in favour of the Junior Championship Boys and Girls to be held in the summer holidays.

March 30, 1938

It was proposed by Mr Holloway and seconded by Mr Vacquerey that the Junior championship meeting should be proceeded with for a one year and that the Clubs should be advised as soon as possible so that Union members could be notified during the Easter Holidays, this was carried. A letter was read from the Bedford County Secretary proposing that Bedford County and Northamptonshire should be merged in a joint effort to issue books of tickets for green fees, after some discussion it was decided that the council was not in favour of this proposition and Mr Catlow was requested to write the Bedford County Secretary to this effect.

16th A.G.M. Northampton Golf Club June 30, 1938

About 20 representatives of the various Clubs were present. The Hon Treasurer presented the accounts for the year which showed a profit of £11.2s.3d.

September 20, 1938

On the proposition of Mr Roe seconded by Mr Catlow it was resolved that a County Tie be adopted in accordance with the pattern obtained, namely a blue tie with the County Rose. The ties to be available at a price of seven shillings and six pence.

November 22, 1938 at 9 George Row Northampton

Mr F.C. Roe President in the chair. A hearty welcome was accorded to Messrs Robertson and W. Hollingsworth as the respective representatives of the Peterborough Milton G.C. and the Castle Ashby G.C. on the occasion of their first attendance at a council meeting. (The two clubs were admitted to membership of the N.G.U. as from the first of January 1939.)

January 18th 1939

The Hon Secretary raised the question of the limitations of the powers of the golf ball at present in use and after a lengthy and interesting discussion in which the majority of the members present took part it was proposed and seconded and agreed that the council of the N.G.U was in favour of the present ball being adopted as the standard ball for the future and that the curtailment or extension of its power was not in the best interests of the majority of golfers or golf clubs.

June 11th 1939

On the proposition that Mr Wild and seconded by Mr Robertson approval was given to Northampton Golf Club's action in reducing Mr C.S.Catlow's handicap to +1. Mr Catlow who was present received the congratulations of members on obtaining such a high standard in his golf. Mr Catlow reported that the Professionals of the County had formed themselves into a body to be known as the Northamptonshire Golf Professionals Association and were desirous of holding a Professional Championship. On the proposition of Mr Catlow seconded by Mr Wareing it was unanimously resolved that the Professionals be allowed to run their Championship concurrently with the County Amateur Championship.

17th A.G.M. July 6th 1939 at 8 p.m.

Mr Wild reported the receipt of the donation of Two Guineas to the funds of the Union from the retiring President Mr Watson. On behalf of the union Mr Wild expressed very sincere thanks for the gift.

Special General Meeting on November 23rd 1939

The Secretary explained that the meeting had been called primarily to decide the desirability or otherwise of a series of meetings during the winter months on various courses with the object of raising money for War charities.

It was unanimously agreed to hold meetings one per month between December and March at Northamptonshire, Kettering, Kingsthorpe and Rushden respectively.

Special Meeting September 26th 1940 at Wellingborough G.C. following the last summer evening competition of the season.

Mr Catlow point out that this Special meeting had been called because Mr Holloway the Hon Secretary had been called away on Government Business and was likely to be away for the duration of the War. Mr Catlow was appointed as Hon Secretary pending Mr Holloway's return. It was unanimously agreed to grant as in former years the sum of 10 shillings to the Greenkeepers of the courses where competitions had been held during the summer.

19th A.G.M. March 20, 1941 at Wellingborough G.C.

During the war the E.G.U. had reduced their charges to 50% of their usual requirement. Mr Wild then said that the Clubs in this county had only been asked for subscriptions in proportion to this. The Council had passed a resolution for profits from the Income and Expenditure account of the N.G.U. to be passed on to the Red Cross at the end of the current year. Mr Wild then gave a summary of the amounts paid to the Red Cross by the N.G.U. and the Clubs in the County and by the Henry Cotton match (16th June 1940 at Northampton G.C. see Chapter 1) and a grand total was something like £500 which the meeting thought was an excellent showing.

The acting Hon Sec reported "As to the position since the War, all ordinary matches, championships and competitions have been cancelled, the Cups are in safe keeping, but we have held a few fourball

List of N.G.U. Trophies held for the duration of World War II by the United Counties Omnibus Company.

meetings on summer evenings and on Thursdays in the winter months in aid of the Red Cross. The question now arises with the very necessary, and ever tightening restrictions of all sporting activities as to whether we should continue to run the competitions at all and if so, when where and how".

(For safekeeping most of the union's trophies together with some from the professionals were kept in the safe in the strong room for the duration of the War by Mr Mills of the United Counties Omnibus Company (see page 49). The Union had a healthy £100 in the Building Society; four players who had earned the County Tie were serving as Officers in the Army).

Under item Vote of Thanks, the acting Hon Sec wish to thank all the Clubs in the County who had so generously helped in all the Red Cross competitions and he pointed out that he didn't include the name of the County Captain Mr Roe as a member of the committee which could form a quorum of three, because he knew that Mr Roe was shortly going away to serve with H.M.Forces.

17th Annual General Meeting 16th April 1942

Daventry G.C. had found it necessary to discontinue play over their course for the duration of the hostilities owing to the loss of land and the requisitioning of the clubhouse. They had been given advice, obtained from the English Golf Union, as to the financial claim they might have upon the government departments. It was hoped that with the advent of the more severe rationing of petrol, Clubs would assist other Clubs less fortunately placed.

21st A.G.M. 27th of May 1943 his worship the Mayor of Northampton, Alderman W Lees (President) in the chair.

Hearty congratulations of the Union were conveyed to the President upon his election as Mayor of Northampton. Northampton Golf Club had generously offered advantageous playing facilities to members of the Daventry Golf Club and had been thanked by the Union and the English Golf Union. The Castle Ashby course had been badly affected by the food production campaign and play was unlikely until after the war.

22nd A.G.M. 22nd June 1944

The Union had a credit balance at the 31st of March 1944 of £157:6:4. The income during the year amounted to £42:15:0 and expenditure to £23:18:8, the Hon Treasurer stated that he hoped to forward the balance of £18:16:4 to the Red Cross fund in due course. Thanks were accorded to Mr W. Lees for his services as President and Chairman of the meeting, to the Northampton Golf Club for the use of the course for the day's competition and of their Clubhouse for this meeting and to the Honorary Officers of the Club.

23rd A.G.M. 24th May 1945

It was resolved, in view of the restoration of basic petrol that arrangements be made for Thursday fourball competitions to be held during the summer on Northamptonshire, Northampton and Kingsthorpe courses. (Note from Author. After World War 2 when the patterns of normal life returned, the Union developed significantly)

25th A.G.M. 15th May 1947

Four Union officials and 25 representatives of the Kettering, Northants County, Rushden and Northampton Golf Clubs were present. The Chairman referred to the death since the last annual meeting of Mr F.C.Wild for many years Hon Secretary and Hon Treasurer of the Union in which he took the keenest interest and expressed deep regret at his passing and representatives stood in silence in respect to his memory. The Hon Sec submitted a report in which he made reference to the affiliation to the Union of the Desborough Golf Club and the position of the Daventry and Castle Ashby Clubs.

21st Feb 1948

The Secretary submitted correspondence with the Peterborough Milton golf club in which it was suggested that the handicap of Mr H. Naylor should be reduced to "plus 1". It was resolved that while they are of the opinion that Mr Naylor's handicap must be kept under review they do not feel it is justified in reducing it to plus1 at this stage and accordingly the Council to consider the question again after the Championship Meeting. (At a later Council meeting in November his handicap remained at Scratch)

26th A.G.M. 22nd July 1948

On the proposition that Mr F.F. Parsons a Past President, seconded by the Hon Secretary it was resolved that the best thanks of the Union be accorded to Mr C. S.Catlow for his conscientious and untiring efforts as Hon Match Secretary since 1936 with congratulations upon the success achieved by those efforts. (Mr.W.Hollingsworth replaced Mr Catlow as Hon Match Secretary)

On the proposition of Mr R. A. Palmer, seconded by Mr C. S. Catlow it was resolved that the thanks of the Union be accorded to Mr J.Atwell retiring president for his valuable service.

13th November 1948

To accept with sincere thanks, the offer of Mr C. S. Catlow to arrange for the provision of a Cup for the Scratch Competition at the County Championship meeting for members under 29 years of age (The Braid's Driver). To authorise the Secretary to re-arrange the rota of the courses upon which the Championship is played, in order to provide for it to take place at Church Brampton every third year. That Mr George Mobbs be invited to Captain the County side in 1949.

NGU Summer Competitions in 1949

27th A.G.M. 12 May 1949

The President referred in terms of sorrow to the death of Mr Harry Naylor, of the County team and great supporter of golf in the County in general and at Peterborough in particular. The members stood in sympathy and memory. The Secretary submitted a request from the Market Harborough Club for transfer to the Leicestershire Golf Union on the grounds that although the course is situated in Northants it would be in the interest of the members the majority of which reside in Leicestershire, and adding that they had received all possible help from Northamptonshire. It was resolved that the Union become a member of the Midland Counties Golf Association.

NORTHAMPTONSHIRE GOLF UNION.

President - A. F. PERCIVAL, Esq.

Twenty-Fourth Annual
County Championship Meeting

TO BE HELD ON THE

Northampton Golf Course, Kettering Rd., Northampton

(By kind invitation of the Committee)

On SATURDAY, MAY 5th, 1951

(Open to Members of all Clubs affiliated to the Northamptonshire Golf Union with a Handicap of 12 or less—Revised under New Standard Scratch Score).

1. NORTHAMPTONSHIRE AMATEUR CHAMPIONSHIP.

36 Holes Medal. The Scratch Cup (to be held by the Club of which the winner is a member) for the best gross score. Winner will be the County Champion for the year and will receive a memento. Second Prize.

Entrance Fee, 5/-   Optional Sweepstake, 2/6.

Concurrently a separate competition will be held under handicap (restricted to 12 or less—revised under new Standard Scratch Score).

First and Second Prizes.   Optional Sweepstake, 2/6.

First round must be started by 1 p.m. ; Second round must be started by 4.45 p.m. Entries, see Regulation 6 below.

2. NORTHAMPTONSHIRE PROFESSIONAL CHAMPIONSHIP.

36 Holes Medal. Cup and Prize. Concurrently a separate competition will be held under handicap as settled by the President of the County Professionals' Association. Entries to Hon. Secretary by 30th April, 1951.

3. INTER-CLUB COMPETITION.

Medal Round of 18 holes (aggregate gross scores), in the *Afternoon* Round only, of the foregoing Competition. Teams of three players, limit three teams per Club.

Entrance Fee, 10/- per team.

REGULATIONS.

1. All Competitors will play on their lowest corresponding County Handicaps for the handicap competition.
2. A Committee appointed by the Union and the Northampton Golf Club will supervise the arrangements on the day of the Meeting.
3. All cards will be issued by this Committee only, and when returned must be placed in the box provided.
4. All points shall be settled by the Committee whose ruling shall be final.
5. Entries for Inter-Club Competition must reach the Hon. Secretary, "Whitelands," 108, Ridge Way, Northampton, not later than Saturday, April 28th, 1951.
6. **Entries must be made on forms, obtainable from each Club or the Hon. Secretary, which must be received by the Committee at the Northampton Golf Club by Noon on Monday, 30th April, 1951.** A starting sheet will be in operation. Partners will be arranged by the Committee. Competitors will be advised of the starting time allotted, and of their partner. They must be ready to play at the time allotted.

So far as supplies permit Luncheons and Teas will be provided at the Club House.

108, Ridge Way,
     Northampton.

J. STEVENSON HOLT, LTD. NEWLAND, NORTH.

W. H. ABBOTT,
     Hon. Secretary.

24th Annual County Championship Meeting 1951

12 Jan 1952

The County Club membership scheme introduced this year was reported to have raised £57, resolved that the scheme be continued for season 1952–53. That the President, Secretary and Treasurer consider organising an Interclub Foursome Matchplay competition with power to act, (The Hollingsworth Trophy launched in 1955). The Secretary reported that the Rushden Golf Club had generously donated £5.5s.0d to the funds of the Union to commemorate the Presidency of Mr R.W.Kilsby, and that with his approval the sum had been placed towards the expenses at the Boys Championship. Resolve to confirm that County Ties may be purchased only by players who have played for the County first team on at least two occasions and by the Honorary Officers.

25 October 1952

Resolved by 12 votes to 2 votes to pay, when requested expenses to a maximum of £4 to each of the three players who may represent the County in the English County Championship.

14 November 1953

The Match Secretary Mr Hollingsworth reported that the Ladies Union wished to hold a Girls Championship and to organise it in conjunction with the Boys Championship. Resolved to raise no objection to the proposal. (22 players entered the Boys Championship in 1954).

13 November 1954

The Hon Sec Mr W. H. Abbott reported that he would like to retire at the A.G.M. in 1956 when he will have served for 14 years.

33rd A.G.M. 23rd June 1955

Present C. S. Catlow Esq. (President) in the chair, W. Hollingsworth (Vice President and Match Secretary) W. H. Abbott (Hon Secretary) G.E.Dazeley (Hon Treasurer) and a good number of members representing Northants County, Kettering, Kingsthorpe and Rushden Clubs. Items included: That the future winners of the Union's Cups other than the Boys and Professionals, be requested to have the cups engraved at their own expense. That the request of the Midland Counties Golf Association for a subscription of £3.3.0 be referred to the Council to decide. (Passed in Nov 1955)

19th November 1955

Upon consideration of a letter from Mr J. Clymer (Norfolk) it was decided to donate £5 towards the purchase of the trophy for the Eastern Counties Foursomes. (A trophy we have yet to win!)

34th A.G.M. Northampton Golf Club 30th June 1956

The meeting expressed its thanks to the President Mr W. Hollingsworth for his generous gift of the beautiful trophy for the Interclub Match play Competition. (The trophy was first won by Kingsthorpe G.C. and has been described as Northamptonshire's F.A.Cup from the passion it generates)

35th A.G.M. Kingsthorpe G.C. 6th July 1957

Mr G.E.Dazeley retired as Hon Treasurer after serving since 1943. The abandonment of the Desborough Golf Club was noted as members had transferred to other courses.

36th A.G.M. 28th June 1958

On behalf of Mr C.S.Catlow and Mr W. Hollingsworth it was asked that the President accept their donation of a handsome silver trophy for the Boys Championship scratch under 15 hereafter known as "The Junior Trophy" The President, in accepting the trophy expressed the sincere thanks of the union to Messrs Catlow and Hollingsworth for their handsome gift.

Mr Catlow reported that the County had been presented with a wooden spoon at the Eastern Counties Foursomes Competition in 1958, it was resolved that the Union present a suitably engraved spoon to this competition for future use.

The achievement of Mr C. S. Catlow in winning the County Championship for the 10th time thus established a British Record. A suitable memento was purchased and presented to Mr C. S. Catlow to commemorate his achievement. This is now in the safe hands of the Aitken family.

37th A.G.M. 4 July 1959

That a County Foursomes Scratch Matchplay competition be instituted and that the generous offer of Mr C. S.Catlow to present a trophy to the Union for this event be accepted with many thanks.

26th November 1960

Resolved to hold a County Dinner to be held at Church Brampton on 24th February1961 and that the President of the English Golf Union Mr Stanley Hunt be invited to attend.

39th A.G.M. 1st July 1961

The balance sheet showed assets of £223.19s.4d. A contribution of £20 from the E.G.U. had been received for the coaching of young players.

25th November 1961

The Hon Match Secretary submitted the report of the Blazer Sub-Committee. It was resolved that the design for the County badge be adopted, that the qualification for the blazer badge be the same as for the County Tie, that the Match Secretary be requested to arrange for the purchase and distribution of the blazer badges.

The Boys Organiser Mr W. Hollingsworth produced to the meeting a silver cup presented by the Past President Mr D. Chamberlain for the Boys Championship, Junior Division. The thanks of the Union were accorded to Mr Chamberlain for his generous action.

40th A.G.M. 30th June 1962

On the behalf of the Clubs, Past officials and golfers in the county, The President (P.G. Cotton Esq.) presented a set of golf clubs, and Mr C. S.Catlow an inscribed silver salver to Mr W. H.Abbott in appreciation for his 21 years service as Hon Secretary. Mr Abbott expressed his great thanks to all concerned.

23rd November 1963

In the E.G.U. County Champions tournament held at Little Aston our Champion Mr R.G. Aitken was only five strokes behind the joint winners, beating several International players.

28th November 1964

Following the revision of the County boundaries Peterborough Milton's representatives stated it would be the wish of their Club to remain with Northamptonshire.

43rd A.G.M. 3rd July 1965

The balance sheet showed assets of £366.16s 5d.Congratulations were accorded to Mr Aitken who broke the course record in the English Championship Qualifying round at Woodhall Spa G.C. The E.G.U. County Champions Tournament will be held on the County Course on 25th September 1966.

1962 The Jones Brothers, Joint Secretaries of the N.G.U.

44th A.G.M. 2nd July 1966

The Hon Secretary reported that the Castle Ashby G.C., whose course was lost a few years ago, had funds which probably exceeded £300 (The sum was £400 in fact) and that they had received an inquiry as to whether the Union might be prepared to take over the funds, to apply it for the advancement of junior golf and to give an indemnity should any claims being made against it in the future. Mr A.P.Foulis and Mr R.A.Palmer referred to a proposal made by the Society of Past Captains which is designed to encourage junior golf. This was welcomed by all present. Resolved that the Castle Ashby Club be informed that the Union would be happy to fall in with their suggestions and to give the desired indemnity and that they may be thanked for their proposal.

The Northampton club had submitted a recommendation that the handicap of Mr Richard G. Aitken be reduced to scratch, the matter was referred to the Council at their autumn meeting and subsequently passed. In 1966 the Union consisted of ten clubs.

45th A.G.M. 8th July 1967

The Hon Secretary reported that the subcommittee appointed him to consider the adoption of a Second Team tie. Details of the design of the tie were given, three appearances were required and the ties would be sold to the players at 17/6 each and that there be no free presentations at this stage Agreed. Mr A.P.Foulis raised the question of appropriate clothing for the County team, referred to the next Council meeting in November.

25th November 1967

Mr J. H. Humphries was invited by the President Mr W. Hollingsworth to Captain the County side in 1968,

Richard Aitken pictured here in 1962 and once described as a man who lived with a golf club in his hands.

Mr Humphries accepted the invitation. Mr J.W. Howkins was appointed dinner secretary. At the request of the selection committee, Mr R. G. Aitken referred to the leagues of Counties which had been established in the last few years and expressed the view that an approach be made to Norfolk, Suffolk, Cambridgeshire, Leicestershire and Lincolnshire Unions to ascertain their views, resolved to proceed.

46th A.G.M. 20 July 1968

The balance sheet showed assets of £1044.4s.2d (including £409.13s.0d from the Castle Ashby fund). The representative from Priors Hall G.C. put forward a proposal from his Club that a County league should be formed, resolved that Corby submit details of the proposal in order that it may be considered by the individual Clubs and at a future Council meeting.

7th December 1968

– Hon Secretary reported that the Professional Championship had been held at Kettering and that £25 had been presented for prizes. He added that there appeared to him to have been occurrences during the year that he did not regard as satisfactory. He understood that the Championship had been won by Richard (Dick) Kemp of Priors Hall. After discussion it was resolved to hand over the administration of the Championship to the Professionals who, it is understood have formed a County Association, no decision was made as to a contribution for prizes.

- It was reported that arrangements had been made for the formation of an Anglian Counties League comprising Norfolk, Suffolk, Lincolnshire, Leicestershire&Rutland, Cambridgeshire and Northamptonshire.
- It was reported that the arrangements made for the coaching of boys, by Messer's Lovelady and Murray would continue, in cooperation with the Society of Past Captains.
- The suggestion made by Priors Hall for a County League was discussed it was resolved that the suggestion be deferred for consideration at some future date.
- Concerning slow play, a circular was to be issued by the E.G.U.
- The Secretary read a letter from Northampton G.C. recommending that the handicap of Mr J. M. Pettigrew be reduced to Scratch, this was not approved.
- Oundle G.C. had received a grant of £5100 from the Golf Development Council to assist in the purchase of their course.
- Following a letter from the Club it was agreed that the County Championship be held at Priors Hall in 1970.
- Mr J. H. Humphries Captain, made the suggestion that a President's badge be purchased to be worn by the President of the year and to include a County emblem. The cost of the 9 carat gold/enamel badge would be £58. (The cost of the badge was found by the Past Presidents of the Union, coordinated by Mr C. S. Catlow). It was also proposed that Past Presidents would be presented with a small memento of the badge (Rejected in 1969).

47th A.G.M. 12th July 1969

The balance sheet showed assets of £1309:19:0d (£417:5:1d Castle Ashby Fund). Mr R. A. Palmer the Hon Auditor stated that the excess income over expenditure figure of £217:13:9d was a good result, too good in fact since this was largely due to the increase in the Club's subscriptions from one shilling per head to one shilling and six pence per head. Consideration should be given by the next meeting of the council to reduce it back to the old rate. (This was subsequently rejected in view of the ever increasing expenditure).The joint Hon Secretaries were given permission to purchase new typewriters. £25 had been spent in fees for coaching by County Professionals.

- County League, observations from the Clubs showed that the idea was not workable and it was agreed that the suggestion be deferred.
- The President Mr N.H.Brinton expressed the thanks of the Union to the Past Presidents and in particular to Mr Charles Catlow for the Presidents Badge which he was wearing for the first time.
- The President presented Mr W.H.Abbott with a cheque in appreciation of his services to the Union over the last 27 years; Mr Abbott thanked the President and the Clubs for their kindness to him and said how pleased he had been to put back a little into the game which had given him so much.

6th December 1969

Mr R. G. Aitken reported that The Anglian Counties League was inaugurated and we had finished bottom of the table halving one match and losing four. The Society of Past Captains had provided sponsorship for Bob Larrett and Conrad Ceislewicz to attend the British Boys Championship. It was further resolved that the Jubilee Dinner be held on the 12th October 1971 at a venue suitable for 150 or so guests. Mr R.G. Aitken became County Captain following the retirement of Mr J. H. Humphries. The E.G.U. Youths International Championship was to be staged at Northants County between August 3-7, 1971.

48th A.G.M. 11th July 1970

The Match Secretary, Mr R.B.Catlow presented his report which included details of a successful County Trial held at Tadmarton Heath G.C., where play was possible on a day when all the Northamptonshire courses were snowbound. This he believed was the first time a trial had been held outside the county. At long last two young boys Bob Larrett and Conrad Ceislewicz had finally broken into the County Team.

The venue for the County Championship was changed at short notice from Priors Hall to Peterborough Milton and attracted an entry of 66 players.

The Annual Dinner again had to be cancelled owing to a very bad weather in February; Mr J.W.Howkins kindly consented to continue as Dinner Secretary.

21st November 1970

Following decimalisation the cost of County Membership Cards was increased from £1 to £1.50 and the Club's fees were kept at $7\frac{1}{2}$p per head. Malcolm Pounds had won all five singles in his Anglian league matches a remarkable achievement. At the Boys Championship a starting list had been operated for the first time. It was agreed that a Charity Tournament be held in August 1971 to commemorate the Jubilee year. Conrad Ceislewicz had a very good run in the English Amateur Championship and we were delighted when Robert Larrett won the Midland Boys Championship.

49th A.G.M. 10th July 1971

The balance sheet showed assets of £1,540.00 (Castle Ashby fund £418.00).The arrangements for the Jubilee Dinner were well in hand, the Grand Hotel, Northampton had been booked for 12th October 1971 and a limit of 140 was agreed to. It was proposed that the handicap limit for the County Championship be reduced from nine to seven.

The Golden Jubilee Charity Tournament was arranged for the 14th August 1971 and it was hoped to raise a good sum for the National Playing Fields Association and Golf Foundation. Mr A. J. Everard was leaving the County and thanked the Union for the pleasure he had had and the distinction of playing for the County during the past few years. It was agreed that Mr Everard's kind offer to present a Cup be put before the Council meeting in November.

The President thanked Kingsthorpe G.C. for the arrangements for the meeting and competitions and declared the meeting closed

N.G.U. Administration 1972-2008

1972 Northamptonshire won the Anglian League First team Shield for the first time under Captain Richard G.Halliday. A record winning margin of $11\frac{1}{2}$ to $\frac{1}{2}$ was recorded in the match against Suffolk.

1980 Northamptonshire won the Anglian League Second Team Shield for the first time under Captain N.B. (Barry) Highfield.They won the first four matches and became Champions before the last match of the season. The Scratch League was started with two divisions.

1983 Mr Barry Highfield (Hon Match Secretary) and the County Captain Mr Ray Beekie defined the standard of dress for County matches as grey slacks, white shirt, County Sweater. 3 Friendlies, 5 Anglian League Matches and the Eastern Counties Foursomes were arranged for the year.

1989 The Vice-President Mr A.F.Stevens wished to place on record the committee's pleasure at Jack Humphries being appointed as Chairman of the Midland Golf Union. This was a great honour which the committee fully endorsed. Thorpe Wood G.C. decided to move across to the Cambridge Union of Golf Clubs. The Levy to members (for 1990) was proposed to be increased by 10p to £1-10p at the December Council Meeting.

1990 Travelling expenses for players increased to 10 per mile for away matches only proposed by M.J.Izzard, their mileage to be monitored by the Team Captains. The Scratch League results were analysed in detail for the first time to quantify County player's performances and to find new players with potential. The total annual cost of players travelling expenses was £430.

1994 On the Vice President initiative, the first County Newsletter (The Official Journal of the N.G.U.) was issued and circulated to all Clubs in October. Six quarterly issues were printed and this proved to be the forerunner of the Annual Union Yearbook championed by future President D.Croxton. Numerous organisations kindly provided sponsorship. A future strategy document "Towards the Year 2000" was presented to President Mr Mike McMahon by M.J.Izzard for comment and action by the Executive Committee.

74th A.G.M. 20 March 1996

The meeting agreed unanimously that the V.A.T. refund (£15,000) should be retained by the Union. The Union had retained reserves of £32,794.

1996

The NGU Mobile Tournament Office was used for the first time at the County Championship held at Kingsthorpe G.C. on June 15th. Costs incurred (£5546) were met from the reclaimed VAT fund.

A computer was purchased to assist Union events and the Competitions Chairman.

An N.G.U. "County Roadshow" was presented by the Executive Committee to 3 Clubs in the Union in order to explain the workings of the N.G.U. and how it aims to help its affiliated Clubs.

Izzard Club Team Trophy presented by President M.J. Izzard Esq and won by Kingsthorpe at the President's Club (Northampton G.C.) on the 12 October.

22 June 1996

Plans to celebrate the 75th Anniversary of the Union were well in hand. The event was held at Wellingborough G.C with a shot gun start for the 27 groups of four and a celebration dinner on the 23/06/1996. A major push on Junior Coaching was proposed by Past President Ian Marshall.

The 75th Year of the Northamptonshire Golf Union, celebrated at Wellingborough Golf Club in 1996

75th A.G.M. 26 March 1997 Wellingborough G.C.

The Treasurer Mr Keith Panter reported a loss for the year of £11,254 in view of many new activities. The Affiliation fee was therefore increased from £2 to £3 per member. At the request of Mr M.E.Wadley Secretary of Northants County G.C. it was confirmed that a new budget had been prepared for the coming year. The Union had retained reserves of £23,089, the Castle Ashby fund had grown to £1549.

The Hon Secretary reported that the Constitution was being redrafted and would include for the first time (in view of current behaviours) a Disciplinary and Appeals Procedure; the E.G.U. model would be used.

Under OAB, Mr Newton from Farthingstone asked if the Union still recommended Match Meals to cost £7, this was confirmed, however if the price was greater, Clubs should be informed prior to the match. (Note from author in 1997, I believe that Match meals should remain an integral part of a game between Clubs as part of the camaraderie between golfers. In 2007 sadly there are few matches played where the teams eat together after changing to jacket and tie, a sign of the times!)

12th Feb 1998

A Secretaries Conference was held at Kettering G.C. The Vice President Dave Croxton was in the chair with 22 Clubs represented. Items debated were Amateur Status, County Cards, Tee Reservations, CONGU Rules 19, 19.8, Communication and Stimpmeter readings.

76th A.G.M. March 25th 1998

The new County Constitution was adopted. Mr David Croxton the newly elected President thanked Mr.Richard B Catlow for his help on this matter and also for a major contribution to Union affairs over several decades and proposed that he be elected as The First Honorary Life Member of the Union; this was seconded by Mr Grainger (Daventry G.C.) and carried unanimously. Mr Catlow in accepting the Honour stated that 28 years ago in 1970 he had to adopt a major reform in allowing the County Championship to be limited to 15 Handicap and below! He thanked the meeting for the honour.

Mr Martin Izzard on behalf of the Executive presented Mr Mike McMahon with a crystal decanter in view of his 17 years service to the Union. Mr McMahon stated that he had really enjoyed his time in helping a small though progressive County and felt he had done an average job!

November 1998

Champion Club Trophy "in memory of Jane Anne" presented to the Union by M.J.Izzard Esq to whom thanks were paid by the President David Croxton and those present at Northampton Golf Club's Annual Trophy night.

1999

The Millennium Fund was launched in collaboration with the N.L.G.A. & N.P.G.A. to assist the development of Junior Golf and fund specific golfers at Northampton College. An attempt was made to relaunch the County Card scheme by Vice President T. Haley and M. Taylor (unfortunately this initiative subsequently failed due to lack of support). A new photocopier purchased cost, £299.

77th A.G.M. 25th March 1999

The Secretary of Northampton G.C. advised the meeting that his Club were to monitor slow play and soft spikes only would be allowed on the course between April and October.

78th A.G.M. 23rd March 2000

The Competitions Secretary Mr Malcolm Evans stated that in 2001 the Union are going to introduce knockout competitions for singles, foursomes and doubles, Clubs were asked to supply the names of the winners of their handicap knockout competitions to make up the draw for the County Knockouts. The Union had retained reserves of £27,983 (£1653 in the Castle Ashby fund). The President David Croxton presented the retiring Junior Delegate Mr Ian Marshall with an engraved putter in recognition of his 12 years of service in that role.

In order to improve communication between the Executive Committee and the Club's committees friendly matches had taken place followed by some conviviality in their clubhouses.

79th A.G.M. 22nd March 2001

The President Mr T. Haley expressed his disappointment at not being able to complete his two-year term of office for personal reasons. Although this was a difficult time for him he did have a pleasant duty to perform. It was proposed that Mr Richard G. Halliday be elected as an Honorary Life Member of the Northamptonshire Golf Union in view of his decades of service to the Union; this was proposed by the President and seconded by Mr R.B. Catlow. The motion was carried unanimously and the President presented an inscribed Silver Salver to Richard as a memento from all the Clubs in the County. Richard Halliday thanked the Union for the honour of becoming only the second Honorary Member, the first being Mr R. B. Catlow.

The retiring County Captain Mr Les Cantrell who had served for the last five years was presented with a

2005 N.G.U. Finals Day at Kingsthorpe G.C. – the Foursomes Final between Rushden's Graham May/Steve Roebuck and Wellingborough's Iain Campbell/Tom Kelly; Referee N.G.U. Honorary Life Member Richard Halliday.

memento from the Union by the President. The late Brian Woodcock took over as President and for the first time in the Union's history held the position for three years.

The expenditure for the year was £54,807 income £56,278 and retained reserves were £29,480. The affiliation fee was increased by 50p to £4 per member (juniors included) E.G.U. fee also £4.

17 September 2003 Fixtures Meeting

The President spoke about the need for Clubs to honour their agreements in the Union's constitution, some were choosing to ignore their obligations on grounds of expediency.

David Croxton the E.G.U. representative spoke on the referendum of the proposed Centralised Handicapping Scheme. In Northamptonshire 7 were for the proposal, 7 against it and 13 no responses. Nationally 573 were for the scheme 419 against and 900 no responses. It was described as highly unlikely that the scheme would proceed in its current format.

82nd A.G.M. 24th March 2004

Mr Mike Taylor was elected President and thanked his predecessor the late Past President Brian Woodcock for his sterling efforts over the last three years; the President also stated that a sub-committee was looking at the feasibility of taking on a full time Secretary and to establish a permanent office in the future. The affiliation fee for the year was confirmed at £5 per member. The President stated that he had received an invitation to the R&A's 250th Anniversary celebration dinner at St. Andrews and would be attending to represent Northamptonshire. For the year ended 31st December 2003, the Millennium Trust had a balance in hand of £6,666. Support payments had been made to numerous youngsters male and female to further their golf and education.

June 2004

Under the Chairmanship of Past N.G.U. President David Croxton the Northamptonshire Golf Development Steering Committee was formed following a meeting at Kingsthorpe G.C. on the 30th of June. All the bodies representing golf in the County were present. This is a pilot scheme of the E.G.U. Development Committee which looks to formulating a unified and structured plan to access some of the £100 millions of funding available from the Government's Sport England initiative. Mr Richard Lobb has been appointed County Golf Development Officer.

An N.G.U. office was established for the first time above Golfers Choice, Barrack Road, Northampton by kind permission of Messrs Geoff and Glenn Keates. (Vacated in 2006).

Annual Council Meeting 9th December 2004

It was agreed that the Secretaries honorarium be £7,500, the Competition Secretary honorarium £1000, mileage allowance 25p per mile. The Union had retained reserves of £33,683 (The Castle Ashby fund had by this time been amalgamated into the Union's accounts). The affiliation fee for both the N.G.U. and E.G.U. was confirmed at £5-50 per head.

The President Mr Mike Taylor presented a discussion document concerning the possible appointment of a full time County Secretary. It was also stated that a seminar would be run at Wellingborough G.C. 29th February 2005 to cover subjects such as Golf Course Risk Assessment, messages from the E.G.U., Criminal Records Bureau Disclosures and news from the N.G.U.

83rd A.G.M. 24th March 2005

A relatively quiet meeting. At the end of 2005 the Union had an income and expenditure of £62,000 and total retained reserves of £44,266. The Junior coaching programme was to be refocused.

Annual Council Meeting 14th December 2006

In line with the E.G.U. and Inland Revenue the mileage rate was increased to 40p per mile. Mr Mick Reed from Kettering G.C. was proposed as Vice President for 2006-7.

The imminent launch of a County Card which can also be used in neighbouring counties was described to the Clubs present.

Right: Les Cantrell N.G.U. President (left) with E.G.U. President Richard Palmer (centre) & N.G.U. Competition Secretary & Dinner Secretary Malcolm Evans at the N.G.U. Annual Dinner Kettering G.C. 2007.

Below: Lincolnshire President David Price, N.G.U. Past President Mike Taylor, Cambridge-shire President Martin Start and Bedfordshire President Trevor Hazell at the 2007 N.G.U. dinner

MAJOR COMPETITIONS

INDIVIDUAL EVENTS, WINNERS ARE LISTED IN APPENDIX 1

The County Championship

The County Championship is the major event of the men's golf calendar. The now 36 hole medal competition is normally held in June on the county's premier courses, initially it was an 18 hole event. The venue is determined by a county rota, the home Club of the incumbent President and significant anniversaries of the Clubs and Union.

The first championship was held not too surprisingly at Northants County on the 11&13 May 1922. It was won by Lancelot Bostock, who scored 81, the lowest gross during the 2 days of the first annual meeting. Other notable scores ranged between 86-106 gross. His father Fred Bostock Esq. presented the trophy to the then Association of Golf Clubs and must have enjoyed presenting it to his son. In 1923 the Championship was fittingly won by the gentlemen who brought golf to the county Dr John Allison from Kettering G.C.

Northants County's players have dominated this event with 34 recorded victories to date, Northampton are a long way behind in second place with 15 victories followed in third place by Kingsthorpe with 6 victories and "little" Rushden with 5 victories. Surprisingly Peterborough Milton has only recorded 4 victories.

Two players Charles.S.Catlow and Richard.G.Aitken have recorded almost unbelievable 11 and 8 victories each during the years (1934-1960) & (1962-1977) respectively. Charles Catlow's victories were a British record and the three clubs he was a member of Rushden, Northampton and Northants County were justifiably proud of such a fantastic achievement. It is interesting to speculate how many more he might have won had it not been for World War Two which prevented play for five years (1940-1945). Charles Catlow was also a fine cricketer and played for the County side as a right hand bat. His cricket career was checked when he partially lost sight in one eye in his early twenties, his first Club in the county was Rushden G.C. which he joined after taking a job in the leather trade in the town.

Richard Aitken's eight victories came as a member of Northampton and Northants County and like Charles Catlow (1937-39) also included a treble between 1962-64. I personally watched his last victory at the old Kettering Road course in 1977 as a twenty two year old from beside the old wooden clubhouse. I was at the time, unaware that this was to be his eighth and last Championship victory in a glittering golf career. I remember Richard playing a delicate pitch shot from the right hand side of the awkward green with soft hands to a back left pin position, at this time he was well respected for his fine short game. As he himself pointed out during a chat at the 2006 N.G.U.dinner this touch leaves the body with age, I could not agree more.

Over their years both gentlemen became synonymous with Northamptonshire golf as players and valued officials with recognition and friends across the country. Charles Stanley Catlow born Darwen Lancashire 21 February 1908 died on the 7th March 1986 aged 78; Richard is now in his 60s retired from a career as a Biochemist and enjoying senior golf. Although I never watched Charles Catlow play since our county golf careers did not overlap, I have competed against and have enjoyed the company of his son Richard Catlow on numerous occasions. It was Richard Catlow who had the honour of striking the opening blow in the Anglian League in 1969. Richard was also Northamptonshire Golf Union's first Honorary Life member having served numerous positions including President (1983-4) and Hon Solicitor for 25 years. He also finished third three times in the County Championship and is a chess player with a regional reputation. The families are in fact related, as the two Richards are brothers-in-law.

During the 1980s and 1990s I was a member of county teams that included Richard Aitken, he is a keen competitor and has a good "brain for the game" and a wicked razor sharp whit. I remember in particular the team returning from the Eastern Counties Foursomes Competition held at Hunstanton in a minibus being driven by Steve McDonald after a particularly non-inspiring weekend.

Looking for a suitable place to stop for a drink I directed the driver to the Chequered Skipper Public House at the delightful village of Ashton near Oundle. After a pint or two we headed back to the bus where someone in the crowd stated "You might not have scored many points, but you know some good pubs" it could have been Richard? I was also watching when Richard holed in one during an Anglian League first team match at Gog-Magog which the press reported a being "Too tough an exam for Cambs" as Richard went on to win his singles. The rest of us lost, notably Tony Lord 6/5 to then amateur Russell Claydon on his home turf.

The Hunstanton thread continues where I witnessed something that Richard did not see another of his holes in one! Whilst I was walking towards the 15th fairway I watch a ball come thundering over the hill on the blind 222 yards 14th hole, it crash solidly into the pin a foot above the hole and appeared to stick there temporarily before dropping gently into the hole below. We waited a few minutes for the players to come over the hill and were delighted to hear that it was Northamptonshire's ball stroked by Richard with a three wood; at least we won that hole! The hole in one was toasted that evening with a glass of claret at dinner supplied by MAX Aitken.

Richard Catlow as one means of distinguishing between Richard Catlow, Richard Halliday and Richard Aitken as they spent quite a lot of time together coined the nickname MAX. At the time, Max Aitken (Lord Beaverbrook's son) was prominent in the newspaper industry, the nickname has stuck!

The Catlow and Aitken families have made an immense contribution to Northamptonshire's golf as players and administrators and whilst a little indulgent on my behalf I formally recognise their input.

On a personal front the Championship has eluded me although I did finish 3rd twice at Kingsthorpe and Northants County in 1982 & 1988. In 1988 tying for the lead after the morning round with Richard Aitken and Conrad Ceislewicz proved too much for me in the afternoon on a tight course. The title was won by the powerful quiet gentlemen Duncan Ellson from Wellingborough G.C. who did not use a driver all day in order to keep the ball in play. From the 1980s the Championship has largely been won by young golfers with a few middle aged men interrupting this trend.

Over the years play-offs have sometimes been required to determine the Champion. A lot of this detail has been lost in the passage of time however two notable ones come to mind. In 1995 County Stalwart Tony Lord was victorious following an

Adam Myers, Northants County G.C., N.G.U. Nett Champion (left) with Dan Wood, Brampton Heath, N.G.U. County Champion in 2005.

64

eighteen hole play off at Collingtree Park G.C.When in a rich vein of form, Lordy also held the County Matchplay and Scratch Foursomes trophies. Ten years later at Northampton G.C. 14 year old Adam Myers and 19 year old Dan Wood participated in a two hole play-off on the 10th and 15th holes after both recorded 140 over the 36 holes. Dan became Champion with scores of birdie par against par par from Adam who collected the Nett trophy the Handicap Challenge Cup.

In 1999 the Championship was unfortunately washed out by torrential rain and had to be replayed later in the year when it was won by Nick Soto from Northants County. The following year (The Millennium year) the trophy was retained by the Club as Adam Print became victorious over his home course. In 2004 Stuart Ashwood became the youngest ever winner as a 16 year old winning the gross, nett and Braid's driver on his home course Northants County. In 2006 England International Gary Boyd broke the course record at Peterborough Milton G.C. with a quality gross 66 on route to a four shot victory over England Boy International Adam Myers from Northants County.

The Millennium County Championship winners: Neil Presto, Peterborough Milton; Braids Driver: Adam Plint, Northants County, County Champion; Richard Aitken, Handicap Challenge Cup with President Terry Haley at Northants County G.C.

Stuart Ashwood age 16, the youngest ever winner of the County Championship with the Nett & Braid's driver Trophies at Northants County 2004"

The Northamptonshire County Champion is invited together with all the other English counties' winners to participate in the English County Champions Tournament. This event has been running since 1962 and won by such names as Faldo, Lyle, McEvoy and Wolstenholme, so the standard is very high, in fact the highest in the amateur game apart from the E.G.U. Brabazon Trophy. The closest we have been to victory was third place in 1966 when Richard Aitken 38, 72 (Northampton G.C.) was five strokes behind the winner at Northants County G.C., and in 1998 when Glenn Keates 73, 74 (also Northampton G.C.) also finished third over the demanding Hotchkin course, Woodhall Spa nine strokes behind winner Gary Wolstenholme MBE from nearby Kilworth Springs G.C. in Leicestershire. Other notable performances were recorded by Richard Aitken 80, 77 for 6th place at Sherwood Forest G.C. in 1962, 81, 76 for 8th place at Little Aston G.C. in 1963 and Bob Larratt (Kettering G.C.) 75, 71 for 4th place at Torksey G.C in 1971.

In 2008 & 2009 the Championship will be held at Kingsthorpe and Northants County G.Cs. respectively as part of the Club's Centenary celebrations.

Northampton's Glenn Keates with E.G.U. President John Scrivener after finishing third in the E.G.U. County Champions Tournament in 1998.

The County Matchplay Championship

This event was first contested in 1987 over the Northants County course where Duncan Ellson became the inaugural winner defeating Tony Lord over his home course. Tony Lord later became Champion in 1994 at Peterborough Milton G.C.

Some players have suggested that this event is actually more difficult to win than the medal Championship since one has to qualify first. In fact, the top sixteen players from the medal championship play each other on a knock out basic over eighteen holes, prior to a 36 hole final, which has recently been played on county finals day in October.

The youngest winners to date were 18 year olds Stuart Hawkins in 2002 and Kyle Cullum in 2003. The oldest was Wellingborough's greenkeeper Ian Marshall in 1990 who had retired in 1989 as County Captain. In 2006, England International Gary Boyd from Cherwell edge carried out the double of stoke play and match play titles at Peterborough Milton and Kettering golf clubs respectively.

The trophy was provided by the N.G.U.

Club Champion of Champions

This tournament was introduced by the N.G.U. in 1996 and is played by the Club's Champions as an eighteen hole medal on finals day. The event is normally contested by about 70% of the county's 27 clubs as some of our nine hole golf Club Champions find it a significant step up against the players from the bigger clubs, however some come along simply to enjoy Finals Day, they are most welcome.

Burly Paul Taylor from Staverton Park G.C. has won the event a record four times including a hat trick (1998-2000). Chirpy Darren Matthews put Woodlands/Farthingstone G.C. on the map in this event in 1997 and interrupted Paul Taylor's run of victories. In 2006, Ryan Evans recorded a fine score of one under par on a windy day at Kettering G.C. to pip his county colleague John Chamberlain by a shot.

The trophy was purchased by the N.G.U.

The County Boys Championship

The Council first proposed the County Boys Championship for the Scratch Cup in 1937 for Boys and Girls during their summer holidays and the first meeting was held at Rushden G.C. in 1938. The Championship for the Girls transferred to the N.C.L.G.A. many years ago. It is the main event on the calendar and one, which has given a lot of pleasure to players, parents and organisers. Eighteen holes was the original format and in 1981 the Championship became a 27 hole event when it was won by Derek Scrowther over his home course Staverton Park G.C. The following year it became a 36 hole event and was also won by a player on his home course (the late Grant Norrie Wellingborough G.C.)

The standard of play has improved considerably over the years, originally scores of between 4-12 over par used to provide a winner. Since 1970, the lads have recorded better scores, Conrad Ceislewicz being the early trendsetter with 2 and 1 over par at Kingsthorpe and Northampton G.Cs. The Championship often acts as a springboard for the player to go on to bigger things and many County Champions have been Boys Champions. Interestingly the trophy has been retained on nine occasions and Duncan Ellson from Wellingborough had a three-year gap between victories, his first victory coming at the tender age of fifteen.

Above: N.G.U. Boys
Champions Alex Izzard
(Northampton), gross
(left) and G. Tibbles
(Northampton), nett,
with Past President Ian
Marshall at Overstone
Park in 2000.

Right: Presentation
table for the 2000
N.G.U. Boys
Championship.

The millennium winner was Alexander James Izzard from Northampton G.C. at Overstone Park G.C. who was victorious two days after his seventeenth birthday – one proud day for the Izzard family. The venue for each event has not been included here due to space considerations but is listed on the trophy. The event always has a nice feeling to it as many proud parents come along to hopefully see their son on the winners rostrum. The event is normally held in early August for boys up to the age of eighteen on the 1st January of the year.

The silver cup was presented by N.G.U. Past President Mr D. (Don) Chamberlain.

The County Seniors Championship

The trophy for the over 55 year olds on the day of the competition is normally held each year in September. The trophy (presented by A.J.Everard Esq.) is awarded to the best gross score over 18 holes medal play. The event has been dominated by players from Northants County and to a lesser degree Oundle and Wellingborough. The trophy has been retained three times by Northants County's George Mobbs 1977-78, Jack Humphries 1979-80 and Richard Aitken 1996-97. Flamboyant John (Snack) Haddon from Northampton was victorious in 1987 and we certainly heard chapter and verse from him at Northampton's Trophies night in November that year. The event was kindly sponsored by Ashbourne Homes between 1996-2004.

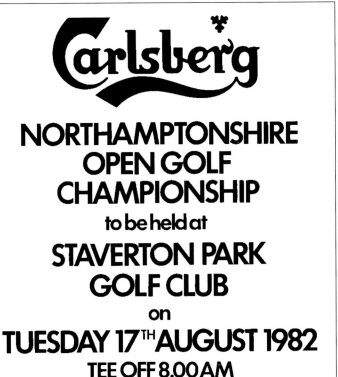

The Northamptonshire Open Championship

The first Open event I have found during my research for this book was held at Northampton G.C. in 1970 and thereafter annually until 7th June 1975. The Championship was for golfers from the Midlands area with a handicap lower than 6. The 1970 winner was Martin Curry 69, 72 Peter McEvoy the famous amateur golfer was third on 146. No one broke par on the "hills and holes" course at Kettering Road.

The event was abandoned after 1975 due to "money grabbing unappreciative youths!" I was actually in the Clubhouse age 20 when the committee made this decision; I did not know how to react and remained silent since I could see both sides of the situation.

The N.G.U. Open as we know it came about following discussions between the County Amateurs and Professionals after the annual

Programme for the first Northamptonshire Open

69

match between the two teams in May 1982. The match was held at Staverton Park G.C. and won by the Professionals 5$^1/_2$-2$^1/_2$ against a below strength amateur team.

When interviewed by the *Chronicle & Echo* newspaper County Captain Conrad Ceislewicz stated "Everyone enjoyed Sunday's match. It was a great success played in the right spirit, I'm sure a Northamptonshire Open would be even more successful". There was clearly a desire for such an event and the inaugural event was held at Staverton Park G.C. on the 17th August 1982 involving twenty professionals and forty amateurs.

Staverton Park's professional Charlie Ray won the event on this day in 1982 and after having a spell in the professional arena came back to amateur golf and now plays competently for their Scratch League team. I am sure that his experiences at a higher level are helping the development of junior golf and the Scratch team at Staverton Park GC.

Over the years the event has received sponsorship kindly provided by Carlsberg and Autohaus Audi. The original mermaid trophy provided by Carlsberg was presented to Ian and Teena Marshall to commemorate many years of involvement with the administration of the event when Autohaus became the new sponsor in 1997. In the "good times" during the late 1980s/early 1990s when there was significantly more sponsorship money available in general, the Professional prize climbed to £1000. This proved to be a good day's work for the fortunate Tim Rouse in 1992 at his home course Northants County G.C. Without our valued sponsors this event would not take place.

Northants County Professional, Tim Rouse, receives the winners cheque for £1,000 from Sponsors Carlsberg at the N.G.U.
Open held in 1992 with Vice-President Ian Marshall in the background.

70

In 2002 at Northampton Golf Club the Autohaus Northamptonshire Open was won by Andy Hare who set was a new professional course record of 66, his 28th in a distinguished amateur and professional career.

In 2006 Wellingborough based professional Simon Lilly recorded the event's lowest 36 hole total at Northants County of 130 which included a fine professional course record of 63 gross. Simon has progressed very well through the amateur to professional ranks and is currently one of the best players in the county. In 2002 Simon was making a living on the P.G.A. Europro tour and won the 2002 Rye Hill event and in 2004 the Heydon Grange event both of which was a significant cheques. Also in 2004 Simon won the final EuroPro Tour event, the PGA Euro Pro Tour Championship at the beautiful Mosa Trejectum course in Spain and with it the top spot in the final Order of Merit (earnings £37,047), this gave him a Category 9 place on the European Challenge Tour for 2005. Another added bonus from winning the order of merit was a place in the Mauritius Open in the December of that year where Simon finished a creditable 11th.

In the Northamptonshire Open, the amateurs have upstaged the professionals six times to date.

The starting sheet for the first Northamptonshire Open held on the 17th August 1982 is given below and makes interesting reading. Although I would have preferred a later tee time having to cross the county from Rushden to Staverton in the breaking dawn light! The Christian names are from my personal memory of the day.

Andrew Hare receives the trophy at the 2002 Northamptonshire Open from sponsor Autohaus Group

Game	Professional	Club	Amateur 1	Club	Amateur 2	Club
1	Simon Ward	CA	Peter Wood	NC	Martin Izzard	N
2	Mike Higgins	D	Richard Aitken	NC	Tony Lack	N
3	Brian Sparks	SP	Derek Scrowther	SP	Rodney Haig	NC
4	N.Watson	D	George Mobbs	NC	M.Stevens	SP
5	B.Medhurst	PM	Anthony Lord	NC	Barry Highfield	D
6	Richard Hudson	-	Nicky Grimmitt	W	David Eborall	N
7	Dick Kemp	PH	Mike McNally	DP	Ray Beekie	PM
8	Kevin Theobold	Ke	Don Tooby	D	Jim Langley	Kg
9	Mike Gallagher	Wo	Jim Dalton	W	Jamie Scholey	NC
10	L.Turner	W	Charley Mace	Kg	Laurie Johnson	NC
11	Richard Lovelady	N	Perry Walker	Kg	John Atkinson	SP
12	Michael Forrest	CA	Steve McDonald	Kg	D.Smith	NC
13	John Freeman	Kg	J.McKeogh	Wo	B.Coleman	CA
14	Peter Barker	PM	John Smith	N	Des Daley	CA
15	Charlie Ray	SP	Steve Langley	Kg	Tim Preston-Jones	NC
16	Brian Mudge	SP	Andy Sibley	Kg	Peter Le-Voi	PM
17	Tim Giles	SA	Jim Dodd	TW	Richard Cole	PM
18	Roger Fitton	TW	Conrad Ceislewicz	NC	Mike Dickens	SP
19	Alf Lovelady	N	Peter Scott	Kg	Ken Billingham	N
20	Stuart Brown	NC	Capper Rose	Kg	Rudy Ragbir	N

Key

BH Brampton Heath	C Collingtree	CA Cold Ashby
D Daventry	DP Delapre Park	F/Wo Farthingstone
Ke Kettering	Kg Kingsthorpe	N Northampton
NC Northants County	O Oundle	PH Priors Hall
PM Peterbo'h Milton	R Rushden	SA St Andrews
SP Staverton Park	TW Thorpe Wood	W Wellingborough
WP Whittlebury Park	- Unattached	

Farthingstone was known as Woodlands in 1982

The County Cup

Northants County G.C. administers this popular event rather than the N.G.U. and I have included it here for completeness of the county scene. The 36 hole scratch competition was originally known as the Newnham Cup since the donor (Harry Draper, Captain Northants County 1960) lived in the attractive Daventry village of Newnham. The trophy was first played for in 1962 at the Northants County Summer meeting strictly for members only. In 1964 George Mobbs won by a shot having taken twelve strokes on the tenth hole (now (2005) the fourteenth) having been in the greenside bunker for two. His bunker shot landed deeply embedded in some sodden hoof marks which required some major hacking to get the ball on to the green. He showed some steely spirit and made six threes on the next seven holes, a lesson to us all.

The format was changed to an open event in 1966 and the name changed to ''County Cup'' in an attempt to attract some of the Midland's better players. In 1988 victory for the Bedfordshire player Angus King was assisted by an almost unbelievable start to the morning round when he recorded scores of 2,3 for an eagle, eagle start. Bedfordshire players clearly enjoyed the course as long standing and respected County player Paul Wharton won the trophy in 1990 followed by young Sam Jarman in 1991. The Club were proud to have a Walker Cup player's name on the trophy in 2003 when Gary Wolstenholme MBE (handicap plus 5) from nearby Kilworth Springs G.C. was victorious. The youngest winner of the trophy was 14-year-old Adam Myers from the home club in 2005. In the early decades of play the trophy was mostly won by players from outside the County however since 1994 Northants players have dominated.

Adam Myers 2005 County Cup winner receives the cup from Northants County Captain Malcolm Peel

TEAM EVENTS, WINNERS ARE LISTED IN APPENDIX 1
ANGLIAN COUNTIES LEAGUE FOR THE
Daily Telegraph SALVERS

The Anglian Counties League was formed at Thetford Golf Club on Sunday October 27th 1968 when representatives from the six counties of Cambridgeshire, Leicestershire & Rutland, Lincolnshire, Norfolk, Northamptonshire and Suffolk were invited to attend a lunchtime meeting in the old clubhouse. The meeting was held in the Dining Room over beer and sandwiches. Roger Trower (Norfolk) had previously been in correspondence with the six counties and all had agreed in principle to go ahead with forming a League.

Roger Trower, then the Captain of Norfolk, chaired the meeting, which approved unanimously to form a league. The ensuing discussions were to draw up a set of basic rules and conditions with the object of the League commencing in April/May of 1969.

Present were-

Cambridgeshire	Andrew Blows (Captain)	Bill Dunn (Secretary)
Norfolk	Roger Trower (Captain)	Derek Rains
Northamptonshire	Richard Aitken (Captain)	
Suffolk	Richard Long (Captain)	
Leicestershire& Rutland	Dr Bill Scott (Captain)	

Lincolnshire- John Bacon (Captain) had written apologising for being unable to attend. His letter expressed the full support of his county and he had confidence that any rules and conditions established would be accepted by his county.

Having agreed to start the League in 1969, it was suggested an approach be made to the Daily Telegraph asking if they would be willing to donate an appropriate trophy. This subsequently came to pass and their golfing correspondents presented a salver in 1970, the salver was first presented to the winning county in 1971.

In 1977, a "B" Team League was formed under similar rules and conditions with counties playing one team at home and the other away on the same day. A shield was presented by P.J.Darton (Captain, Cambridgeshire Area Golf Union) for annual competition.

A Northamptonshire player, Richard Catlow M.A., L.L.M. (Cantab) who was playing with his brother-in-law Richard Aitken at Thorpness G.C. on Sunday the 13th April 1969, struck the first blow in the league. The ball apparently finished in a bush!

The pair were a formidable combination over the years; one of their major highlights was in winning the English Golf Union's Presidents and Guest Trophy in 1983 (during Richard Catlow's N.G.U. Presidency) with a score of 63 pts again at Thorpness G.C.

The league matches now consist of teams of eight players, who play four foursomes in the morning starting at 10 a.m. and eight singles in the afternoon, starting at 2 p.m. In the early days of the competition some teams consisted of twelve players but this was changed to the current format in 1977. The six teams, which compete for the two shields, play five matches on Sundays throughout the summer months. This often allows players from our land locked county to play at seaside courses in Norfolk, Suffolk and Lincolnshire at such marvellous venues such as e.g. Hunstanton, Felixstowe Ferry and Seacroft which often requires a change of playing tactics at these different tests of golf. When the first team is playing at home, the second team will be playing away and vice –versa. Sadly, these matches are not watched by more than a handful of spectators since the standard of golf is high, par figures often losing matches. The N.G.U. President travels to support the A team, the Vice President with the B team.

Continuing the social/supporting theme it is interesting to note that the A&B teams used to hold an annual dinner dance (1971) at the Spencer Arms, Chapel Brampton, where players and their golf widows could meet one another at the end of the season, the event was quite popular.

Northamptonshire A team have played local rivals Leicestershire & Rutland even before the start of the Anglian League and to date (2008) have Won 7 Lost 33 and Drawn 2. The fixture against them in fact dates back to 1922 where our first victory came at Kingsthorpe in 1938[9].

The majority of matches have been played at Northants County, Peterborough Milton, Luffenham Heath and Rothley Park. Longcliffe also features prominently on the results sheet and was the venue in 1983 where

Leicestershire's Steve Adams and I survived being stuck by lightening on the par five twelfth hole. Both of our wives were pregnant at the time and we had to very carefully manage the news when we arrived home without any bad side effects. I felt the impact all down my left side and Steve felt it all down his right side, so we surmised that the minor bolt came down between us. It simply knocked us to the ground, as we looked at each other we nodded our heads to each other as a way of communicating "Oh my god! we are still alive" though soaked with rain and grass from the fairway. We then walked towards each other and embraced each other in a state of bewilderment. My body was "tight" for a few days and I felt slightly "dazed and dopey" fortunately my heart rhythms had not been affected by the blow.

My poor mother heard the news on the local radio before I had a chance to show her that I was in fact all right. I often refer to my son Alex as the "Thunder Child", since both Steve Adams and I might never have seen our first born. Driving past Junction 23 the Loughborough turn on the M1 even now brings back bad thoughts of what might have been. For the record Leicestershire won the match, again!

The second team matches against Leicestershire started in 1947 at Kettering G.C. and the early matches were played at Kettering, Kirby Muxloe and Kibworth. To date (2006) the Northamptonshire B team has Won14, Lost 33 and Drawn 7. Complete details of the scores and venues can be found on the Leicester& Rutland G.U. website[9]. Despite the fact that the morning foursomes only count for one third of the total points available the result in the morning has a major impact on the overall match result. This is more a psychological effect rather than a rational argument. I have carried out this analysis for Northamptonshire together with an analysis of the score margins which are given here on pages 75 and 76.

This clearly demonstrates that even a slender win in the morning provides sufficient momentum for good pickings from the singles in the afternoon. In fact if the foursomes are lost 3 matches to 1 or worse there is at least a 71% chance of losing a match. The scores over the years tend to be clustered around the midpoint and many matches are decided on a few key points during the game. To date we have only succeeded in winning the A league and the B league twice in 1972/1990 & 1980/2002 respectively. In any season the five matches played have 12 points at stake each, the percentage of victories has a significant impact upon the final league position as shown on page 76.

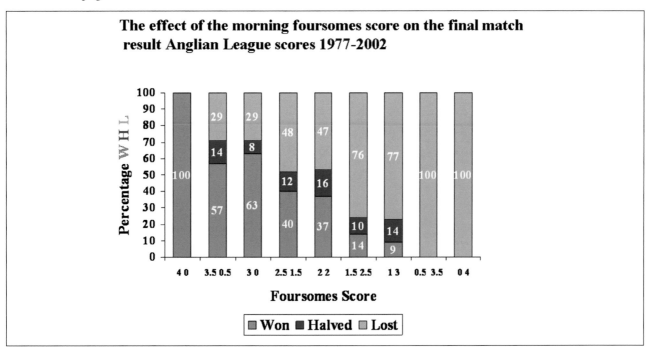

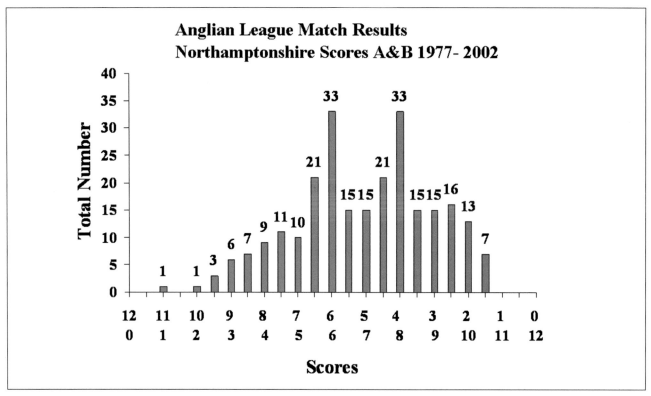

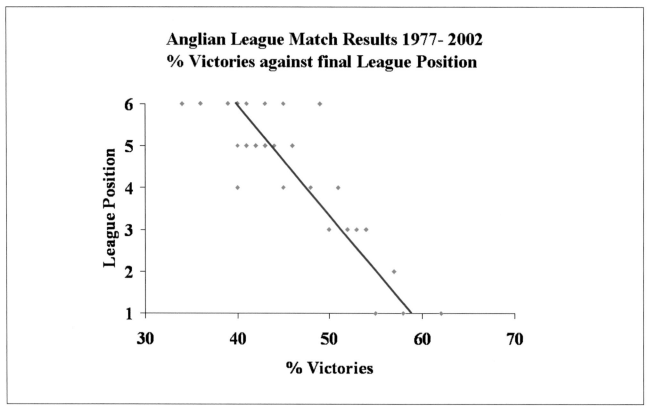

In our four winning years (1972, 1980, 1990, 2002) the percentage of victories for the whole season over the sixty points available was 68, 55, 62, and 58%, in reality one simply needs to develop the winning edge. The individual match results are given in Appendix 1.

Interestingly the success of the 1972 team was predicted by the County Secretary/Match Secretary in his annual report to the Council in 1971. A "youth first" policy for the second team was first introduced at this time. Both men had vision for the future of Golf in Northamptonshire.

An example of how close the matches actually can be is given below for our winning B Team in 2002 (Captain Richard Brown). Even half a point can swing a match both ways and during each game individual shots can mean the difference between victory and defeat. The games have over time followed a similar trend, start (holes1-6), middle (7-13) and the finish (14-18).We have been weak over the middle & finish through the years compared to other counties especially Leicestershire & Lincolnshire. However, during the County's winning years such as 2002, we had the winning edge over these holes.

The last match of the season took place against our great rivals Leicestershire at Willesley Park in Ashby–de-la-Zouch. I arrived to watch the afternoon singles equipped with a camera and was pleased to note that after half a dozen or so holes, most of the team were up in their matches. The winning putt which came at the 17th hole was greeted with much jubilation from the team and officials, the Leicestershire players and officials had respectfully retired to the clubhouse to allow Northamptonshire their moments of glory.

It was very nearly a very special day; we actually could have won both the A& B Leagues for the first time in our history if the A team had not lost at home to Leicestershire&Rutland at Wellingborough G.C by a slender margin. The telephones and mobiles were buzzing around 5 p.m. on that warm sultry afternoon as the squad of players and officials realised what had been achieved tempered with the frustration of a near double.

I had personally waited patiently for 22 & 12 years respectively for the opportunity to photograph such emotional scenes having been a member of the winning 1980 B and 1990 A teams. I have been fortunate to be present at three out of four Northamptonshire Anglian League victories and wore the County Rose that evening at dinner with a warm glow and great pride.

Let us hope we do not have to wait so long for the next Anglian League victory, my camera is ready in waiting.

Northamptonshire winning teams consisted of the following players:-

1972 A Winners: Richard Aitken, Tony Bishop, Richard Catlow, Richard Halliday (Captain) Jack Humphries, Malcolm Pounds (All NC), Bob Gray (PM), Bob Larratt (Ke), Jim Pettigrew & Conrad Ceislewicz,(N).

Match Results

v Leicestershire (Northampton G.C.)	Won 8-4
v Cambridgeshire (Newmarket G.C.)	Won $6\frac{1}{2}$-$5\frac{1}{2}$
v Suffolk (Peterborough Milton G.C.)	Won $11\frac{1}{2}$-$\frac{1}{2}$ * league record, half came in foursomes
v Norfolk (Northants County G.C.)	Won 9-3
v Lincolnshire (Torksey G.C.)	Won $6\frac{1}{2}$-$5\frac{1}{2}$
	Points $40\frac{1}{2}$ from 60=68 %

Name	Matches	Fours	Singles	Name	Matches	Fours	Singles
R.G.Aitken	5	$3\frac{1}{2}$	4	R.G.Halliday	5	$1\frac{1}{2}$	3
A.D.Bishop	1	1	1	J.H.Humphries	5	$2\frac{1}{2}$	3
R.B.Catlow	2	1	$\frac{1}{2},\frac{1}{2}$	R.Larratt	3	$2\frac{1}{2}$	2
C.R.Ceislewicz	4	$3\frac{1}{2}$	3	J.M.Pettigrew	5	$4\frac{1}{2}$	$3\frac{1}{2}$
R.J.Gray	5	$2\frac{1}{2}$	$2,\frac{1}{2},\frac{1}{2}$	M.Pounds	5	$4\frac{1}{2}$	$2,\frac{1}{2},\frac{1}{2}$

Northamptonshire, Anglian League A Winners 1972.
Back row: F. Saxby (N.G.U. Vice-President), R. Catlow, J. Pettigrew, M. Pounds, R. Aitken, A. Bishop, P. Meacock (N.G.U.
President); Front Row: J. Humphries, C. Ceislewicz, R. Halliday (Captain), R. Gray, R. Larratt.

1980 B Winners 5 matches Barry Highfield Captain D, Martin Izzard (N), Rodney Haig (NC). 4 Matches Peter Scott & Steve McDonald (Ki). 3 Matches David Evans (NC), Kevin Newman (N). 2 Matches Ian Marshall (W), Mike Haddon (Ki). 1 match Malcolm Scott (PH), R.Hall (Ke), Bob Killip (N), Nick Grimmitt (W), Jimmy Ellis (PM), Jonathan Payne (Ke) and Tony Lord (NC).

Match Results

v Leicestershire (Scraptoft G.C.)	Won 7$^1/_2$-4$^1/_2$
v Cambridgeshire (Kettering G.C.)	Won 9-3
v Suffolk (Aldeburgh G.C.)	Won 6$^1/_2$-5$^1/_2$
v Norfolk (Barnham Broom G.C.)	Won 7-5 Shield won after 4 matches
v Lincolnshire (Staverton Park G.C.)	Lost 3-9
	Points 33 from 60= 55%

Name	Matches	Foursomes	Singles	Name	Matches	Foursomes	Singles
J.Ellis	1	0	1	R.Killip	1	1	0
D.Evans	3	1	2	A.M.S.Lord	1	0	0
N.Grimmitt	1	1	0	I.Marshall	2	1	1
M.Haddon	2	2	2	K.Newman	3	2$^1/_2$	0
R.Haig	5	4	3	S.McDonald	4	2$^1/_2$	1
R.Hall	1	1	1	J.Payne	1	0	$^1/_2$
N.B.Highfield	5	3	3	M.Scott	1	0	0
M.J.Izzard	5	3$^1/_2$	4	P.Scott	4	1$^1/_2$	2$^1/_2$

Northamptonshire, Anglian League B Winners 1980 Left to right A.M.S.Lord, J.Payne, R.A.Haig, N.B.Highfield (Captain), M.J.Izzard, P.Scott, K.V.Newman, D.Evans.

1990 A Winners 5 Matches John Evans & Peter Flude (Ki), Ian Marshall (W). 4 Matches Mike Lynch (NC), Greg Shelton (PM). 3 Matches Darren Jones (Ki), Michael Pask (Ke), 2 Matches Adam Print (NC). 1 match Ian Achurch (NC), Ray Beekie (PM), Martin Izzard (N), Martin Herson (PM), Ronnie McIlwain (PH).Richard (R.S. Dick) Biggin was the non-playing Captain.

Match Results

v Cambridgeshire (Gog Magog)	Won 8-4
v Leicestershire (Peterborough Milton G.C.)	Won $6^1/_2$-$5^1/_2$
v Suffolk (Wellingborough G.C.)	Won 11-1
v Norfolk (Northants County G.C.)	Won $6^1/_2$-$5^1/_2$ Shield won after 4 matches
v Lincolnshire (Stoke Rochford G.C.)	Lost 5-7

Points 37 from 60= 62%

Name	Matches	Foursomes	Singles	Name	Matches	Foursomes	Singles
I.Achurch	1	0	0	M.Lynch	4	3	2
R.Beekie	1	0	0	I.Marshall	5	3	$2^1/_2$
J.Evans	5	$4^1/_2$	$3^1/_2$	R.McIwain	1	1	0
P.Flude	5	$3^1/_2$	$2^1/_2$	M.Pask	3	2	$2^1/_2$
M.Herson	1	1	0	A.Print	2	1	1
M.J.Izzard	1	0	1	G.Shelton	4	3	2
D.Jones	3	1	3	J.Wilson	3	3	$2^1/_2$

Northamptonshire, Anglian League A Winners 1990. Back Row: G. Shelton, P. Flude, M. Herson, M. Pask, D. Jones, R. Beekie, J. Wilson, I. Achurch. Front Row: J. Evans, M. Izzard, M. McMahon (N.G.U. Vice-President), R. Biggin (Captain), A. Stevens (N.G.U. President), I. Marshall, M. Lynch.

2002 B Winners Twin brothers Roger & Colin Green, Tom Duck (NC). Gavin Condon, Dominic Jessup, Simon Tootell, Stuart Young (N). Stuart Hawkins (W). Adrian Firman & I.Symonds (PM). Greg Croxton (CA) and Matt Bearman (S). Richard Brown (W) was the Captain.

Match Results

v Norfolk	Lost $5^1/_2$-$6^1/_2$
v Cambridgeshire	Won $7^1/_2$-$4^1/_2$
v Lincolnshire (Kettering)	Won 7-5
v Suffolk	Won $6^1/_2$-$5^1/_2$
v Leicestershire (Willesley Park)	Won 8-4
	Points $34^1/_2$ from 60= 58%

Name	Matches	Foursomes	Singles	Name	Matches	Foursomes	Singles
M.Bearman	5	$2^1/_2$	2	R.Green	3	$1^1/_2$	2
R.Brown	4	$^1/_2$	$1^1/_2$	S.Hawkins	2	0	$^1/_2$
G.Condon	1	0	1	D.Jessup	4	$1^1/_2$	3
G.Croxton	4	0	$1^1/_2$	I.Symonds	2	$1^1/_2$	1
T.Duck	3	$^1/_2$	2	S.P.Tootell	2	0	1
A.Firman	1	1	$^1/_2$	J.Ward	1	0	0
C.Green	4	1	2	S.Young	3	$^1/_2$,$^1/_2$	3

For the record, the table is incomplete since the result sheet for the Cambridgeshire match cannot be located in either county!

Northamptonshire, Anglian League B Champions 2002. Back Row: R. Green, R. Duck, G. Condon, S. Young, S. Hawkins, A. Firman, M. Bearman, C. Green. Front Row: G. Croxton, M. Taylor (N.G.U. Vice-President), B. Woodcock (N.G.U. President), R. Brown (Captain), J. Crouch (N.G.U. Team Manager), S. Tootell, D. Jessup.

Left: Northamptonshire's Richard Catlow who struck the first blow in the Anglian League in 1969 addresses those assembled at the Millennium celebrations held at Seacroft G.C.

Right: Menu Card for the Anglian League Millennium Celebrations.

Anglian League Dinner 2000

To celebrate the Millenium

NCGU

L&RGU

CAGU

The Crown Hotel,
Skegness, Lincolnshire
Saturday 7th October 2000

Chairman, Anglian League:
Andrew Blows, Cambridgeshire

LUGC

SGU

NGU

The six Counties that make up the Leagues celebrated the Millennium at the Crown Hotel, Seacroft, Lincolnshire following a proposal by the author. The day consisted of a round of golf followed by the Celebration Dinner. To add to the festivities a hole in one was recorded by former N.G.U. Junior Delegate Keith Bass who retired to the coast and is now a member of Sheringham G.C. It was appropriate that Richard Catlow who struck the first blow in the league and several others who were at the first meeting were able to be present at this special dinner. The Loyal Toast was proposed by R.A.C.Blows, Esq Chairman of the League, The Anglian League was proposed by John Rawden, Esq., response was by R.A.C.Blows & The Guests was proposed by Northamptonshire's Richard Catlow.

In the Millennium year Suffolk carried out a clean sweep of the trophies winning the A, B and Junior Anglian League Trophies, a unique achievement which had never happened before. The annual match played against Suffolk is played for the Easterbrook Salver in memory of Chris Easterbrook who made a huge contribution to Suffolk golf as an administrator. The combined scores from the day of the A & B teams determine the winner; to date the Salver has been won five times by each county. There is a good deal of good camaraderie between the teams, possibly as we are both less likely to win the league and therefore simply enjoy the day.

The results demonstrate that Lincolnshire and Leicestershire & Rutland have dominated the winning podium since the league started. We have over the years tried to analyse why this is the situation. There appears to be a correlation with the size of the county in terms of the number of golf clubs and number of quality golf courses. The table below demonstrates this point I believe, although this is not the complete picture which may also depend upon coaching budgets and player's commitment. Four victories from sixty eight attempts is Northamptonshire's total, a teacher might say" can do better, more homework and practise required"

Northamptonshire Captains
Anglian League 1969-2008

A	B
1969-71 Richard Aitken NC	1977-1983 Barry Highfield D
1972 Richard Halliday NC	1984-87 Rodney Haig NC
1973-74 Peter James W	1988-89 Martin Izzard N
1975-6 Michael Duck NC	1990 Alan Linney N/NC
1977-78 Laurie Johnson NC	1991 Martin Izzard N
1979-80 Jim Dalton W	1992-94 Malcolm Scott PH
1981-2 Conrad Ceislewicz NC	1995 Steve McDonald Ki
1983-5 Ray Beekie PM	1996-2000 Tony Smith W
1987-1989 Ian Marshall W	2001-03 Richard Brown W
1990 Richard Biggin NC	2004-5 Peter Scott Ki
1991 Tony Stevens N	2006-7 Dominic Jessup N
1992-95 Tony Lord NC	2008- Jim Campbell Ke
1996-2001 Les Cantrell NC	
2001-3 Tony Lord NC	
2004-5 Richard Brown W	
2006-7 Neil Presto PM	
2008- Richard Brown W	

Anglian League Counties Composition

County	Number of golf Clubs	Nine hole Courses	Number of members	Life Anglian League position A&B
Lincolnshire	57	13	21,000	2,1
Leicestershire and Rutland	32	3	13,000	1,2
Suffolk	31	11	14,000	3,3
Norfolk	32	10	13,000	4,5
Cambridgeshire	29	7	10,000	5,6
Northamptonshire	**27**	**8**	**10,000**	**6,4**

ANGLIAN LEAGUE BOYS

The league was formed in 1979 and matches were first played that year. In 1980 the trophy which the teams competed for was kindly presented by Granville Haskell from Suffolk. The Northamptonshire County Boys team have registered some success in this Anglian League campaign, twice lifting the trophy in 1982 & 1984. In 1982 the team consisted of the likes of Richard Dalton, Derek Scrowther, Steve Langley, Michael Pask, Jamie Scholey et al. An East & West qualifier is held to determine the finalists, the venue for which is moved around the six counties which participate to give neutral venues where ever possible.

It is clear that over the years Lincolnshire, Norfolk and recently Suffolk have a system, which produces many good young "lads". For example Tony Jacklin, Mark James, Jim Payne, Jamie Moul and several other less recognised players such as David Rose, James Crampton, Jonathan Herbert, Paul Streeter and others. Many of these "lads" have firmly put English Golf on the world map, especially with Tony Jacklin's Open & US Open victories in 1969 and Mark James experiences in the Ryder Cup.Surely inspiration to us all!

Northamptonshire's boy coaching system has produced two players who have become full England Internationals (Robert Duck Northants County 1997 and Gary Boyd Cherwell Edge 2006&7); they both have an inner passion for the game, great drive, great short games and the desire to improve through practicing the correct swing.

In 2000 Northamptonshire Boys reached the final but were beaten by a strong Suffolk team at Seacroft G.C. Lincolnshire. Let us hope we can stop Suffolk and Lincolnshire's recent domination of this particular event and bring the trophy back to the County after a gap of over twenty years.

EASTERN INTER COUNTIES FOURSOMES

This is one of the most enjoyable events of the yearly county calendar, which requires the players to play 90 holes of golf over a three-day period. A practise round on the Friday is followed by two days of 36 holes. Only the fit survive this gruelling test and it is interesting to note that very young and older players do not regularly feature on the starting sheets, stamina for golf and this event maximises between 25 to 45 years of age. Most golfers hope for an easy win by for example 7/6 to preserve their stamina although this happens infrequently. Nine Counties participate. The event has largely been held at Hunstanton and Seacroft links although it briefly visited Royal West Norfolk G.C. in 1958 &1959.

The matches are played in sixes so that each pair is playing two matches at once against two different counties. Northamptonshire for example would play Essex and Leicestershire Saturday a.m., Beds and Lincolnshire Saturday p.m., Cambs and Hertfordshire Sunday a.m. and Norfolk and Suffolk Sunday p.m. In recent years the standard of golf has been high, I particularly remember being five under par gross after 10 holes at Hunstanton G.C. and 1 down to BB&O and five up on Lincolnshire. However seaside links breezes sometimes affects the scores produced; on quality putting greens in May and June those golfers with a honed putting stroke often score points.

This event saw one of the most amazing set of holes in one in the history of the game by two handicapper Bob Taylor, a member of Scraptoft Golf Club and a Leicestershire & Rutland County player. During the practice day for the 1974 Eastern Counties Foursomes on the Hunstanton Links, he holed his tee shot with a 1-iron at the 188-yard 16th. The next day in the first round of the competition, he repeated the feat this time with a six iron since the wind had changed on the tide. When he stepped on to the 16th tee the following day his partner jokingly offered him odds of 1,000,000 to one against holing-in-one for a third successive time. There was a small group of spectators surrounding the green who had gathered just in case. Bob Taylor again selected his six iron and amazingly holed-in-one to the astonishment and cheers of everyone present. Over the years I have spoken to several people who were present at the time, they all say it was as though time stopped for a few seconds as they contemplated the significance and improbability of what had just happened.

The hole itself is a very difficult par three with a two-tier green and four bunkers and is badly affected by those North Norfolk winds. Bob Taylor became Leicestershire & Rutland County President during the same period that I held that position for Northamptonshire in 1996-98; we have often dined together at functions and chatted about this feat and this beautiful golf course. Poor Bob has become so famous with the story that he is often asked to relive it, since people still find it unbelievable. The bet was in fact taken on jokingly since Bob said "Oh go on then, let's have a penny on it" He is still waiting to be paid for that famous day in May 1974. An engraved seat has been placed beside the tee by the club in honour of this magnificent achievement. The odds of achieving a hole in one have been calculated in America to be 3,708 to1 for a top amateur. Bob Taylor's achievement therefore had a probability of about 50 Billion to1. On this particular green when the wind blows from the tee, uphill putts with the wind are faster than downhill putts into the wind!

Playing in sixes brings about some interesting situations especially on the putting green. For example if a Northants ball was close to the hole it might well be conceded by our friends from Suffolk although competitive Leicestershire would ask for it to be tapped in. A total of 8 points can therefore be collected over the weekend although there are many of us who have come home without a single point.

Kingsthorpe's Steve McDonald has experienced the highs and lows of this event and once captured 8 out of 8 at Hunstanton with Northants County's David Evans in 1978. This total equalled Bob Larratt & Jack Humphries score from the 1972 event however it is of note that Bob& Jack played top pair whilst David & Steve played last pair. This beat the previous best total of $7\frac{1}{2}$ from 8 by Richard Aitken and partner in 1971. It could also be argued that there are no easy games in this great event. Steve's low of 0 from 8 happened in 1991 at Seacroft, he was severely leg pulled all weekend by his Kingsthorpe colleague Darren Jones and nicknamed "blobby". Undeterred by the friendly banter Steve went on to become County Champion the following weekend at Kettering, such is the nature of this fickle game.

When playing in this event for the first time the scores as each game progresses can be very confusing. I remember once playing at Hunstanton and being 3 up on a pair from Cambridgeshire and 3 down to a pair from Hertfordshire after six holes. The "Eastern Counties" format was used twice by the N.G.U. for the Hollingsworth Trophy Final in 1978&9 but proved to be unpopular with the players and has not been repeated.

At Hunstanton G.C. greenkeeper Ian Marshall from Wellingborough who is used to getting up early in the morning found he was awake and bored at 4:30 a.m. Rather than kill time waiting for breakfast he went for a quick nine holes on his own and claims to have scored 3 under par over holes 1-4,14-18! Ian never indicated if he helped cut the greens which we later found were running at 13 on the stimpmetre. Northamptonshires best performance to date has been runners up in 1967 and 1989. I have been unable to find details of the team which played in 1967. The team who finished runners–up in 1989 are given below. The County Captain at the time Ian Marshall still believes we would have probably won the event if Leicestershire had not completed a clean sweep of ten points out of ten on the Sunday morning (a very rare accomplishment). The following points were recorded:-

	Club	Saturday	Sunday	Total
1st Pair John Wilson & Conrad Ceislewicz	NC	$3^1/_2$	2	$5^1/_2$
2nd Pair Darren Jones & John Evans	Kg	$1^1/_2$	$2^1/_2$	4
3rd Pair Richard Cole & Greg Shelton	PM	$2^1/_2$	3	$5^1/_2$
4th Pair Ian Achurch & Anthony Lord	NC	$^1/_2$	1	$1^1/_2$
5th Pair Ian Marshall & Martin Izzard	W/N	4	2	6
		12	$10^1/_2$	$22^1/_2$

The Northamptonshire Team, Eastern Counties Foursomes Runners-up at Hunstanton G.C. 1989.
Left to right: J. Evans, I. Achurch, M. Izzard, A. Linney (Selector), C. Ceislewicz, G. Shelton, I. Marshall (Captain),
D. Jones, R. Cole, A. Lord, J. Wilson.

85

This was the last time this magnificent event was played at Hunstanton G.C., numerous letters flew about the ten counties during that winter and at one stage it looked as though the event might come to Northamptonshire (kindly offered by Northants County G.C.). However since it has always had a seaside feeling, it was appropriate that after Les Pepper had discussed the position with Lincolnshire the event crossed the Wash over King John's treasure to the links course at Seacroft G.C. (Skegness) near to the Gibraltar Point Nature Reserve. Les continued to look after the fine details and the overall running of the event till his death in 2005. We have been fortunate to see such a commitment to this event from a man with a passion for the game; we will all miss his sense of humour and individual style. Les (L.C.Pepper) made this his event in his County Lincolnshire coupled with some assistance from helpers from the Club.

Les was born in his father's cottage on the edge of the Burghley Park G.C., which is now close to the A1. Les lived most of his life in Stamford; a man with good strong hands Les worked with wood for a great deal of his life and also played golf for Lincolnshire. I first met him at Staverton Park G.C. in 1977 when he was there to support their B team along with his little dog "stumpy". I was somewhat taken aback when he openly critisised the Lincolnshire players on the course during the foursomes, that was Les Pepper's way. Back to Seacroft, Les was often found patrolling the course in a buggy checking out the speed of play, golf course and weather conditions and the sobriety of some of the Officials! Les Pepper worked timelessly for the game; he certainly made an impact and is missed by many.

The late Les Pepper "doingadmin" at Seacroft G.C.

In 2004, the Northamptonshire team achieved their highest ever points total in the competition during the golden anniversary of the tournament when the team collected 24 points, finishing in third place. The points scores in 2004 were Matthew Bearman & James Dunkley 6 Pts, Jeremy Creffield & Neil Presto 5.5 Pts, Tony Lord & Glenn Keates 4.5 Pts, Neil Connolly & Adrian Firman 4 Pts, Richard Brown & Stuart Hawkins 4 Pts. In fact since the event has been held at Seacroft G.C. Northamptonshire have finished third twice.

The much enjoyed visits to this seaside resort generates a complete contrast between the town's main street with flashing lights, discos & nightclubs, the green or brown seaside links and the peace and isolation of the Nature Reserve at the bottom of Drummond Road at Gibraltar Point.

In 2005 Cambridgeshire scored a remarkable tally of 17 points on the Sunday which included a clean sweep of ten out of ten in the morning. This feat was last achieved by Bedfordshire in 2000 and Leicestershire in 1989.

I am certain that there are many players and officials who could tell some wicked stories or yarns about their experiences in the event however as they say "when the lads are away the lads will play". There are four little cameos I can tell here without fear of recrimination.

At Seacroft G.C. in 1990 County President Tony Stephens promised Darren Jones (Kingsthorpe G.C.) and Michael Pask (Kettering G.C.) a cheque for £50 if

N.G.U. County Captains in action at Seacroft G. C. during Easter Counties Foursomes. Anthony Lord, Northants County (left), and Neil Presto (Peterborough Milton).

they won eight out of eight matches and it looked as though the President was going to pay out with the final match on the final green. Tony had his cheque book in hand and was beginning to write until a 35 foot birdie putt flashed into the hole from Suffolk and the cheque was torn up right under Darren's nose. The pair recorded a very creditable $7\frac{1}{2}$ out of a possible 8 points.

Over dinner on the Friday evening at Seacroft G.C. two pairs from Kingsthorpe and Northampton G.Cs. were discussing how they best prepared for the golf the following day, one pair went to bed early and one pair visited the town for a few drinks. After the morning foursomes the two pairs met in the clubhouse when the famous quotation was delivered " Early to bed, early to rise get you're a**s beat six and five, pissed out of your head, sleep on the floor win your match six and four". It is the subtle balances "work hard/play hard" which we sometimes get wrong. The names of Stones & Crowson spring to mind!

Also at Seacroft G.C. an amusing incident occurred on the practice ground which is between the 1st and 18th holes. Players teed off on both tees and proceeded to hook balls onto the practice ground when the players got to their balls they found they were sat side-by-side within a foot of each other. Since both matches were playing Titleist Professional number 1 balls without markings on neither pair could identify their ball, consequently both pairs lost the hole to their opposition who were giggling on both fairways!

Sir John Betjeman poem "Seaside Golf" given in Chapter 11 reminds me of the splendour of the Hunstanton and Seacroft links and captures the essence of links golf.

Champion Club Northamptonshire & England 1984-2007

This event for the 34 English counties was introduced by the E.G.U. in 1984. Three players from each county make up their team who play a gruelling 36 hole medal with two out of three scores to count. In 2005 the test was made even more demanding with all three scores to count. In Northamptonshire the Club with the lowest aggregate score in our County Championship represent us at national level. Northants County and Peterborough Milton have been most successful with the occasional interjection from Kingsthorpe, Northampton and Wellingborough. We have not yet managed to win the event but have been 4th, 5th and 6th over the years. Perhaps our best chance of victory came in 2002 when the event was held in Northamptonshire at Northants County, Peterborough Milton qualified that year thereby removing any chance of a possible home advantage and 26th place was recorded.

The winning Club receives the de Montmorency Trophy to hold for the year. For many years, members of the E.G.U. Council and Executive committee played annually at Sunningdale for the de Montmorency Trophy as an 18-hole foursomes event under handicap. This was won by R.G.Aitken & R.B.Catlow in ca 1978. Because of disappointing annual turnouts, the de Montmorency Trophy transferred to the winner of the English Champion Club tournament initiated in 1984. The trophy is named after Reymond Hervey De Montmorency q.v. born October 6, 1871, Gondah, India died December 19, 1938, Sunningdale, Berkshire. Research[16] demonstrates that the trophy was originally the President's Cup donated by Lt. Col. P.C. Burton O.B.E. and won twice in its first two years by R.H. de Montmorency as a singles competition at Woodhall Spa. He played cricket for England (1897 – 1899), was a well known English International Player who joined Stoke Poges G.C. as the 100th Member in 1908, a two times winner of the St Andrews New Club Eden Trophy (1923&4) and was Housemaster at Eton. His golf swing is depicted on the 1930 Wills Famous Golfers Cigarette cards number 16.

The winners of the de Montmorency trophy represent England in the European Champion Club Tournament which is held in October or November where two out of three scores count.

On a recent visit to Stoke Poges (now Stoke Park) G.C. for their 2005 Captain's Day I happened to be seated for dinner just below a honours board for the RH de Montmorency Bowl Challenge Cup presented by the Club in 1939. This brought about strange feelings of coincidence since in 1996 I had donated a salver for the winning Northamptonshire Champion Club team. Perhaps one day I will be able to photograph my salver along side the English de Montmorency Trophy and the European Club Cup Trophy, now that certainly would be something for Northamptonshire to celebrate.

CHAPTER 4

THE NORTHAMPTONSHIRE LADIES COUNTY GOLF ASSOCIATION

Everyone has talent.
What is rare is the courage to follow the talent to the dark place where it leads.
Erica Jong

N.L.C.G.A. HISTORY

1927 The Cecil Leitch Trophy was presented at Northants County G.C. by Miss Leitch to the winners Kingsthorpe G.C.

The 1927 Kingsthorpe Ladies team, inaugural winners of the Cecil Leitch Trophy.

1928 Miss Grieg (Northamptonshire) & Miss Enid Wilson (Derbyshire) participated in the "Eves" Ladies Northern Foursomes at Woodhall Spa G.C. Their photograph together with two other ladies walking towards the sixth green on the famous Hotchkin course appears in the large black minute books, which can be viewed in the bar at the Club and in their Centenary book[10]. Their picture is reproduced below.

1930 The Northamptonshire Ladies County Golf Association minutes were started.
      – The County Championship was instituted in 1930, when Lady Annaly from nearby Holdenby Manor presented the Trophy at Northants County. G.C.

Left to right: Miss Grieg (Northamptonshire) & Miss Enid Wilson (Derbyshire) Miss M.J. Monks & Miss N.E.Nevell (Preston)
walking to the 6th green during the "Eves" Ladies Northern Foursomes at Woodhall Spa G.C. in 1928"

1931 In the Cecil Leitch Trophy the Clubs playing were Peterborough, Walton Heath, Northants County, Northampton, Rushden, Kettering, Kingsthorpe and Wellingborough.

1932 The Ladies County Championship was held for the first time.

1935 N.L.C.G.A. took over the running of the Cecil Leitch Trophy from Northants County G.C.

1936 County Division was Cambridgeshire & Huntingdonshire, Norfolk and Suffolk.
      – Walton Heath G.C. disappeared.

1937   The two Peterborough Clubs amalgamated (Peterborough Walton/Gordon and Peterborough Milton Hall) to form Peterborough Milton G.C.

– County greensomes competition was introduced and played at Kingsthorpe G.C. it is now possibly the Handicap Foursomes.

1938   A SSS for Peterborough Milton G.C. was implemented (The New course opened on the 14th July 1938).

1939   Mrs Phipps presented the Junior Cup which was played at the County Championship for Ladies 11 Handicap and above; the second eight qualifiers compete for the Bronze Championship.

1946   The County Committee was reconvened after World War II.

– Northants County and Peterborough Milton received County Green status.

1948   A County Mixed tournament was introduced, Mrs D. Cooch presented the trophies, format Ladies Greensomes a.m. and Mixed p.m.

1949   The Junior Championship would now be called the Phipps Cup and played for at the County Championship.

1952   The English Ladies Golf Association was formed (E.L.G.A.).

1953   The Ladies County Foursomes tournament was introduced.

1955   Mrs A. Timpson presented the Runner-up Cup for the County Championship.

– Swannell Salver donated by Mrs Kath Swannell. At this time the Championship had 3 separate match plays, the Championship, [first 8], the Swannell Salver and the Phipps Cup, [handicaps 11 and over]

1959   The Bouverie Bowl was held independently from the Championship for the first time, medal a.m. foursomes p.m.

– Peterborough Milton were asked to hold the first Bouverie Bowl, but were unable to do so, it was therefore held at Northants County G.C. and has remained there ever since.

1961   The first 9 hole Girls Championship was held at Wellinborough G.C., Mrs Collier of Wellingborough donated the Junior Cup, and Mrs Cooch donated the Handicap Cup.

1963   The Bouverie Bowl was played over 2 days, Medal round on the first day, Handicap foursomes on the second day.

1970   The County Committee took over the running of the Girls Championship, 4 trophies held at Wellingborough G.C. were handed over to the N.L.C.G.A. by Mrs E. Gilbert, and two of these trophies were used for the runners-up of the County Foursomes.

1972   The County 1st Team played Leicestershire, Nottinghamshire and Lincolnshire and won through to the Sub Divisional Finals where they were beaten by Staffordshire.

1973   The first youth organizer was appointed - Mrs Angela Duck of Northants County.

1974   The Veterans joined the N.L.C.G.A.

– Mrs Carol Gibbs nee Lefeuvre represented Great Britain and Ireland in the Curtis Cup in San Francisco G.B. & I 5 - U.S.A. 13. [Carol is a Northamptonshire member]

1977   Miss Cecil Leitch former British Women's Golf Champion died aged 86 years, she won the title in 1914, 1920, 1921 & 1926 and presented the much sort after Cecil Leitch Trophy at Northants County G.C. in 1927.

1978   The Coronation Medals were played on separate days in conjunction with the National Playing Fields; it was originally played in conjunction with the Bouverie Bowl.

– New County colours were introduced - Navy and White.

– Mrs Russell donated a County Flag.

1979   The County Captain's badge was purchased.

– The Professional Women's Golf Association formed.

1980   The N.G.U. allowed girls to play in the Boys Championship as a separate competition, if any girls enter the N.L.C.G.A. have 2 cups available for presentation. This was the first Girl's Championship since 1964.

1982 The Phipps Cup Match play was dropped from County Championship [Championship and Swannell Salver only]
- Bronze Championship introduced. [trophy is the Phipps Cup].
- The Past Captains Association formed.
- The introduction of County week being held over 3 days.

1985 National Playing Fields Competition discontinued.
- Coronation Medals and Captains Day separated from the National Playing Fields.

1986 Charity Final was introduced - Playing Fields Trophy.

1987 A new Metal County Badge was purchased.
- Mrs Irene Hart, President presented the County with a New Flag.

1989 New County Colours were introduced - Kingfisher Blue.

1990 A new format was introduced for the County Championship - [36 hole] first 16 best gross play Matchplay, first Matchplay winners go into Championship and losers into the Swannell Salver.
- The November Delegates meeting open to all N.L.C.G.A. members without voting powers.

1991 Scratch League formed, Trophy donated by Mrs Judy Ray Oundle G.C.

1992 Mrs Gleeson provided a new Silver Band on the Bouverie Bowl Trophy.
- Introduction of a Competitions Secretary.
- A clock was presented to Kingsthorpe G.C. for the many years the County have used their clubhouse for Delegates Meetings.

1993 Mrs Sue Hennigan & Mrs Phil Cook of Peterborough Milton G.C. represented the County in the L.G.U. Centenary Foursomes at St. Andrews.
- Centenary year for Oundle, Northampton and Wellingborough G.C.s.

1994 The Handicap Foursomes trophy was presented by Mrs Muriel Curtis Kettering G.C.
- Handicap Foursomes no longer played at Northants County G.C. the first time for many years.
- Society of Past Captains joined the N.L.C.G.A.
- A Presidents Badge was purchased and presented to Mrs Peggy Coker Northants County G.C.
- The sad death of Mrs Laura White Kettering G.C. a former County Captain.
- Mrs Stephanie Wright Northants County. G.C. appointed as Deputy on the E.L.G.A. Committee

1995 Miss Susanne Sharpe Peterborough Milton G.C. was chosen to train with the England Team in Spain at Las Brisas near Marbella; Suzanne represented the England Ladies in the Spanish Open.
- The Charity Trophy was refurbished by Mrs G. Wild Northants County G.C.
- Northampton G.C. attained County Green status.
- Introduction of ladies 4 Counties 36 hole scratch competition.
- Junior Quaich Trophy presented by Mrs S. Wright.
- Team Shield presented by Mrs A. Duck.
- Miss Kelly Hanwell Northampton G.C. was selected to play for the under 18 England Team and played in the Home Internationals, she also trained with the Intermediate Team.

1996 Mrs Janet Halliday Northants County G.C. was appointed as Northamptonshire's Standard Scratch Assessor [ELGA appointment]
- Miss Kelly Hanwell captained the English Schools team v Scotland and Wales, both matches were won, Kelly also won the Daily Telegraph Junior Championship at Hanbury Manor, which won her trip to Lake Nona U.S.A. for the Finals.
- A runner-up shield for the Cecil Leitch competition was purchased.

1997 Miss Kelly Hanwell started a 4 year scholarship to the University of Arkansas, USA
- Introduction of County Fourball competition in place of the County Foursomes Championship which has been lacking support. [The County Foursomes Trophies were given to Northants County for safe keeping].

– The sad death of Mrs Hilda Castel Wellingborough G.C. a former County Captain.
– Wellingborough G.C. presented 2 trophies in memory of Mrs H. Castel, [The County Fourball Trophies].
– Mrs Judy Ray appointed ELGA Junior Area Manager Midlands Division 1.
– Centenary year of the Goodyear Cup.

1998 Introduction of a new Handicap system.
– The sad death of County President Mrs Peggy Coker Northants County G.C. and Past President Mrs Kath Lock Kettering G.C.
– Appointment of Mrs S. Wright on the E.L.G.A. Committee.
– Northamptonshire Millennium Committee formed from members of N.G.U. and N.L.C.G.A. to raise money to help the golfing youth of the County.

1999 Mrs Carol Gibbs Cold Ashby G.C. ex Curtis Cup player appointed as England Selector, and County Training Officer.
– Miss Roseann Youngman Oundle G.C. won Flight 2 England Girls Challenge at Theydon Bois G.C.

2000 Due to personal reasons Mrs Carol Gibbs resigned as England Selector, Mrs Angela Duck took over the post.
– Mrs Kirstie Jennings Northants County G.C. was appointed as E.L.G.A. Junior Development Officer.
– Miss Roseann Youngman Oundle G.C. won the Midlands Division 3 Abraham Trophy; in the National Final she won Best Gross, winning a small trophy and E.L.G.A. pin. [Abraham Trophy is a Nett competition] Roseann also qualified for the English girls Championship at Sheringham G.C. and was selected for England Regional Training Squad.
– Miss Alison McArthur Northampton G.C. won the Four Counties Championship.
– The sad death of Mrs Kath Swannell Northampton and Northants County G.C. age 96 years, Kath had been a Past County Captain in 1955 and County President in 1974.
– The first Millennium Ball was held at Wickstead Park, Kettering, 300 attended from all clubs in the County.
– The Millennium Committee raised £15,000 in their first year.
– Sarah Carter (Northampton G.C.) reached the Semi Final of the Ladies Midland Championship at Spalding G.C.

Millenium Golf Ball for the celebrations & events

2001 Miss Roseann Youngman selected by ELGA to play in the U16 Scottish Championship at Drumoig G.C.Winner of the Midlands Schools Championship at Chesterfield G.C. unable to play in Final because of exams. Winner of the England Schools U16 Championship setting a course record at Blankney G.C. [Gross 73 and 70].Winner of the U21 Prince of Wales Challenge Trophy at Woburn G.C. [Duchess Course] Trophy held at Woburn. Selected for the U18 Elite Squad. Qualified for the Junior Tour Final at Chart Hills G.C., unfortunately had to forgo this as date clashed with 1st England Elite Training Date. Selected to play in match - U18 England Girls v U16 England Boys at Parkstone G.C. Devon Selected North of England U16 Amateur Strokeplay Championship at Pannal G.C. for ELGA Team, qualified 36 holes 4th of girls, 2nd of English girls.

– Miss Lucinda Davies Peterborough Milton & Miss Emma Parr Northants County selected for Midlands ELGA Regional Training Squad

– Miss Kelly Hanwell winner of the Midlands Ladies Close Championship held at Peterborough Milton G.C.Winner of the Intermediate Section of the English Strokeplay Championship.

– Miss Christine Allen Brampton Heath G.C. winner of the Golf Foundation Special Needs Award Category, presentation made at Wentworth G.C.

– 1st and 2nd team Badges purchased. [County Colours].

– Four Counties Scratch Competition abandoned - Quaich Trophy presented by Mrs Stephanie Wright to be used for junior matches.

– Team Trophy presented by Mrs Angela Duck to be used for runner up team trophy at County Week.

– The sad death of Mrs L. V. Everard Kettering G.C. Past County Champion, County Captain and County President.

Kelly Hanwell 2001 Midland Ladies Close Champion pictured here at Overstone Park G.C. with Northants County Ladies Golf Association Captain Sue Aitken

2002 Miss Roseann Youngman won the Faldo Series at Forest of Arden G.C. She was also selected to represent England in the Quadrangular Match in Rome, Selected to play in the Under 18 Team Championship at Esbjberg G.C. Denmark.Roseann was a member of the winning England team in the Girls Home Internationals at The Heritage, Dublin and won all matches she played. In the foursomes, Roseann partnered Felicity Johnson; the pair won matches their matches by 5/4 against Scotland, by 2/1 against Wales and by 5/4 against Ireland. In the singles, Roseann won 2up against Scotland, 3/1 against Wales and by 4/2 against Ireland.

– Also selected to play for England in the Under18 England Girls v Under 16 England Boys match at Parkstone G.C. During this rich year she also Captained the English Schools v Welsh Schools at Ashburnham G.C. England halved with Wales, Roseann won both her matches.

– She was also selected for the Under 21 Elite Squad.

– Roseann Youngman & Emma Parr won the Team Trophy at the English Ladies Under 23 Championship at Saunton Sands G.C.

– The Junior team won through to the Midlands Matchplay Final at Beeston Fields G.C. Beeston Fields G.C.

– Miss Alexandra Banham Elton Furze G.C. was selected for the E.L.G.A. Midlands Eagles Squad.

– The sad death of Mrs D. Cooch Northants County Past County Captain 1947.

Roseann Youngman in her England colours with the Stroyan Trophy at the Girls Home Internationals in 2002

2003   Miss Roseann Youngman invited to a Masterclass at Celtic Manor G.C., 8 girls from G. B. & I were invited. Swing analysis from Butch Harmon and brothers, followed by a competition. Winner of the Midlands Girls Championship at Worfield G.C. [Course record Gross 71].Winner of National Schools Championship at Trentham G.C.Selected to play in the U18 European Team Championship at Torino G.C. Italy, qualified 1st flight [[8th out of 17 teams].Played in The Italian Ladies Championship at The Circolo Bogogno, Nr Milan.Selected to play in the U18 Girls Home Internationals at Pyle and Kenfig, Wales [England winners]. Selected to play in the U18 English Girls v U16 English Boys match at Pleasington G.C. [Girls won 121/2 to 51/2].

– Mrs Gillian Curley Northants County & Mrs Anita Lawson Farthingstone G.C. winners of the Midland Foursomes Championship.

– Miss Georgina Dunn Peterborough Milton G.C. winner of Midlands Area 3 Abraham Trophy.

– Miss Emma Parr selected to represent ELGA at U16 Scottish Strokeplay Championship at Drumoig G.C. Scotland.

– Jane Petts Northampton G.C. winner of the Goodyear Cup.The Goodyear Cup first played in 1897, Trophy presented to Leicestershire by Mr J. W. Jansen of Northamptonshire in 1896 [Handicap Competition for Leicestershire, Northamptonshire and Warwickshire]

– Mrs Gill Spencer Wellingborough G.C. presented with a Silver Clock from Midlands ELGA for her fine organisation of the Coronation Medal Final held at Wellingborough G.C.

– Junior County Badges purchased [County colours].

– Mrs Carol Gibbs selected to play for the Seniors Midlands ELGA Team v North, South and Scotland.

– Carol awarded the Chronicle and Echo Sports Volunteer of the month for services to Sport.

2004   County Ladies beat Lincolnshire, Nottinghamshire and Leicestershire at county week played at Scraptoft G.C. Leicestershire. Team went forward to the sub-divisional finals at Sherwood Forest G.C. Nottinghamshire; unfortunately they lost out by 1/2 point to Warwickshire who were the winners.

– County junior team beat Nottinghamshire, Leicestershire and Lincolnshire to win through to the Midlands E.L.G.A. Matchplay final at Stoke Rochford G.C. teams competed Staffordshire, Northamptonshire and Bedfordshire. Winners were Staffordshire with Northamptonshire runners-up.

– Mrs Shirley Chapman Wellingborough appointed Chairman of Midlands Division ELGA.

– Miss Kelly Hanwell won Best Qualifying Round in the Midland Ladies Championship at Stagsdon G.C. Bedfordshire. Kelly and Roseann won the magnificent Team Trophy [Trophy hadn't been won by Northamptonshire since 1939].

– Miss Roseann Youngman selected to play in The French U21 Championship at St.Cloud, France.

– Miss Karin Poolton Overstone G.C. won the Midlands Area 3 Abraham Trophy.

– Miss Emma Parr winner of the 4 Counties Championship at Northants County G.C. [Gross 72].

– Miss Boo Haig Northants. Co. lost on countback for the nett Cup [Nett 71]

– Miss Megan Liddington Daventry G.C. won the Nett Cup at the Midlands Challenge played at Flempton G.C.

– Miss Georgina Dunn winner of the ELGA Rose Spoon.

– Miss Charley Hull Kettering G.C. won through to the Wee Wonders National Final to be held at St. Andrews G.C.

– Miss Megan McLaren Wellingborough G.C. selected for the Midlands ELGA Birdie Squad.

– Charley [10 years] winner of the Ladies Health Perception Tournament at Turnberry G.C. part of her prize is to play in the Ladies Weetabix Pro Am in 2005.

– President Mrs Pam Giles received an invitation from Prince Andrew to attend a dinner celebrating The Royal and Ancient's 250th Year.

– Introduction of the CONGU Unified Handicap System.
– County Vice Captain's badge purchased.
– County Partnership Committee formed, representatives from the NGU, NLCGA, PGA and Millennium Committee.
– Mrs Carol Gibbs selected to play for the Seniors Midlands ELGA Team v North, South and Scotland.

2005 Miss Rachel Smith Northants County G.C. winner of the Goodyear Cup held at Wellingborough G.C.
– Meghan McLarin and Miss Rebecca Gee [Juniors] Wellingborough G.C. Nett overall in the Midland Ladies Foursomes Championship at Haverhill G.C., they also achieved 2nd Best Gross P.M.
– Miss Charley Hull selected for the Midlands ELGA Birdie Squad.
– Miss Kelly Hanwell Northants County was appointed ELGA Regional Development Officer.
– County ladies team beat Lincolnshire, Nottinghamshire and Leicestershire at county week played at Coxmoor G.C. Nottinghamshire. Team presented with the Rosie Bowl.

The Northamptonshire Ladies team and officials at Scraptoft G.C., Inter County Week winners 2004. Back Row (LtoR) Gillian Curley, Angela Duck, Rachel Smith, Kirstie Jennings, Roseann Youngman, Sarah Carter & Carol Gibbs; Front Row (LtoR) Lucinda Davies, Heather Williams, Susan Hennigan, Pam Giles, Sue Aitken & Kelly Hanwell.

– sub-divisional finals beat Cambs & Hunts., Warwickshire and Caernarvonshire & Anglesey at Copt Heath G.C. Warwickshire a wonderful achievement. Team presented with trophy.
– National County Matchplay final at Brancepeth Castle, county Durham, teams were Yorkshire, Hampshire and Gloucestershire - Yorkshire were the winners (see Appendix for full results).

– Ladies county team awarded Northamptonshire Team of the year for their outstanding achievements in reaching the national finals for the first time in their history The E.L.G.A. Press release which is reproduced here provides a nice glow. "What Praise" E.L.G.A. 1 November 2005.

– Northamptonshire Ladies' drive to transform themselves from "golfing minnows" into major players on the national scene has been recognised with an award. This year, for the first time, the Northamptonshire ladies' team reached the finals of the English County Championship and their achievement has won the Northamptonshire Sport Team of the Year award. They beat challengers from the worlds of cricket, rugby and hockey to take the title and will now represent the county in the BBC East Midlands Sports Awards in December. The recognition is reward for the Northamptonshire ladies' determination to change their golfing fortunes. The county is one of the smallest in the country with 27 clubs and had suffered from a long tradition of defeat." We were minnows in a sharks' pond and serial wooden spoon winners!" said Kirstie Jennings, a county player, Northamptonshire ladies' committee member and E.L.G.A.'s national girls' development officer.

A four-year plan, involving considerable investment and a structured approach to training, was put in place under the guidance of former Curtis Cup golfer, Carol Gibbs, who was then county training officer. The effort paid off. In 2000, Northamptonshire won their first county week match in 13 years. In 2004, they won county week for the first time in 33 years and went on to the Midlands sub-divisional finals where they narrowly missed going through to County Finals on points.

This year they made no mistakes, and joined Yorkshire, Gloucestershire and Hampshire in the finals at Brancepeth Castle finishing fourth.

– Mrs Carol Gibbs selected to play for the Seniors Midlands ELGA Team v North, South and Scotland.

2006 Miss Alexandra Banham 17 years qualified for the Midland Schools Final at Belton Woods G.C. Qualified for the Final of the Faldo Series. Selected to play in a Junior Mixed Match versus a Junior team from Thailand at the Warwickshire G.C. Selected to play for England Schools versus Scotland Schools at Hillside G.C. [England won match]

– Miss Charley Hull 12 years won nett Cup at the 4 Counties Championship at Wollaton G.C.

– Charley, Megan McLaren & Rebecca Gee won the nett team prize in the same event. Selected for the Super Birdie Sqaud. Qualified for the Wee Wonders Final at St. Andrews G.C. [2nd in age group]

– Miss Rachel Smith Northants County G.C. winner of the Goodyear Cup at Hinkley G.C. [3rd time Rachel has won this competition].

– Miss Hannah Mulliner 16 years Northampton G.C. nett trophy winner of the Midlands Challenge at Stratford on Avon G.C. Winner of the Abraham Trophy prize at the Midland Girls Championship at Park Hill G.C. Leicestershire.

– Mrs Carol Gibbs selected to play for Midlands ELGA Team v North, South and Scotland.

– County ladies team attended the Sports Award dinner at De Montfort Hall. Charley Hull received a judge's award for special achievement.

– Kelly Hanwell and Kirstie Jennings took up significant positions in E.L.G.A.

2007 E.L.G.A. E.G.M. vote carried, will be renamed E.W.G.A. (English Women's Golf Association) and become a company.

– Northamptonshire will now be part of Midland South Region Buckinghamshire, Berkshire, Oxfordshire, Warwickshire, Worcestershire and Herefordshire.

– Tim Rouse professional at Northants County appointed as training officer for the Ladies County Team.

– Sad death of Mrs Dot Sleath former County Treasurer.

– Sad death of Mrs Janet Gubbins a Past County Captain.

- Northamptonshire Ladies 2nd Team played in the Matchplay Final at Gainsborough G.C.
- Bronze Championship will be played on a separate day in 2008.
- Committee Blazer Badges purchased, colour of blazers changed to Navy [committee members to purchase own blazers].
- Ann Lones Overstone Park G.C. winner of the Bronze Division of the English Challenge Bowl.
- Daventry & District G.C. celebrated their Centenary Year.

N.L.C.G.A. COUNTY TROPHIES

COUNTY CHAMPIONSHIP TROPHY
Presented by Lady Annaly. If the Trophy is no longer played for, the trophy is to be held at Northants County Golf Club.
COUNTY CHAMPIONSHIP RUNNER UP TROPHY
Presented by Mrs A Timson in 1955.
SWANNELL SALVER
Presented by Mrs K Swannell in 1955.
BRONZE CHAMPIONSHIP TROPHY
Presented by Mrs R T Phipps in 1939. This Trophy was played in conjunction with the County Championship until 1982.
BOUVERIE BOWL
Presented by Miss Bouverie in 1910 to the Northants County Golf Club. The N.L.C.G.A. took over the running of this competition in 1930 when it was played in conjunction with the County Championship until 1959.
CECIL LEITCH TROPHY
Presented by Miss C Leitch in 1927 to the Northants County Golf Club. The N.L.C.G.A. took over the running of this competition in 1935.
CECIL LEITCH RUNNER UP TROPHY
Presented by the N.L.G.A. in 1997.
HANDICAP CUP
Presented by Mrs Cooch in 1948.
COUNTY FOURSOMES TROPHY
Presented by not known. This Trophy is held at Northants County Golf Club until the competition is re-introduced.
COUNTY FOURSOMES RUNNERS UP TROPHY
Donated by Wellingborough Golf Club, presented by Mrs E Gilbert in 1970. This Trophy is held at Northants County Golf Club until the competition is re-introduced.
GOODYEAR CHAMPIONSHIP BOWLE
Donated by Mr J. W. Jansen in 1896.

The major trophy that individuals compete for is described below:-

Northamptonshire Ladies Championship

The Championship was instituted in 1930, when Lady Annaly from nearby Holdenby Manor presented the Trophy at Northants County G.C, it was first played for in 1932. The Championship has been won by many well known ladies and of course there have been a few nice surprise victories. It was stipulated presumably by the donor that if the trophy is no longer played for, which appears quite unlikely, the trophy be held at Northants County G.C.

Prior to this gross competition perhaps the first N.L.C.G.A. event, a Nett Ladies Championship was held over the Kettering links on 1st October 1896, before a large crowd of spectators. The championship prize was the Goodyear Championship Bowl donated by Mr J. W. Jansen. Ten Lady Golfers from various Clubs entered. In donating the trophy, the donor regretted the absence of any Kettering ladies. He attributed this to the fact that the Club did not possess a ladies room and donated five pounds towards such a building. The scores recorded are given below.

	Gross	HCP	Nett
Mrs C.W. Phipps, Northampton	123	28	95
Miss Britain, Northampton	122	26	96
Mrs Lucas, Stamford	126	18	108
Mrs E. Bull, Northampton	122	12	110
Mrs W. Hope, Wellingborough	141	30	111
Mrs F. Bostock, Northampton	145	28	117
Miss Dickin, Northampton	145	28	117
Mrs S. Spurgin Northampton	158	29	129
Mrs Pendered, Wellingborough	172	33	139
Miss G. Hughes, Wellingborough	179	36	143

The list of Ladies County Champions is given in Appendix 1.

Since the formation of the N.C.L.G.A. several ladies have made a major contribution to county golf as players and officials, their contributions are described below:

Mrs Sue Aitken Northants County G.C.

Sue was County Captain in 2001, a 1st team player. Sue has made a huge contribution to junior golf and will become Lady Captain of Northants County G.C. in their Centenary year in 2009.

The late Mrs Peggy Coker

Peggy Coker made a huge contribution to ladies golf as County Secretary for many years, responsible for bringing the N.L.C.G.A. constitution, and Cecil Leitch rules up to date, also L.G.U. Handicap Advisor for 10 years. Mrs Coker was Lady Captain at Northants County G.C. in 1971 and Lady President in 1995.

Susanne Dickens Peterborough Milton & Northampton G.Cs. (1993-present)

Suzanne was born in Stamford in 1971 and spent a large amount of her amateur career at Peterborough Milton G.C before migrating across the county to Northampton G.C. In her amateur days, she played hockey for Cambridgeshire and represented Cambridge at tennis, at the same time as representing Northamptonshire at golf. Suzanne was Northamptonshire County Champion 1993-95, a losing finalist in the English Amateur Championship 1994 and Liphook Trophy winner 1994. Suzanne represented England between1994- 95 and was the Frilford Heath Scratch Salver Champion in 1995.

Suzanne turned professional in Oct 1995 and competed in 10 events in 2003 where her best finish was tied for 31st in the Spanish Open, that year she won the W.P.G.A. Order of Merit title in the UK. In 2004, Suzanne improved her performance in the Spanish Open finishing tied for 17th place, also that year she won the inaugural Ladies 9-hole English Golf Championship at Great Chart G.C. Kent. In 2005 she posted a career best finish of tied for 8th place at the Arras Open de France Dames, she finished 97th on the Money list. In 2006, Suzanne played in sixteen tournaments with a best finish of 12th in the Ladies English Open at Chart Hills G.C. and finished 113th on the New Star Money list. In the winter, Suzanne coaches at Thorpe Wood G.C. Peterborough.

Her interests away from the golf course include all sports, music, cinema, fitness training, taebo, wildlife and countryside farming.

Mrs Angela Duck Northants County (1950s-present)

Angela was born in Staffordshire where she became a member of Brocton Hall and Beau Desert golf clubs in the 1950s. At 16 years of age, she was down to a handicap of four and a member of the Staffordshire county team. Angela played in the British Girls Championship aged eighteen and was selected for the Home International team. Angela won the Staffordshire County Championship in 1960 and 1962 and the Midland Championship twice. Internationally Angela won the Spanish Open in 1969 and the Swiss Open in 1972. Angela moved to Northants County G.C. in 1963 and became Club Champion in seventeen successive years starting in 1985. In 1991, she played for the English Seniors team vs Europe in France and was runner-up in the English Seniors Ladies Championship at the magnificent Burnham and Berrow course in Somerset.

Angela has played for Northamptonshire ladies from 1966-2005 and won the N.C.L.G.A. County Championship in 1972, 1984, 1985 and 1988. With husband Michael, they were Northants County's junior delegates for ten years. Angela was also an England selector for E.L.G.A. for five years.

Carol Gibbs (Nee Le Feuvre) Cold Ashby & Wellingborough G.Cs. (1966-present)

1966-68 Jersey Champion
1966-68 Runner up Channel Island Championship
1968 Runner up English Girls Championship, English Girl home international team
1969 English Girls Champion, English Girl home international team
1970 English Girls Champion, British Girl Champion (the first English girl to hold both girls' titles in same year), under 23 British Stoke Play Champion and English Girls home international. team
1971 English Ladies home international team
1972 English Ladies home international team, Dutch international ladies open Champion
1973 Runner up English Ladies Championship, Runner up Avia Foursomes with Micky Walker, under 23 British Stroke Play Champion, British Vagliano team v Europe, English team member of the winning European Team Championship in Belgium, British Team touring Australia, English Ladies Home International team.
1974 English Ladies Home international team, South Eastern Champion, Avia Foursomes winner with Carole Redford, Curtis Cup Team v USA in San Francisco, Hampshire County Girls Champion 1968-70, Hampshire County Ladies Champion 1970-74&6, Hampshire County 1st team player 1968-1976
1998-2006 Northamptonshire 1st Team player
1989-92 Northamptonshire County Champion
1993&4 Runner up Northamptonshire County Championship
1997 Runner up Northamptonshire County Championship
1998 Northamptonshire County Champion
2000 Northamptonshire County Champion to date the only Captain (1999-2000) to win the Championship while Captain
2001, 2002 &2004 Runner up Northamptonshire County Championship
2002-2005 Represented the Midland Seniors against the North, South and Scotland
2003 Northamptonshire County Champion
2004-7 N.C.L.G.A. Training Officer. Note from author, this contribution had a significant effect on the recent successes achieved by the N.C.L.G.A. ladies.

Miss Kelly Hanwell Northampton & Northants County (1997-present)
1993-97 N.C.L.G.A. Girls Champion
1995-present represented the N.L.C.G.A.
1996 Semi-finalist in the English Girls Championship, represented England in the Home Internationals.
1997 won the English Schools championship at Sherwood Forest G.C., represented English Schools against
    Scotland and Wales and Captain of the girls squad, Daily Mail finalist at the Lake Nona U.S.A.
1997-2001 Attended a golf scholarship in Arkansas 1997-2001
2002, 2006 & 2007 N.C.L.G.A. County Ladies Champion
    Having worked in local government and at Northampton G.C. the 2006 Northamptonshire Champion
    joined the E.L.G.A. /E.G.U. Golf Development team in May 2006 to encourage adults and juniors to start
    and stay in the game of golf. Kelly is one of six E.G.U./ E.L.G.A. regional development officers and cur-
    rently works with the counties of Bedfordshire, Cambridgeshire, Leicestershire & Rutland, Norfolk,
    Northamptonshire, Nottinghamshire and Suffolk.

Miss Emma Parr Northants County (2002-present)
2002 under 16 English Schools Golf Championship with rounds of 76, 79.
2003-2005 N.C.L.G.A. Girls Champion
2004 Winner of the 4 Counties Championship at Northants County G.C. Gross72.

Mrs Judy Ray Oundle G.C. 1989-present
    County Captain 1993-94, County Secretary, 1st Team player, Club Captain, 4 years as Junior Area Manager
for Midlands ELGA, 4 years as County Junior Organiser, involved with County Juniors for over 15 years, currently County President until 2010.

The late Mrs Kath (W.T.) Swannell Northampton & Northants County (1904-2000)
    Kath Swannell began playing golf at the age of 13 in 1917, and made a significant contribution to County golf.
Mrs Swannell was clearly a "good brain" and helped Gil Sibley in his compilation of Northampton Golf Club's
Centenary book[1]. Her memories of events from1920-1940 particularly the Cecil Leitch Trophy are clearly won-
derfull. Mrs Swannell played her first county match in 1925, she was County Champion five times
between1937-1958 (1937, 39, 46, 48 & 58).
    On the administration side Mrs Swannell was County Captain 1956/57 & N.L.C.G.A. President 1974-78. Mrs
Swannell was Lady Captain at Northants County G.C. 1949, she was also Hon Secretary & Treasurer from 1930-
1964, a commitment which may not be repeated ever, especially in current times when many officials last less
than five years. Kath Swannell lived at lot of her life for the enjoyment and development of golf in the county.
Mrs Swannell clearly had an interest in natural history and wrote a short piece on the wildlife of the course,
which demonstrated considerable warmth for the subject in Neil Soutar's Northants County book[5].

Mrs Glynis Wild 1985 - present
    Glynis was County Captain twice, a first team player for over 10 years, a significant contribution to the County
and especially team golf. Her partnership with Glenda Abbott was renowned as a fine foursomes pairing winning
many County matches.

Mrs Vera White Northampton G.C. 1989-present
    Vera was County Captain in 1997-98, 1st Team player. Vera has made a significant contribution to County and
Club juniors, she was County Junior Organiser for several years, and is currently involved with County junior
training, responsible for bringing some very good golfers through [e.g. Kelly Hanwell].

Miss Roseann Youngman Oundle & Wellingborough G.Cs. (1998-present)

1998 Ladies Bronze Championship winner

1999 Winner of Flight 2 England Girls Challenge at Theydon Bois G.C.

2000 Winner of E.L.G.A. Midlands Division 3 Abraham Trophy

2001 England Schools under 16 Champion, Prince of Wales Amateur Golf Challenge Under 21 winner, represented England against England Boys.

2002 Represented England in Quadrangular Match in Rome, Under 18 European Team Championship Denmark, Home Internationals at The Hermitage Dublin and against England Boys at Pleasington. Butch Harmon Master Class Celtic Manor.

2003 Midland Schools Champion Wellingborough G.C. course record 71, Midland Girls Champion Worfield course record 73 & 71, European Team Championship Torino G.C. Italy team finished 8th, Italian Ladies Championship Milan. National Schools Champion Trentham G.C. (see photograph on p.246, Chapter 9). Under 21 Elite Squad member, Under 18 British Girls Champion Newport. Team Captain for England Schools vs Wales Ashburnham G.C. Wales

2004 Selected to play in the French Under 21 Championship St Cloud G.C.

2005 County Champion at Kingsthorpe G.C.

2006 Roseann with Emma Parr won the Team Trophy at the English Ladies Under 23 Championship at Saunton Sands G.C.

NORTHAMPTONSHIRE LADIES COUNTY GOLF ASSOCIATION
COUNTY PRESIDENTS 1948-PRESENT

1948	Mrs L. Everard	1986	Mrs Kath Lock
1968	Mrs Cesily Wilson	1990	Mrs M. Curtis
1972	Mrs L. Everard	1994	Mrs Peggy Coker
1974	Mrs Kath Swannell	1998	Mrs I. Hart
1978	Mrs Marjorie Hollingsworth	2002	Mrs Pam Giles
1982	Mrs D.Cooch	2006	Mrs Judy Ray

NORTHAMPTONSHIRE LADIES COUNTY GOLF ASSOCIATION
COUNTY CAPTAINS 1930-2008

1930 May	Mrs Gill Phipps	1971	Mrs Muriel Hutcheson
1930 September	Mrs Shirley Everard	1973	Miss Jill Douglas
1931	Mrs Helen Mobbs	1975	Mrs Angela Duck [resigned]
1933	Miss Bryan	1976	Miss Jill Douglas [substitute]
1934	Mrs Gill Phipps	1977	Mrs Janet Gubbins
1935	Mrs Gill Phipps	1979	Mrs Hilda Castel
1937	Miss Dorothy Wooding	1981	Mrs Glynis Wild
1939	Miss Marjorie Troup	1983	Mrs Glenda Abbott *(continued overleaf)*

Golf in Northamptonshire

World War Two		1985	Mrs Laura White
1946	Miss Marjorie Troup	1987	Mrs Shiela Carr
1947	Mrs Dorothy Cooch	1989	Mrs Judy Ray
1949	Mrs Toseland	1991	Mrs Glynis Wild
1951	Miss Pat Spencer	1993	Mrs Pam Giles
1953	Mrs Gill Phipps	1995	Mrs Anne Cobley
1955	Mrs Kath Swannell	1997	Mrs Vera White
1957	Marchioness of		
	Northampton (Virginia)	1999	Mrs Carol Gibbs
1959	Miss Pat Spencer	2000	Mrs Sue Aitken
1961	Mrs Cesily Wilson	2002	Mrs Sue Hennigan
1963	Mrs Shirley Everard	2004	Mrs Heather Williams
1965	Mrs Phyll Clarke	2006	Mrs Gill Spencer
1967	Mrs Marjorie Hollingsworth	2008	
1969	Mrs Kath Lock		

CHAPTER 5

THE ENGLISH GOLF UNION,
THE ENGLISH LADIES GOLF ASSOCIATION,
& THE MIDLAND GOLF UNION

A man must love a thing very much if he not only practises it without any hope of fame and money, but even practises it without any hope of doing it well.

G. K. Chesterton

E.G.U.

THE English Golf Union (E.G.U.) was established in 1924 at a conference in Manchester on the 13th February prompted by a suggestion from the Lancashire Union of Golf Clubs". At the meeting 23 representatives of 15 County Unions, representing 459 Clubs, together with 2 representatives from the Midland Counties Golf Association (Mr Spencer Newey General Secretary from Worcestershire and Mr Carl Bretherton Match Secretary from Warwickshire) and by invitation Mr Norman Boase the Chairman of the Championship Committee of the Royal & Ancient were present. The Lancashire President Mr J. Rayner Batty was voted to the

Chair, and the Lancashire Secretary Mr.A.S.Wright was asked to act as Secretary for the meeting, which then formally agreed that a Union should be formed, a step that was welcomed on behalf of the R&A by Mr Boase.

Representatives from Yorkshire, Lancashire and Cheshire were appointed to finalise the drafts of the Constitution and Messrs A.S.Wright & Geoffrey Tweedale were appointed Joint Hon.Secretaries. Mr J. Rayner Batty subsequently became the first President of the E.G.U.

It would appear that the principal reason for the sudden formation of the E.G.U. was to satisfy the urgent desire of the Royal & Ancient Golf Club of St Andrews in their wish to see a uniform system for the Standard Scratch Score (S.S.S.) and Handicapping being applied to courses and therefore a uniform system of handicapping.
The very next day another meeting was held, this time in York where a Joint Advisory Council was formed consisting of four representatives from each of the four National Unions, whose "role would be to deal to deal with what had become a vexed question, the S.S.S. for courses and handicapping". Mr M.E.Whitehead from Leicestershire and Rutland was present to represent the interests of the Midlands Counties Golf Association. This body was rechristened the Council of National Golf Unions (C.O.N.G.U.) and today still looks after S.S.S. and Handicapping for England, Ireland, Scotland and Wales and is one of the main interfaces with the R&A.

There had long been Irish and Welsh Unions, dating back to the 1890's and a Scottish Union had been formed in 1920. The oldest Golf Union in the world is in fact the Golfing Union of Ireland, which was founded in 1891. The E.G.U. became the governing body for male amateur golf in England and on their recommendation it became necessary for all English Counties to organise themselves into unions to satisfy the requirements of the R&A.

A second meeting was held in May 1924, where the draft Constitution was approved and officers elected. At this meeting the Royal Liverpool Golf Club offered its course and a trophy for the English Amateur "Close" Championship for the "Warwick" vase which was gratefully accepted by the E.G.U. This trophy has become the principal trophy for an Englishman to win and was first won in 1925 by T.F.Ellison who retained the trophy the following year at Walton Heath. The trophy is played for under matchplay conditions, 18 holes for the rounds

followed by a 36 hole final. Some very famous Englishmen including Guy Wolstenholme, Michael Bonallack, Mark James, Nick Faldo and recently Paul Casey have won it. Players from our County often enter the event, which has a maximum handicap limit of two although our best performance in recent times came from Robert Duck in 2001 who reached the fifth round and Gary Boyd in 2006 who reached the quarter final losing to the eventual winner Ross McGowan. Previously Charles Catlow had reached the last sixteen. In 2007 Gary Boyd from Cherwell Edge lead the medal qualifying with rounds of 70+64 at Royal St Georges & Royal Cinque Ports respectively but was knocked out in the first round at the 19th hole.

The first part time Secretary was paid an honorarium of 25 guineas per annum. By 1938 the work-

Gary Boyd at the Home Internationals in 2006 at Pyle & Kenfig G.C. Wales when Gary recorded his and Northamptonshire's first full international point

load had grown to such a level that the first full time Secretary was employed who operated from a one room office in his own house! Following this the EGU rented accommodation at Woking prior to acquiring its own premises at Upper King Street Leicester in 1986. During the 1990's it became obvious that a National Centre was needed in England to facilitate the requirements of a growing game. In 1994 it was announced that the E.G.U. had negotiated with Mr Neil Hotchkin to purchase his course, the buildings and some 180 acres of surrounding land at an estimated cost of £8 million. This was according to Paul Baxter the Secretary of the E.G.U. the biggest decision to be taken in the Union's history and was described in the Times as a marriage made in heaven, John Flanders Chairman of the E.G.U. and old friend of E.G.U. Past President Neil Hotchkin acted as "marriage broker". A second course (The Bracken) was subsequently built at Woodhall Spa to complement the existing Hotchkin course, which has been correctly described many times as one of the best inland courses in the world.

In 1984 the *Golf Magazine* of America voted the Hotchkin course the twenty seventh best course in the world, in the English magazine Golf 's rankings it has consistently been in the top fifteen reaching third place in 1994. It has recently been extended to a challenging 7047 yards. The Bracken course and the E.G.U. headquarters were officially opened on the 27th May 1998 by the E.G.U. President John Scrivener, Chairman and Treasurer John Flanders who also presented Neil Hotchkin and his wife Sallie with silvers salvers to mark the occasion.

The town of Woodhall Spa has many hotels, which initially were set up to look after the many visitors from

The E.G.U. Headquarters at Woodhall Spa

London who used to arrive by train to enjoy the waters. Nowadays the health tourists have been replaced by visiting golfers. Perhaps the most famous is the Petwood Hotel, which between 1943-45 became the Officers Mess for several R.A.F. Squadrons including the famous 617 Dambusters Squadron. The E.G.U. use this hotel for accommodation of its committee members where they take post dinner coffee in The Squadron Bar which is tastefully embossed from floor to ceiling with Dambuster memorabilia. The room, which is open to the public, has a unique atmosphere and should be visited as part of the Woodhall Spa experience. The two courses offer contrasting challenges since the Bracken course is relatively straight forward woodland course with greens which are very difficult to read whereas the Hotchkin is a real challenge requiring long straight shots to avoid the heather and gorse and some of the deepest bunkers in golf.

The short par three twelfth hole in particular has witnessed some considerable drama over the years for example during the 2000 Brabazon Trophy the leader of the event at one over par, Daryl Berry from Yorkshire a scratch handicapper scored 14 when unable to escape from the deep left hand bunker (see picture below). A Club member playing in the monthly medal also found this deep cavern and proceeded to score 35 for the hole during eighteen embarrassing minutes. This makes the road bunker at the 17th on the Old Course at St Andrews sound easy! The hole also witnessed amazingly a half in one by Albert Wilson and Leslie Henshaw in 1982, the odds of this happening are incomprehensible, and I wonder who bought the round of drinks.

Nowadays the E.G.U. has grown in to a massive operation with a multimillion-pound turn-over with scores of permanent staff and many willing voluntary committee men who administer the game to the 34 Counties, 1900 Clubs and the 700,000 male golfers in England.

The "Home of English Amateur Golf" at Woodhall Spa is simply a venue that must be visited preferably in August when the heather and gorse paint the Hotchkin Course with subtle shades of pink and yellow and fill the clear air with their aromas.

At Woodhall Spa there have been many remarkable rounds played over the Hotchkin course by many famous players. One of the most notable matches occurred in 1969 and comprised two Open Champions who took on two Lincolnshire County players for a small wager on a

The green of the 12th hole at the home of English Golf, Woodhall Spa where a half in one was recorded in 1982.

damp grey December morning at 10 a.m. It is astonishing to think that Lincolnshire's R&A Champion Golfer of the Year (Open Champion 1969) Tony Jacklin and American Tom Weiskopf (Open Champion 1973) were playing golf "up the road". Weiskopf used borrowed clubs and shoes and even managed five birdies from the back tees, what is even more remarkable is the fact that the match took place on Christmas Day[10]. After the match and a spell in the clubhouse the "Champions" were entertained by the course owner Neil Hotchkin and his wife Sallie at Wormesley House which is set back from the third fairway on the Broadway.

Mr Neil Hotchkin, a marvellous man, who saw so many facets of life lived into his 90th year and was very proud of Woodhall Spa G.C. He was welcoming to so many golfers over many decades of the last century and could often be seen driving around the course and inspecting what must have felt like his back garden. Mr Hotchkin had his own views on how the game should be played, notably over judging distance where Neil was insistent that the golfer should "use the eye" and not become a slave to 150 yardage markers.

I remember in particular visiting Woodhall G.C. for a committee meeting in 1996 with my young son Alex (AJ) in tow age 13. The meeting overran by one hour and during this time Neil noticed that Alex was as usual trying to wear out the putting green. Realising that the young lad was at a loose end, Neil suggested Alex might relax for a while in the clubhouse and enjoy a drink as Mr Hotchkin's guest and to give the grass a rest. For the record Alex had a glass of coke kindly paid for by Neil Hotchkin "The Woodhall Legend".

This was a unique day for the author; I often revisit these emotions at Woodhall Spa and often "see" Neil on the Hotchkin Course at Woodhall Spa G.C.

Woodhall Spa without Mr Neil S Hotchkin TD, DL will never be the same again.

E.L.G.A.

The English Ladies' Golf Association (E.L.G.A.) was formed in 1952. The management of the Association is vested in the annually elected Executive Committee. The Committee consists of a President, eleven members elected by the four Divisions and two English members of the L.G.U. Executive Council. In addition to the Executive Committee there are sub-Committees dealing with the various aspects of Ladies' golf in England, for example, Finance, Girls, Handicapping, National Championships, National Training, Rules & Regulations, Selection, Venues, World Class, ELGA Trust Management and ELGA Trust Marketing. The Executive Committee is supported by a team of professional and enthusiastic staff headed by a Chief Executive Officer. See the "Secretariat" page for further details on their website[12].

Prior to 1952 golf in England came under the jurisdiction of the Ladies' Golf Union, which as the governing body of women's golf in Britain, decides essential policy regarding golf generally and deals with International events. One could suggest the L.G.U. is the Ladies equivalent of the R&A and in fact their offices are only a sand iron from each other at St Andrews.

The headquarters of the English Ladies' Golf Association has been based at Edgbaston G. C. Birmingham since 1988. There are over 1,780 ladies' sections of golf clubs affiliated to the Association in England, resulting in a membership of over 135,000. The game of golf became increasingly popular at the end of the 1980s and as a result there was a surge in new course development. This came to an abrupt end in 1990 with the economic recession, and a number of major projects which had been started, failed before completion. However, there are many new golf courses attracting a new and inexperienced club membership and in particular, most of these are proprietary owned.

The work of the Association is varied but its overall objective is to further the interest of Women's golf in England. This involves the Association dealing with all the areas detailed above and in particular trying to raise the profile of E.L.G.A. This means ensuring representation at meetings with other bodies, by marketing the organisation in a more professional way and by working with Government departments to tap in to the funding streams that we know are available to National Governing Bodies. The challenge for the future is to bring more people into the game and retain those who are already participating. This has involved E.L.G.A. in developing a whole sport plan for golf in England and working with the English Golf Union and the Professional Golfers' Association. This is the England Golf Partnership.

In 2004 the E.L.G.A. adopted the C.O.N.G.U. system of handicapping, which now means we have the same handicapping system for women and men in Great Britain and Ireland. This gave E.L.G.A. equal representation on the C.O.N.G.U. Executive Council along with other women's and men's governing bodies which is a significant step forward to safeguarding handicapping in the future. Golf is a very individual game governed by discipline of both mind and body. It differs from many of the other ball games in which the player reacts to someone else's actions. The player is solely responsible for their own actions. With a system of handicapping, two players of a very different standard can have a good, competitive game, and this is valuable in encouraging beginners that are starting in the sport, as they are able to compete at club level at an early stage.

The National Championship is held in May each year and in addition, there are Stroke Play, Mid Amateur, Girls', Under 15, Under 13 and Senior Championships. A county golf championship is held for the counties in England and Wales and the winners of the four divisional finals qualify to play in the County Championship Finals.

Senior, Ladies, Junior and Girls' teams are selected to represent England in events held in Great Britain and Europe. At present England are the holders of the Girls' and Senior Home International titles. England training is given the highest priority and over 100 players are involved in the World Class training programmes, funded by a Lottery award. Each receives coaching from golf professionals appointed by ELGA throughout the country. In addition, four Elite Squads receive training in autumn and spring at home and overseas under the guidance of Director of Coaching Pat Smillie, Physiotherapist Lynn Booth, and a Sports Psychologist, Karl Morris.

The Association is also responsible for the organisation of several handicap events. The winners of the Silver and Bronze Medal competitions organised in the clubs are invited to take part in one of eight National Finals. The Australian Spoons competition is organised for Bronze Division players and every club is entitled to enter the Rose Spoon competition and Open Challenge Bowls meeting. The Abraham Trophy competition is for girls of any handicap who have not reached their 18th birthday before the 1st January each year and aims to find the most improved player.

In 1982, the E.L.G.A. Trust Fund was formed to provide girls with financial assistance for some of their expenses. Help with the purchase of essential equipment, the cost of coaching and competing in championships can be offered to girls applying through their Counties. E.L.G.A. is extremely grateful to the clubs who support this fund by their annual contributions.

Funding of the work of the Association is from contributions from every female member of an affiliated golf club in England. The current subscription fee is £5 which gives an annual income of just over £650,000. The amount collected may only be changed by agreement of the members at an Annual General Meeting.

ELGA is also very fortunate to be in receipt of Lottery funding awarded to the World Class programmes. These funds are for training our talented young players and the top amateurs, thereby releasing ELGA income from subscriptions, which has been mainly diverted into Junior Golf Development and the appointment of a Team of Development Officers.

The E.L.G.A. website ref contains significantly more information.

Locally we have two ladies who are significantly involved with E.L.G.A., in May 2006 Northants County's Kirsty Jennings took on a new role in the organisation, Kirstie had previously spent five years spearheading E.L.G.A.'s golf development plans and in her new role with England Golf, she will specialize in child protection and equality. Her appointment is for the position of Compliance Officer for England Golf, a partnership which brings together ELGA, the English Golf Union and the Professional Golfers' Association, supported by the Golf Foundation and Sport England. Also in May 2006 our ladies County Champion Kelly Hanwell also from

Northants County joined the England Golf development team in a role to encourage adults and juniors to start and stay in golf. Kelly is one of six E.G.U. / E.L.G.A. regional development officers and will work with the counties of Bedfordshire, Cambridgeshire, Leicestershire & Rutland, Norfolk, Northamptonshire, Nottinghamshire and Suffolk.

In fact, Northamptonshire are the most progressive county in England for the development of England Golf Partnerships having piggy backed on to the fine work of the existing Millennium Committee, which was largely driven by N.G.U. Past President Dave Croxton from Cold Ashby G.C. We are very much in the spotlight since the various National organisations are watching our progress, this book will also hopefully make a statement as a snapshot in time of how our county's golf has evolved. In January 2007, a Partnership Ball attracted an attendance of 200 people at Wicksteed Park, which generated £3000 for county golf; (see Chapter 13 for more information on this subject).

From September 2007 because of E.L.G.A's modernisation review, they have been incorporated as a company limited by guarantee and known as the English Women's Golf Association since January 2008. Looking to the future, new mission statements have been designed to support their strategy of Driving Women's Golf by:
- improving communications within the organisation
- improving the image of women's golf
- helping women achieve equality in golf
- improving services to members and clubs
- putting more focus on volunteers
- giving women and girl golfers more opportunities to improve.

The Midland Golf Union

M.G.U.

The Midland Golf Union (M.G.U.) as we know it today evolved from a number of organisations, which already existed. The original predecessor of the Midland Golf Union was a body known as the Midland Counties Competition (1895 to 1921). Prior to this, certain gentlemen of the Staffordshire Club had sought to form such a body in 1893, and again in 1894 but the Committees of both the Warwickshire and Worcestershire Golf Clubs had decided not to take up the matter. The Midland Counties Competition was formed in 1895 to run the annual competition for the Midland Counties Strokeplay Championship and the Midland Club Team Competition and remained as the governing body for those competitions until 1921. Several other organisations were formed around this time and during the early part of the twentieth century, their history and composition are described overleaf.

The East Midland Union of Golf Clubs (1895 to 1914?)

The East Midland Union of Golf Clubs was also formed in 1895. Membership of this Union was confirmed to Clubs in the Counties of Nottingham, Leicester, Derby, Northampton, Lincoln and Rutland. A championship meeting was held annually. This Union does not appear to have survived the First World War.

The Professionals and the Ladies (1897)

Although not officially involved with amateur male players, it should perhaps be mentioned that the Midland Professional Golfers Club was formed in 1897, and the Midland Professional Championship was started in the same year. The inaugural meeting of the Midland Counties Ladies Championship was also in 1897 when Staffordshire, Worcestershire and Warwickshire were involved, and the following Clubs accepted the invitation – The Worcestershire, Kings Norton, Kenilworth, South Staffs, Hagley, Coventry, Sutton Coldfield, Kidderminster and Stratford-on-Avon.

The Midland Golf Association (1906 to 1921)

Formed in 1906 by the amalgamation of four Midland Golf Unions two reasons being:-
1. "a means by which they could 'manage' their own immediate affairs without constant appeal to a governing body in the North (the R.& A.!), a body which they regard, with perhaps little injustice, as one whose chief characteristic is indifference to their particular needs as inland golfers"; and
2. To establish the rules for the new inter-County matches.

The Midland Counties Golf Association M.C.G.A. (1921 to 1984)

Formed in 1921 by amalgamating the Midland Counties Competition and the Midland Golf Association.

The Midland Group (1955 to 1984)

Formed solely for the purpose of holding the qualifying event in the Midlands for the English County Championship. By amalgamating the M.C.G.A. and the Midland Group, The Midland Golf Union (M.G.U.) was formed in 1984. This body was formed for the purpose of bringing together all the Counties in unison and forming an association for the strengthening and furtherance of golf in the Midlands. (The concept of this Union was conceived following a long conversation between John Flanders, M.C.G.A. President at the time and Ray Baldwin (the late Secretary of the M.G.U.) at the Midland Open Amateur Championship in 1981 at that lovely and demanding course Little Aston.
Membership of the M.G.U. through the years has been largely restricted to County Unions as follows:-
Nottinghamshire (formed 18th May 1899) - one of the first four Counties to join in 1906
Lincolnshire (formed February 1900) - did not however join until 1921
Worcestershire (formed November 1905) - one of the first four Counties to join in 1906
Gloucestershire (formed January 1906) - one of the first four Counties to join in 1906. Moved from the Midlands to the South-West region in 1925.

Warwickshire (formed March 1906) - one of the first four Counties join in 1906.

Leicestershire & Rutland (formed June 1910)

Derbyshire (formed in 1913 - no records available)

Shropshire (formed in 1913 - no records available)

Northamptonshire (formed in 1921)

Staffordshire (formed in May 1923)

Bedfordshire - joined the Midland Counties in February 1924. Moved to the South-East in 1947.

Herefordshire (formed in 1949) and then amalgamated with Shropshire on 15th December 1956.

Cambridgeshire (formed February 1950).

There were also a few Clubs who joined before their Counties had been founded such as Trentham in Staffordshire and Uppingham in Leicestershire & Rutland who were members in 1907, whereas in 1914 there were Northants County of Northamptonshire, and Penn, Rudyard Lake and Trentham of Staffordshire.

In recent years the Midland Golf Union has consisted of Cambridgeshire, Derbyshire, Leicestershire & Rutland, Lincolnshire, Northamptonshire, Nottinghamshire, Shropshire & Herefordshire, Staffordshire, Warwickshire and Worcestershire. In 2000 the ten Counties contained 144,000 male golfers.

The Midland Golf Union organise many events including the English Golf Union's regional qualifier for the English County Championship where the ten Counties attempt to qualify for the national finals against qualifiers from the Northern, South East and South West regions. The teams consist of six players playing 36 holes medal all six scores to count which is a very demanding format since if a player breaks any rule the whole team is disqualified! The Midlands has been mostly represented by Leicestershire & Rutland, Lincolnshire, Staffordshire and Warwickshire. To date Northamptonshire have yet to win the qualifier.

Midland Counties have become English County Champions 15 times, Staffordshire leading the way with 6 victories, Warwickshire 5, Worcestershire 3 and Lincolnshire 1. It is interesting to note that from these 15 victories the three counties, who have the largest number of players (18-20,000) to draw from, have all been victorious in this event apart from Worcestershire. Is it the absolute quality of the courses that their golfers play on, the number of players who contribute monies to provide coaching or a winning mind set?

Northamptonshire have had several players who have represented the Midland region often against the South-West region over the years as detailed below:–

Player/Years	Club	Played	Won	Halved	Lost
Lancelot Bostock 1920-37	Northants County	6	2	0	4
D.S.Bruce 1920-37	Peterborough & Luffenham Heath	26	12	1	13
Richard G.Aitken 1964-69	Northampton	10	6	0	4
Conrad R.Ceislewicz 1972	Northampton	2	1	0	1
Ryan Evans 2007-8	Wellingborough	4	2	1	1
Robert Larratt 1972-3	Kettering	4	2	1	1
Nick Soto 1999-2000	Northants County	4	1	1	2
Anthony M.S.Lord 2002	Northants County	2	0	1	1
Gary Boyd 2007	Cherwell Edge	2	2	0	0

Golf in Northamptonshire

The yearly Midland Order of Merit which is examined by regional and national selectors consists of eleven midland venues with romantic names such as the Beau Desert "Stag", Shifnal "Ox", "The Gog", Leicestershire " Fox", Lincolnshire "Poacher" and Kedleston "Goose".

The major event in the yearly calendar is the Midland Open Amateur Championship which attracts many players from outside the region. In 2007 the highest playing handicap was 1. The name of the Championship has changed several times since its inception in 1895, for example in 1974 The Midland Counties Amateur Strokeplay Championship was played at Northants County and won by future Open and Masters Champion A.W.B. (Sandy) Lyle.

It is currently played over two days on two adjoining courses; its traditional home for many years (1976-2000) was Little Aston and Sutton Coldfield. The event now moves around the region to for example, in Nottinghamshire Coxmoor & Hollingwell, when the competition is played typically in June, the rough at these two magnificent courses is called the "pink" due to the lovely hues produced by the heather and the grasses.

In Northamptonshire, Northampton and Northants County Clubs have been used as venues in 2001&2007. In 2001 the event was won by the "south western extrovert" Matt Lock who competed sporting a pink Mohican hair cut and scored 279. Previous winners include famous players such as Peter McEvoy, Gary Wolstenholme MBE and more recently Luke Donald.

Northamptonshire boys have featured fairly well in the Midland Boys Championship with victories by Bob Larratt in 1970 at Blackwell score 145, Tim Giles in 1973 at Blackwell score 141 and Robert Duck in 1994 at Longcliffe score 145. Tim Giles went on to represent England at Youth level and was a member of the team that played against Scotland in 1975, this team also included Sandy Lyle from Hawkstone Park. There is a picture of the team which hangs in the golf complex at Hawkstone, which shows Tim proudly wearing his Northamptonshire County Colours.

In 1983 Northamptonshire Boys won the East Midland League by winning all four matches played, Richard Dalton from Wellingborough G.C. was Captain. The winning team is shown below.

1983 Northamptonshire, East Midland Boys Champions:

Back row: Neil Connolly, Michael Pask, Scott Dowell, Derek Scrowther, Steve Langley, Jamie Scholey, Glyn Evans, John Deakin, Darren Jones, Martin Herson.
Front Row: Les Pepper, M.G.U., Junior Delegate, Richard Dalton (Captain), Keith Bass N.G.U. Junior Delegate.

114

At youth level Neil Presto, Peterborough Milton and Andrew Lynch, Northants County won the Midland Youths Championship in 1998 & 1999 at Stoke Rochford with scores of 285 and 277 gross respectively. In 1997 Nick Soto and Robert Duck, both Northants County won the Midland Club Team Championship at Little Aston & Sutton Coldfield with a score of 149. Northamptonshire boys have yet to qualify for the English Golf Union's Boys County Championship although teams from Worcestershire 1986, Nottinghamshire 1991 and Shropshire & Herefordshire 1992 have won the gruelling three day final having qualified as the top team from the Midland qualifier.

At men's level the three man team from Northants County won the Midland Club Team Championship in 1997 at Sandwell Park with a score of 149. Northamptonshire's Senior team have also featured on the winner's rostrum when in 2001 they won The Midland Senior County Team Championship at Birstall with a score of 389. The six man team's score consisted of Rodney Haig 75, Malcolm Pounds 78, Richard Aitken 78, Richard Halliday 79; Martin Harris 79 Jim Dalton's score was discarded as five from six scores were required.

Northamptonshire Ladies have also had a degree of success in Midland Competitions as early as 1902 when Mrs Phillips from Northampton won the Midland Counties Ladies Championship with a score of 161 and also finished runner up in 1912. In this event Mrs Nielson also finished runner-up in 1914. Angela Duck won the Midland Ladies Championship twice.

Many hard working officers such as John Flanders, Jack Humphries, Brian Purse, John Tickel, John Stubbings, Barry Kay and in particular the late Ray Baldwin & Les Pepper who acted as Secretary/Treasurer and Junior Organiser for at least twenty years have lovingly looked after the affairs of the M.G.U.

From Northamptonshire the late Jack Humphries was Captain of Northants County G.C. in 1986, County Captain in 1968&9, President of the Northamptonshire Golf Union 1984-85, Midland President in 1988&9 and Chairman from 1990 until his death in 1993. Jack was a great lover of the game and gave decades of service to many organisations. He was also very fond of natural history and painting china, which he also fired. Jack had a very direct approach to life and people and I remember one story in particular, which to me characterised the man.

In 1977 whilst playing the annual friendly against Bedfordshire where the teams compete for the "Highfield Shield" (a personally hand crafted wooden shield donated by the late Past President Barry Highfield) I cautiously approached Jack who was sat on a walking stick at the back of one of the greens to enquire about the state of the match. "How's it going". "I am three down", I stated in an attempt to engage Jack in conversation realising he had been sat there for an hour or so "You're the worst!" came the rapid response which caused me to three putt and hasten my eventual downfall! I later found out that he was actually joking. At a tender age of twenty two I was not receptive to that style of humour!

As I became more involved in golf administration and my flat belly joined the round belly "Club" we often used to chat about natural history, subjects such as the Green Woodpeckers that would visit his garden in Quinton and shout the ringing call across the lawn and when at Hunstanton how well the sound of the Curlew "coorrleeee" would travel across the salt marsh or golf course.

Jack also served on several English Golf Union committees notably the executive committee in 1988. Jack was also well known in R&A circles. Unknown to many golfers Jack had a wide knowledge of Robert Burns's poetry and was a talented Scottish Country dancer, which he also taught. His arty nature was also expressed as talented painter of china, which he fired in his own kiln. Jack made an enormous contribution to the game both as a player and as an administrator. Jack presented The Humphries Quaich to the M.G.U. which is competed for in the Midland Mid-Amateur event for player from 40 years of age. In 2004 the trophy was won for the first time by a Northamptonshire player, Anthony Lord one of the "lads" that Jack encouraged at Northants County G.C. who has become one of the county's stalwarts. Anthony or Lordy as he is known scored 69 against a CSS of 71 at Wollaton Park G.C. which reduced his handicap to scratch for the first time in a distinguished playing career for Club and County. Lordy also became a father in 2004 and Midland Captain in 2007, Jack would have been very proud of him!

Past President of the N.G.U. Jim Dalton (1988-90) from Wellingborough G.C. was also President of the Midland Golf Union in the 1990s.

Another Past President from Northamptonshire (1992-94) and a good friend of the late John Henry (Jack) Humphries was Mike McMahon the Chairman of the Midland Championship Committee and as he would say, doing an average job! Sadly we lost this jovial man in 2005. Several of the M.G.U. officials also serve on the E.G.U. various committees in order to represent the views of the Midland Group and its Counties.

A significant amount of the information on the Midland Golf Union and other areas has been taken from the late Ray Baldwin's book[13]; I hereby formally and personally thank him for permission to use this information. I remember him encouraging me with this book at a Championship at Little Aston G.C. saying, "With your passion boy, you'll do a nice job".

R.J.W. Baldwin's contribution to the game was recognized in 1997 when he was presented with the prestigious Gerald Micklem Award by the English Golf Union, for those who have made an "outstanding contribution to further the interest of Amateur Golf in England". Ray Baldwin sadly passed away in 2004 and I think it is fair to state that the amount of work and commitment given by Ray to the Midland Golf Union as Treasurer and Secretary in unlikely to be surpassed ever. In fact his workload was taken over by three people in 2005.

In 2007 Anthony Lord from Northants County G.C. became Captain of the Midlands, a fitting reward for someone who has given a lot to the game over the last 28 years. He came in to office at the 2006 November Council Meeting. I felt quite proud of him as he collected the Captain's badge; I was also present at Staverton Park G.C. in September 1979 when "Lordy" made his first appearance on the county scene.

Northamptonshire's Winners of Midland Golf Union Events 1895-2008

Midland Boys Championship
1970 R.S. (Bob) Larratt from Kettering at Blackwell, 145
1973 T.J. (Tim) Giles from Northants County at Blackwell, 141
1994 R.M. Duck (Robert) from Northants County at Longcliffe, 145
E.G.U. County Junior County Championship - Midland Qualifying
2007 Adam Myers from Northants County 70+63=133 (New Course Record), Individual winner at Oswestry G.C.

Champion of Junior Champions
2003 Gary Boyd from Northants County at Market Harborough, 136

East Midland Boys League
1983 Northamptonshire (Captain Richard Dalton)

Midland Youths Championship at Stoke Rochford Lincs
1998 Neil Presto from Peterborough Milton, 285
1999 Andrew Lynch from Northants County, 277
2004 Gary Boyd from Northants County, 282
2005 Gary Boyd from Northants County, 282

Midland Youth League
(1997 Runners Up to Shropshire & Herefordshire, final played at Ramsey G.C. Cambridgeshire)

116

1997 Midland Youth Team. Left to right: N. West, D. Roberts, S. Tootell, N. Soto, D. Spragg, J. Howitt, R. Harris, R. Duck.

Midland Officials, President Barry Kay (right) & Past President John Price (centre) with Past Club Captain & N.G.U. Vice President Mick Reed at the N.G.U. Annual Dinner 2007.

Midland Club Team Championship
1997 R.M.Duck & N.Soto from Northants County, 197

Midland Mid-Amateur
2004 A.M.S. Lord from Northants County at Wollaton Park, 69

Midland Senior Championship
2006 Richard Cole Peterborough Milton, 71 at Ladbrook Park

Midland Senior County Team Championship
2001 Northamptonshire at Birstall Leicester, 389
2005 Northamptonshire at Burghley Park 379

Midland Senior Club Team Championship
2003 R.Cole & J.MacCallum from Peterborough Milton at Lincoln, 152

117

CHAPTER 6

THE GOLF CLUBS OF
NORTHAMPTONSHIRE

"What other people may find in poetry or art museums, I find in the flight of a good drive."

Arnold Palmer

THIS chapter gives a taste and flavour of Northamptonshire's courses between 1876-2008. With the limited space available here for such a demanding task I have focussed on their evolution and included notable winners of individual and team trophies together with any unusual events that have occurred. There are currently 27 Clubs who are affiliated to the N.G.U. & N.L.C.G.A. Further in depth information can be found in their websites which are listed in the references section[14]. The chapter also describes courses that have disappeared from the county.

Anyone looking at a map of the county would instantly comment upon its unique shape. It is almost an ellipse in shape and some seventy miles long and only twenty miles wide at its broadest; this does include the original Soke of Peterborough, which severed its ties with Northampton in 1888 and became part of the enlarged county of Cambridgeshire in 1974. The underlying geology has a major effect upon the quality of the courses where the effect of course topography, drainage of water, soil structure and grass species plays a major role. The soils above the Oxford Clays regions tend to suffer from severe alternate water logging and desiccation and have tended to be avoided by course constructors.

The geology of Northamptonshire is almost entirely made up of sedimentary strata pertaining to the Jurassic period (195 to 135 million years BC). The exceptions to this trend are patchy deposits of Quaternary glacial sands, gravels and till from the Wolstonian glacial cycle and the alluvial deposits found in the main tributary valleys of the river Nene. Although the Jurassic period is associated in palaeontology with the greatest abundance of dinosaur remains ('The Age of the Reptiles'), this picture is somewhat misleading locally since no significant dinosaur fossils have ever been recovered from the county. The county is mostly lowland along the Nene valley with the higher land being situated mostly to the south west with only a few areas above six hundred feet *(see Figure on opposite page)*. One of the highest points in the county is located at Cold Ashby G.C on land owned

Northamptonshire - Altitude

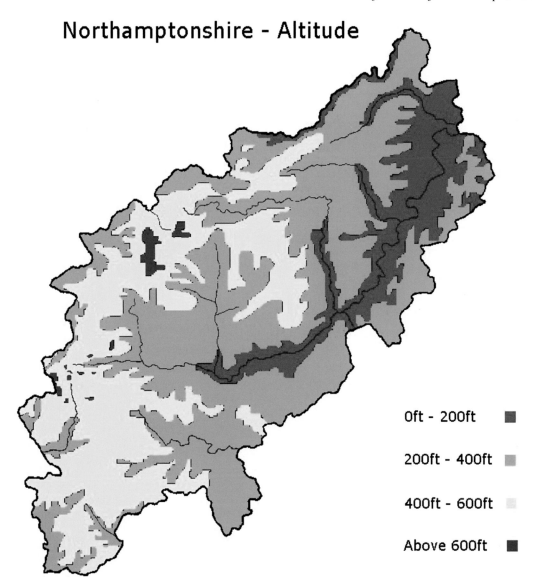

Oft - 200ft ■

200ft - 400ft ■

400ft - 600ft ▫

Above 600ft ■

by farmer and member Mike Lill who administered the running of the county boy's junior league for many years.

The current twenty seven golf courses are mainly centred around the county town with the remainder spread as far and wide as to the far north-eastern corner of the county close to Peterborough and to The Wolds in the south-western corner near to Brackley as shown on page 120. If Cherwell Edge G.C. play Peterborough Milton G.C. for example, this would entail a round trip of some 150 miles. Fortunately this does not happen very often, although now that the Hollingsworth Trophy is decided by a random draw, the chance is more probable than when the competition was partially regionalised.

Included in this chapter are what I considered to be the most demanding holes in the county in order to break the list like nature of this chapter. These are my personal choices and I look forward to debating this element with any readers.

Northamptonshire Golf Courses in 2008

My Top 18 Holes in Northamptonshire

1. Northants County White 454 yards, Par 4.
2. Cold Ashby Elkington Nine White Tee 366 yards Par 4.
3. Northampton White Tee 523 yards Par 5 Wood Way.
4. Overstone Park White Tee 128 yards, Par 3 Blackthorn Lake.
5. Kettering White Tee 503 yards Par 5 Poplars.
6. Staverton Park White Tee 357 yards Par 4.
7. Northants County White Tee 402 yards Par 4.
8. Whittlebury Park Royal Whittlewood Red Course White Tee 198 yards Par 3.
9. Wellingborough White Tee 426 yards Par 4 Carp.
10. Peterborough Milton White Tee 448 yards Par 4 Cottons Fancy.
11. Northants County, White Tee 443 yards Par 4.
12. Collingtree Park Blue/White Tee 192 yards Par 3.
13. Farthingstone White 213 yards, Par 3 Knightly Way.
14. Kingsthorpe White 398 yards Par 4.
15. Priors Hall, White Tee 217 yards Par 3.
16. Northampton, White Tee 166 yards, Par 3 Waters Leap.
17. Wellingborough, White Tee 456 yards Par 4 Redhill.
18. Collingtree Park, White Tee 543 yards, Blue Tee 602 yards Par 5.

120

Abington Park ca 1960-1995, 2007-

Abington Park's pretty little nine hole course course in November 2007, the tall hazards of what was originally two hunting gates at the entrance to the parkland come in to play on the 61 yards 4th hole.

This pretty little 9-hole course is located within the park on land to the left-hand side of the large boating lake and as I remember it was lush green pasture when I was a child in the 1960s, and may have been used occasionally for grazing by the nearby farm on Wellingborough road. The first knowledge of the park was at the time of William the Conqueror. A survey ordered by the king that was completed in 1086 described the land as belonging to Richard Esquire a Norman, who probably held it since he furnished arms and men for the invasion of England. It was originally the grounds of Abington Manor that were opened to the public in 1897, Northampton's first park. It is interesting to note that Joseph Grose, a local motor pioneer was fined for speeding close to the park in 1898 for travelling at a dangerous 15 miles per hour.

The course provided an excellent route for people young and old to try out the game using a couple of clubs and a putter. It has a length of 510 yards, the longest hole the 3rd at 75 yards, the shortest the 9th at 41 yards. The Northampton County Council are responsible for the facility and originally hired out golf equipment from a small brick building located next to the first boating lake. Numerous Northampton golfers have hit their first shot there.

During cold snowy winters such as the famous one of 1963, the course was closed and used for sledging, since holes such as the third, fifth and sixth all had good long slopes. As an eight year old during that long cold winter the family spent many happy Sunday mornings there. I remember in particular my sister crashing our sledge into one of the giant snowballs which had been rolled down from the top at Abington Park Crescent. Well I thought it was funny!

This little course was where I hit my first golf shot in 1965, a five iron to the 45 yards 1st hole. Even now in 2007 after many conversations, the number of golfers with fond memories of the course who claim to be the course record holder still amazes me, I have no recollection of a single round. My personal life eclectic was seventeen can anyone better that?

Our son Alex also started playing golf there with my mother "Gran" as his caddie and scorer, a card from five-year-old "one jab" Alex is reproduced below for those like myself with an emotional disposition.

The facility was closed in 1995 for over 10 years due to vandalism, personal threats to the cashier and the continual break-ins at the hire centre.

In 2007, the course was re-opened by the council and for security reasons equipment could be hired from the office next to the bowling green. There were some new golfers who made the journey down to the course. Unfortunately the course once again suffered from vandalism and many of the flags and holes were stolen. It is an interesting thought especially for cosmologists on how one could steal a hole!

We can only hope that things improve and it is again used more often in 2008/9 and encourages youngsters to take up the game. I look forward to taking our grandchildren there with Alex as caddie.

Brampton Heath Golf Centre 1995-present

The development of William Rice's brainchild is very much a success story. The opening champagne buffet ceremony was conducted in a large heated marquee and followed by Noel Hunt's famous entertaining golf show.

It is also one of the best draining courses in the county and is rarely closed. It hosted the County Boys Championship in 2003 on a warm July day, the N.G.U. AM-AM in 2004 and the Family Foursomes in 2006. It has become an extremely popular venue as a pay and play course and has a significant membership who are now winning county events.

Between 2001-2005 Club member have recorded several notable victories in county events. Kevin Purkis won the Higgs Bowl at Kingsthorpe G.C. and together with A.Clarke the Stableford Cup played at Oundle G.C. In 2003 Dan Wood and Matt Bird should have won the County Fourball Knockout Trophy, however in the final at Cherwell Edge G.C. on the last hole with the match all square the golfing gods struck. With his partner out of the hole, one of their opponents (Dean Roberts Northampton

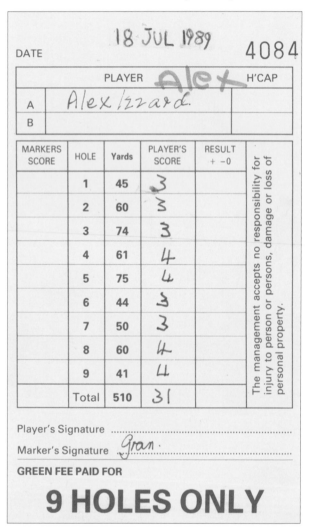

Score Card from Abington Park's Pitch & Putt course recorded by five year old "one jab" Alex Izzard.

Brampton Heath, aerial view of the clubhouse and course

G.C.) holed his third shot from 153 yards for a winning birdie 3 having dropped out of a ditch! It was never meant to be a fair game! Also in 2003 Professional Carl Sainsbury won the Northamptonshire Open with a score of five under par over the composite course at Cold Ashby G.C. The Club have also produced the 2005 men's County Champion and Braid's Driver winner chirpy Dan Wood who also won the Scratch Foursomes with friend Matt Bird from "over the fence" Northants County, the Champion of Champion's event and just for good measure the home club's medal Championship. Dan embarked on a golf scholarship in America. Also in 2005 the men's team won the Scratch League Division 3 trophy.

The driving range is extremely popular especially during cold winter evenings. The range and the challenging nine hole short course have been used by both the N.G.U. and M.G.U. for player training.

In August 2007 a new course record of 66 was set by Dan Wood during a rich vein of form, he is clearly enjoying the American experience. Also in 2007 whilst looking at the starting sheet for the Izzard Club Team Trophy I thought a typo had been made with the name M. Forgione three times on the starting sheet. After due consultation I was pleased to welcome three generations of the Forgione family to Wellingborough G.C. Having won the trophy the previous year at Silverstone G.C. they were present to defend the trophy. Young Michele Junior handicap 5, Michael handicap 3 and Michele Senior handicap 13 enjoyed the challenge of the course, the social-ising and the camaraderie as always and despite not defending the trophy, these Italians made a significant con-tribution to the day.

In November 2007 the Club have decided that play should commence from the current par 5 tenth tee until further notice. Another innovation introduced is colour coded daily green fee tags to help in respect of mar-shalling on the course; these can be obtained from head professional Alan Wright in the well stocked shop.

A winter league is also run each year and has proved to be quite popular with members on this well draining course, which catches a lot of the weather, thrown in to the county off the Atlantic from the south-west during this time of the year. Many holes do not face south west and therefore the wind irritatingly blows across many holes.

Being adjacent to Northants County G.C., balls often cross the fence notably on the Club's old 11th hole now the 2nd and Northants County's 8th hole. Since Northampton G.C. is also a short distance away it is surprising that a triangular match has not been arranged yet. All that is needed is a suitable sponsor/trophy donor, come on chaps, let's set this one up.

Burghley Park 1890-present

This course was originally listed firstly by the Golfers Handbook in 1913 and secondly in 1921 under Northamptonshire but probably always belonged to the Lincolnshire Golf Union (see www.lugc.co.uk/history). The confusion may have arisen as a result of boundary changes. I include it however for completeness due to our many contacts with the Club over the years. The course was designed by J.D. Day in 1890 and opened in October 1890 with a 9 hole course. It has always prided itself on the quality of its fast smooth greens.

The famous English golfer, Ryder Cup player and 1999 Captain Mark James started his golf at Burghley Park as a junior member. His book "Into the Bear Pit" which describes the 1999 Ryder Cup and the background to some of the worst golf behaviour by the American team ever seen on a golf course proved to be quite controver-sial, although I personally found it to be a good read. Normality was restored at the event held at The Belfry in 2002 when great sportsmanship and camaraderie shone through. As predicted, non-playing captain Sam Torrance, the man who had sunk the winning putt in 1985, cried when Paul McGinley holed the winning putt. Sam and the U.S.A non-playing captain Curtis Strange had a massive influence on this particularly emotional Ryder Cup after the horrors of the 11th September 2001 and the 1999 Ryder Cup. Together they were instrumen-tal in restoring the beauty and spectacle and camaraderie of this great event.

Going in to the singles tied at 8-8 Sam and Curtis's singles order and the golf played by some of our less fan-cied European rookies (Phillip Price, Pierre Fulke and Paul McGinley) largely influenced the outcome as the Europeans were victorious by 15$\frac{1}{2}$ -12$\frac{1}{2}$.

The comments from Davis Love and Jim Furyk summing up the sportsmanship of the event and golf itself:

Davis Love "I would not have Darren Clarke as a friend if it was not for the Ryder Cup".

Jim Furyk "Paul McGinley is a wonderful gentleman. I had never met him before. I told him afterwards that I'd made a new friend this week". Long may golf continue to be played in that manner.

In 2005 Club member John Price became the President of the M.G.U.

Castle Ashby 1913-1945

The Club was first mentioned in 1913; the private 9-hole course was laid out on the Castle Ashby Estate, the seat of the Compton family the Marques of Northampton where the membership was 150. The Marques's moth-er was apparently involved in its design and the course was somewhere "in fields" near to Easton Maudit. The Clubs pavilion was situated on some flat ground close to a brook on the road leading from Eastern Maudit to Yardley Hastings.

Castle Ashby House the seat of the Compton family, the Marques of Northampton where inspiration for construction of a course came from The Marques's mother.

The title of Marques of Northampton was created in the Peerage of the United Kingdom in 1812 for the Earl of Northampton. An earlier Marques of Northampton was William Parr, brother of Queen Catherine Parr, who was created Marques by Edward VI in the Peerage of England, lost the title under Mary, and was granted a new creation of the title by Elizabeth, again in the Peerage of England. The present (Compton) Marques holds the subsidiary titles of Earl of Northampton (1618), Earl Compton (1812), and Baron Wilmington (1812), the first in the Peerage of England, the latter two in the Peerage of the UK. The families are major land owners and have two major estates: Castle Ashby and Compton Wynyates.

The Club was wound up a few years after the 1939-45 World War since the land was badly affected by the national food production campaign. The funds remaining (£400) were passed over to the N.G.U. in the 1960s and held as a separate fund for the development of junior golf until 2002 when they were amalgamated with the Union's reserves. It was a popular venue for the town's golfers especially from Northampton G.C. some of whom were also Castle Ashby members, notably Bill Hollingsworth donor of the Hollingsworth trophy.

Peggy Durant, Northampton's Lady Captain 1972 and a Life member of Northampton G.C. played there and

*Reproduction of the course layout
at Castle Ashby*

remembers the location and the layout of the course very well.

Following our conversations Peggy and her son Nick drove out to the Easton Maudit/Castle Ashby area to establish its grid reference. After Nick a Chartered Architect had this information, he looked at the topography and the memory of the holes displayed in the land by the satellite system Google Earth, this information combined with Peggy's memory of the holes was combined to reproduce the course layout that disappeared over sixty years ago. This is reproduced here and I thank them both most sincerely for their diligence and this remarkable piece of detective work.

A larger copy has been passed on to the archivist at the house.

Cherwell Edge 1981-present

Cherwell Edge is Northamptonshire's furthest south and west golf club. Originally nine holes, the now 18-hole course is situated on both sides of the road leading in to the village of Chacombe from the B4525 about a mile from the town of Banbury. From its relatively humble beginnings, the Club has grown significantly over the years. The Newman family have been involved for decades, father David is currently Secretary and son Jason is the Professional.

Cherwell Edge Clubhouse under moody skies.

A driving range was first introduced in 1994, resculptured, and refurbished ten years later. One of the Club's most amazing occurrences was an albatross which occurred on the 370 yard 14th (old 5th hole) by Kevin Cole. This was in the late 1990s following a powerful drive across the blind left hand dogleg. Knowing Kevin, I am sure he would have upheld the round of drinks tradition and I would not mind betting there was a significant bar bill. Kevin also added the N.G.U. 2002 Champion of Champions trophy, played at Collingtree Park, to his list of achievements.

In 2006 England International Gary Boyd handicap +4 won the prestigious prize of Local Sportsman of The Year at the Northamptonshire Sports Awards ceremony held on the 1st November at the Northampton Saints Rugby Club, Franklins Gardens. Over 300 people attended the celebration ceremony which also witnessed county cricketer the spin bowler Monty Panesar collect the premier award of Sports Personality 2006. At the same ceremony Gary's fellow county team member Adam Myers (Northants County) collected Runner Up in the Young Male Sports Achievers section. Northamptonshire golfers collected two of the 41 prizes given out that day. Both sets of parents were justifiably glowing with pride. Chic and Pauline Boyd have driven thousands of miles supporting their talented son Gary who has firmly put Cherwell Edge on the map.

Also in the autumn of 2006 Gary won his first full English international point, and first international victory in the Home Internationals in Wales and the Asia Pacific Open Amateur Championship at Mission Hills in China respectively. In 2006 his aspirations were to be selected for the Walker Cup team, before becoming a professional golfer. The R&A included Gary in the 22 man squad selected to prepare for the event and he subsequently became travelling 1st reserve. The 2007 bi-annual match against the Americans was held in September at the magnificent Royal County Down G.C. in Ireland, one of my favourite golf courses in the world. Gary actually turned professional in November 2007.

Other highlights of 2006 were Adam Riddall winning the N.G.U. County Boys Match play title and Gary Boyd setting a new course record of 63. One Club competition which raised a bit of a titter was the Match Play trophy which was played over 18 holes between Club stalwart David Newman and of course Gary Boyd. Gary predictably won despite Dave trying to talk him out of it!

Members also have use of their sister club Silverstone G.C. it is slightly unusual though creative to have access to two courses some ten miles apart for around £700, however the arrangement works very well for both clubs involved.

Things are on the up, down at "Chirpy Cherwell".

Cold Ashby 1974-present

What an evolution over 30 years is my reaction when considering "Crocker's Dream" or as I often joke with my fellow N.G.U. Past President and proprietor David Croxton "Not a bad effort for an ex Milkman".

David originated from Worcestershire, the son of a dairy farmer and began to carve out a career with the Milk Marketing Board as a project manager. This would have meant hiking his family around the country and forever changing schools, houses etc. David had a desire to run his own business and this coupled with the original owner's (Alpha Green) desire to get it off their hands, a business plan was put together. Three months later in 1978 David had Cold Ashby G.C. on a 99 year lease from farmer Mick Lill. The rest they say is history.

The original 18 hole course opened in July 1974 on the western slopes of Honey Hill on land originally known as Bunkers Hill farm. Being at one of the highest points in the county it commands some superb views notably towards Warwickshire. It also has some considerable hills to be climbed during play which are also used for Skiing when conditions are right!

The course was lengthened in 1983 and to mark the occasion, David invited future Ryder Cup winning Captain Ian Woosnam to play club professional Simon Ward in an exhibition match. Both players were superb ball strikers and Woosy allegedly drove the ball over the top of "Cardiac Hill" (the old 5th hole, now the 7th on the Elkington nine) leaving a simple wedge to the green. Most mortals cannot get anywhere near to the top of this 30 degree hill and end up playing a mid iron or wood off a sloping lie.

The Club has always had a warm welcoming atmosphere which I once enjoyed rather too much during the 1970s. On a warm summer evening in the converted farmhouse clubhouse whilst chatting and drinking with Dave Dazeley time simply drifted by! For safety sake I was not allowed to drive home and spent the night under a blanket in the corner of the converted farmhouse. This scenario was almost repeated during the research for this book, though not through drinking alcohol.

In February 2007 after a heavy overnight snowfall I ventured over to the club to take some photographs of the snow covered course. Driving down the hill was a test as I was the first car to go down the hill. Having taken my photographs in a snow storm it took me over an hour to get back up the hill to the side road and at several stages I was genuinely worried about even returning home. I felt quite isolated and thoughts of asking Mick Lill to get his tractor out occurred several times.

Cold Ashby G.C., anyone for Skiing?

The current clubhouse which was extended in the early 1990s has an Open Championship Gallery which is thought to be the only one in existence with pictures back to the first winner Willie Park in 1860. It was compiled by the late Sydney Cruickshank. The extension was opened by Ryder Cup player Paul Broadhurst and European Tour Player Andrew Hare on the 22nd June 1993.

Now that David is involved with the E.G.U. he may be trying to lure The Open to Northamptonshire for 2021 the Centenary of the N.G.U.! To return to reality, many events have been held at Cold Ashby G.C. as a result of the Club's generosity, long may this level of course courtesy be extended to male and female golfers from all the clubs in the county. David and Wendy's sons Jim and Greg are both employed in golf, Jim is the Secretary of the P.G.A. Northern Group and Greg is learning the ropes at the "bottom of the hill". Greg was N.G.U. Team Manager and is editor of the N.G.U. annual yearbook.

During the 1980s with many USA aircraft station in England the high ground and transmitter at the top of the course became a frequent flyover point for pilots during training, it was not unusual to have a pair of A10 tank busters flashing low across the course and interrupting the peace of our golf.

In 1989 club Professional Kevin Dickens finished runner-up in the Belgian Open to Gordon J Brand who scored 273 for the four rounds. Several members including Roger Hart and Paul Douglas travelled over to support Kevin for the final round and had a thrilling experience. Also in 1989 the Club's team qualified for the grand finals of the Vauxhall Team Classic of Britain and Ireland at St. Pierre eventually finishing fifth.

In 1990 and 1991 Ivan Oliver Captained the Northants Juniors and became N.G.U. Boys Champion in 1991,

Ivan became the Club's first player to represent the county receiving his County Colours in 1990. Before turning professional, Ivan represented the county approximately 50 times. Ivan is famous as a great ball striker and used to practise so much he wore out the sweet spot on his irons.

One of the Club's most famous members was Carol Gibbs a multi County Champion (5 times in Northants N.C.L.G.A. & 6 times in Hampshire & the Isle of Wight) and a former British Curtis Cup player. Carol continues to be a major driving force in the N.C.L.G.A. and Carol's husband Rod is a Past Captain of the Club. Carol was very much involved in the preparations for the Millennium Golf Ball and together with David Croxton welcomed everyone to the Wicksteed Park venue and introduced the cabaret artists who were all from our county's golf clubs. It was a special night for the 250 or so who had gathered to celebrate a once in a lifetime event. Carol has continued to be involved with the Millennium committee and organisation of the County Golf Ball which was staged for the seventh time in January 2007. Monies raised from the event go towards the development of Junior Golf in the county. Carol and Rod now play more of their golf at Wellingborough G.C. but also maintain their links with Cold Ashby.

A further 9 holes known as the Elkington nine were added and opened on the Captain's Day in July 1995 heralding the dawn of a new era at 27 hole Cold Ashby. This was also the year when the club reached the Hollingsworth Trophy final for the first and only time, losing to Kingsthorpe G.C. In 1998 the men's team won the Inter Club Handicap League and A.D.P.Brearley the Handicap Challenge Cup. The N.G.U. County Championship was played there in 1999 and after a torrential downpour was sadly washed out and had to be replayed later. The Championship was won by Nick Soto from Northants County G.C. with scores of 69, 71 over the composite course. In 2000 the team of three from the club won the Izzard Club Team Trophy and in 2001 Fraser Carnihan followed Ivan Oliver (1992, 95) as the second Club winner of the N.G.U. Braid's Driver. In 2003 P.Mason and A.Clark lifted the N.G.U. Stableford Cup when the event was played at the home club.

In 2005 the men's team again reached the Handicap League final losing the final to Kingsthorpe G.C. again, success came however in the N.G.U. Finals day played at Kingsthorpe G.C. for Aidan Tallentire and John Chamberlain in the Fourball final, Fraser Carnihan won the N.G.U. Order of Merit and reached final qualifying for The Open.

In 2006 following promotion in 2003 the Club celebrated their greatest success to date as N.G.U. Scratch League Division 1 Champions. Following this success one of their major contributors to the victory, their one off character, crazy Fraser Carnihan embarked upon a career in the professional ranks. Watch out Ian Poulter, Fraser might compete with your colourful clothes! Also in 2006, Duncan Burgess (Big Dunc) won the Glenmuir National Club Captain's Cup following victory in the National Final at The Belfry. Big Dunc won the trophy in style with a birdie on the final hole. He had an eight foot put for victory after an approach with a five iron and did a Paul McGinley.

The Club has employed its fair share of talented professionals e.g. Simon Ward, Kevin Dickens, Tony Skingle (aka Elvis), Andy Hare and Shane Rose who between them have collected nine Northamptonshire Open titles. Course records abound, Andy Hare was also a winning member of the 1991 Walker Cup team and a member of the 21st PGA Cup team in 2003. Some of the teaching methods employed became well known throughout the county for their eccentricity e.g.

"The way to play golf is to go up to the ball and hit it, but to get it to go further hit the bloody thing harder"
Tony Skingle 1991.

The Midland P.G.A. Cold Ashby Classic is held there annually, it is unknown if any of these professionals employ Tony's strategy!

Since the course is completely surrounded by farm land it is quite rich in Nature. Whilst playing "Cardiac Hill" one July evening in the 1980s I heard the characteristic call "quick, quick, quick" of the rare migrant game bird the Quail coming from the farmland close to the green. Thinking that I was doing the right think for the bird watching community I put the news out on the grapevine. Over the next few days the corn field was badly

Looking towards the green on the par four second hole of the Elkington Nine at Cold Ashby G.C.

trampled by birders trying to get a view of this rare elusive bird and the crop was ruined, my name would have been mud with land owner Mick Lill if he had known it was me. Some ten years later whilst seated next to each other at a dinner we somehow got on to the subject and I had to put my hand up, this brought roars of laughter from Mick, typical of the man, I hid my embarrassment.

2nd Hole (20th) Elkington Nine White Tee 366 Yards Par 4

The stroke index 5 hole requires two accurate shots and has in fact been described by some golfers as quite fiddly; however all the hazards are natural. The tee shot has to be aimed over a tree on the corner of the dogleg with a medium iron, too far left and you will either be blocked out by a tree on the left hand side of the fairway or in the lateral water hazard, too far right and the ball will disappear into dense undergrowth and be lost. The second shot is to a long narrow green which has a hill covered in gorse to the right which comes down close to the green. In a recent N.G.U. Scratch foursomes event held at the Club two pairs with a combined handicap of two recorded a 9 and a 7 during the morning round!

Collingtree Park 1990-present

Collingtree Park aerial view of the course & clubhouse 2006

Left: Seve Ballesteros in Northamptonshire during the 1995 British Masters.

Below: The British Masters in Northamptonshire held at Collingtree Park in 1995 and 1996.

The opening of the Club in May 1990 was a glitzy affair involving TV personality and comedy script writer, Barry Took who became their first captain. The course is close to junction 15 of the M1 and is one of the toughest layouts in the county. It has twice hosted the British Masters in 1995 (14-17 September) and 1996 (28-31 August) as well as several P.G.A. Senior Tour events. The 1996 event was the fiftieth anniversary of the British Masters.

This was probably the biggest event to have ever come to the County. It was amazing to have most of the 1995 Ryder Cup team playing in Northamptonshire with the likes of Colin Montgomery, Seve Ballesteros, Ian Woosnam, striding our fairways. In 1995 Sam Torrence led the Collingtree British Masters through the second and third rounds, and the title eventually came down to a battle between the Scot and New Zealander Michael Campbell who were the last pair out on the course. Coming down the stretch, the 26-year-old New Zealander had surged one ahead with three consecutive birdies, however after a three putt at the 16th hole and sharing the 17th in par the pair came to the 18th hole all square. Torrence hit his tee shot, down the left-hand side into the short rough, whereas Campbell hit his tee shot even further left into the water. After a penalty drop, the powerful New Zealander smashed a huge 3 wood 257 yards over more water onto the island green. This forced the issue and smoking Sam ripped his second shot also onto the green. Both players were 30 feet from the hole on the two-tiered green and rolled up to 3 feet from the hole, Campbell holed for his par whilst Torrence stroked in a winning birdie putt to the cheers of the local crowd. This win took the 42-year-old to the top of the money list leaping over the younger Colin Montgomery. For the record Sam Torrence scored 67, 66, 68, 69 =270 18 under par.

The N.G.U. was asked to help with the scoring & marshalling of both events and a lucky few were invited to play in the 1996 Pro-AM. N.G.U. President, Ian Marshall, played with moody now TV commentator Howard Clark. Angus McLeod, the late Brian Woodcock and I played with future US Open Champion Retief Goosen. I'll never forget his opening shot from the first tee, which had a ball flight completely different to mine, and also went 40 yards further! The 1996 One2One British Masters had its share of trauma and it was such a shame that the greens were not in the best of order. Colin Montgomery was extremely vocal on this subject, since it was the first qualifying tournament for the 2007 Ryder Cup. Seve was on the course and scored 73 in the first round and complained as he left the final green that his Ping putter had changed colour on the greens, along with his stroke, it has "dyed". The lunch provided that day was superb and one felt privileged to be sat in your home town around

133

Front Cover of the Brochure for the British Masters held at Collingtree Park G.C. in 1995.

Front Cover of the Brochure for the British Masters held at Collingtree Park G.C. in 1996.

tables which contained the cream of European golfers.

The 1996 event was won by Robert Allenby from Australia, with scores of 69, 71, 71, 73 = 284 four under par, following a one hole play-off with Miguel Angel Martin. The greens returned to normal later that year and have consistently been of a good pace.

In 2000 Luke Hillier won the inaugural Boys Matchplay Trophy beating James Ward from Overstone Park 4/2 in the final. Both sets of parents walked the course to watch the match as good supporters of their N.G.U. Boys Squad members. This was the first running of the event conceptualised by Past President Ian Marshall and organised by Stuart Pitcher the past N.G.U. Junior Delegate over their home course Wellingborough G.C. The trophy was donated by Wellingborough members John and Doris Redden who invite all four sets of parents from the

Luke Hillier, N.G.U. Boys' Match Play Champion 2000, centre, with Trophy donors, John and Doris Redden in the Leather Room at Wellingborough G.C.

semi and final to attend a meal and presentation ceremony in the sumptuous clubhouse. This has become a tradition of the event. This was a very special day; I shall never forget the look in proud mum's eyes as I photographed the family group complete with trophy in front of the fireplace in the leather room.

In the middle of the successful 2002 Ryder Cup week, former Open and US Open Champion Johnny Miller returned to Collingtree Park Golf Course to review the progress of his first Johnny Miller Signature Design golf course in the UK and Europe. The Club had been recently purchased from the PGA European Tour Courses and taken into private ownership, with the owners already investing in new facilities. Miller on his flying visit said: "It is a great feeling to return after more than 10 years to a place of creativity and beauty, to see design ideas mature into a tremendous golf course. When ground was broken for the Collingtree Park Golf Course in the late 1980s, I commented at that time, when asked, that my sense of immortality is having golfers take divots out of me forever. Twelve years is not forever, but certainly a fine beginning to that objective. No two holes on the course are the same and water comes into play on 10 of the 18 holes. The devilish fifth hole, a par-three challenge, and the signature 18th hole have gone a long way to fulfilling my ambitions for the course. After speaking with members and others who have played the course, as well as seeing what has been achieved here at

Collingtree Park Ladies Team, Cecil Leitch winners 2005

Collingtree Park, it is apparent that the standard of golf in the club is very high. I have seen the plans for the new clubhouse and, from what I have been told; it would appear that, once completed, the new clubhouse combined with the outstanding golf course will afford the members and their guests with one of the most outstanding golf experiences in the UK. I look forward to returning to Collingtree Park for a longer stay in the future."

A new clubhouse and Greens restaurant has recently opened and provides a good atmosphere and views of the 18th, one of the county's most demanding holes.

The Club has to date produced two County Champions namely Ian Dallas in 1996 at Kingsthorpe with a total of 72+67=139 and Peter Langrish–Smith who was victorious in 1997 at Peterborough Milton with scores of 73+72=145 and for good measure both players were rewarded with the Nett Handicap Challenge Cup. This was after Peter (nickname Hugh Jars) had won the N.G.U. County Match Play Championship in 1995, some regard this as the "true County Champion" since the player has been through both medal and Match-Play formats. The debate continues. Following these successes Brendan Moss came a close second to Glenn Keates in the N.G.U. Medal Champion at Wellingborough G.C missing out by a single shot with scores of 74+73=147 in 2003.

The Club registered its first N.G.U. team trophy win in 2005 when the men's team won the Scratch League Division 1 title after twice being runners up in the Hollingsworth Trophy in 1999 & 2004. Also in 2005 the Ladies team won the Cecil Leitch trophy together with Ian Tait's Higgs Bowl victory during his first ever N.G.U. event which generated great celebrations especially at their annual trophy presentation evening.

The Club has recently added the home of the Explanar® Golf Academy to it's facilities so pop down and see my old Portugolfe mate Tony Clark (TC), let him describe the new technology to you, are better still let him explain it!

12th Hole Blue/White Tee 192 Yards Par 3

Looking towards the clubhouse from behind the green, 12th hole at Collingtree Park G.C.

The choice of the 12th hole has not been an easy one. My home Club's par-5, 601 yards uphill Lighthouse hole (Northampton G.C.) was an obvious candidate together with the par four 12th at Kingsthorpe. However the final choice is Collingtree Park. The hole has many degrees of difficulty, including a tee shot across water and lateral water hazard to the left and the contoured green, which somehow appears closer than the yardage. The hole is also frequently played into the wind to complete the degree of difficulty.

18th Hole White Tee 543 Yards, Blue 602 Yards Par 5

I have selected this as my most demanding finishing hole ahead of the 407 yard par 4 at Kingsthorpe G.C., the long gone 455 yard par 4 at Northampton's old Kettering road course and the fiddling and difficult 320 yards par 4 at Wellingborough G.C. This was a difficult choice especially being the last hole; I placed it above Kingsthorpe since it is mainly the tee shot which is critical there and above Wellingborough's 18th due to its length. Northampton's Kettering Road final hole was rejected largely since it no longer exists, but would have been a very close second due to the demanding tee shot and second to a two-tier green surrounded by seven bunkers.

The hole demands three accurate shots with water on the left hand side and out of bounds down the right hand side of right to left sloping fairway. There are very few amateur golfers who are capable of reaching this green in two shots, consequently the third is played over water to the county's only island green which is also two tiered to complete the difficulty of the hole. It is rumoured that during the 1990s one of the county's best ball strikers

The only full island green in the county, the 18th at Collingtree Park G.C.

Shane Rose reached the green in two from the very back tee with a driver and a long iron, his poor back must have been stretched almost beyond its limits. The hole has seen its fair share of fun and disasters.

Daventry and District 1907-present

Daventry and District G.C. is still effectively a nine hole course par 69 as it approaches its centenary despite attempts to move to 18 holes in the past, the hilly nine hole "Borough Hill" course requires considerable local knowledge and has become a "Hollingsworth graveyard" for many teams. The short par 3 2nd hole catches out many players, at the green a deep cavern to the right and out of bounds to the left demands accuracy from the tee. On the 17th hole the second shot has to be nestled on to a green perched on the side of a hill, from the green there are fine westerly views of Daventry Reservoir/Country Park and on a clear day some of the Cotswolds/Warwickshire hills.

The Club has produced four N.G.U. Presidents, the late Peter Meacock, whose family connection with the

The 18th green at Daventry and District G.C.

course go back decades (1971-72), Jim Punch (1980-81), Richard Catlow (1983-84) and the late Barry Highfield (1985-86). The Club's location at Borough Hill looking over Daventry town is on the site of two Iron Age forts and the Roman encampment including the remains of a Roman villa beneath the sixth fairway. When the Hollingsworth Trophy was introduced in 1955 the club was one of the first to register its name on the trophy in 1956 and 1960. A third victory came in 1969, their last appearance in the final was in the first 3 cornered "Hunstanton Foursomes" final in 1978 played at Northants County. A final I should have played in, possibly against Walter Dunn, Barry Highfield, Dick Clarke, Don Tooby, Derek Scrowther et al but was dropped by non playing captain Tony Stevens despite not losing a game on the way to the final. Northampton won the final and on reflection in later years childishly (age 23!) refused to join the celebrations back at the old Kettering Road clubhouse. The three cornered final was repeated the following year but proved to be unpopular with the players, the final reverted to its standard format the following year.

In 1977 Derek Scrowther recorded the Club's first and only victory in the N.G.U. Higgs Bowl at Wellingborough G.C. prior to him turning professional and making a living in Scandinavia. According to the Internet, Derek has spent time in Norway and more recently Sweden but has maintained his links with the county and played in the 2006 N.P.G.A. Pro-Am in Portugal in February.

Barry Highfield was Club Champion ten times, N.G.U. Anglian League second team captain for a record eight years and captain of the winning 1980 team. He donated the personally hand carved wooden Highfield Shield which is played for in the annual friendly match between Northants and Bedfordshire. Neville Barry Highfield passed away, age 64 in 2000, and we miss the "Worm Burner's" sense of humour and company. A stone sundial bearing his name was erected in his memory from monies collected by club members.

In 2001 the club became N.G.U. Scratch League Division 4 champions and in 2005 they became Scratch League Division 5 Champions and will celebrate their Centenary in 2007.

For a long time it was thought that the Club had been formed in 1916; however a recently discovered minute from a 1937 committee meeting states that "the Club had been formed 30 years ago". A centenary book will be published and numerous events took place during the year, the highlights of which were tournaments and dinners arranged for the middle of August 2007.

Delapre Park Golf Complex 1976-present

Delapre Park Golf Complex is located in the heart of Northampton next to the A45, and close to Brackmills Industrial Estate. Well known P.G.A. Professionals John Corby and John Jacobs designed the original complex, including the Oaks course, in 1974. It has matured into a fine, established parkland complex with facilities to suit golfing of all standards. The courses are set in 260 acres of parkland, the complex includes, the Oaks 18 hole course (white 6117 yards par 70), the Hardingstone 9 hole course (par 32 opened in 1991), two nine hole Par 3 courses, a nine hole pitch and putt, a large practice putting greens and a 40-bay covered, floodlit driving range. The Oaks and Hardingstone courses have full automatic irrigation systems, to ensure the best possible playing conditions for the many thousands of rounds, which are played there each year. The Oaks Course has many mature established Oak trees, which add to the challenge posed to the golfer. Between 1976-2003 PGA Professional John Corby was a "permanent figure" and guided many thousands of aspiring golfers in to the game together with stalwarts such as John Cuddihy, Alan Wright, Greg Lunn et al. John Corby retired from the Club in 2003; Professional John Cuddihy continues to teach golf and is thought to be their longest serving employee having started there in 1983.

Significant changes occurred in 2003/4 when the Northamptonshire County Council decided to reprofile and

Delapre Golf Centre

in 2007 the complex is now part of the Jack Barker's Golf Company. A new professional shop (American Golf) has been created together with a new downstairs coffee bar/casual area and their title has changed to Delapre Golf Centre. The centre consists now of the original Delapre Oaks and Hardingstone courses, the two nine hole par 3 courses have been named as the Abbey (1302 yards) and Jacks (1272 yards) and of course the pitch and putt and putting green. The centre is well recognised too as a place for a good value lunch.

There are an interesting set of rules to set the tone and encourage the players:-

Jacks Rules

No yob's or snobs…Not scruffy, not stuffy!
Dress smart, clean and tidy…No effort, no chance!
Mind your language.. A foul shot's alright, not a foul mouth!
Check your footwear…Remember you're playing golf, not football!
Be courteous and friendly to others…It costs nothing to be civil!
Respect each other…Respect the course, respect for the game of golf!
No sharing…1 Person, 1 bag, 1 fee = 1 game!
It's only a game… And golf's meant to be fun!

I remember playing what is now the Jacks 9 hole course during the early 1980s and almost holed in one on the first hole, the ball finished 1 inch short of the cup. My tee shot with a wedge nearly generated a round of drinks even though we were playing in very dense fog when I could not even see the green!

The Club has produced some county winners notably in 1979 when C.A.Fletcher won the N.G.U. Higgs Bowl at Kingsthorpe G.C. and the Costello brothers S.J. & L.J. who became N.G.U. Family Foursomes winners in August 1996 at Oundle G.C. with a score of 34 Stableford pts. The donor of the Family Foursomes trophies N.G.U. Past President H. (Bert) W. Colton, Esq. made a special effort, driving over from Rushden to Oundle to present them on their fourtieth anniversary. It was interesting listening to this calm elderly gentleman described how he and his wife considered the design and format of the trophies. The silver salver trophy considered appropriate for a gentleman, the elegant "Old English" silver trophy appropriate for a lady.

As a fellow Rushden based N.G.U. Past President I felt quite proud to be included in the photograph of the winners, despite missing out by a single point with my son and partner young Alex (AJ) Izzard. The most famous win for the Club was undoubtedly Mick McNally's County Championship and Handicap Challenge Cup victory in 1985 where the colourful character won at Peterborough Milton G.C. Mick was a considerable talent and played a significant amount of his golf for Warwickshire where his home club was Coventry Hearsall. He was a member of the Warwickshire team who qualified for the E.G.U. County Finals in 1976 &1978 and twice runner up in their Matchplay Championship to legends Andrew Carmen in 1976 and Ronnie Hiatt in 1978. He was a great putter and used to literally hit it with pace "straight at the f****** hole" which in time he became famous for. Wellingborough's Ian Marshall played quite a few foursomes matches with him and became used to Mick's approach and many five footers "coming back". Mick also won the N.G.U. Scratch Foursomes with Richard Cole from Peterborough Milton G.C. collecting the Catlow Salvers in 1987. He has not been seen locally for a considerable time and I doubt if I would recognise him in 2008.

In 2004, the Club became the inaugural winners of the N.G.U. Scratch League Division 5 trophy and continue to provide a suitable route for people and coming in to the game. These new golfers are what are needed to maintain and expand the total number of golf club members in England which are currently dipping approximately 12,000 per annum since its peak of 700,000 in 2004.

Desborough G.C.

Golf was played somewhere in the area between 1947-57.

Dunsmore (near Rugby) 1908-1916

Little is known of this 9 hole course. The Warwickshire centenary book[15] states that the course was in Clifton Road a mile from the station. It is thought to have been Rugby School Golf Course. In 1912 the Club consisted of sixty members. In view of the dates it is doubtful that they were ever affiliated to the N.G.U. and inclusion here is simply for historical completeness.

Elton Furze 1993-present

Elton Furze G.C.

The 6279 yard par 70 18 hole course was opened in 1993 and is set a few miles south of the Cathedral City of Peterborough down Bullock Road. It has two loops of nine and many of the holes are located in mature woodland within Furze Wood, these are combined with holes featuring ponds and slopes which make an interesting challenge. The course is geographically in Cambridgeshire and is unusual since the Club's men are affiliated to the Cambridgeshire Area Golf Union whereas the ladies are affiliated to the Northants Ladies County Golf Association.

144

The Cambridgeshire Team, Eastern Counties Foursomes winners 2007 contained 3 members from Elton Furze G.C. Jody Greenall (Captain) Ed Conduit & Adam Pike.

The current men's course record holder is Ed Conduit with a score of 63 gross, he is a Cambridgeshire county player though represented Northamptonshire as a youngster. In 2006 the ladies won the Cecil Leitch trophy and retained it the following year with victory against Collingtree Park at nearby Peterborough Milton G.C. Also in 2006 The Elton Furze team of Jody Greenall, Ed Conduit & Adam Pike finished 22nd of 34 counties whilst representing Cambridgeshire in the annual E.G.U. Champion Club Tournament played at the fantastic Stoke Park Golf Club in Buckinghamshire. Jody Greenall led the way with scores of 72, 71 which could have been a lot better but for 2 pieces of misfortune in his 2nd round. On the 8th hole Greenall hit a fairway bunker shot which caught the lip, popped up onto the fairway and rolled down the slope hitting his bag thus incurring penalty strokes. Things were to get worse on the 11th as Greenall holed out for par from 2 feet only to see the ball hit the steel rim at the bottom of the cup and pop back out. Ed Conduit and Adam Pike had contrasting rounds. Conduit couldn't keep it on the golf course in his first round and returned an 81. In the 2nd round though he straightened up off the tee and scored a highly commendable 71. Adam Pike was 2 under after 6 in the first round before a double bogey 5 on the treacherous 7th and a poor finish saw him signing for a 75. In the 2nd round he never got it going and finished with an 83. The course was in fantastic condition and played every ounce of its 7000 yards in testing breezy conditions.

In 2007, the men's team competed in the final of the Goddard Cup at Saffron Walden narrowly losing 7-5 to

Champions Gog Magog. Also in 2007 County Captain Jody Greenall from the Club help steer Cambridgeshire to their first ever Easter Counties Foursomes victory at Seacroft G.C. with a 2 day points total of 26 points. Jody Greenall/Shaun Malone scored 6.5 points; Ed Conduit/Adam Pike scored 5.5 points out of a possible 8.

The single storey clubhouse has been designed to blend in with the surrounding area and offer good views of the course. Locally it has a reputation as a friendly and welcoming Club which I found to be well deserved whilst visiting to research this book; I was even treated to a free pint!

Goddard Cup 2007

16 September 2007
Saffron Walden Golf Club

Foursomes

ELTON FURZE GC	Points	Result	Points	GOG MAGOG GC
Aaron Jones Adrian Randall		4&2	1	Elliot Fletcher Anthony Richardson
Adam Pike Ian Pritchett	1	5&4		Clive Corcoran Mark Dean
Ed Conduit Paul Farrance		1 hole	1	Neil Hughes Tom Williams
Jody Greenhall John Summerfield	1	4&3		James Stammers Craig Thorburn
	2		2	

Singles

ELTON FURZE GC	Points	Result	Points	GOG MAGOG GC
Jody Greenhall	1	2&1		Anthony Richardson
Adam Pike	1	3&2		Mark Dean
John Summerfield	1	3&2		Clive Corcoran
Aaron Jones		3&2	1	Elliot Fletcher
Adrian Randall		2&1	1	Craig Thorburn
Paul Farrance		3&1	1	Neil Hughes
Ian Pritchett		1 hole	1	James Stammers
Ed Conduit		2&1	1	Tom Williams
	3		5	

Match Result

ELTON FURZE GC	5
GOG MAGOG GC	7

Embankment Golf Club 1975-present

The course is located on the south side of Wellingborough close to the river Nene in the grounds of Wellingborough School. The course meanders around the school grounds so hazards such as Rugby posts come into play. The members are an enthusiastic bunch and are good supporters of county social events; there are about 175 members currently. The Club Champion regularly takes part in the annual N.G.U. Champion of Champions event and appears to relish the challenge against the "bigger Club Champions". The Club are also regular attendees of the Izzard Club Team Trophy which is held at the end of the season in October. In fact, the Club are quite proud of their affiliation to local and national organisations, which was granted in 1992.

The Embankment Golf Club at Wellingborough

The white course measures 3462 yards, SSS 56 for the men SSS 59 for the ladies. The shortest hole is 87 yards, the longest 352 yards; stroke index 1 is a par three, the 3rd length 219 yards which requires a good blow.

Many holes have trouble to the left so hookers beware. Ground under Repair during the summer months includes Cricket Squares, jumping areas & white lines for sports pitches. In the winter obstructions include Rugby and Football Posts where relief can be taken. In line with some other flat courses, the Club helps some young people in to the game and also provide a facility for older players wishing to play golf without too much stress in their later years. A gem of a local rule states "Any ball striking sports equipment from tee to green must be replayed without penalty". With the limited space available for all the school's sports, the possibility of a

147

cricketer hitting a golf ball out of bounds exists albeit at a very low probability!

I popped in there recently and found the members and green staff, to be very hospitable. The kindly provided milky coffee was consumed outside accompanied by discussions about golf in general on a warm slightly damp October morning.

This little "cameo" reflected the friendly nature of a sometimes competitive game and set me up for the challenges of the day.

The Firs Club 1935-1939

This little nine hole course was established by Northampton's future (1962) Captain Mr W.H. (Bill) Chapman on rough fields adjoining Harlestone Firs[4p140]. Mr Chapman used to hit a few balls in these fields and eventually generated nine holes once the tenant farmer finally agreed to a peppercorn rent. There were no bunkers and only natural hazards such as hedgerows and gorse bushes. The course became very popular especially for golfers from Jimmy's End (St James End) Northampton. During the early stages of the 1939-1945 War, Mr Thorn the tenant farmer was forced to plough up the course in order to provide potatoes to help the County's shortage of food.

The card of the course was as follows:-

Hole	Yards	Strokes Front 9	Strokes Back 9	Bogey
1	306	5	6	5
2	114	17	18	3
3	232	7	8	4
4	220	9	10	4
5	207	11	12	4
6	361	1	2	5
7	308	3	4	5
8	144	15	16	3
9	160	13	14	3

Bogey 36 Length 2052 yards

Farthingstone Hotel and Golf Course 1973-present

Established in 1973 the 6299 yards par 70 course is located in open countryside to the north and west of Towcester. The course is located below one of the county's beautiful ancient woods (Mantles Heath) where badgers and nightingales give the ancient woodland a special atmosphere on most warm summer evenings. The initiative to develop a golf club and complex in this location came from Don Donaldson who is to date the owner; Don has witnessed both the boom and relaxation of golf in the county. The hotel has 16 rooms, two snooker tables and a squash court for the energetic golfer.

Many of the holes have names derived from the surrounding area such as the 1st Fox Hole, 7th Mantles Trail and 17th Ridge & Furrow. Some holes are named after local personalities such as the extremely demanding 11th Gallagher's Lakes named after professional Mike Gallagher. At 198 yards from the white tees the shot is played

The Clubhouse at Farthingstone G.C.

over water to a narrow green cut into the side of a hill, a par here is always welcome. During a recent Hollingsworth Trophy match, a half in two was recorded, both sides felt that they should have won the hole or indeed have lost it!

Mike Gallagher was Professional at the Club for many years during the late 1970s/80s before spending time at Peterborough Milton G.C. The "kid from Kingsthorpe" went back to Farthingstone in 2006. Mike is one of the best players the county has produced; he played in two Open Championships in 1977 and 1981. He has a great passion for the game and has retained this in to his senior years. He started his professional career as Alf Lovelady's assistant the same time that I started my amateur career in 1969 at Northampton's Kettering Road course. Having spent the day working in Alf's shop, Mike would offer a tempting bribe to us young juniors if we played a few more holes in the evening with him. This was an offer we could not refuse and would typically play up to the par fifth green and back down the 15th hole to the old wooden clubhouse and a glass of coke. The evening concluded with a short trip round the corner on our bicycles to "George's chip shop" and Mike's kind purchase of free fish and chips!

In 1978, A.Deakin won the Stableford Cup over his own course and in 1980 J.F.McKeogh won the Higgs Bowl at Oundle, these singles victories were followed by Carl Leeson and Nick Pyne in1985 as the pair became N.G.U.1985 County Scratch Foursomes Champions at Kettering G.C. They were the last pair out on the course and temporarily upset the author who was on the first tee ready to participate in a play-off with another pair! Congratulations were in order for "Crazzy Carl and Ordered Nick". Nick Pyne also became the N.G.U. Handicap Challenge Cup winner in 1994 played at Northants County G.C.

Darren Mathews is their multi Club Champion and became both N.G.U. Champion of Champion in 1997 at Northampton G.C. and Matchplay Champion in 1999 defeating Kingsthorpe's John Evans at Kettering G.C.

The Club's men won Scratch League Division 2 in 1995 and spent a season in the "premiership" actually Division 1. Fourball matches are clearly a preferred format at Farthingstone since the N.G.U. Fourball Matchplay trophy has twice been won by their members. In 2001 Ian Donald & Steve Chalcroft lifted the trophy and P. Butterwick and S. Bird retained it the following year.

In 2003, the men's team reached the Hollingsworth Final for the first time in the club's history narrowly losing 3-2. Mike Taylor became the Club's first ever N.G.U. President when he came into office in 2004. The 4th hole is named Taylors Woe however there is no direct connection. As N.G.U. President Mike was invited as Northamptonshire's guest to attend the 250th Anniversary of the formation of the R&A at St Andrews. A function Mike clearly enjoyed and is still describing the meal and events to date. At this event one notable signing occurred, initiated by E.G.U. Championship Secretary John Walker who managed to persuade the legendary Arnold Palmer to sign future E.G.U. President Richard Palmer's menu "Best wishes from Palmer to Palmer".

Arnold Palmer what a man for golf, indescribable.

In 2007, Ian Bell won the N.G.U. Higgs Bowl at Northampton G.C. with a score of Nett 68 off a handicap of 11.

The course has the longest hole in Northamptonshire the 14th at 606 yards Alexander's Mirth, which is rarely reached in two and requires two accurate shots to set up the pitch to the green. The fairway has a slope towards the out of bounds to the left and a large tree in the middle of the fairway to affect the second shot.

13th Hole White 213 Yards Par 3, Knightly Way

This is a very demanding hole at the far end of the course which has out of bounds all the way down the left hand side and close to the sloping green. In fact if the ball is to finish near the pin it must either hug the out of bounds or be drawn in with a long iron or wood. The wind often blows left to right across the hole to add to the hole's difficulty.

The Ryder Cup in Northamptonshire guarded by N.G.U. Vice-President Mike Taylor and President the Late Brian Woodcock.

13th Hole, Knightly Way

Great Harrowden Hall 1876-1895

In the known history of the Hall the estate of Earl Fitzwilliam was used by the Great Harrowden School for Daughters of Gentlemen between 1876-1895 for ladies entertainment which included golf. This location which is now the home of Wellingborough G.C. very likely, had a course lain out in the grounds, since old golf balls in the form of a Gutty Ball have been found there by the Club's Past Captain Ken Ellson .

If one is to be critical concerning the early origins of golf in the county it is highly likely that a course existed here, especially since the Earl had a private course on his other estate at Milton Hall Peterborough. There is good evidence to prove this[3] since the *Wellingborough Illustrated* wrote at the turn of the last century "Wellingborough has the distinction of being a great educational centre, and probably one of the most notable colleges in the Midlands for education of daughters of gentlemen. This is about two miles from the town. The climate is salubrious and the splendid grounds of Harrowden Hall present a picture of unique sylvan charms. The Hall realises the ideal of a college which is at once an efficient school and a refined home". Some sixty acres were set aside for golf and riding whilst cricket, hockey and tennis were also played vigorously on the remaining 100 acres of the grounds. Unfortunately, to date, I have not been unable to establish a firm date when golf was first played here.

The most famous young lady that came to the Great Harrowden School for Daughters of Gentlemen was Princess Kaiulani of Hawaii who was sent to the school in 1889 age fourteen. She was described as being an outstandingly beautiful young woman who was idolised by the Hawaiian people; this is confirmed by the photograph on page 59 of Wellingborough's Centenary book[3]. After returning to her beautiful island of Oahu she tragically died at the tender age of twenty-three. Some 20,000 people attended her funeral. Her family, some of whom have visited Harrowden Hall since her death presented to Wellingborough Library a beautiful book describing her short life.

One of the school's lady golfers may have used the gutta percha ball found by the late Wellingborough Club's Past Captain Ken Ellson some time around 1885. The solid gutta percha ball was first introduced c.1848; it was made from the sap of the Palaquium genus of trees which are native to South-East Asia. The name comes from the Malayan name "gueta" meaning gum and "percha" meaning cloth. The ball has been mounted on a plinth and is looked after by his son Duncan Ellson. See illustration page 2.

Harborough Road 1908-1914

A nine hole course existed opposite the hospital[15], its end date is unknown but most likely corresponds with Kingsthorpe G.Cs. move to Gypsy Lane in 1914. This was in fact Kingsthorpe's first location.

Harringworth 1894-1902

Little is known of this course apart from its start and end dates.

Hellidon Lakes Hotel Golf & Country Club 1990-present

Situated to the south west of Daventry this 27 hole golf course has some of the finest views in the county especially on warm summer evenings, sunsets westerly over the Warwickshire hills as far as the eye can see can be spectacular. The original eighteen holes were opened in 1990 and a further 9 holes added in the year 2000. The

A cold bright winter view from the veranda at Hellidon Lakes G.C. with views towards Warwickshire and a single Crow

hotel is situated in 220 acres of rolling countryside on the borders of Warwickshire and Northamptonshire and has 110 bedrooms and suites two restaurants and a spa/leisure club. Many of these rooms have the spectacular view. The hotel and clubhouse are set in a commanding position overlooking the 18th green; dinner from the Lakes restaurant during an evening sunset can be quite beautiful. A total of seventeen lakes are spread evenly across the three loops to punish any wayward shots and the course can be quite hilly.

In 2004, the course underwent some radical changes notably to the original seventeenth and eighteenth holes. The three loops of nine are now named Red, Blue and Green yardages from the medal tees are: Red: 3,321 yards. Blue: 3,277 yards and Green 2,791 yards. The 296-yard 17th par four and 158 yard 18th are both new. The original 18th hole was a long par four over the lake which could be driven by strong players; those less able were forced to go clockwise over 400 yards round it. "It was too silly," said Professional Joe Kingston. "It was almost a par seven for those who played it the safe way". The changes to the layout have given the course a better balance and more variety. The shorter green nine has been designed with hotel guests and juniors in mind.

The Club's first male county player was Paul (P.M.A.) Hutchings who played the game with "gay abandon" using power as his main weapon. Paul was also Club Champion in 1993 and 1996. Paul and his brother Graham became well known on the local golf scene during the mid 1990s prior to their departure from the county. In 2004 the Club's first victory in a N.G.U. tournament came when R. French and R. Trim became Foursomes Champions at Overstone Park G.C. when they were victorious over Oundle's B.Harrison and A.Gow with a margin of 4/3. In 2005 the Club reached their first ever Semi-Final of the Hollingsworth Trophy against local rivals Staverton Park G.C. Staverton went on to become Champions.

In 2007 they are part of Marston Hotels who are in turn owned by QHotels.

Holdenby Manor c.1900- c.1945

Holdenby has Royal connections dating back around 400 years. This was once the largest 'house' in England, where Queen Elizabeth I stayed, and was also the prison of her successor Charles I. The nine hole course was laid out in the 20 acre grounds of the then Lord Annaly's estate who occupied the house between 1905-1945, the holes measured between 151 and 293 yards. During my research for this book, I have found no proven record of the start and end dates for the formation and closure of this "course".

John White Golf Club 1970-present

John White Golf Course and Club House.

John White Golf Club is a friendly little pay-and-play facility located in the once homely town of Rushden the course is located left of the A6 just before the turn to Wymington. The Club was one of the first golf clubs in the U.K. to receive money from the National Lottery Fund to purchase the land required to enhance the course that is open to visitors today. The old wooden clubhouse/cricket pavilion which dated back to the 1930s was demolished in 1998 to make way for the smarter new brick building which has a lounge bar overlooking the course and a large function room. The nine hole parkland course, has a length of 1,520-yards and a par of 27. Junior golfers are most welcome.

In October 2005, ownership of the clubhouse and course reverted to the club members from the tenants GRS Properties. Also in 2005 a new amateur course record of 53 was recorded by the Chairman Allan Bowman in the July medal, Marion Johnson is the Club's E.G.T.F. teaching professional. A separately owned 20 bay driving range is situated next to the clubhouse.

In April 2006, a newsletter was launched and the membership currently is approximately 180, the course is maintained by a greenkeeper who has 40 years in the trade. Catering is provided by Hinde Catering Ltd and the clubhouse can seat up to 120 guests for weddings, birthdays parties etc. It is a very friendly little club, a drive and a three wood from our back garden in Newton Road, Rushden.

Kettering Golf Club 1891-present

A traditional Sunday morning fourball match finishes at the 18th hole Kettering G.C., in 2008 it is the county's oldest surviving golf course.

Kettering G.C. is the oldest surviving course in the county and is still on its original site in 2008, it has a length of 6057 yards and a SSS of 69. It was started in September 1891, after the nine hole course was laid out by St Andrew's Old Tom Morris, $^3/_4$ of a mile from the railway station. A bus met every train to transport the golfers to the course fare 6d. In 1891 the 18-hole course was nearly 3 miles in length. In 1891 the numerous hazards included the railway (Midland Region), roads, hedges, hurdles, gorse and whins. The longest hole was 510 yards the shortest 130 yards. In 1895 the entrance fee was £1&1 shilling, Subscription £1&1 shilling 6 (d) pence, at that time the membership was 90.

One of the earliest known reported matches with a complete score was between Kettering and Northampton G.Cs. on the 1st March 1894 on the Kettering Links[9]. These events were keenly contested since some Northampton members were also members at Kettering. The man who brought golf to Northamptonshire Dr J Allison played number one for the home club and defeated Northampton's Norman Dawson by 3 holes. In these matches all 18 holes were played and Northampton squeezed home by 3 holes largely due to game 3. Dr Allison has the first hole named after him "Allison's" and his picture hangs in the clubhouse.

KETTERING *vs* NORTHAMPTON 1 MARCH 1894

Kettering		Northampton	
Dr Allison	3	Mr N Dawson	0
Mr A Simmons	0	Rev H Stewart	4
Mr W Milsom	0	Mr B B Muscott	9
Mr T C Fraser	0	Mr W R Henderson	4
Mr C Saunders	4	Rev W H Deane	0
Mr E Mobbs	6	Mr J Haviland	0
Mr R B Wallis	0	Mr R C Scriven	1
Mr R Abbott	0	Mr A E Anderson	1
Mr R Barlow	3	Mr W G Hobbs	0
	16		19

The current course has not changed too significantly from the original layout and has an out and back route with the par five 8th hole the "Farthest" from the clubhouse which is the hole's name. The front nine has a demanding par three the 186 yards 7th hole Pond Side, which attracts may balls and also dragonflies. The back nine has two holes with very sloping greens, the par four 14th 418 yards "Buccleugh's" requires an accurate approach shot to hold the right to left sloping green. The 16th 453 yards par 4 stroke index 1 hole "Oak" has a green which is set across the second shot and sloping away from the approach shot. Par figures on these holes are most welcome but often not achieved. The 1st and 2nd holes were modified from the original layout when the A14 was constructed, a new two tier green was constructed on the 1st and new tees were put in on the 2nd and 3rd making the holes more of a dog-leg to the right. The tee shot on the 3rd now has to carry the fishing lake.

Over the years the Club has produced four men's County Champions, the 1920s being their most dominant period with legend Dr J. Allison 1923, W.J.Thompson 1924&27 and relatively more recently R.P. (Bob) Larratt in 1971. During the 1920s/30s the club registered several victories in the N.G.U. Higgs Bowl and Kettering members J.Hutchinson and A.L.Hart won and retained the trophy at the Club in 1953-4. In total the club has 13 names on this trophy including most recently young scatterbrain Richard Cooper in 1989 and brothers Simon and Andrew Lilly in 1994 & 2000 respectively.

Bob Larratt was a member of the 1972 N.G.U. team that won the Anglian League A shield for the first time, also in 1972 the N.G.U. Seniors Trophy winner was T.H.Goode, and the trophy was retained the following year by W.Griffiths, their only successes to date in this event. Bob became a Professional golfer in 1973 and moved to Kibworth G.C. Leicestershire and is now making an impact at Senior level. In June 2005 Bob fired a flawless final-round 69 to snatch the PGA Senior Club Professional Championship at King's Lynn, Norfolk. The European Seniors' Tour regular had two reasons to celebrate – winning his first major PGA title and seeing his wife Judith return to caddying duties for him after serious illness. Bob finished tied for 35th place in the 2006

Kettering G.C. Presentation evening 2007, Charley Hull (left) Ladies Club Champion (their youngest ever winner), with Kevin Theobald (centre) Club Professional for the last 25 years and Simon Lilly Professional associated with Kettering on the European Challenge Tour. In the background is the picture of Dr John Allison, the Scot who founded the Club in 1893, he is still keeping his eye on proceedings.

Senior British Open with scores of 72, 72, 75, 71=290 +10 over the Ailsa course at Turnberry Scotland. His final round included a hole in one at the 171 yard, par-3 4th hole with an 8-iron shot. Bob also has qualification for the America based Champions tour.

Professional Kevin Theobald (originally from Corby) has been in residence since 1982 and in 2007 notched up twenty-five years at the Club. I wonder if they have a gold watch for him! Kevin has brought many young players in to the game especially when teaching over at the driving range at John White G.C.

Left-hander Michael Pask became the N.G.U. Handicap Challenge Cup winner in 1984 on his own course. Michael studied at St Andrews University and became Universities Champion prior to embarking on a career with the late Mark McCormack's company IMG and is doing quite well for himself. The last time we met was at Wentworth where I was treated to a nice piece of corporate hospitality. In 1991 Michael teamed up with Darren Jones for the Eastern Counties foursomes at Seacroft G.C. (Skegness) and became a formidable pair, winning 7$\frac{1}{2}$ out of 8 Matches. That was one very fun weekend for all involved, the camaraderie was great. Michel's ball striking ability was phenomenal and we still talk about him now, especially as he hit a sand wedge all weekend to the 156 yards par 3 10th hole.

One of the best players the Club has produced is Simon Lilly. Simon burst on to the county scene when he won the N.G.U. Braid's Driver in 1994 and turned professional in 1998. After a relatively quiet spell Simon won the final event of the 2004 P.G.A. Euro ProTour at the beautiful Mosa Trejectum course in Spain and also finished top of the final Order of Merit for the year which gave him a place on the European Challenge Tour for 2005. For the record Wellingborough G.C. based Simon scored 73, 68, 67 = 8 under par to collect the £20,000 cheque. Simon currently has a significant advantage over the rest of the local professionals and twice won the N.G.U. Autohaus Open in 2005 and 6. In 2006 at Northants County G.C. this included a new professional course record of 63 in the afternoon to add to his morning round of 67, Simon won the event by 10 strokes from the nearest professional and 7 strokes from our English International amateur Gary Boyd (Cherwell Edge).

However in 2004 to prove it's not just a game for youngsters Jonathan Payne made it a hat-trick of wins in the club championship – an amazing 25 years after he first won the title, his 36 hole total of 140 won the trophy by four shots from the younger "uncut diamond" Lee Smith.

A vintage period for the club in the Hollingsworth Trophy was between 1982-1992 when their six final appearances generated four victories and the team also won the N.G.U. Scratch League Div 1 title in 1991 for the first time.

Northamptonshire County Cricketer Brian Reynolds was a member at Kettering. He made such an impact locally as a sportsman that a book *"The Times and Life of a Northamptonshire Sportsman"* was subsequently produced[16] in 2000. Brian Reynolds played 426 matches, 732 innings 65 not outs scoring 18,640 runs, highest score 169 including 21 centuries, 95 half centuries, average 27.95, 254 catches 45 as wicket keeper 20 stumpings, 4 wickets for 284 runs best 1 for 0 average 71.00. Brian Reynolds played County Cricket from 1950-1970 and coached the county team for 25 years. He was also 12th man for England on a number of occasions.

Brian Reynolds was coach to one of the world's fastest bowlers, Northamptonshire's Frank "Typhoon" Tyson in the 1950s. Watching Tyson bowling in 1954 at the County Ground Fred Trueman, Tom Graveney, not to mention coach Brian Reynolds, swore he was the fastest bowler that ever lived. Tyson was the only great fast bowler capable of quoting Shakespeare or Wordsworth in between knocking stumps out of the ground. "I wandered lonely as a cloud that floats on high o'er vales and hills," he would chortle. "Shut up, Frank," they would chorus back, "or you'll be lonelier than you've ever imagined." My father used to joke to me that a Tyson ball was coming as he bowled tennis balls to me as a young lad at Eastfield Park a mile or so from the County ground as he tried to emulate the great man. My connections with cricket are largely through my father (Lesley Donald Izzard) and my great grandfather W. Izzard who played for Northamptonshire in 1908. My efforts at cricket saw me become wicket keeper at Cherry Orchard School because "the boy can't run very fast, but is good at diving!"

At Kettering G.C. Brian Reynolds won the Club Championship (Championship Bowl) three times in 1966, 1973 and 1975. On the 21 May 1966 he scored 74, 77 to take the title and at his best held a handicap of three.

Golf in Northamptonshire

Brian Reynolds was born in Kettering and has never lived away from the town, as well as his major contribution to cricket and golf he also played football for Kettering Town and Peterborough United.

On the family side the arrival of his two children also contained a golf connection. The family's life changed dramatically on Saturday the 27th April 1968. The day before Brian's wife Angela had been admitted to hospital five weeks before their first child was due suffering with high blood pressure. Brian was due to compete in an Inter-Club match at Kettering and just prior to leaving the house phoned the hospital to enquire about his wife's condition. The Doctor asked if he was sitting down and then broke the news that Angela had had a baby boy (Ian) and that ten minutes after baby Ian had arrived another child Sue had been delivered, undiagnosed twins! He was told that there was little point in visiting at this time, he dropped out of the team match and with time to kill had a social game with David and George Buckby. In the book describing his sporting life[16] Brian states "I was in such a state of shock I played the worst golf of my life that afternoon". In 1986, the 17-year-old twins recorded an unusual double when Sue became Head Girl at Southfields School and Ian was Head Boy at Kettering Boys School.

Brian Reynolds' contribution to his native County has been immense and is echoed by the following quotations.

"Throughout the long history of the County Cricket Club, there have been few, if any, individuals more committed and dedicated to Northants cause." – L.A.Wilson Chairman 1977.

"In his own mind he is not only a cricketer, he is a Northamptonshire cricketer." – John Arlott.

In times that are more recent one of the Club's very young ladies is Charley Hull who is already making a large impact on the golf scene. The 10 year old girl from Burton Latimer is being hailed as one of the best young golfers in the world. Charley Hull's swing has been described by one top golf coach as "unbelievable" for her age. At the tender age of nine she became the youngest ever winner of the Health Perception L.G.U. Championship at Turnberry on the 26 September 2005 (see Chapter 11 success at National level). Charley is becoming quite a celebrity and has been interviewed by the BBC and has recently been the subject of an article in the January 2007 edition of *Golf World*, one of the sport's leading magazine. Her father Dave is also a member at the club and like many parents with talented children is burning up a lot of rubber on the roads. In August 2007 she appeared on BBC2 instructing three young boys and girls how to play the game and also had to judge who had the most promising swing, what a star!

A new clubhouse was constructed in 2000 which now hosts the N.G.U. Men's County Dinner. The donors of the N.G.U. Scratch league Division 2 trophy was Club Past Captains R.P. (Paul) Seddon who also opened the nearby private Woodlands Hospital in June 1990 and Don Bates. The Club has produced 6 N.G.U. County Presidents to date and uniquely the late Brian Woodcock was in office for 3 years (2001-4) partly due to the untimely resignation of the previous incumbent and also Brian's dedication to the game. Mick Reed (Captain 1987) became the 7th Kettering N.G.U. President in March 2008. Mick is in fact a good low handicap player and has represented the Club in both Scratch League and Hollingsworth Trophies; together with Graham Dolby they won the County Scratch Foursomes in 1992 over their home course. This was the second time the trophy had been won by the Club following R.Allen and Tony (A.J.) Wooton in 1975 and for good measure, the trophy was retained the following year by Jonathan Payne & Simon Lilly at Northampton in 1993.

In November 2007 Steward Cheryl Oakes picked the National award of "London Pride E.G.U. Steward of the Year". After receiving the award from John Roberts MD of Fullers and Craig Wagstaff E.G.U. Finance Director Cheryl stated "I'm over the moon to have won this award, I love Kettering and get a real buzz when I enter the clubhouse, when someone's had a bad round I like to put a smile back on their face- and its something I love doing". In addition to the trophy Cheryl won two tickets for a day's play at Lord's and accommodation. Who will Cheryl take with her, Mick Reed? Watch this space!

Kettering golf club's steward Cheryl Oakes (Centre) the 2007 Fuller's Steward of the Year winner with left John Roberts (Managing Director Fuller's Beer Company) & Craig Wagstaff (EGU Finance Director).

5th Hole 503 Yards Par 5 Poplars.

This hole is effectively a double dogleg, which requires the tee shot to be gently faded around the out of bounds to reach the ridge and furrowed fairway, a straight shot will end in the trees and rough on the left-hand side, forcing the player to lay up short of cross bunkers. The second shot has to be carefully positioned to avoid having to draw the third shot around the poplar trees. For good measure, the green is slightly raised and two-tiered. The third shot is one of the most difficult shots to judge as the green is quite open and many shots invariably end up short of the pin. It is rarely reached in two blows.

The fifth green at Kettering Golf Club

Kettering Working Mens 1894-1910

Formed in 1894 by Dr Allison the course of six holes was in the North Park, it was last mentioned in 1910.

Kimbolton 1906-1914

Although now in Cambridgeshire, Kimbolton is listed by Ray Baldwin[13] as one of Northamptonshire's extinct courses. The 9-hole course was formed at Stonely two miles from Kimbolton station and eight miles from St Neots station. It measured 2366 yards long Bogey 38. The course had five bogey four, one bogey three and three bogey five holes. The shortest hole was the sixth hole 138 yards the longest was the fifth at 551 yards. It was a natural course with no made bunkers, no sand or furze. It contained a brook, which had to be crossed twice, and was hilly with very good turf. It had a membership of 30-60 and a playing season of October to April.

Kingfisher Hotel, Golf & Country Club 1995-present

This pretty little 9 hole layout close to Deanshanger was designed by the 2006 President of the E.G.U. Donald Steel. It has an 18-hole par of 70 length 5552 yards from the white tees. The hotel has 28 double rooms together with a Lakeside Restaurant and is often used for team building, family fun days and specialist events. They are also licensed for civil wedding ceremonies. Coarse fishing in the lake often provides a departure from golf. There are approximately 100 members. On the County golf scene, the club have participated in finals day and are regulars at the Izzard Club team Trophy.

Kingfisher Golf Club

Kingsthorpe Golf Club 1908-present

The Club was founded 1908 by a group of employees from the "Union Bank" now part of the "Natwest Bank" in the Drapery, Northampton. The course was nine holes off Harborough Road close to the current cemetery. In 1912 land was acquired in the area known as Gypsy Lane to establish an 18 hole course and the Club moved to its current location on the outskirts of the town from the Harborough Road location in 1914. The course was "laid out" by one of the well-known architects of the day Charles H Alison who was Secretary at Stoke Poges G.C.,

Aerial view of Kingsthorpe G.C.

an associate of the more famous Harry Colt who had built the earlier course. Harry Colt is thought to have modified the course during the 1920s. The course provides a challenging yet fair test of golf synonymous with the design skills associated with Colt the legendary architect. Accuracy off the tee is paramount to afford the golfer the opportunity to hit the right part of the small undulating greens. Many birdie opportunities are on offer if you can achieve this, whilst par becomes tough if you are off line or faced with downhill sloping putts.

In previous years without the current modern transport infrastructure, it was a popular venue with townsfolk since the number eight bus stopped right outside the entrance. Kingsthorpe are members of the Society of 1908 Golf Clubs, which was established during the year the Clubs were formed. The society consists of Clubs from as far and wide as for example Stoneham in Hampshire, Kingsknowe in Edinburgh and Vale of Llangollen in Denbighshire. Kingsthorpe members are able to play at many of the societies Clubs through mutual courtesy arrangements.

The Club have produced six N.G.U. County Champions and six Presidents. The course used to almost back on to Northampton's Kettering Road course and there is a story of a golfer teeing off at Northampton in the 1960s and ending up at the clubhouse at Kingsthorpe, name unknown!

First played for in 1962, the *Chronicle & Echo* Foursomes Tournament was an extremely popular event played at the Club in May and ran for over 40 years. In 2000, the competition changed to the Hakko Team/Camden Motor Group Foursomes and was last competed for in 2003. The late Alex Good, Past President of the N.G.U. 1977-78 inaugurated the competition.

The so-called "Chron and Ech" became a very popular event. So much so, that a waiting list for prospective teams was needed. The format was foursomes match play, with two pairs participating out of the team of five. Matches were played over a two-week period, on Tuesdays and Thursdays with a semi-final and final on the Saturday of the second week. In each round 18 holes of golf were played, I remember the first pair from a particular team (Insurance Society Dan Dare, Nick Grimmitt *et al*) coming in seven holes up and being quite chirpy in the bar about the next round, unfortunately, the second pair lost eight holes down so they were out! If necessary, sudden death was played by both teams to determine the result and matches for the next phase of the competition. The teams came from many different areas of life and this helped in providing discussion on and off the course and variety for the event.

I personally had great fun in the competition as an Old Northamptonion starting in 1980 for well over twenty years with club stalwarts David Sharpe and Jim Howkins together with Northampton members Kevin Newman, Alan Linney & Bob (R.T.F.) Willoughby. The semi-finals were followed by a nice lunch and the final was arranged to conclude at 7 p.m. in preparation for a presentation buffet which was available for all teams, wives and supporters at 8 p.m. The trophy winners are listed in Appendix 1, N.A.L.G.O. & Old Wellingburians collecting a record six victories, one ahead of the Scottish Association. N.A.L.G.O. the National Association of Local Government Officers were allegedly given time off to practise according to the rumour machine. The trophy was presented to the winning team, by the Mayor of Northampton ably assisted by Miss *Chronicle and Echo*. This was often the Mayor's first event in office and the evening celebrations were well supported in a relaxed, friendly atmosphere.

Alex Good was very proud of his concept and glowed quietly in the background. In his youth he trained alongside Olympic champion Eric Liddell, immortalised in the film *Chariot's of Fire* for winning the 400 metres in the 1924 Paris Olympics. I often think fondly of him, notably when I walk where much of the film was made, West Sands beach at The Home of Golf St Andrews, he was a true gentlemen. Alex was also a swimmer and trained the first Scotsman to swim the English Channel named Ned Barney.

A new purpose built clubhouse was completed in

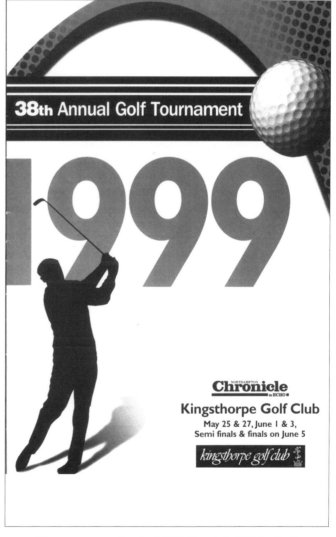

The programme for the 1999 Chronicle & Echo Golf Tournament.

Golf in Northamptonshire

Right: N.A.L.G.O. Chronicle & Echo
Champions 1979 – Left to right:
Tony (Archy) Bishop, Jim Dalton,
Brian D'Hooghe, Councillor Fred
Desborough the Late Mayor of
Northampton and Tony Stevens.

Below:
Kingsthorpe G. C., Hollingsworth
Trophy Winners at Northants County
in 1999.
Back Row: G. Thomas, D. Jones,
S. McDonald, J. Crouch, P. Harris,
S. Blundell, S. Crowson.
Front Row: P. Croxford, P. Stones,
M. Jones (Captain), D. Roberts,
K. Spence

2004 with considerable assistance from the members that own building companies.

In 2006 during the playing of the Adams Cup the front nine holes was completed in a record five under par gross 28 by Northampton's team Captain Dean Roberts. The Adams Cup which was originally known as the Hospital Cup it was presented by H.W. Adams in 1936 as a singles competition off handicap. Dean's card included birdies on the 1st, 2nd, 3rd, 8th, & 9th holes. Having kept the run going on the back nine with a couple of birdies and bogeys, Dean stood on the 18th tee requiring a birdie 3 to equal the long standing amateur course record of 63 set in 1985 by Steve MacDonald. Pressure took over and a gross 67 ensued which was still a fine effort, but left him with a feeling of what might have been. According to the Club's Secretary John Harris, you only get a birdie on that hole if you are playing like a dog!

Also in 2006 the Club won the Hollingsworth Trophy for a record twelfth time, four victories ahead of their great rivals Northampton G.C. This rivalry stems from the close proximity of the two courses in the town between the formation of both Clubs in 1893 and 1908 to the present time. This is despite Northampton's move to Harlestone in 1990 and the continual interchange of members between the two Clubs. Only time will tell and it reminds me of the English-Scottish scenario.

Steve McDonald's 1985 score was recorded without the current long spring faced drivers and long travelling golf balls and stands as a testimony to his amazing touch from 40 yards to the pin. He will talk you through the round if you are interested, as he can still see it in his memory.

Steve made a great impact as a player at County level starting in 1977 against Leicestershire & Rutland on the 24th April at Kettering G.C. where he played number two in the foursomes (with Northampton's Kevin Newman) and two in the singles. His last appearance was at Grimsby G.C. on the 03/09/1995 when the Anglian League B team were solidly beaten 9-3 by Lincolnshire despite having five highly rated Kingsthorpe players in the side. The Frank Bruno World title fight the night prior to the match and the quality of the out of hotel entertainment clearly had a significant emotional impact on their ability to sleep. Losing the foursomes 0-4 was the start of bad embarrassing day!

Steve often played number one in the batting order and I still wonder if two many "early baths" affected his confidence in the long term.

Steve's Club colleague "the Engineer who likes to fish" Peter Scott also represented the N.G.U., Peter's first match was also in 1977 in the autumn against Lincolnshire on the 4th September 1977 with "rentapartner" Kevin Newman at Northshore G.C. Skegness where the pair won 4/3 playing top. One of Peter's greatest day's came the following year in 1978 in the Anglian League match against Cambridgshire at Staverton Park G.C. when he won the foursomes 4/3 with ex County Wicketkeeper Laurie Johnson and his singles by 8/6. Cambridgeshire's R.Boorman feeling the intensity of Peter's golf over those 27 holes.

1977 marked my first appearance for the N.G.U when I played with rentapartner at our home Club Northampton on the 03/07/1977 when we won 1 up in the foursomes and I gave the Suffolk player a "dog licence" in the afternoon singles. All four of us were part of Captain Barry Highfield's "Spunky Young Pups" team which would go on to win the Anglian B League Shield in 1980.

Steve McDonald and Peter Scott later became Anglian League B Team Captains in 1995 and 2004 respectively; Kevin has two teenage sons who are becoming fine players at a tender age. My son Alex has now taken my place in the Club's Scratch League Team and I am certain the late man (worm burner Barry) would be proud of what his "pups" have achieved.

14th White 398 Yards Par 4

The hole is played across the valley up and over a slight hill to a long thin green which has an out of bounds hedge on either side. There is also a small dip in front of the green which makes the second shot difficult to judge. The green is also one of the most difficult to read on the course and is no more than 10 feet wide at it's furthest point. In days gone by, one could see the 10th, 11th and 12th holes on the old Kettering Road course from here.

Whilst playing the hole in the 1980s, I hooked my tee shot into the hut behind the 12th green which forced an explosion of players from inside the hut, who were sheltering from the rain. As I arrived at the scene it was clear I was not popular with the wet golfers especially when I claimed a free drop!

Evening light with singing blackbirds at the fourteenth green at Kingsthorpe Golf Club

Market Harborough 1898-present

The first 9 hole course was set out by David Duncan, the professional from Northampton G.C. who had taken up the post there in 1897 for a period of four years. The Club was founded at the end of the Victorian era on the 16th August 1898 and at that time consisted of 71 male and 42 lady members. The course, which was extended to eighteen in 1993, is located at Little Oxenden about two miles to the south of the town.

The Club's first meeting was held in the town at The Three Swans family hotel and posting house. At this meeting many local dignitaries were present including William Henry (E.J.) Symington who was a founder member; his presence was often easily detected by the whiff of an expensive cigar! The Club's first committee was largely the town hierarchy. Fox hunting connections and the local countryside attracted many personalities to the area who would often stay at the Three Swans, this was a regular visiting spot for the Whyte-Melville family, both George and his father John were captains of the Royal and Ancient Golf Club of St Andrews and George clearly made a big impact locally (see Chapter 2). The town and its surrounding countryside inspired George to publish a book simply called *Market Harborough* in 1861.

The opening day for the Club was on the 20th October 1898 two months after the first meeting at the Three Swans. The bogey score was 86 for the 2370 yards course and caddie fees 3d per round. Fences around the greens (as also used in the next century by Rushden G.C. up until the late 1980s) were used to keep the grazing cattle off the putting surface. At Rushden G.C. sheep rather than cattle were used. The local rules allowed a player to replay the shot if it struck the post or wire around the green and another local rule allowed a player to lift and drop from a ball lying in dung presumably after cleaning the ball. A nice job for the caddie! The Club-room was in "Flint's Cottage" located just opposite the entrance to the Club on the Market Harborough to Northampton road. A bout of scarlet fever broke out in the cottage owed by the Flint family which resulted in members clubs being moved to a boarded-up shed precipitated discussions about a new Clubhouse. In 1923 a new "Club-room" was opened on the 13th September followed by an exhibition match between the Club's professional Arthur Flint and Len Holland professional at Northants County. Holland winning the exhibition singles at the seventeenth.

The Club joined the Northamptonshire Golf Association (later Union) in November 1922 on the invitation of County Secretary Mr G.A.T. (Tubby) Vials a member at Northants County. The Club came under the jurisdiction of the Northamptonshire Golf Union until 1949 when it moved by mutual consent to Leicestershire & Rutland Golf Union in 1950. The last event run by the N.G.U. was probably the four-ball best ball bogey handicap limit twenty off $^3/_4$ handicap on the 20th August 1949, it was won by two local members with a score of 5 up.

The late Richard.S (Dick) Biggin captained Northamptonshire's winning Anglian League A team in 1990. Dick was also a member at Market Harborough in the 1960s. Dick was a member of the team, which won the Leicestershire & Rutland mixed foursome title in 1964 against a heavily fancied Rothley Park team. This was in fact the first time that the Club had reached the final, which was described as the closest final in the history of the event won with a score of one hole. Having spent a lot of time with Dick watching N.G.U. county matches, I would lay a sportsman's bet that Dick's putter made a significant contribution to the proceedings and that he enjoyed describing it in the clubhouse! He was a nice man.

The Club has only had seven professionals in over one hundred years as described in the Club's centenary history book[17]. Northamptonshire's Gary Boyd became the Midland Golf Union's Champion of Junior County Champions on the course in 2003, with a four under par score of 71+ 65 to take the title from Lincolnshire's Robert Harris on count back, local rule. Gary's second round equalled the amateur course record and included seven birdies. Gary received the Les Pepper trophy which was purchased with monies received from the Golf Foundation when Les was awarded the Henry Cotton award by them. The Ladies course record on this day was broken by Katrina Holford from Staffordshire with an excellent 69 gross to give her a comfortable victory in the ladies event.

Northampton Golf Club 1893 -present[1,4,25]

Norman Dawson was a prominent local Boot and Shoe manufacturer, a keen churchman, fisherman, fine golfer and a visionary. From his lofty Cliftonville home over-looking the River Nene, close to his favourite stretch of fishing water below, he saw the possibility of a golf course in the rise and fall of the fields nearby. Together with a group of influential golfing friends, he was successful in obtaining a lease of the desired field area. Gourley Dunn, a member of a Scottish family of golf architects, was summoned south to assist in planning a nine-hole layout just a mile from the town centre. A local scribe, writing at the time, stated, "The situation is well adapted to the game with hedges and a stream to cross. The ground is undulating." J.Tabor, a fellow "Scottish Professional/Groundsmen and Clubmaker" was employed to teach aspiring, local golfers from his small wooden hut, which contained unsophisticated gardening and cutting tools to maintain the course, and so, on the 1 July in 1893, golf was established in Northampton's Ancient Borough. At that time the greenkeepers equipment consisted of little more than a barrow, a spade and a shovel.

The Club initially consisted of some 45 members, male and female with local dignitary, Lord Spencer – "The Red Earl" – as President and John Haviland as the Club's first Captain 1893/4. In 1895 the entrance fee was £3 3shillings with a subscription of £2 2 shillings. One of the oldest trophies played for at the Club was presented by Norman Dawson (Captain 1895) and John Haviland. The name "Dawland" combines the names of the two donors. In earlier times it was played for under medal conditions, it was first completed for in 1896 and won by Arthur F. Forster. Up until the First World War the trophy was typically won with a score of Nett 80 which exemplified the difficulty of golfing conditions at the then nine-hole Kettering Road course and the clubs/balls available. The trophy is now presented to the winner of the eighteen-hole bogey competition played on the Saturday of the autumn meeting.

The Spencer Cup is actually one year older being first played for in 1895 and now that the Club is located near to the Althorp estate has become even more special as a trophy to be won. The Club and the whole county were numbed on the 31 August 1997 when "our" Lady Diana Spencer Princess of Wales was tragically killed in Paris. The recent concert on the 1 July 2007 at the new Wembley Stadium in her memory was conceptualised by sons William and Harry. Initially it reminded me of that horrible day ten years ago however the concert then lifted me to go forth and try to finally win this trophy which has eluded me for the last 30 years.

The Club's first Secretary, W.G. Hobbs, employed at the Capital and Counties Bank, was a reputed former Mayor of Cambridge. Several of the members were also members of the County's first golf course Kettering G.C. that was formed in 1891 and used to make the pony and trap journey to their nine-hole course laid out on land owned by the Duke of Buccleugh.

The conditions at the Club's first nine-hole course, which was close to, the current St Andrews G.C. were far from satisfactory. "The grass was rank and unyielding". The tenant farmer insisted on his grazing rights and so for much of the growing season golf was impossible. After two years, the Club again in the words of a local writer, decided to "flit". He further wrote, "An excellent site was obtained on the other side of Northampton at Kettering Road, a mile and a half from the town centre, close to houses and allotments, ideally suited to the game". Perhaps our ancestors had unconsciously been preparing the members for such a course. The soil was composed of sand and limestone and drained well. There were so many undulations in the terrain because of quarrying that the area was known locally as "The Hills and Hollows" or "Little Switzerland" – loved and sometimes reviled by countless golfers over the years to come.

The legendary "Old" Tom Morris, four times Open Champion 1861-1867, was asked to travel south to design the new nine-hole course. He had also received a similar request from the nearby Wellingborough Club and so travelled south from St Andrews to fulfil both obligations.

Along with Norman Dawson, these two worthies set out in December 1894 to lay out the nine holes on the undulating surface at Kettering Road, a course that was to be the Club's home for the following ninety-five years.

**The original Northampton Golf Club course at Kettering Road December 1894
designed by Old Tom Morris**

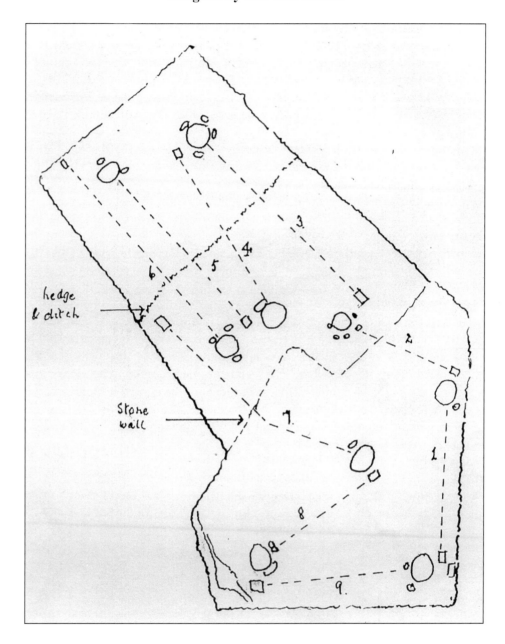

Details of holes

Hole	1	2	3	4	5	6	7	8	9
Yards	270	220	340	300	350	400	440	130	260
Par	4	4	4	4	4	4	5	3	4

Old Tom Morris and Norman Dawson's layout ran in a different direction from that enjoyed by members since the conversion to 18 holes in the 1920s. This is particularly noticeable on the first hole, which became the 18th when the old ninth green became the 18th green. In addition, it is highly likely that the green of the 440 yards par five seventh hole became the green for the 305 yards 2nd hole.

The land used by the Club had a colourful past since Danes and Saxons lay buried there after years of struggle for supremacy. The land had also been quarried for limestone but by the time the Club moved there it had become a "place of concealment by prowling rascals". On a summer's evening with a setting sun these velvety excrescences which were almost volcanic in effect gave every type of lie imaginable and provide the players with the utmost variety of shots. Uphill or hanging lies were the order of the day with entrancing greens tucked away amongst the miniature pyramids.

These lies certainly taught me the art of chipping and to how to shape the flight of the ball. As a 14 year old and now a member in a "real golf club" in 1969 there were very strange lies compared to my first experience of golf at Abington Park and what I had seen on the television.

The Club was keen to embrace the membership of the Ladies who played a significant part in its history. One lady, Mrs.G.J. Phillips, gained national fame by being selected for the English Ladies side against Scotland early in the twentieth century and won her match by 4 and 3.

One of our members who has recently become a Life Member is the timeless lady Dilys Tyrell who kindly provided the following information about the Club during that period. The information was lovingly extracted by Dilys from the Central Library in the Town from their microfilm records:-

The Mercury January 31st 1896

"H.M.B" contributes an interesting article on "Golf in Northampton" in this week's number of *"Golf"* the article being illustrated by four illustrations from negatives by Mr Henry Manfield. The writer refers at length to the characteristic features possessed by the Northampton links, and concludes "The Club numbers 85 players of whom, 25 are ladies; several of the gentlemen are also member of the Kettering Club. The entrance fee is £3 3s, and the annual subscription £2 2s. Earl Spencer, K.G. is president of the club. The clubhouse is a mean building with painted wooden roof, conveniently situated at the entrance to the ground. It contains a luncheon room, dressing-room, general smoking room, ladies club room and dressing room, and was put up by the club, but the ornamental surroundings, the handsome flag and flag-post, and the scrubs, ivy, and rose trees were presented by two members – Mr C.C. Becke and Mr. H. Manfield"

Northampton v. Wellingborough January 29th 1896

This match was played at Northampton on Thursday, resulting in a victory for the home team by 33 holes to love.

Wellingborough	Northampton	
A.E.Villar	Bruce H Muscott	10
G.Nicholson	Elliot Bull	3
H.Dulley	A.J.F.Forster	5
P.G. Dulley	R.G.Scriven	8
W.W. Robinson	A.E.Phipps	1
H.W. Miller	G.N.Stewart	0
A.Laycock	F.Hill	5
0		33

Having popped in to Wellingborough's clubhouse in July 2007 just prior to The Open Championship as part of my research for this book, I truly felt the links and friendliness of the past interactions between the two Clubs. This was amplified when their professional David Clifford asked me to deliver the balls won by Northampton members during the recent Wellingborough Cup. My three Titleist Pro V1Xs, won as a result of a two on their fourth hole were soon in my bag ready for action.

In Victorian days and for many years early in the twentieth century, golf was a game for the elite, with local dignitaries' prominent members. Northampton was no exception who's membership included: leading Boot and Shoe Manufacturers, church Dignitaries and Town Councillors enjoyed a round of golf away from their duties. The Town Clerk, Borough Transport Manager, Chief Constable and Chief Engineer were at one time members and distinguished Captains. One can readily assume that many leading questions on local affairs were discussed and perhaps resolved in the bar room at Kettering Road a room where golf stars of former years- Walter Hagen, Dai Rees, Peter Allis and Henry Cotton were entertained after exhibition matches on the "Northampton links".

In its early years the Club became well established, prosperous and with a future to look forward to. Just prior to the First World War, 107 acres of land to the north of the original nine-hole course was purchased to make it an 18-hole course on the 2 May 1915.

For those golfers and Northamptonians with a good memory, this was the land beyond the footpath behind the fourth green and from the winter tee on the sixteenth hole when looking north. Willie Park of Musselburgh, Open Champion 1875 designed the layout. Only four of the old greens were retained the 2nd, 5th, 7th and 9th. Owing to the conflict and the difficult post war years it was not until 1922 that the new nine-holes were finally joined to the Victorian layout and began its full eighteen hole history. The course then consisted of holes 1-4 and 16-18 on "The Hills and Hollows" and the remaining eleven 5-15 as parkland holes on the new land "Behind the Pioneer towards the Sunnyside area". The Club was particularly well placed where buses from the town and outlying districts converged and set the players down almost in the clubhouse. The activities of the Club at this site up to 1990 are thoroughly well described in Gil Sibley's 1993 Centenary book[4].

After many years of debate, which started in 1950 initiated by the Town Council's master plan for housing/development, the Club finally moved to its current site at Harlestone in 1990. The last round of golf was played at Kettering Road on the 5th October and the new course was officially opened when Captain David Prior drove in at 9 a.m. the following day. My lifetime eclectic of 41 (21+18) at Kettering Road was therefore preserved from the potential ravages of today's spring faced drivers and new golf balls which would have challenged my total.

Like many members, I look back with great fondness of my time at the Hills and Hollows between 1969-1990. With the new equipment reaching 480-490 yard holes such as the 5th & 6th with a driver and a nine iron would be easily achievable. This can't be right and the new equipment is destroying the true test of many classic courses. At the age of fifty two I hit the ball as far now as I did 30 years ago and I certainly don't go to the gym. Am I becoming an old fart? My son and fellow golfer A.J. Izzard assures me that I am there already!

The new course at Harlestone has matured over the last seventeen years to a good test of golf where the opening four and the last three holes are particularly challenging. Interestingly the same could have been said of the Kettering Road course although I am sure that the Golf Architect Donald Steel was unaware of this when

NORTHAMPTONSHIRE GOLF UNION.

President - A. F. PERCIVAL, Esq.

Twenty-Fourth Annual
County Championship Meeting

TO BE HELD ON THE

Northampton Golf Course, Kettering Rd., Northampton

(By kind invitation of the Committee)

On SATURDAY, MAY 5th, 1951

(Open to Members of all Clubs affiliated to the Northamptonshire Golf Union with a Handicap of 12 or less—Revised under New Standard Scratch Score).

1. NORTHAMPTONSHIRE AMATEUR CHAMPIONSHIP.

36 Holes Medal. The Scratch Cup (to be held by the Club of which the winner is a member) for the best gross score. Winner will be the County Champion for the year and will receive a memento. Second Prize.

Entrance Fee, 5/- Optional Sweepstake, 2/6.

Concurrently a separate competition will be held under handicap (restricted to 12 or less—revised under new Standard Scratch Score).

First and Second Prizes. Optional Sweepstake, 2/6.

First round must be started by 1 p.m. ; Second round must be started by 4.45 p.m. Entries, see Regulation 6 below.

2. NORTHAMPTONSHIRE PROFESSIONAL CHAMPIONSHIP.

36 Holes Medal. Cup and Prize. Concurrently a separate competition will be held under handicap as settled by the President of the County Professionals' Association. Entries to Hon. Secretary by 30th April, 1951.

3. INTER-CLUB COMPETITION.

Medal Round of 18 holes (aggregate gross scores), in the *Afternoon* Round only, of the foregoing Competition. Teams of three players, limit three teams per Club.

Entrance Fee, 10/- per team.

REGULATIONS.

1. All Competitors will play on their lowest corresponding County Handicaps for the handicap competition.
2. A Committee appointed by the Union and the Northampton Golf Club will supervise the arrangements on the day of the Meeting.
3. All cards will be issued by this Committee only, and when returned must be placed in the box provided.
4. All points shall be settled by the Committee whose ruling shall be final.
5. Entries for Inter-Club Competition must reach the Hon. Secretary, "Whitelands," 108, Ridge Way, Northampton, not later than Saturday, April 28th, 1951.
6. **Entries must be made on forms, obtainable from each Club or the Hon. Secretary, which must be received by the Committee at the Northampton Golf Club by Noon on Monday, 30th April, 1951.** A starting sheet will be in operation. Partners will be arranged by the Committee. Competitors will be advised of the starting time allotted, and of their partner. They must be ready to play at the time allotted.

So far as supplies permit Luncheons and Teas will be provided at the Club House.

108, Ridge Way, Northampton.

W. H. ABBOTT, Hon. Secretary.

24th N.G.U. County Championship held at Kettering Road 1951

Northampton G.C. view from the right side of the 15th hole

Above: Inside Northampton's old Clubhouse at Kettering Road.

Left: Annual Trophies Night in the 1980s at Kettering Road

he designed "Harlestone". The new course maintains it links with the old course's "Hills and Hollows" as similar land exists in the village of Harlestone.

This disturbed ground in the north of the village bears witness to the tradition of quarrying which must have began in the days before Duke William of Normandy's followers founded the great castle of Northampton in the 12th Century [18]. Northampton Castle was used as a seat of parliament until 1380 and was demolished in 1662 by order of Charles II because the town supported the parliamentarians during the Civil War. Most of the remaining stonework was later carried away by Victorians for building work in the town. The site became a railway station (Castle Station) in 1859 and continues to be a major link to the capital.

The Northampton Golf Club line-up in 1970. Left to right: Alf Lovelady (Professional), L.G. Hasdell (Secretary), W. Hollingsworth (President), Mrs J. R. Tong (Lady Captain), G. B. Pyke (Captain), R. L. Clarke (Competition Secretary).

Aerial view of the Northampton's course at Harlestone

The view from the clubhouse veranda across Harlestone Lake is probably one of the best in the country especially on a warm summer evening with the velvety evening light from a setting sun. The lake often holds good wildlife such as Herons, breeding Mute Swan, Tufted duck, the occasional darting Kingfisher and also one of the county's rarest mammals the high flying Daubenton's bat. It is also home to several species of damsel and dragon flies.

There have been two very unusual episodes on the 611 yard par five 12th hole. The first was an Albatross two by Northampton junior member Jamie Lloyd on the 14/06/1993 using two drivers when the hole measured 590 yards during regular play and was witnessed by his playing partners Robert Page and Robert Harris.

Junior member Robert Harris had become a low handicap member and was set to become a valued long term member of both the Scratch League/Hollingsworth team, Robert had been picked to represent the Club for his first Hollingsworth appearance at Oundle G.C. Sadly Robert was taken from us by the deadly strain of meningitis on Masters weekend the 12 April 1993 age 16. Future Club Captain in 2007, father Martin somehow found the strength to be present at Oundle a few weeks later where Robert would have hit his first representative shot for the Club. That day we played for the Harris family Martin, Sue, Philippa and their late son Robert, the team won the match 4-1. I cried on the way home, emotionally it was too much for me.

Jamie Lloyd's Albatross on the 12th is one of the longest recorded in the history of golf, currently 5th. Jamie Lloyd was also the first player to record a hole in one at Harlestone, interestingly he achieved this aged 13 on the 13th hole on the 13th of December 1990, lucky for him, though not for his father Trevor who had to purchase the traditional round of drinks for a packed clubhouse.

The second memorable happening on this hole was by the very powerful player Lee Corfield, from Burnham & Berrow G.C., who put the ball on to the green with a drive and a wedge! (Unbelievable but true). This occurred during a practice round for the Midland Open Amateur Championship on the 28/06/2001 with the new Titleist Pro V1 ball and a Callaway ERC II Trampoline-faced driver. He jokingly admitted that he actually scored five by trying to make an eagle. He is still "putting for dough" and made an impact on the regional and national golf scene he (nickname Box in view of his stature) was an English International and runner up in the The Amateur Championship 2004 prior to turning professional in 2005. The Amateur Championship returned home to St Andrews as part of the events, which commemorated the 250th anniversary of the R&A in 2004.

At Harlestone, John (J.A.) Smith became the first member to ace all four short holes from 1999-2007 as described below.

1999 5th hole 128 yards, nine iron.

2002 16th hole, 131 yards, eight iron, one bounce and into the hole

2005 13th hole 152 yards, seven iron, thinned a complete fluke. John was playing with Club character " FFing Frank Bustin" who commented "Well done".

2007 2nd hole, 164 yards five iron.

During this rich vein of form John played the course 1092 times, his average is therefore an impressive 4 from 4368, not that he is counting!

The course at Harlestone has recently adopted a strongly recommended soft spike rule for the summer months along with one or two other clubs in the Union in order to improve the quality of the putting surface. There is much debate around the Club's bar area about whether or not this will work; only father time and the weather know the answer. Continuing the fun hole in one scenario, Merve Hughes a relatively long standing member, in 2002 had a "drive in one" when his tee shot from the 11th tee found the bottom of the hole on the nearby 7th green, Merve's round ?

Long serving administrator Thomas Charles Austin (T.C.A.) Knight who had been Club and County Secretary for many years was elected the Club's fifth President in 1991 and has guided the Club as it has moved and developed.

The Club has produced 15 N.G.U. County Champions, many N.G.U. officials and the occasional English International such as Conrad Ceislewicz who was selected for England Boys vs Scotland in 1970 age seventeen; he won his foursomes match and was victorious in the singles by 2/1. Richard Aitken recorded four of his County Championship victories whilst a member of the Club between 1962-1964 &1968, the Club then had to wait a further 30 years for a further victory. This was achieved by Glenn Keates over the Harlestone course in 1998 with scores of 74, 70=144 during the afternoon round Glenn joined the Club's so called "15Club". His afternoon round started 4, 2, 4, 3, 2 to join a small band of players who have scored 15 or less over the first five holes. Glenn also became County Champion five years later in 2003 at Wellingborough with a solid performance 71, 75=146, in the Match Play Championship Glenn was victorious in 2000.

The Hollingsworth Trophy which has become one of the premier trophies was donated by Past Club and County President Bill Hollingsworth (see section later in this chapter) who incidentally was the N.G.U. Higgs Bowl winner in 1948. The trophy has "come home" on eight occasions between 1964-2003.

In the Scratch League the Club's men have spent most of their time in Divisions 1 & 2 with a single success in Division 1 under the Team Captaincy of Jon Lloyd in 2002 and four Division 2 titles between 1980 and 2000.In 2005 the team were demoted to Division 3, the first time in the Club's history due to poor commitment from some of the players, but bounced back to Division 2 in 2006. The scenario almost sounds like Dave Bowen's Cobblers football team! The ladies have achieved much success in the Cecil Leitch trophy with twelve victories, the latest coming in 2002. In 2007, they reached the semi-finals at Rushden G.C. narrowly losing out to Collingtree Park G.C.

176

In recent times, Sarah Carter and Kelly Hanwell have dominated the ladies Club Championship with three and four victories each between 1994 -2004. In 2006, Ladies County Champion Kelly Hanwell joined the England Golf development team, which encourages adults and juniors to start and stay in golf. Kelly is one of six EGU / ELGA regional development officers and she works with the counties of Bedfordshire, Cambridgeshire, Leicestershire & Rutland, Norfolk, Northamptonshire, Nottinghamshire and Suffolk.

In 2007 a new course record was established on the recently established "green" course by bar stalwart Bobby Bason who was incidentally (we are not allowed to forget it!) the last trophy winner at "Kettering Road" in 1990. The 71 year old, 5 foot 2 inch giant stormed round the 5178 yards course in 96 shots. The record score card commemorating this "feat" hangs in the spike bar next to "Bobby's seat" where if you have the odd half an hour, he will talk you through the two nines of 49&47!

Long serving members include Tony Stevens Past President of the N.G.U., the current President Tom (T.C.A.) Knight a Past Secretary of the N.G.U. The Late Past President John Arthur Eyton- Jones was a member for sixty years and witnessed golf as a junior member through to Club President in 1991. Peggy Durant a Past Lady Captain (Captain 1972) became the Club's first Lady Life Member in 2005, Peggy was followed by Dylis Tyrell who was also unanimously and emotionally voted in as the second lady Life Member at the 2007 A.G.M. These two ladies have over 110 years of membership between them, their contributions to the Club is immeasurable and greatly appreciated.

3rd Hole White Tee 523 Yards Par 5 Wood Way.

This is the first of Northampton's signature holes. The tee shot needs to be directed towards the right side of the sloping fairway will end in the centre of the fairway, anything down the centre or left will tend to run off into the semi-rough on the left-hand side. A blocked tee shot brings the small pond into play on the right-hand side of the fairway. The second shot for the majority of players is laid up short of a water hazard, which crosses the fairway 40 yards from the green. The shot, being played through an avenue of trees, with water hazards and rough on both sides. The longer hitter has the choice of laying up or flying this hazard to reach the green. The third shot if required is a relatively easy pitch. The large green slopes back to front and the sound of woodpeckers drumming, often acts as a sonic backdrop to putting especially in the spring. I know of only one albatross on the hole, this was scored by Club member Scott Bailey in fog on a temporary green and found by

The par 5 third hole at Northampton G.C.

177

the author. Those players present in the bar that morning counted it as "half an albatross". Despite its relatively high stroke index, it is one of the most difficult holes on medal days.

16th Hole White Tee 166 yards, Par 3 Waters Leap.

This hole demands an accurate tee shot to a narrow green over water. I have selected this hole just ahead of the 16th at Northants County and Wellingborough due to the wind factor affecting the difficulty of the shot to the green. The current "crazy" W shaped green at Northants County G.C. was taken into consideration and ignored in view of its lack of reward for a good shot. The 16th at Wellingborough was rejected in view of the large tree in the middle of the fairway which causes problems on the tee shot for high handicappers. The 16th at Harlestone has overtones of the 12th hole at The Masters Augusta since the fate of the ball is unknown until it has pitched on the green. The wind whips around both holes; the tee shots at the Masters are affected by the wind funnelling down and through Amen Corner, tee shots at Harlestone's signature hole is affected by westerly winds blowing down the local valley and across Harlestone Lake. Although only 166 yards when played into a wind low handicappers typically hit clubs such as a 3 iron, down wind it can be as little as a 7 iron.

In 2003 during a match involving the author and three low handicappers all four players recorded birdie twos, after the excited players had settle down there was a long debate as to the total number of 25 pence "bits" recorded. My "ready reckoner" calculates it to be 9, Dean Roberts make's it 5, Andy Carter has no idea!

The 16th hole at Northampton and views across Harlestone Lake after winter snow falls

Northamptonshire County 1909-present

To give a flavour in a few pages of what many consider to be the County's premier club is an almost impossible task. The Club has been involved in both play and administrative activities since its inception. I look forward to reading their centenary book in 2009 which is being collated by President Bruce Clayton; this will extend Neil Soutar's book[5] which was published in 1995. It could be argued that in this chapter I have not devoted enough attention to N.C.G.C., this is delibertae on my part, in order not, to impact upon their Centenary compilation.

The construction of the original course started in April 1909 and the course opened for play the following year. The distinguished golf course architect Harry S Colt laid out the original 18 holes. Harry Sharpland Colt became the first secretary at Sunningdale and designed the New Course there also the East and West Courses at Wentworth, Swinley Forest, St. Georges Hill, the Eden Course at St. Andrews and 115 others around the world. For further information on these courses visit the Colt Association website. The layout at Northants County has stood the test of time very well as relatively few major alterations have been instigated, the most notable of which were carried out by James Braid, in 1947, when the pattern and arrangement of many bunkers were altered and the 18th green was relocated to its present position in front of the clubhouse.

The route to complete 18 holes has been tweaked a few times notably to the displeasure of Charles Catlow[5 p130], in the bar there is still some considerable debate as to which way to go from the third green down the eighth (the

Aerial view of Northants County, the clubhouse, practise grounds, 1st, 9a & 18th holes.

original 3rd) or as at present, down the fourth (the original 13th). Charles Catlow was a legend in the County and his record of 11 County Championship victories is unlikely to ever be beaten. It is interesting to note that one of these victories was achieved with the aid of a bicycle to protect an injured leg[7]. I wonder if this would not be permitted these days; however I can find no rule/decision in the books which actually prevents him using a bike. After all is this very different from using a Power Caddy?

A further 3 splendid holes (7a, 8a, 9a) designed by course architect and Past Captain Cameron Sinclair, were opened in May 2004. These now provide a 9 hole loop returning to the clubhouse, for those wishing to play 9 or 27 holes. During the autumn in particular the course shows off its beauty as a traditional inland golf course with undulating woodland, gorse, heather and fine pine woods. The course is partly bisected by the national railway line to Rugby and the current 10th-14th holes are located in the "field" to the south west of the line. The sound of the train is therefore a characteristic feature of the course and the golfer sometimes has the dilemma of do I play the shot before or after the train passes.

With a course of this maturity each hole has trees and a hazard on both sides of the fairway and accuracy off the tee is a must. This can be clearly seen on the internet from satellite systems such as Google Earth where it is also possible to see the front of the clubhouse, members cars parked in the car park and in the future in to the veranda and bar!

Following a major review in 2005 by Cameron Sinclair and the committee, the course was extended to 6750 yards off the back tees to ensure that the round is still challenging with today's equipment. This included some new and reshaped bunkers and a major change to the entrance to the 6th hole.

The late Sidney Drown and Richard Aitken are thought to be the only members to have holed in one on all four short holes during their golfing careers. It is of interest to note that coincidently both players' homes were in Weston Favell Northampton on streets that run parallel to each other; their houses were a pitching wedge distance apart. Other notable records include Jim Smith's Albatrosses and it is believed he is the only player to have recorded albatrosses on the two par fives. This was achieved in successive summers in the late 1990's the first was recorded at the 2nd hole with a drive and a six iron, the second on the 18th hole with a driver and five wood. On both occasions this generated great debate amongst the Dawn Patrol "Committee" concerning the number of "bits" to be paid. In typical miserly fashion the intelligentsia agreed on six bits two for each shot under par, Jim's claim for 16 was rejected!

In 1985, the Club celebrated its 75th anniversary and a number of events were organised to mark the occasion. These included a professional exhibition match, and an anniversary dinner. Shropshire's Sandy Lyle was due to play in the exhibition match but having won The Open Championship at Royal St Georges, had other commitments. The exhibition match was preceded by a golf clinic by Tommy Horton. In the exhibition match Club professional, Stuart Murray returned the best score of 71, followed by Stuart Brown, with 72, Bernard Gallagher 75 and Tommy Horton, 76. The dinner dance was attended by 150 members and guests in a marquee close to the 18th green. Also during the year, the English Ladies Stroke-Play Championship was held at the Club in August and won by Miss Patricia Johnson, who went on to become a leading professional on the ladies world golf tours. Fittingly, the Club also won the Hollingsworth Trophy that year for the first time since 1972.

Rumour has it in 1986 when the highly talented and former European Tour rookie of the year professional the late Stuart Brown played the front nine holes for the first time he birdied them all. In recent years Northamptonshire County Golf Club has been the venue for many National amateur golfing competitions including the English Schools National Championships (1997), English Golf Union Carris Trophy (1994) and the British Girls Open Tournament (1992). In 1994 the Club members were proud to see junior member Robert Duck collect the Carris Trophy (see chapter 11) for the detail. In addition, for six years from 1997 until 2002, the course was the home of the Regional Qualifying for The Open Championship. The final of the E.G.U. Club Team Championship was played over the Brampton course in 2002 and in 2004 the E.L.G.A. Closed Championship was held there.

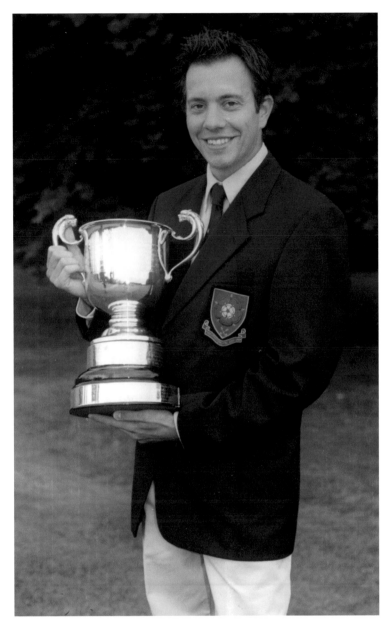

A Champion's smile from Nick Soto, N.G.U. County Champion in 2001.

In the Millennium year the N.G.U. County Championship was held there and won by home player Adam Print. At the presentation, Club and county stalwarts Richard G. Aitken and Richard G. Halliday were presented with a bottle of champagne each.

In 2005 long serving Club and county stalwart Tony Lord became Club champion for a third time and reduced his handicap for the first time to plus 1. Also in 2005 two lady pairs represented the Club at national level. Sarah Carter and Kirsty Jennings having won the Deterding Cups the previous year reached the national finals of the Daily Mail Foursomes Competition narrowly losing one down to Cowdray Park. Gillian Curley and Annie Haig qualified for the L.G.U. Peugeot Coronation Foursomes which attracted over 30,000 entries. Having won the regional final at Wellingborough with a score of 43 pts they won a dream trip to the home of golf, St Andrews. Their 27 pts scored in atrocious conditions saw them finish in 7th place behind the winners from Stoke Rochford. Also in 2005 fourteen year old Adam Myers won the English Boys Under 16 Stroke play championship (McGregor Trophy) at Ratcliffe-on-Trent G.C. with a total of 286 for the four rounds.

In April 2006 N.G.U. referee chirpy Jeff Jacobs ran the London Marathon. Runner number 47241, Jeff managed to get round in a creditable time 4 hours and 1 minute and 21 seconds and finished in 12,132th place raising approximately £2,000 for his charity VICTA, Visually Impaired Children Taking Action. He tells me that he is even faster going round the golf course! In June the course hosted the Midland Golf Union's E.G.U. qualifier where Warwickshire became the county to represent the Midland Region at the Nation Finals at Princes in Kent. Anthony Lord was elected Northamptonshire's first ever Captain of the Midlands for the period 2006-2008 succeeding Warwickshire's Peter Holt. Also in 2006 the club were awarded the Junior GolfMark Award by the England Golf Partnership in recognition of their hard work and dedication to junior golf. This award developed by the E.G.U. and E.L.G.A. identifies and acknowledges junior friendly facilities in England. The clubs are evaluated on coaching and playing, club environment, child protection and duty of care.

The end of the season "curtain closer", the Hollingsworth Trophy is often held on the course in October and

Two members of the Duck Dynasty, Mike and Tom, County Foursomes winners over their home course Northants County in 1997.

the combination of stiff competition, jangling nerves and the autumn colours make for a wonderful Sunday's entertainment. I have personally enjoyed the feelings of both winning and losing this magnificent trophy at "Brampton". One special day in 1996 as President of the N.G.U. I was fortunate to play as a member of the winning team (Northampton G.C.) and had the pleasure of presenting the trophy together with Mary Bird (Bill Hollingsworth's daughter) to Northampton's team captain Gary (G.P.A.) Addington.

For many years, the N.G.U. annual dinner was held at the Club in March until the event became very popular and a new venue was required. This was achieved by Malcolm Evans, President of Priors Hall G.C. the N.G.U. Dinner Secretary who single handidly promoted this event, which resulted in a move to Kettering G.C. when their clubhouse was extended in 2000. A typical number for this dinner is 110. Malcolm has been a member of several clubs including Priors Hall, Burghley Park and has recently become a member at Northants County. Malcolm has severed on the N.G.U. Executive Committee for over ten years now and rightly so should become President at a suitable time in his life.

69-year-old Richard Aitken currently holds the lifetime eclectic for the course with a score of 39.

Richard Aitken's Eclectic Card at Northants County 1969-2007

Hole	Par	Score	Hole	Par	Score
1	4	3	10	4	3
2	5	3	11	4	3
3	3	1	12	3	1
4	4	2	13	4	3
5	4	2	14	4	2
6	3	1	15	3	1
7	4	2	16	4	3
8	4	2	17	4	2
9	4	3	18	5	2
Total	35	19		35	20

One albatross, 11 eagles and 6 birdies =39 strokes (31 under par). This is one element of Richard's extensive golf achievements, which also includes four trophies at Northampton G.C., 21 trophies with the N.G.U. and 41 Trophies at Northants County.

In 2007 the Club hosted together with Northampton G.C. the prestigious Midland Golf Union Open Amateur

Championship which is a 72 hole event with the final 36 holes being played at "Brampton". The winner, plus 2 handicapper George Wollgar from Chesterfield G.C. holed his second shot at the 1st in the afternoon on his way to a fine gross 67 and a winning total of 274, 8 under par. Also in 2007, the P.G.A. Senior Club Professional Championship was held there in early May and won by Donald Stirling professional at Wien-Sussenbrunn in Austria by five clear shots.

The Club have enjoyed a long associated with the N.G.U. and N.C.L.G.A. and have produced scores of county players, men and ladies County Champions and officials. Centenary celebrations are planned for 2009, which will include a week of celebrations during August. In addition the membership of 850 will be invited to many other celebration events throughout 2009.

1st Hole White 454 Yards, Par 4.

I have selected this as my most demanding starting hole slightly ahead of Peterborough Milton and Daventry club's opening holes. From the quiet sanctuary of the back tee one aims the tee shot at the Express Lift's tower (Northampton's somewhat ugly "Lighthouse"). The large bunker on the right hand side of the fairway is there to catch the wafted tee shot. The fairway bunker which crosses the hole does not come in to modern play and a new set of bunkers has recently been added. The green is subtly bunkered and slopes left to right and slightly downhill from the approaching second shot. A par on this hole feels like a birdie and will often win the hole in match play. The occasional eagle

Above top: Northants County Captain Chris Thompson receives the Scratch League Division 1 Trophy from Dave Croxton in 1999.

Opposite: N.G.U. County stalwarts Richard Aitken (left) and Richard Halliday receiving a bottle of Champagne each from President Terry Haley at the Millennium County Championship held at Northants County G.C.

has been recorded notable by Bedford-shire's eighteen stone "Honey Monster" Angus King in the 1988 County Cup who just for good measure also eagled the 2nd hole. An amazing start from a local gentle giant.

The hole has witnessed many sudden death situations especially during the Hollingsworth Trophy and Open Qualifying competitions where the pressure of being watched by up to a hundred spectators can affect the smoothness of the swing. Some became heros, some wilted away, such is our game. The recent changes to the bunkering have made the hole even more challenging.

Right: Northants County Captain Richard Halliday receives a commemorative plaque from E.G.U. President Bill Bryce after hosting the Champion Club event in 2002.

Below: The green at the 1st Hole at Northants County G.C.

The 7th green at Northants County G.C.

7th Hole Northants County White Tee 402 Yards Par 4

The recently extended tee on the edge of the reservoir gives the hole the feeling of almost shooting down a funnel and the shot has to be accurately placed to avoid bunkers left and right. The second shot, frequently comes up short of the pin on the steeply sloping green, shots finishing above the hole are extremely difficult and frequently require three putts. The green actually slopes away from the player and to the right and the only "easy" putt is straight up the hill.

11th Hole White 443 yards par 4.

This hole typifies golf at Northants County. A hole close to the railway with all the elements of the great course. Although relatively short as a par four from the yellow tee, it requires the player to be on his game. The tee shot has to be straight and positioned between jungle on the right and a copse to the left of the twelfth green, the second shot with between a 5-9 iron is directed towards a sloping green with out of bounds to the right and behind. When the green is fast do not place your ball above the hole as the putt will be rapid. This end of the course is more remote and has a lot of wildlife such as Siskin, Fox, Buzzard, Sparrowhawk, Green Woodpecker and Badger. In 2008 a new "tiger" tee has been added further extending the hole which has restored the hole's former degree of difficulty.

The 11th green at Northants County G.C. plus train!

Oundle 1893-present

The original 1893 layout was a nine-hole course with a par of 32 and the current extended 18 hole course is still on its original old stone quarry site of Bailey Hills on Benefield Road half a mile west of the beautiful stone town. The site originally was used as a picnic site for the townsfolk. The quarrying past is most noticeable around the current 18th green where the mounds around the green dictate the need for an accurate approach shot to this 376 yards hole.

P. (Phil) G.Cotton Secretary during the Second World War years was made a life member in 1950 in view of his sterling service under great difficulties and elected President of the N.G.U. in 1961, the Club's only President to date.

A description of the Club between 1962-1987 was lovingly compiled by Major Guy Richardson[19]. Notable highlights during this period reproduced here included-

1960-1965, this period witnessed the awakening of the Club and the start of many developments, which included water to the greens, improvements in the clubhouse such as washing and toilet facilities, using funds raised by the members who paid for these changes. At the time the 9 hole 51 acre course was rented on an annual tenancy from the landlord Major David Watts-Russell cost £128 per annum less £25 per annum for grazing rights below the old 6th green. The greens were protected from the grazing cattle by barbed wire fences which sometimes caused the members discomfort when trousers, skirts etc were caught by the barbs when stepping over them. This course was looked after by one man George Pyewell and the layout lasted until 1967. At this time, the total wage bill was £10 a week!

The 18th Green and Clubhouse at Oundle G.C. 2008

There were 150 members and in 1963, Norman Kitchen was elected President. Food for match meals often consisted of a tasty pork pie bought from Saxby's of Wellingborough and it is believed that John Saxby provided the Saxby Cup which is played for annually in view of the Club's bulk purchase of the family's pies. The local beer (Smith's North Street Oundle) cost 1/2d a pint and whilst having a short shelf life was good and flavoursome. Keg beer arrived at this time locally in the shape of Watney's Red barrel although the Club opted for its closest rival, Flowers Bitter from Luton. The Club Championship for the Watts Russell Cup was played as a 27 hole event which took about $5^1/_2$ hours to complete the 9 holes three times. Dinner dances were held in the town at the Talbot Hotel. At the end of 1964 entrance fees were introduced cost £2.2.0d per head.

1965-1975, during this period the course was extended twice, initially to 13 holes which was completed in 1967 and secondly to 18 holes completed in 1971. The cost of conversion to 13 holes was £430. The most significant event was in 1967 when the original 9 holes covering 51 acres were purchased from the landlord at a cost of £10,100. The membership had grown to 317 in 1972. Also during this period a new Clubhouse was constructed and opened on the 12th September 1974, this was coincident with the connection of mains water and electricity. The opening ceremony was followed by a buffet lunch and a 10 hole one club challenge played as a fivesome medal. Twenty seven teams played, each team consisted of three men, a lady and a beginner. Each team member carried a wooden club, a low or medium or short iron and a putter. After the opening shot which could be played with any club the rest of the shots had to be played in strict rotation. The event was a big success. Interclub matches were popular and meal costs were 50p per head. In 1973 Club member P.Coffey won the N.G.U. Stableford Cup at Kettering G.C.

1976-1980, this was a period in the Country of very high inflation, which affected us all, and at Oundle the Club Rules had to be changed to allow above inflation increases to occur in order to meet the ever-rising costs. This resulted in a few years when the annual subscription was increased by ca 50%! In 1977, there was a waiting list of 150 and the N.G.U. Family Foursomes was played at the Club and won by Mr & Mrs George Mobbs from Northants County.

In 1980, wide wheeled trolleys became fashionable, Dutch Elm disease from the previous year had generated much firewood and the cost of match meal rose to £2. In late June 1980, 73 years old former three times Open Champion Henry Cotton visited the Club and as one of his trademarks instructed many members in the use of a spare tyre to strengthen the wrists and help the strike of the ball. The visit was arranged by Phil Cotton; Henry scored 72, two over par and was entertained to dinner by the committee at the Falcon Fotheringhay. Henry's post dinner speech entertained the whole house. 1981 was a vintage year when Martin Herson was runner up in the under 14 gross section at the N.G.U. Boys Championship and Club Champion, the Club gained promotion to Scratch League Division 1.

In 1982, the Clubhouse was extended by building a second storey costing £49,757. 80 and the extension was opened in November by Major Watts-Russell. In 1984 Eddy MacGuiness was made a Vice President in recognition of his many years of service particularly as Greens Chairman. In 1985 Bill Sloan became N.G.U. Seniors Champion and the Club were narrowly beaten in the final of the Hollingsworth Trophy 3-2 at nearby Peterborough Milton G.C. Club Captain Ron Cuthbert almost motivated the team to their greatest ever success. In 1993 during the Club's centenary year, a three cornered Stableford match was played over three courses against the other two county courses who were also celebrating their centenary year Northampton and Wellingborough on the 15th May 1993. The match at Wellingborough G.C. included a hole in one at the eleventh hole by the author which helped Northampton's cause, since they won the event by just 3 Stableford points. Selfishly I suggest that my hole in one won the event for my home club Northampton G.C. I "only" bought one round of drinks (absolutely my pleasure) at Wellingborough G.C. despite beer begging phone calls from the other two clubhouses prior to sitting down for the tri-cornered centenary dinners. A hole in one in a tri-club centenary match was unique.

In 1996 the N.G.U. Family Foursomes was held at the course when the donor N.G.U. Past President H. W. Colton, Esq. made a special effort, driving over from Rushden to present the pair of trophies on their fortieth anniversary to the winning pair from Delapre G.C. In fact, the Club have often given up the course up for this event and also the Boys Championship, kindly helping to spread the load across the County's Clubs for these N.G.U. events.

Four new holes, all par fours were added in 1995 on agricultural land to the right of the old fourth green with views from e.g. the 6th hole stroke index 1, 473 yards looking towards the spire in the town and Barnwell to the right. This gave the course a better balance. Internal out of bounds on some of these new holes (not one of my favourite features on any course) adds to the degree of difficulty and a pond, one of my favourite features attracts passing wildlife such as ducks, moorhen, coot and the occasional wading bird. Continuing the wildlife theme which is quite a feature of this area, it is one of few courses where a beautiful raptor the Red Kite can regularly be seen as they breed in the surrounding woodlands of the once extensive Rockingham Forest. Past Club Secretary Gordon Brooks became N.G.U. County Secretary in 2001 and served until 2004 when Dave Foly took over the Club position until 2007.

In 2005 the clubhouse was refurbished, N.G.U. President Mike Taylor was kindly asked to open the new building at the opening ceremony. The new building contains the upstairs Cotton Room restaurant, the name of which is derived as follows. The story links, both club members and The Open Champion Henry Cotton (1934, 37, 48). Members Phil & Esme Cotton both made a major contribution to Club affairs before during and after the Second World War. Phil became County President and his wife was Lady Captain 4/5 times. They owned a shoe shop in the town "Cottons". Although not related to the great champion they first met each other at his home/golf club, whilst on holiday in Penina Portugal.

The County Championship, Northamptonshire men's blue riband event was held there in 2007. Once again as in previous years I had the task of deciding the pin positions for the Championship, a demanding job considering today's golf technology and a relatively short course. The Championship was won by young Ryan Evans with a score of 70+68=138; Ryan also collected the Braid's Driver. Despite the showery day all the players made nice comments on the condition of the course and N.G.U. President Les Cantrell thanked the Club whole heartedly in view of their commitment to make it a success. Les described it as retiring Secretary Dave Foley's swansong. In September, each year the "Oundle Putter" an open better ball competition is held which frequently attracts a good field from surrounding clubs.

Success at men's county level has been largely achieved by the club's seniors. In 1976, Frank Overson was victorious, followed in 1981 by G. E. Collison, Frank Overson again in 1983, W.(Bill) Sloan in 1985 and more recently, John J.V. Smith in 1999, all victories coming in the 18 hole N.G.U. Seniors Trophy. In team events the Club have reached the Hollingsworth Final twice in 1957 and 1985. In 2004, the men's team won Scratch League Division 4. The ladies team won the Cecil Leitch trophy for the first time in the Club's history in 1996 and retained it the following year.

Overstone Park Hotel, Golf & Leisure Resort 1994-present

Aerial view of Overstone Park G.C.

This 6478 yards par 72 course is situated on the far eastern edge of the town on land, very close to Overstone Scout Activity Centre. Some Northamptonian Scouts of my generation may remember this area fondly from days in the past. I used to spend time there as a cub scout in the 1960s and specifically remember the swimming pool which had a temperature close to freezing, it was very unlike the warm one in the Leisure Centre at the Club now, which does not have leaves, twigs and the odd dead bird floating in it.

Set amongst 165 acres of Victorian parkland it was designed by Donald Steel and established during the 1990s golfing boom in 1994. The Clubhouse was officially opened on the 5th November by Sharon Davies MBE. The location was also considered by Northampton G.C. during their deliberations on moving from Kettering Road prior to their move to Harlestone. The course is set amongst mature trees and enjoys good views over lakes, nearby countryside and the impressive Overstone House.

Overstone House originally Overstone Hall was acquired in 1832 by Lewis Lloyd for a small sum of £117,000, a grade 2 listed building had 119 rooms, set in 40 acres of grounds, with three lakes, an old carriage block, walled gardens and farm buildings. The house was designed in 1860 for Lord and Lady Overstone by William Milford Teulon to reflect their status and took six years to complete. Sadly, Lady Overstone passed away in 1864, and didn't see her project completed. The exterior walls are stone from quarries in the north of the county and the golfing connections are maintained since the original oak timbers came from the Forest of Arden. In 1929, it was converted to the Overstone School for Girls, which existed for 50 years until July 1979.

The school occupied the main house, carriage block, stable and farm buildings but because of the financial demands required to maintain a crumbling Victorian estate, the House together with 70 acres of land was eventually transferred after being initially sold to property speculators to the New Testament Church of God in1980. On the 16th of April 2001 a fire started in one the upper rooms, possibly the dormitory; best known to the girls as "gallery" and a major proportion of the building was gutted as the fire raged for 12 hours. Some 40 fire engines attended the blaze. Sadly most of the best-loved features, including the extraordinary wooden staircase, the library and parquet flooring were destroyed, the one third of the house that survived is still used as the National Centre for that organisation.

Ex-pupils of the school keep in touch through the Overstone Association (225 members), their eldest lady joined the school in 1931.At a recent reunion held at the Aviator Hotel, Sywell 37 ladies gathered to share memories over lunch. A recent estimate for restoration of the House to its former glory was £35million, so there is little chance of it ever becoming a new palatial clubhouse! The current views of the boarded up building are rather sad considering how elegant it must have been.

The course has some challenging holes, one of which the devilish fourth hole Blackthorn Lake, 128 yards I include in my top 18. The short and tricky par four, fifth hole Watermark, 268 yards has twice seen hole-in-one albatrosses. The first by former Club professional Brian Mudge during a Captain-Pro challenge in 1995 with a driver. The base of the pin is not actually visible from the tee and Brian was first alerted to this wonderful achievement by the Late Sydney Cruickshank who was sat at the back of the green doing some marshalling and did a little jig in celebration. The second was by a Lincolnshire County player, Steve Dixon during an Anglian League match with a five wood.

Perhaps the most difficult hole is the long 177 yards par 3 seventeenth Brae Head, which has seen much drama, notably during the Hollingsworth Trophy. It is known as the Club's signature hole. The demanding tee shot has to carry a lake to a narrow sloping green and a par there often wins the hole. To add to the degree of difficulty wind often sweeps across the hole either from the lake on the right or from the direction of the clubhouse
There are 114 Scandinavian style wooden lodges on the complex. They have a variety of locations such as lakeside, golf course and woodland. Owners benefit with free membership of the health club and golf course. The leisure club has the latest state-of-the-art equipment for fitness, diet and healthy living, together with a 17 metre pool, maintained at a nice warm temperature of 30C. The second floor bar and Terrace Restaurant look out over the1st and 10th tees and the par 5 18th hole with its heavily bunkered green.

Left: Overstone Park's demanding 4th hole.

*Below:
Overstone Park G.C.*

On the county scene N.G.U., victories to date are James Ward, Boys Champion in 2001, and E.Chapman Singles Match play Champion 2004. On the team front they have climbed from division four in 2000 up to division one in 2005, a fine achievement. In 2007, James Barker became Northamptonshire's E.G.U. Gold Medal at the Izzard Club Team Trophy and will represent the county at the national finals over the Hotchkin course to be held at Woodhall Spa in 2008.

Amateur Club Champion Richard Dalton (son of N.G.U. Past President Jim Dalton) & Northants County professional Tim Rouse jointly hold the course record of 67. Richard is a very good sportsman and was a fine local cricketer before taking up the challenge of golf, clearly ball size or colour does not matter to him. Perhaps we should have a Titleist golf ball with a seam on it to make the game more difficult!

4th Hole White Tee, 128 Yards, Blackthorn Lake

Although only a short hole, requiring no more than a 9 iron the hole is a little gem. Set at the bottom of a small valley, the tee shot over water to a small, sloping green requires much precision since the wind often seems to swirl around this area. The lateral water hazard continues on to the left of the green and catches many tee shots. When we have held N.G.U. events here are rules official is specifically allocated to this hole to answer the question "Where do I drop" In a county match there a few years ago despite the quality of the players a half in five occurred during the morning foursomes matches. There is a well established hedge to the right of the green just beyond the out of bounds margin. In 2007 during the N.G.U. Open, Oliver Nightingale from Silverstone G.C. recorded a hole in one, "this sounds like an expensive round of drinks to me".

The only other hole I seriously considered as my fourth was Peterborough Milton's Rabbits Corner, which was placed a close second.

Peterborough Gordon/Walton 1894-1937

The Club was formed on the 13 Oct 1894. In 1895 the entrance fee was 10 shillings and 6 pence and an annual subscription of £1 1shilling and had a membership of 112. Matches were played against Wellingborough G.C. as early as 1897. The 9-hole course was situated at Orton, 2½ miles from Peterborough and the clubhouse was "The Gordon Arms". The ground was clay soil such that summer play was impossible due to luxuriant grass, the greens were fair and many natural hazards were present on the course, which was 2 miles round. In 1906 the membership was around 100. The course was adjacent to Walton Station and in 1921 the name changed to Walton. The Club closed in 1937 and amalgamated with Milton Hall.

Peterborough Milton Hall 1928?-1937

The 6th Earl Fitzwilliam had a 9-hole course built in the late 1920s quite literally in his back garden at Milton Hall, Milton Ferry Peterborough. In the 1930s he approached Peterborough Gordon/ Walton with a view to amalgamation and a move to Milton. The amalgamation resulted in the current Peterborough Milton site, which was designed by James Braid and opened in 1937/8.

Peterborough Milton 1938-present

This is one of the premier Clubs in the county formed originally by the amalgamation of the two courses described above; the original James Braid layout has been modified slightly and is currently 6541 yards Par 72. The layout which skirts the grounds of Milton Hall often has views of the hall as a backdrop, notably the par four 4th hole (Rabbit's Corner) and the Par 5 13th hole (Fitzwilliam). The 13th hole also has the original reed thatched Clubhouse located beyond the green. The course was constructed by R.Strutt & Co from Paisley and opened on the 14 July 1938, when the Captain of the new Club H.B.Hartly hit the opening tee shot. This triggered off a race for the ball as a souvenir which was won by his chauffeur.

The parkland course has many good holes some of which were badly affected by Dutch Elm disease during the 1970s, however the character of many of the holes has largely returned thanks to an active reforestation programme. This is particularly true of the 3rd and 4th holes. The 4th Rabbits Corner 420 Yards Stroke Index 2 is a hole characteristic of great designs, the tee shot has to be accurately placed and reasonably long and the second is played to a long narrow green with bunkers each side. The famous Par 4,10th hole is known as Cotton's Fancy because Henry Cotton eulogised about it in a golf magazine article. The narrow two tier green with a hollow in front is extremely difficult to hit especially with a long iron in one's hand. In the 1990s installation of an automatic watering system has led to a significant addition to the course, Lake Temptation serves as both a water storage facility and a dominant feature on the 1st and 18th holes. The finishing holes, which start at the par 4 14th Hole the Ha Ha, represent one of the toughest finishes in the N.G.U.

During my playing career for Northampton, the two Clubs have generated a good rapport between players and we often had fun post matches. These included for example a throwing competition across the lake at Northampton's 16th hole a long driving competition (not won by Jimmy Ellis!) and a one club five iron challenge at Peterborough Milton G.C. The challenge, which was open to all players cost two pounds was played up across and down the 1st, 2nd and 18th holes lowest score takes all and buys the beer! Having completed the first two holes someone suggested we played from the 18th tee to the first green for a bit of fun and Jimmy Ellis holed out! Try and contemplate the shot the next time you are on that tee, we fell about laughing; it looks impossible with a five iron but truly happened. Jimmy refused to buy a round of drinks, claiming it was not a true hole in one, everyone accepted this apart from "Coley" who was thirsty.

Recently the off course facilities have been upgraded with a half a million pound extension to the clubhouse. This development included the incorporation of a new entrance, an improved restaurant and bar areas and a new locker room.

In 2005, County Players Neil Presto (Chewy) and Richard Cole (Coley) played some superb foursomes golf over the Hotchkin Course at Woodhall Spa and reached the Semi-Finals of the prestigious tournament the Central England Open Men's Foursomes. They were narrowly defeated on the 19th hole by the eventual winners P.Wardle and A.King from Gosforth G.C. Prior to this Coley had also been involved in the final stages of this competition with fellow member Ray Beekie when they reached the semi-finals in 1988 narrowly losing one down to the eventual winners T.Elvin & J.Gibson.

Peterborough Milton's three times N.G.C. Scratch Foursomes winners Neil Presto (left) and Ian Symonds in 2000.

In 2005 Neil Presto was awarded the "County Player of the Year" award at the N.G.U. annual dinner and in 2006 became a playing N.G.U. County Captain having represented the county for the last ten years. He continued his winning ways during the autumn with long term partner Ian Symonds as they won the Finney Shield. This is a Foursomes Championship held annually at Harborne G.C. their morning score of 67, 3 under par was a fine effort on a wild day when the event was reduced to a single round due to bad weather. This was a nice addition to their three victories in the N.G.U. Scratch Foursomes (2000, 2001 & 2004). The Symonds theme continues in 2006 as Ian's brother Daniel and Rob Fredericks, won the East Anglian Open Foursomes at Hunstanton Golf Club, Norfolk on Sunday 23rd April. They lead the Saturday qualifying with 38 Stableford points in the morning and amassed a further 31 points in the afternoon as conditions became more windswept. In the match-play final on the Sunday they won on the 19th hole. The trophy has also been won in the past by Rushden wrestler Doug Joyce & Jim Dalton (N.G.U. Past President) and nicely retained the following year by his son Brian after his father had passed away also partnering Jim Dalton.

The N.G.U. County Championship was held over the course on June 17th 2006 and won with a score of 69, 66 (a new Amateur Course record) by England International Gary Boyd from Cherwell Edge G.C. Also in 2006 Richard Cole became the Midland Senior's Champion at Ladbrook Park G.C. with a gross score of 71, level par of his scratch handicap. At his ripe old age Richard is one of the lowest handicap golfers in England, a good friend and a good egg!

In December 2006 Club vice Captain Bob Bellamy had a unique happening just before Christmas, when recording three eagles on the front nine holes. The fun started at the first hole, with a chip in for an eagle three and after a quiet spell on holes up to the eighth, the fireworks started again with a driver and the seven wood to two feet for a second eagle. This was the first time he had recorded two eagles in a game of golf in his life, though more was to come. Incredibly, his nine iron tee shot on the 145 yard par three ninth took one bounce and finished in the bottom of cup for Bob's third eagle of the day, and his third hole-in-one. Quite a feat considering that play was on temporary greens. He was unable to play the back nine, because of a board meeting at the Club, such is the role of vice captain. As the clubhouse was empty at the time, the customary round of drinks was only enjoyed by his playing partners on their return.

In August 2007 the amateur course record was equalled twice in a day during the Club's Pro-Am. County Captain Neil Presto's round of 66, five under par, included an eagle at the first and birdies at the 3rd, 12th, and 13th to match his Club mate and fellow county player Adrian Firman's record. Gross 66 was also recorded that day by Matt Morris the professional at Hatchford Brook G.C.

At county level the Club has produced many champions and officials over the years although surprisingly only four County Champions. In the new century 3 victories in Scratch League Division 1 (2001, 2003, 2004) demonstrates the quality of players present. Recent N.G.U. County Captains include Ray Beekie (1982-3) and Neil Presto (2006-2008). Their most recent N.G.U. President was Terry Haley (2000-1).

In July 2000 Terry and I travelled together up to St Andrews for The Millennium Open. Arriving at 9.45 p.m. on the Wednesday evening we were fortunately able to watch the eventual winner Tiger Woods playing a few holes. To watch the now 13 times Major Champion enjoying himself as a relaxed young lad without the usual hullabaloo at the Home of Golf against a setting sun from the shoreline of West Sands road was indeed special. This win was to be the first leg of "Tiger's Slam" when he became the first player ever to hold all of the current Majors. Tiger is one of the greatest players ever to have played the game, if not the greatest, the press are currently pontificating on whether becoming a father might affect his drive and desire to try and beat Jack Nicklaus's record of 18 Majors. Personally I cannot see it making any difference; he has such a strong mind and has been great for the game. After winning the 2007 USPGA Championship Tiger needs five more majors to equal Jack's amazing record and stated that this victory was special to him since it was the first one since the arrival of daughter Sam. The debate on who has been the greatest player in the game continues, although some argue it is simply a question of when rather than if!

10th Hole Cottons Fancy White Tee 448 Yards Par 4 Stroke Index1

Cotton's Fancy the
10th hole at
Peterborough
Milton G.C.

One of Henry Cotton's favourite holes requires two accurate shots that have to negotiate the tree-lined fairway, including one beautiful large tree on the corner of the dogleg and a narrow, two-tiered green. Before the advent of spring face drivers the second shot was often played with a long iron as dictated by the course designers. There are only four positions for the hole on the green none of which makes the putting particularly easy. The horse chestnut tree on the right-hand side make chipping difficult for the leaked second shot and a par here is most welcome.

Priors Hall (Corby Golf Course) 1965 -present

Corby Golf Club.

Priors Hall, length, 6636 yards par 72, was constructed by Corby Urban District Council on the land originally leased from land owned by Stewarts and Lloyds Mineral Extractors Ltd. The land was originally used for iron ore extraction by open-cast working. The course is crescent shaped arising from the original workings by the company. Constructions of the course started in 1962 and play commenced in May 1965 tickets, golf balls, tees and chocolate being issued from temporary wooden huts. The official opening took place on Sunday 23rd of July 1967, which included a fourball match including local pro Dick Kemp, Northants County's Stuart Murray, Ryder Cup Player Eric Brown and 22 year old future Open Champion Tony Jacklin from neighbouring Lincolnshire. The list of the fourball's achievements locally and globally is amazing, too great to be repeated here.

Nº 575

URBAN DISTRICT COUNCIL OF CORBY

Official Opening

of

Priors Hall Golf Course

by Councillor J. F. Stevens, J.P.
Chairman of the Council

on

SUNDAY 23rd JULY 1967

at 2.30 p.m.

followed by

Fourball Match between Professionals

| ERIC BROWN | DICK KEMP |
| TONY JACKLIN | STUART MURRAY |

PROGRAMME 1s. 6d.
Prize of Golf Bag value £12 for winning number

Score Card from the Opening Day Fourball at Priors Hall 23 July 1967

Hole	Yards	Par	Eric Brown	Tony Jacklin	Dick Kemp	Stuart Murray
1	378	4	4	5	4	6
2	386	4	4	4	4	3
3	486	5	6	4	4	6
4	425	4	6	5	4	4
5	165	3	3	5	3	3
6	477	5	7	5	4	5
7	403	4	3	3	3	4
8	170	3	3	3	3	3
9	370	4	3	4	4	6
		36	39	38	33	40
10	425	4	4	4	4	5
11	380	4	5	6	7	4
12	205	3	4	3	3	3
13	476	5	5	7	4	5
14	389	4	5	4	5	7
15	215	3	4	3	3	4
16	390	4	4	4	4	3
17	407	4	4	4	4	5
18	489	5	4	4	4	4
		36	39	38	38	40
			78	77	71	80

Local knowledge and Dick Kemp's skill ruled that day!

In addition, on that day, Richard Aitken met Sue Catlow for the first time, which subsequently resulted in their successful marriage; this is one of the Club's little known claims to fame.

In the 1980's Corby District Council changed the name of the course to Corby Public Golf Course however in terms of word of mouth it has always been called Priors Hall Golf Club. With the 2005 name changed to Corby Golf Course it will be interesting to see how long Priors Hall remains. I suspect it will be at least a generation. Many golfers in the east of the county started their golf here, especially some of our elder statesmen. Getting your ball into the starting shoot was one primary requirement to get on to a popular course. This method did promote the occasional dispute with some of the fiery Scots present. Links with Scotland are maintained with the only burn in the county, The Parley Burn which comes in to play on the 2-6th holes is a water hazard in which the sleepers are considered part of the burn.

Priors Hall has produced some outstanding county players most notably Malcolm Scott and Ronnie McIlwain (County Champions 1984 & 1986 and 1993 respectively). Malcolm was also County Matchplay Champion in 1989 & 1991 and Ronnie collected the N.G.U. Braids Driver in 1989). Malcolm Scott has also seen some considerable success in the N.G.U. County Scratch Foursomes event with county team mate Anthony Lord (Northants County). They were victorious in 1989, 1994, 1995 and 1998 and are currently the only pair to have won the event four times, one ahead of Neil Presto and Ian Symonds, from Peterborough Milton.

The N.G.U. Higgs Bowl has also been won several times by the Club with victories by Bill Sloan in 1976, Steve Jarret in 1982, Gerry Cummins in 1983 and young "baby faced" Chris Haggerty in 1990. The pair of Paddy

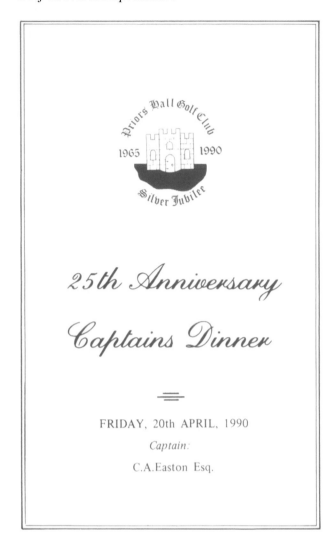

Above: Anthony Lord, Northants County (left) with N.G.U. President Dave Croxton and Malcolm Scott, Priors Hall, N.G.U. County Scratch Foursomes Winners 1998.

Left: Priors Hall Golf Club's 25th Anniversary Dinner Programme

McLean & Ronnie McIlwain became the first pair to retain the N.G.U. Stableford Cup in 2004&5 at Northampton and Wellingborough G.Cs. respectively. Tommy Sheridan won the County Singles Trophy in 2001 at its first outing.

Prior Hall is still the only Club to have won the Hollingsworth Trophy three years in a row (1973-5). Since those "heady" days when member numbers/players handicaps/players commitments have stabilised they have only reached the final once more in 1987 at Peterborough Milton. I played in this final and have to say that I witnessed one of the best shots I have seen for a long time. Playing against Greg Shelton & Mike Lynch our game was quite tight playing the tenth hole Cotton's Fancy. After we had both found the fairway from the tee Mike hit a three iron which pitched on the top level of this demanding green and sat down" like a butterfly with sore feet". This set the tone for the back nine, which Mark Britten and I eventually lost, convincingly to Greg & Mike. I can still see the shot when I play the course.

With reference to Club officials, two gentlemen Jack Marr and Phil Ackroyd have both been Captain twice. The Club has produced several officials for wider organisations, notably Malcolm Evans Captain 1983, President of the Club (2002-present) and Competitions Secretary of the N.G.U. (1995-present). Malcolm Scott Captained

198

the N.G.U. Anglian League B team for three years and recently Terry Arnold became Secretary of the M.G.U. A Silver Jubilee 25th Anniversary Captains Dinner took place in 1990, which was well attended and enjoyed by the dignitaries present including Jim Dalton N.G.U. President. In 2005 the Club changed its name to Corby Golf Course and are managed by Ruspro Ltd working with Corby Borough Council. Club members however have "kept" the name as Priors Hall.

15th Hole White 217 Yards Par 3

This is a long and difficult par three hole, I have selected it from this point of view and also emotionally since the tee shot during the 1970s was hit towards the fire spitting glowing furnace of the steel-works in the town "The Corby Candle". The hole has remoteness also on its side at the northern end of the course. The hole has a narrow wide green and has bunkers short right and left to catch any loose tee shots. To add to this, it is often played in to the north wind. Interestingly during the official opening day fourball in 1967 only two players recorded a par at the hole. I also considered the par four 15th at Peterborough Milton G.C. and the par three 15th at Collingtree Park G.C. before my decision in favour of Priors Hall.

The par 3 15th at Corby Golf Course.

The Pytchley Golf Lodge 1995-present

Established in 1995 as a driving range and then with an academy style course in 2000 it has become a popular venue for golfers who are starting out and looking to improve their game. The course was designed by Roger Griffiths Associates of Rugby is par 34 and 2574 yards in length, all greens were set to U.S.G.A. standards for year round playability. The facility also includes a large well stocked American Golf superstore equipped with video teaching facilities. There are resident P.G.A. professionals available and the store is one of the largest in the UK.

In 2003, the Club won their first N.G.U. event the, Izzard Club Team Trophy at Northampton G.C. the team consisted of Lee Creamer, Ian Wilson and Chris Penney with a combined total of 116 Stableford points a massive 10 clear points from runners up Collingtree Park. The trophy was retained the following year at Cold Ashby G.C. when the team of Mark Brimley, Mike Charter and Richard Wright amassed 38, 34 and 31 respectively for a total of 103 Stableford points narrowly piping runners-up Staverton Park by a single point. The floodlit driving range is open 7 days a week and the new Ironside bar provide refreshments, hot and cold snacks in a relaxed atmosphere.

In 2007, the Club won the Izzard Club Team Trophy for a record third time at Wellingborough G.C. the team of Kelvin Mayers 42pts; Michael Steventon 40pts & Richard White 29pts amassed a total of 111 points narrowly piping the home team. At the evening meal there was much talk around the tables of where bandits could be found in the county!

Pytchley Lodge 9th hole.

The driving range at Pytchley Lodge.

Rushden 1919-present

Rushden & District G.C. as it used to be known started life in 1908 on land close to nearby Stanwick by a group of wealthy boot and shoe owners, the course is believed to have consisted of six holes. Mr G. A.Wetenhall inaugurated the Club's first competition, presenting a silver trophy. The first recorded winner was Mr G.S. Mason in 1908.

The Club's badge above has an interesting history[14], which is reproduced here. The leather bucket is symbolic of the leather trade that dominated this area. It is shown here in the canting arms of the Pemberton family. In the 15th century the Pemberton family settled in Rushden, they were a prominent family in the area for 200 years,

Rushden Golf Club.

employed at the courts if succeeding Kings and Queens in such high offices as Members of Parliament and High Sheriffs. They were very instrumental in the development of the Rushden district, including the building of the present Rushden Hall incorporating parts of the hunting lodge that had been set up in the Norman Conquest era of the 11th century.

The heraldic lion is depicted due to the course being laid out on land owned by the Duchy of Lancaster. The Higham area was passed down to the family of Ferrers in the 12th century. In 1226 Henry III granted the town to his son, Edmund Duke of Lancaster. This is the era of the sovereign change from the Plantagenet to the House of Lancaster, and remains crown land to this day, thus making H.M. the Queen the Lady of the manor. The Lion's stance is known as Passant Guardant.

The golf course is laid out on land that was originally used for agriculture. The wavy lines in the 4th

Ladies at Chelveston/Rushden Golf Club 1923.

Rushden Golf Club's Captain Kevin Barclay (left), with Past Captains Nigel Richards (Centre) and Martin Cox at the 2007 N.G.U. Dinner

quadrant of the shield represent the Ridge and Furrow style of ploughing that was commonly used. These contours are still readily visible and make for an interesting variety of stances when addressing the ball.

The current location on Kimbolton Road half a mile from the outskirts of Higham Ferrers was opened in 1919. A recently found photograph originating from a car boot sale depicts two lady golfers standing outside a pavilion ready for play in October 1923 at Chelveston. In view of the slope in the photograph from left to right, and the fact that the pavilion is at a greater height that the footpath, this may well have been taken from just outside the entrance to the ladies changing rooms of the current clubhouse in 1923. Since the two ladies are wearing the same attire it is also tempting to speculate that these were team colours for 1923. The lady carrying a golf bag appears to be leaning on a white gate which was probably used to keep the sheep away from the pavilion; she is thought to be a member of the Mason family. The photograph is reproduced on page 202.

The Club dropped it's "& District" from their title in 1986. The 6249 yards Par 71 course uniquely consists of only 10 holes on its 78 acres. N.G.U. legend Charles Catlow the 11 times County Champion was a member there for a time and the current par three 5th and 14th which share the same green are named after him. He was asked to approve the design and made minor modifications, notably the design of the small mound to the right of the green and the Club reciprocated by naming it "The Catlows".

Being at the centre of the original shoe trade, Rushden had regular visits from celebrity customers, among

The Rushden & District G.C.Team, Hollingsworth Trophy finalists 1976
Left to right: L Everard, J Callaghan, J Vollmar, R Allen, M Rye (Captain), D Edwards, R Everard, D Roberts,
M Allen, B Sharkey and K Bottomley.

them golfing legend, Bobby Locke, the South African who won The Open Championship in 1949&1957. Bobby Locke often played the course to break in a new pair of shoes and was made an honorary member. A faded photograph of Bobby Locke with three club members (J.A. Sharpe, R. Mackellar and R.W. Kilsby) hangs in the clubhouse. In 2007, there are about 360 members of whom 120 regularly play competitions throughout the week. Any more and there would be chaos on the course; however there are now plans to extend the course to 18 holes and build a new clubhouse. Members voted in favour of this in November 2006 by a great majority and the projected completion date is 2010. The new clubhouse might be sited on Water Lane to improve member's access out on to the now busy B645 Higham Ferrers to Chelveston road.

The Men's invitation day is one of the highlights of the season and I enjoyed the camaraderie over many years with partner Jeremy "Scoopy" Smith their greenkeeper and Ian "Mars Bar" Dickerson their multi Club Champion and past course record holder. These two nicknames refer to Jeremy's legendary chipping action and Ian's in mouth ability (no hands required) to unwrap, consume and expel the wrappings of a complete king sized Mars bar. Passing the clubhouse frequently during the 36 holes competition ensured that sufficient fluid was consumed to avoid any possible dehydration in the summer sun! On one occasion as a result of this intake and a nice relaxing dinner, I walked the two miles home to my house in Newton Road Rushden complete with golf clubs on the powercaddy and wearing a suit and tie! It only took an hour and I collected my car the following day.

The water feature in front of the short par three 3rd hole is affectionately known as "Sharkey's Pond" a reference to the Past Captain who was instrumental in its construction. One dry summer, Brendan was searching for the drain and managed to locate it by falling down into it. The spectre of a mud covered Past Captain can be

Left: Gary Boyd Cherwell Edge N.G.U. 2007 Champion of Champions and Rushden's greenkeeper Jeremy Smith the 2007 N.G.U. Singles Champion at Rushden G.C. on finals day.

Below: Rushden Golf Club's 3rd hole, with Sharkey's pond & easy pickings for Lewis Miller who aced it twice in a day in 2007.

occasionally spotted on misty moonlit nights as the ghostly figure tries to hide his embarrassment!

On the playing front the Club have produced a run of five N.G.U. County Champions between 1932-1936 with four times winner R.W.Kilsby's run being broken by the notable Charles Catlow in 1934 who also won the Higgs Bowl in 1936. In 1961 J.A. (Jimmy) Sharpe won the N.G.U. Scratch Foursomes with partner E.G. Freeman from Northants County and also the Higgs Bowl in 1966, he also became N.G.U. President in 1969. The men's team have reached the Hollingsworth Trophy final once during the hot autumn of 1976 narrowly losing 3-2 to Peterborough Milton, their only final to date. In 1983 the Club were promoted to Scratch League Division 1 and remained there for a single season.

In 1999 and 2002 the Club won the Izzard Club Team Trophy at Peterborough Milton and Wellingborough G.Cs. respectively. The 1999 Team of D.Felce, R.Smith and T.Sibcy amassed 105 pts were clear victors by 4 points over Collingtree Park, T.Sibcy also won the individual prize with 44pts.The 2002 team of Gary Jackson 33pts, John McGuirk 33pts and Steve Roebuck 27pts amased a total of 93 points to narrowly beat the home team.

In 2005 Graeme May and Steve Roebuck reached the N.G.U. Foursomes final at Kingsthorpe narrowly losing 2/1 to two of my Unilever work colleagues Ian Campbell & Tom Kelly from nearby Wellingborough G.C.

The Club have produced five N.G.U. Presidents and H.W. Colton Esq. President 1957-58 presented the pair of trophies for the annual Family Foursomes competition.

Rushden is a friendly club and very welcoming to visitors; new members will be actively sought when they convert to 18 holes in 2010. The friendliness at the Club was typified recently, when my wife and I visited to take a few pictures for this book of the par three 3rd hole. After chatting to the Green's Chairman Bryan Barwick and greenkeeper Jeremy Smith over a couple of pints and a glass or two of red wine, It was time to go home two hours later!

At one stage, Jeremy and I used the same child minder for Jeremy's Joshua and our Natalie. The children got on well together, and four year old Natalie used to sing a lovely little child's rhyme she made up one-day, "Joshua, Joshua, sweeter than orange squash youa". How sweet & creative.

Ten years later, young Joshua was hitting a nine iron on to the third hole with no hint of his father's legendary scooping action! In 2007 this hole (113 yards) was amazingly aced twice in a day by 15-year-old Lewis Miller on the 3rd September. The Club's Junior Champion first ace came at 2 p.m. with a gap wedge whilst playing with Joshua and he repeated the feat at dusk six hours later when playing with one of the Club's junior organisers. The pair did not know Lewis had pulled of what is thought to be 40-million-to-1 chance until they reached the green. A day to be remembered for the rest of his life and one to tell the grandchildren.

Also in 2007 Jeremy Smith became the N.G.U. Singles Champion, scooping up the trophy over his manicured course by 3/2 against Dennis Sleath from Northants County G.C. during Finals Day. This was a great day for the Club, the competitors & officials were warmly welcomed and looked after extremely well. This together with Past Captain Gordon Rising's appointment as N.G.U. Vice President 2008-10 and the probable expansion to eighteen holes has firmly put the Club back on the golf map.

Silverstone 1991-present

The Club transferred to the N.G.U. in 2001 from the Berks, Bucks & Oxon golf union largely due to their location and are now active participators in N.G.U. affairs. They have recently hosted events such as the Family Foursomes and Izzard Team Trophy. The Club has to date produced two county players Simon Williams and Matt Bearman who are now members at Northampton G.C.

The oak woods around the course, which are part of the ancient Whittlebury Forest complex, have contained over the years one of Britain's finest and rarest butterfly the Purple Emperor. I saw one example of "His Majesty" in 1979 long before the golf course existed and still look for the insect if playing the course in July or August.

Silvertstone Clubhouse

His Majesty spends a great deal of time resting on the top of oak trees looking out for the female of the specie and to chase off other males. The tree is known as the master oak and the insect flies down to drink from muddy puddles, dead rabbits and other leaking wildlife for its salt supply. It's yellow proboscis being used to probe such delicacies. More recently, I have not been successful in finding the much-prized insect, so I probably need to hit the ball in to the rough more often so I can scan the oak trees, which are home to His Majesty.

Father and son combination of Carl & Simon Williams registered their first N.G.U. success when they won the 2002 N.G.U. Stableford Cup at West Park G.C. with scores of 38+42=80 pts, not a bad effort over 36 holes for a pair with a combined height of almost thirteen feet, weight 35 stone. They are now members at Northampton G.C. and in 2006 Simon had reduced his handicap to scratch. In 2007, Simon embarked upon a golf scholarship in the U.S.A. at the University of Iowa; Carl has played in the Hollingsworth team.

Their sister Club is Cherwell Edge G.C.

St Andrews Hospital 1960-present

This course is located on Billing Road close to Northampton School for Boys and provided an interesting challenge especially some of the par 3 holes. The course in Northampton is set amongst 100 acres of land has 18 tees and 9 greens and is currently cared for by Nigel Phelan and his 3 staff. It became a private club in 1974; a clubhouse located at Lime Tree Cottage was established in 1999.

St Andrews Hospital G.C. looking north on a summer's day.

The course record of 67, four under par is held by Stuart Pitcher their 1996 Club Champion, Stuart made a significant contribution to county golf as N.G.U. Junior Delegate between 1999-2004. Stuart's meticulous preparation for events and his junior reports were a firm foundation to encourage many young lads on their way in to the game of golf and life.

I strongly suspect that one of Stuart's proudest moments was at Seacroft G.C. in 2000 when the County team reached the Anglian Boys Final. The boys eventually going down to a strong Suffolk team who packed plenty of punch! Two future full England Internationals, our Gary Boyd from Cherwell Edge G.C. and their Jamie Moul from Stoke by Nayland played on that sunny day by the North Sea together with the twin brothers Colin & Roger Green from Northants County. The camaraderie in the Crown Hotel that night prior to the match will last forever. Ask Jon Lloyd or Ian Marshall who were present. Like Stuart they have all made a significant contribution to junior golf in the county, Stuart is now a member at Wellingborough G.C.

Looking out over the Wash on that day towards Norfolk, we had a clear view only interrupted by sand, birds and seals; now in 2007 the view is interrupted by a wind farm. This pollution of the view is largely due to the current government's policy on energy.

In 2003, St Andrews won their first silverware in a N.G.U. competition with a thrilling victory over Kingsthorpe in the Inter-Club Handicap League final. They beat the Kingsley Road outfit by 12 holes to 11 in a tense day's play at Collingtree Park G.C. despite making a number of changes from their original semi-final line-up due to player absences. With daylight rapidly fading a delighted St Andrews team celebrated when Andrew Pearson's 12 inch putt for victory was graciously conceded by the Kingsthorpe pair. St Andrews team for the final was: Phil Godfrey, John Nightingale, Simon Pearson, John Wilcox, Nigel Phelan, Nigel Cole (Capt.), Tommy Timmins, Eddie Condon, Andy Birkett, Bill Jenkins, Andrew Pearson, Bill Fitzsimmons. Also in 2003, a new website was launched.

In June 2006, two Captains achieved aces on the same day at separate Captains away days. Lady Captain Chris

Gore holed out on the 237 yards 14th hole at Windmill Village G.C. Coventry and Immediate Past Captain John Nightingale holed out during Captain's weekend on the 156 yards 3rd hole at Gloucester G.C., a full report appeared in the local paper the Chronicle & Echo. Also in 2006, the 10th &11th tees were enlarged such that in 2007 the 10th became the 1st and vise versa in order to ease congestion.

The course has a considerable amount of wildlife including Kingfisher, the rare Lesser Spotted Woodpecker and in the past the elusive Hawfinch.

Stanwick 1905-1919

Matches were played between Stanwick and Wellingborough between 1905-1914 and in 1919 came under the name of Rushden & District G.C. Stanwick was in fact not a registered Club but a group of players who played there. Six holes had been laid out on fields belonging to the "Squire of Stanwick" Mr Wetenall. At the end of the First World War the holes had been ploughed up which prompted a moved to Rushden where the conditions for golf were better. Rushden's Club Championship is called The Wetenhall Cup

Staverton Park 1977-present

The complex is situated on the outskirts of Daventry adjoining the centuries old village of Staverton and enjoys some superb views towards neighbouring Warwickshire. Local farmer David Green commissioned Commander John Harris, with the help of architect Bryan Griffiths in 1975, to design and build a new style course to take advantage of the countries fast progressing golf boom. Along with the beautiful stone clubhouse the 6583 yards par 71 course was built rather uniquely for the time with U.S.G.A. Specification Greens. The greens were made large, with each one averaging over 1000 square feet and free draining. The course is played on either side of a large hill with several large ponds coming into play that attract much wildlife, such as

Above: The Staverton Park team Scratch League Division 2 Winners inside the old clubhouse at Kingsthorpe G.C. 2002.

Left: Paul Taylor, Staverton Park G.C. N.G.U. Champion of Champions 1996, 1998-2000.

Moorhens, Coots and Little Grebe which can often be heard with its bubbling call. Continuing this wildlife theme, the first club emblem became the Badger because of the Sett situated to the left of the then 1st hole, now the 10th. Crows were also common on the course and one family famously terrorised golfers for several months by stealing balls from the fairway, driving one deranged member to strap his loaded 12-bore shotgun to his bag before play, to wreak revenge on the thieves. Visitors to the Club were amused by the local rule that was created to accommodate the situation.

The Club's first Professional (1977-79) was the now world famous David Leadbetter. Lesser known in these days but still highly regarded as a coach. David had many visits from aspiring South African and Zimbabwean Tour Professionals. Legend has it that 1994 Open Champion Nick Price used to hit balls - perfectly struck with a persimmon driver flush off the paving slabs outside the shop onto the Practice Ground. At the Club juniors still play today for The Leadbetter Trophy, which was kindly donated by David some years after his departure.

Brian Sparks (1979-84) with his brother Phillip moved from Barton on Sea on the South Coast to become the next Professional. He carried on the tradition of coaching and established a then famous Junior Academy, which helped establish several Professional and Low Handicap Amateur golfers. One of Brian Sparks's young assistants Charlie Ray who went on to secure his European Tour Card and won the first N.G.U. Open in 1982 that was hosted by Staverton Park. Charlie regained Amateur status in the 1990's and went on to win the Club Championship in 2005.

While on the subject of Club Champions, it cannot go without mention the incredible achievement of club member Paul Taylor. Starting as a junior member Paul, who achieved a handicap of Plus 3, went on to win the Club Championship an amazing 13 times up to 2003 including 10 straight wins. He also won the N.G.U. Champion of Champions a record 3 times in succession from 1998-2000. This was during a time when Staverton Park could field a Scratch League team where the highest handicap was two. David Shandley, Simon Brown and Michael Franklyn are all players that have held plus handicaps.

With its location the course seriously catches the storms in the autumn which come in from the south-west and I do not know many of their Scratch League players who are not big ball strikers apart from one little chirpy chap. One man who came into the frame in this respect was David Shandley who was capable of some prodigious drives. David regularly used to fly the ball over the tree and bunker on the right of the current first hole with little effort and pure timing. This legendary striker together with Paul Taylor certainly enhanced Staverton's reputation as a place where the driver was king. I particularly remember playing a Hollingsworth Semi-Final there with a young powerful and somewhat raw Glenn Keates and being surprised to have either an eight or nine iron to the 500 yards par five second hole. This was new territory for me as a mid fourty year old with an aging swing and back. A half in five brought a rueful glance from the youngster, who had calculated an eagle three; however, Northampton won 3-2, "drive for show and putt for dough".

Strangely, despite their standard, no male Staverton player has ever won the County Championship and to date David and Sue Turbayne remain the only members who have won any of the Counties prestigious trophies, namely the Family Foursomes in 2000, the millennium event held at Northampton G.C. and Sue's N.C.L.G.A. County Championship victory in 1999.

As a Club, the teams have had some excellent successes. The Hollingsworth Trophy win of 1980 remains one of their most memorable victories; even though they went on to win this trophy again in 1993 and 2005. Along with Collingtree Park they are also to date the only three times winner of the Inter Club Handicap League achieving victories in 2000, 2004 and 2006. In 2008, the Men's Scratch team won Division 2 to gain promotion to the elite Division 1 and will attempt to win this division for the first time in the Club's history in 2009. Surprisingly the Club has only hosted one County Championship, this being in 1981 when Kingstorpe's Mike Haddon won the title in wet and windy conditions. The N.G.U. officials could not believe the scores the young man produced in such terribly difficult conditions. I was away and saved the personal embarrassment of a couple of 80s.

Staverton Park has long been a supporter of the National Amputees Society and has hosted the National

View from the 6th Hole at Staverton Park G.C. across rolling hills.

Championships, which attracted entries from all over the world. This has a phenomenal attraction to golfers and non-golfers.

Staverton Park has always hosted Professional competitions, notably the Midland Professional Championship (one of the oldest in golf professional history) as well as the Midland Professional Matchplay Championship. Many top players have competed and won in these events. The likes of Peter Baker, Mark Mouland, Brian Waites, Carl Mason, Ross McFarlane and David Russell have all featured here. The most notable however was Ian Woosnam who played in the championship in 1980. Still trying to breakthrough, the following year he had some success in Africa and on the European Tour and became a world number one player before the next decade.

Brian Mudge took over as Club Professional in 1984, continuing in the Leadbetter/Sparks coaching tradition, and having been Assistant Professional under Brian Sparks since 1979 and lived all that time in a caravan that was parked behind a hedge shielding the 9th green. Brian developed the business and his reputation as a Club Professional solely until 1989 when planned development of the adjoining hotel prompted him to ask his brother Richard, himself a reputable Club Professional from Tunbridge Wells in Kent, to become his business partner at Staverton. In 1991 business failures of the owner caused Staverton Park Hotel and Golf Club to go bankrupt and temporarily close. The golf course operation continued with the brothers helping it through its administration period. In 1993, having served 14 years at Staverton Brian moved to Overstone Park in Northampton to serve another 14 years there. His brother Richard is now Head Professional and has been in office for his 19th year, one of the longest serving in the County.

The Hotel that has 240 rooms in 2008 is now owned by the De Vere Group and is one of the main Business Training and Conference Centres in the Country. The course has had a relatively new clubhouse built for it with adjoining leisure club. Unfortunately, Dutch elm disease devastated the course's majestic trees during the 1980's. The golf challenge at several holes was weakened by their removal and of course will never be quite the same. The sixth hole nominated in the Counties top 18 holes was one such hole affected (see description below).

Staverton is and continues to be one of the finest and still improving courses in the County.

6th Hole White Tee 357 Yards Par 4.

This hole was originally a very formidable challenge and is rated stroke index 1. The hole is played up a steep hill with out of bounds to the right. A long thin bunker used to be present on the right hand side of the fairway to catch any faded shots and two tall elm trees used to guard the approach to the large but sloping green. Nowadays despite the modern equipment and the loss of the two elm trees its degree of difficulty is partially maintained by the wind and the slope, which still make this hole a challenge. I also strongly considered the recently extended and reshaped 240 Yards par 3, sixth at Northants County G.C. and only rejected it in terms of a balanced compilation.

Stoke Albany 1994-present

Stoke Albany G.C.

The Hawtree designed Welland Valley club officially opened in April 1995 following a champagne reception in a purposely provided marquee. Speeches made by the Club's dignitaries, N.C.L.G.A. President and N.G.U. President Ian Marshall together with a happy forward looking atmosphere, some warm nibbles and some champagne induced rosy cheeks helped to reduce the chill of the cold morning temperatures.

The 18-hole par 71 course (6175 yards) has spectacular views over the surrounding picturesque countryside. Water comes into play on nine of the holes and especially features on the 9th, 10th & 11th holes. The course drains well such that temporary greens are only occasionally required. The Clubhouse and Fairways Restaurant has a relaxed welcoming atmosphere. Adrian Clifford is the professional who runs BigRedGolf. The Club are also an England Golf Foundation Starter Centre. The website is very modern and up to date; and is one of the few to contain a Safety Risk Assessment and a very comprehensive e-brochure. In 1999, the Club became known as Stoke Albany Golf & Country Club.

In 2002 the team of Andrew Bruce, Pam Sayles, Duncan Burgess, the deputy "pro" from Cold Ashby and Ryan Evans won the Millennium trophy held at Cold Ashby with a total of 91 Stableford points. The Club are becoming active participants in the county's events having hosted the Seniors Championship in 2002 won by Richard Cole from Peterborough Milton G.C. Continuing the senior's theme home player Aurthur.J.Lenaghan won the gross and Nett Championship held at Cherwell Edge G.C. in 2004 and alongside Gordon Shields and Barry Stone, also collected the team award. Also in 2004 Ladies vice-captain Pam Sayles had a year to remember after achieving her first-ever hole-in-one on the 15th in August only to repeat the feat four weeks later in the Ladies Monthly Medal. The men's team were promoted from Scratch League Division 4 that year too and enjoyed a single season up in Division 3.

In 2006, the Club were proud hosts of the Junior County Championships, the Ladies Cecil Leitch Semi Finals and a County Seniors' Match vs Lincolnshire, many favourable comments were made on the facilities, and it was nice to have good support for county events. Several Open events took place in 2007.

Scott Marlow won the 1996 N.G.U. Match Play Championship played at Overstone Park G.C. at the time a County Player and then a member of Kettering G.C. Scratch handicapper Scott the 2005 Club Champion also holds the course record with scores of 32+33=65 six under par set during the June 2005 medal. The following year Scott was runner up in the event to rapidly improving youngster Ryan Evans who also won the Priors Hall G.C. Championship. Junior Captain for 2007 is Shaun Davis who reached the semi-final of the N.G.U. Boys Match Play final in 2005 and won the 2006 N.G.U. Boys Championship held at Stoke Albany with a score of 72+72=144. Two promising golfers and two nice lads who have recently transferred to Wellingborough G.C. Ryan Evans became N.G.U. County Champion at Oundle G.C. in 2007 played a total of 70+68=138.

The course is also one of the few places in Northamptonshire where one can see the one of the county's special birds the rare and elegant Red Kite.

Thorpe Wood 1975 –present

The course was developed as one of the first major leisure projects during the expansion of Peterborough and has been recognised as one of the leading Pay-as-you-Play course in the country. The course was designed by Peter Alliss and Dave Thomas also designers of the famous "Ryder Cup" course The Belfry. It is set up as a challenge and rewards golfers of all levels and abilities. The Par 73 course is slightly undulating; it has a length of 7086 yards from the back tees and is rarely closed. The Club were originally members of the N.G.U. from 1975 but transferred to the Cambridgeshire Area Golf Union in 1989. In 1986 J Dodd won the Club's first and only N.G.U. trophy the Stableford Cup at Kettering G.C.

There is a Golf Club attached to Thorpe Wood that has membership available. Green fee rates are quite competitive and there are after 3 p.m. times available at special rates on weekends. Coaching is available through Gary Casey P.G.A. Professional or Suzanne Dickens P.G.A. Member and Ladies European Tour Player and Simon Fitton. Simon is in fact the fourth generation of "Fitter's" to be a P.G.A. professional. In 2004, Simon became the P.G.A. Rookie Assistant of the Year.

Director Roger Fitton oversees the day-to-day running of the facility. The Professional shop is part of the Europro Group. Catering facilities are provided at the adjoining Woodman pub/restaurant. The Club's President is Wyndham Thomas C.B.E. who is together with Mr D. (David) and Mr R. (Roger) Fitton one of three Honorary Members.

Thrapston 1895-1910

Instituted 1895 the course was on the estate of Mr Sackville Chairman of the Huntingdon County G.C. A match was played against Wellingborough in 1898; the Club was last mentioned in 1910.

Towcester 1896-1914

Instituted 1896 as a 9-hole course within 3 miles of the station, the "circuit" was 2380 yards, hazards were hedges, streams and old railway cuttings. The membership was 30 in 1896. In 1905 the Club was reconstituted as Whittlebury G.C. and had a membership of 40. The 2522 yard Bogey 40 course was situated in Whittlebury Park and contained one bogey 3 hole at 121 yards and 5 bogey five holes having lengths between 284-380 yards. The Club was last mentioned in 1914.

Wellingborough Golf Club 1893-present

The 11th Hole at Wellingborough G.C. during the Autumn

This Club has to date played golf on three separate sites. Old Tom Morris laid out the first nine-hole course on the 16th November 1893 at Nest Farm. Having come down from St Andrews the night before, the course was laid out in the morning followed by a foursomes match played with three amateurs on the new course in the afternoon. The three amateurs were Messers. Allison, Simmonds and Fraser from nearby Kettering Golf Club. The match was staged for the edification of the members and was watched by some thirty ladies and gentlemen. The golfers from Kettering did not play to their potential largely as a result of the behaviour of the moving, talking crowd of members. Tom Morris and partner "winning comfortably" assisted by some of Tom's clever approach shots with his patented cleek and clever putts on the rough greens that were less than a day old! The first committee met up at the Hind Hotel in the town a week later to draw up the rules of the Club. This was also the venue for the Club's first dinner in 1895.

Golf course construction was booming at this time and in 1893 some 74 Clubs were built around the world including Killarney in Ireland and Northampton and Oundle in our county. In their centenary year letters of mutual congratulations were exchanged between Wellingborough and Killarney together with an exchange of visits. Killarney Golf and Fishing Club put on A Cead Mile Failte as a special welcome to the members from Wellingborough. The Club's first course was as follows: -

Hole No. 1 Railway (233 yards) The country, with the exception of a few tussocks, ant-banks, and furrows is plain sailing with a generally good lie.

Hole No. 2 Crab Corner (250 yards) A drive of 150 yards will clear a lot of small whins. If you slice badly you will foozle your ball on to the Midland Railway line, or into a high hedge. The next stroke requires care, or you will drop into a hazard, as the green is placed on a small triangular piece of turf, with whins, briars, paths, hedges, stunted trees and a dry ditch surrounding it.

Hole No. 3 Land's End (450 yards) As you tee off you find, about fifteen yards in front of you, a double hazard, consisting of two pollard trees, with a whitethorn bush behind them. If you get a drive between 160 and 200 yards your ball will be among some young whins about two feet high. In the other 300 yards the lie is none too good, but there are no large hazards.

Hole No. 4 High (242 yards) This will require a few artificial bunkers.

Hole No. 5 Old Tom (317 yards) This finishes up with a tree and hedge hazard, the hole laying about twenty yards on the other side.

Hole No. 6 Tabor (366 yards) If you pull you get on to a bridle road, amongst some old grass grown cart-ruts. If you slice ever so little you go into a hedge, as the ground hangs that way very much. Straight ahead are dry ditches, high bushy thorn trees, iron stone pits dotted about, which pleased Old Tom immensely. This and the next are the two most sporting holes on the links.

Hole No. 7 Windmill (283 yards) This is up a steep hill, the green being well guarded on the approach side by a ring of thorn trees, with a long deep pit to the right; to the left is a smaller one.

Hole No. 8 Nest (440 yards) This stretches away over hedge, dry ditch, and tree hazards down to a green in a corner, well guarded on two sides of a triangle by a small pond, ditch and hedges.

Hole No. 9 Home (265 yards) There is a hedge and tree hazard to cross. If you slice you are liable to get among some farm buildings, where it is proposed to make a temporary clubhouse.

The turf was described as good and always dries as the course "lies high". Later in 1893 there was a request to use "part of the hovel at the farm buildings" as a clubhouse and that with the permission of the tenant" would get the hovel made secure if possible against thieves, and fit for use as a place of shelter. The tenant was paid £2 10s 0d. An estimate for alteration of £4 10s 0d was accepted and also an offer to supply a pendant lamp for 11s 6d. A member kindly supplied a stove but the tenant was to be asked whether she entertained any objection to the Club putting up a coke fire and flue. It is believed that the Club's first course was known affectionately as "Nest". The first competition took place on the 29th March 1894 and was won with a score of gross 126. The first President of the Club (1893-1907) was George Charles Wentworth Fitzwilliam, who was an Etonian and Captain of the Northamptonshire Imperial Yeomanry.

The first clubhouse was very much in the style of a railway carriage but was replaced in 1910 by a New Pavilion. The first club match was played against Northampton, Kettering Road on 13th December 1894 at Nest Farm and reported in Golf.

December 21 1894 GOLF

Northampton	Holes	Wellingborough	Holes
Rev Mr Stewart	0	Mr.A.G.F.Forster	0
Mr.Truscott	6	Mr.H.Dulley	0
Mr.E.R.Bull	0	Mr.P.E.Dulley	0
Rev Mr.Deane	0	Mr.C.Nicholson	4
Mr.Anderson	0	Mr.W.W.Robinson (Captain)	0
Mr.Scriven	6	Mr.J.Pendered	0
Mr.F.Hill (Captain)	1	Mr.J.C.Laycock	0
Mr.Marshall	0	Mr.C.Pell	5
Mr.Hamilton	1	Mr.W.H.Hope	0
Mr.Jansen	1	Mr.W.F.Mills	0
	15		**9**

Despite the fact that Wellingborough lost the match, the sandwiches, butter, bread, cake and two bottles of Scotch Whisky provided by the home Club demonstrated that they were very good hosts. This was the start of a good relationship between the two Clubs, which ultimately resulted in the two Clubs competing annually for the Wellingborough Cup on a home and away basis. The first Club Championship was played in April 1896 and won by William Wills Robinson who was also the Club's first Captain and first Secretary.

The second "Old" course at Wellingborough was laid out by Tom Williamson and opened in 1923 on the same date as two other new courses designed by Williamson; Belton Park Lincolnshire and Beeston Fields Nottinghamshire. The area was known as the Waterworks or Bushfield Site and golf was played there until 1975 when the Club moved to its current location at Great Harrowden Hall. In 1923 the membership was 105 gentlemen and 50 ladies. The "Old" nine-hole course was about one mile from the town centre on the Kettering road the A509. The original location now has houses built upon it on roads with names such as Wentworth Avenue, Braid Court and Curtis Mews.

The Board of Agriculture and Fisheries closed the course on the 26th September 1926 owing to an outbreak of foot and mouth disease. Within a week Northampton G.C. opened its doors free of charge to Wellingborough members and Kingsthorpe followed suit in November. Forty members had played on both courses by the time Wellingborough re-opened. Contributions amounting to £3.50 from these members were used to purchase a cup to be presented to Northampton G.C. and an ink stand to Kingsthorpe G.C. The cup was presented to Northampton G.C. on the 16th September 1927 and became known as the Wellingborough Cup. Generous gestures of this nature strongly typify the spirit that exists within this wonderful game. This theme was continued between the two Clubs and Northampton's Professional Alf Lovelady acted as Wellingborough's Professional one day a week between 1959-1962.

The cup was originally awarded to the player returning the best score over eighteen holes bogey until 1989 when it changed to fourball betterball. The competition is played alternately on each course. In the foot and mouth year of 2001 the cup was competed for appropriately at Wellingborough. This was the first time that the competition had been played on the Club's new greens, which have been completely rebuilt to provide a dryer and more playable surface. There have been two breaks in the competition in 1988 and 1991 due to administrative "issues".

The trophy has often been won by players with higher handicaps since scores of at least forty five Stableford points have become the accepted norm. The low handicap men do sometimes have their days, for example Northampton's Chris Hopewell and Glenn Keates in 1994, 46 pts and Wellingborough's County B team Captain Richard Brown and Graham Smailes 45pts in 2003. In the new Millennium the Wellingborough Cup continues to be a popular event however the fun of the event is being ruined by the speed of play, where rounds have recently taken 5 $\frac{1}{4}$ hours!

Just before the Second World War there were 125 gentlemen and 65 lady members. After the War in 1945 the membership had fallen to 84 men and 49 ladies. During the late 1960's considerations were given for a move to a new location, after several abortive attempts a more promising prospect appeared involving a local builder and Past Captain of the Club Ron Tann, an auction of vacant parts of the Harrowden estate and Great Harrowden Hall was planned. The arrangements were finalised in 1974 when it was decided at an historic meeting of the Club to purchase the Hall and grounds at a price, which was eventually finalised at £125,000. The plans for a new course and clubhouse at Great Harrowden Hall were eagerly worked on by various sub committees and the old course closed on the 28th April 1975. At the "Old" course the ladies of the Club were responsible for catering and were ably assisted by the Saxby family who supplied the necessary provisions and helped with the service.

The Saxby family have a distinguished connection with the Club and have provided Presidents, Captains and Club Champions and John Saxby was elected Centenary year Captain. On the county scene John Saxby was Boys Champion twice and County Champion in 1965. John Saxby is currently President of the club. The "Old" course amateur record was 68 gross by Peter James and the professional record was 66 by Rodney King.

Great Harrowden Hall was built around 1719 and has an interesting history that is thoroughly well documented in the Club's centenary book[3]. The building underwent some considerable changes during its conversion to a clubhouse for the members whilst retaining some of the beautiful qualities of a listed building. The "Drive-In" at Wellingborough's third and current location took place on May 2nd 1975, which was followed by a cheese and wine reception. On the golf scene the ladies were very hard to beat and won the Cecil Leitch trophy seven times in nine years from 1973-81 whilst the men completed the Hollingsworth and Scratch League double in 1984.

Individual successes around this time were achieved in 1974 by Chris Hodgson who became County Champion and Parson's Cup winner together with Duncan Ellson who became the County Boys Champion at Kettering with a score of 76 gross. Duncan (DK) also won the trophy over his home course in 1977 with 75 gross with Nick Grimmitt as runner up. Duncan became County Champion in 1988 at Northants County where he played the entire two rounds without using a wooden club. This kept him out of the deep rough, which has been specially grown up for the Championship. Duncan's brother Chris together with Peter Hulme won the County Scratch Foursomes at Peterborough Milton in 1981. Glenda Abbott dominated the ladies championship in the 1970s and 1980s winning the trophy a record fourteen times.

In 1993 there were two or three surviving members who had played on all three Wellingborough golf courses. One of them Peter James (Club Captain 1977, N.G.U. President 1982-3) has in his possession a hickory shafted club that was made for his father by the Club's first professional George Craddock. George Craddock gave the Club forty five years of service and used to cycle to the Club from his home on The Drive. During this time he only ever had one week off as holiday. He was granted Honorary Membership at a lavish presentation dinner.

Continuing the theme of long service is the current professional and green keeper. Professional David Clifford has been in residence since 1983 and will soon complete 25 years good service at the Club. David originates from Nottingham and before moving to the Club was assistant professional at Chilwell Manor and Breadsall Priory. In 1992 he became Captain of the Northants P.G.A. and won their Matchplay Championship a couple of times in the early 1990s. Claims to fame on the course include driving the third hole and in 1985 David recorded the first and only hole in one on the 18th hole. This albatross was "shot" using a driver on this very tight finishing hole and is unlikely to be repeated.

Greenkeeper Ian Marshall joined the Club in 1979 and has made many notable contributions both on and off the course. He was a member of both B and A County Union teams that won the Anglian League shields in 1980 and 1990, Parsons Cup winner in 1981 and 1999 and County Match Play Champion in 1990. Ian became a scratch golfer at the age of fifteen and at nineteen played two rounds in The Open Championship narrowly missing the cut for the weekend by a single shot. He proudly carried out the job of N.G.U. Junior Delegate for twelve

N.G.U. trophy winners 2006 (left to right) Jonathan & Glenn Harris, Stableford Cup & Family Foursomes, Charles Higgins Club Captain, Shaun Davis Junior Champion, & James Whitmore, Higgs Bowl. The Family Foursomes "Ladies" Salver" was omitted from the photograph simply to produce a balanced picture.

years and was instrumental in setting up the County Junior Coaching Scheme and became County President in 1994-96. Further success for the Club at county level came in 2006 when Glenn & Jonathan Harris won the N.G.U. Stableford Cup at Whittlebury Park G.C. on the 2nd September with scores of 42+40=82 points. This completed a notable double for the father and son combination who had in August won the N.G.U. Family Foursomes with a score of 42 points at Brampton Heath G.C. on a very windy day. This was a very nice spell for Glenn since a large turnout of around 140 greeted him to welcome him as Captain on his "Drive In" in November. There was some hilarity generated as Charlie Higgins (Immediate Past Captain) handed him a shovel to hit a teed up ball, Glenn duly obliged much to the delight of the crowd before officially driving in!

In 2007 the tried and tested pair of Ian Marshall & Roger Butler reached the quarter finals of the Central England Open Men's Foursomes held annually on the Hotchkin course at Woodhall Spa G.C. Lincolnshire at their first attempt. Perhaps they may go on to become the County's first ever winners in this prestigious event which has been held annually over this magnificent course since 1958.

Left: Carp the 10th hole at Wellingborough.

Below: Redhill, the17th hole at Wellingborough G.C.

9th Hole White Tee 426 Yards Par 4 Carp

This is perhaps Wellingborough's most demanding par four and rightly has a stroke index of one. The tee shot played downhill across the carp filled pond has to be gently faded to reach the safety of the fairway. A straight tee shot will finish in the rough left of the fairway and too much fade brings another pond into place on the right side of the fairway. The uphill second shot, will require the

219

right club to reach the long well guarded green. The green slopes back to front and quick putts are often found here after greenkeeper Ian Marshall has been out with his mower. A par at this hole provides a nice flavour to go with one of wife Teena's legendary Pasties or Eccles cakes and a cup of coffee at the halfway house. This husband and wife combination is part of the fabric of Wellingborough G.C.

17th Hole White 456 Yards Par 4 Redhill

Once again, I had some difficulty in my final choice for the seventeenth hole and rate this hole just ahead of Northants County, Hellidon Lakes, Overstone and Peterborough Milton's penultimate holes. The tee shot is critical and played to a small gap between a large oak tree and copse to the right and a line of trees and bunker to the left. Any shot hit to the right prevents any attempt to reach the green in two, any shot to the left it blocked out either by the line of trees or a second stand of trees some 60 yards from the green. The length of the hole ensures that a driver is required from the tee. Having found the fairway the second shot played slightly up hill needs to be accurately played with a long iron to a green with a narrow entrance. In many monthly medals there are not many pars recorded on this demanding hole.

Whittlebury Park Golf and Country Club 1991-present

The current set up was originally known as West Park on land that was originally hunting ground for Medieval Kings. Whittlebury Park was in the middle ages part of the ancient Royal Hunting Forest of Whittlewood. In 1820 the land was transformed into a deer park by Lord Southampton with the retention of many of the mighty oaks, some of which are amongst the oldest in England. On the original "1905" course play was by invitation

The demanding eighth hole on the Royal Whittlewood Red Course at Whittelbury Park Golf and Country Club

only, a carriage was sent to Towcester railway station to collect the guests, a local caddy was provided, and a golden guinea was expected as contribution towards the upkeep of the course. The current layout of 36 holes has to be respected and is a good challenge for the golfer. In 2006 the P.G.A. Midland Match play Championship was held at the club on the 7 May and was the reinvention of one of the Midlands oldest and most prestigious professional events.

The Atrium was opened in July 2004 and proves a popular venue for social events. It is situated in the very heart of the Parkland course is reputedly one of the largest clubhouses in Europe. It was nominated by the Mirror group for Clubhouse of the Year Award in its first year of opening. There are several bars and restaurants, the Golfers board room can accommodate up to 20 whilst the Terrace dining room is capable of seating up to 75 guests. There is an abundance of natural light to assist good views of the Park. A paved patio area has fine views of the 1905 course. The Atrium is currently used for a multitude of events from Celebration lunches, Banquets, Dinner Dances, Weddings, Theatre style presentations, Sales meetings, Product Launches and Exhibitions. It also houses the Unique Indoor Golf Centre and Pro shop.

From a personal point of view the four loops of nine are a very good test of golf often played under big moody skies with ancient oaks which provide a backdrop to remind us years gone by. The various ponds are a notable feature and hold a good deal of wildlife. The tranquillity is only spoilt by the close proximity to Silverstone racing circuit, though fortunately racing does not happen every day.

The park also includes the Whittlebury Hall Management Training Centre, Hotel and Spa. It is one of Northamptonshire's largest hotel conference venues, with 211 bedrooms, 65 meeting & training rooms, all complemented by a superb spa. So if you need a couple of nights of pampering and a game of golf this could be the spot for you, though make sure you take the credit card.

In 1998 David Goodrham from the home club won the Higgs Bowl. In 2006 the Club reached the final of the Hollingsworth Trophy for the first time narrowly losing 3-2 to Kingsthorpe G.C.

In 2006, the Club's lowest handicapper was ex Professional, Neil (N.A.) Connolly, who currently plays off a handicap of plus 2. Originally from Staverton Park and Warwickshire Neil served the N.G.U. as Junior Delegate. As an amateur, Neil won the Warwickshire Boys Championship in 1986, the Amateur and Matchplay Championships in 1994. He has subsequently moved to Northants County.

8th Hole White Tee Royal Whittlewood Red Course 198 Yards Par 3.

A long carry of 180 yards over a large lake is required to reach this narrow green, which is well bunkered to the right and beyond, and only 18 yards wide. The tee shot is played from a sheltered spot amongst a small copse which makes club selection difficult as the wind can swirl around this "corner" of the course.

Inter-Club Trophies

The men play for several trophies, which provide a good variety of formats The Scratch League and the Hollingsworth are the "majors". There is also the popular Inter Club Handicap Trophy, which was launched by Past President the late Mike McMahon in 1997 and the Izzard Club Team Trophy launched in 1996.

The N.G.U. also launched Singles, Fourball and Foursomes March Play competitions in 2001, which each Club provides players from each category. The competitions are held across the county on a knock out basis with a final played in October at Final's day. The winners of all these events are documented in the N.G.U. annual yearbook, which is published in March to coincide with the N.G.U. annual dinner.

The major ladies inter-club trophies are the Cecil Leitch and Scratch League Shield.
The men's Scratch League has been dominated by Northants County, the men's Hollingsworth by Kingsthorpe,

Golf in Northamptonshire

the ladies Cecil Leitch by Northants County and the Ladies Scratch League by Northampton & Northants County.

Appendix 1 contains a list of trophy winners.

Scratch League 1922-2008 Men

The Scratch League as we know it today was originally played for as the Inter-Club Challenge Cup between 1922-1966. It was presented for play by W.P.Cross Esq (Northampton G.C. Captain 1915) in 1922 and first won by Northants County with a 3 man total of 250 at the First Annual Meeting held on the 11th&13th of May 1922 at Northamptonshire County G.C.

W.P.Cross was successful in several mixed events at Northampton G.C. and was the first peacetime event winner of a "Sealed Handicap" bogey event involving twenty players held on Christmas Day 1918.

Between 1922-1966, the trophy was won 18 times by Northants County, 12 times by Northampton G.C., 3 times by Rushden and Peterborough Milton G.Cs., twice by Kettering G.C. and once by Kingsthorpe G.C. Between 1966-1979 the trophy was unfortunately not played for.

The idea of a County League was first proposed by Priors Hall in 1968 at the December council meeting and it was agreed that the suggestion be deferred. The initial proposals were firmed up by the N.G.U. and circulated to Clubs; the issue was discussed in the summer of 1969 at a council meeting. Observations from the Clubs showed that the idea was not workable. The concept of a county league lay dormant until 1979 when a new format, which was agreeable to the Clubs, was accepted.

The Scratch League was formally launched in 1980 and two divisions were formed consisting of eight and seven Clubs respectively. The format of matches consisted of a team of ten players, four singles and three foursomes was played until ca 1990 when the format was changed to eight singles played in handicap order. The played in handicap order was introduced by the N.G.U. as a way of evaluating players performances and to identify new players for county golf. Since the introduction of this format, the results have been analysed annually by the N.G.U. for this purpose. In 1997 Kingsthorpe G.C. proposed that players position should become a "Captain's Pick" rather than by handicap order, this proposal did not find favour with the Clubs and the proposal was rejected by the council 15-4 votes. Kingsthorpe's original proposal has recently been revisited following pressure from some Division 1&2 players. This was debated in detail by e-mail during 2007 and passed to the N.G.U. Competitions Committee for consideration. I predict that no change will happen in 2008/9.

When attempting to analyses a player's performance there are two factors, which need to be considered, firstly the annual won, lost, halved scenario, which most simple analyses produce as a percentage. However when we look at a yearly and a long-term analysis it is also important to realise that the number of points a player has contributed to the team's performance should also be taken in to account.

For example if a player plays two matches and wins once, he will have a percentage success rate of 50% and contributed 1 team point, contrast this scenario with a player who has played all eight matches winning four games also with a success rate of 50% but has contributed 4 team points. I have developed a scientific equation (The Izzard Index), which takes in to account both situations resulting in the definition of a player's success. The N.G.U. Match Committee notably at the start of each season uses this information for A&B team selection. An example of this analysis for Division 1 2005 is given in Appendix 1.

Since 1980, the beautiful trophy has been presented annually to the Scratch League Division 1 winners. The donors of the Scratch League Division 2 trophy were Kettering's Past Captains R.P. (Paul) Seddon and Don Bates. In 1996& 2004 in view of the growing success of the competition and more Clubs' participating, trophies were provided by the N.G.U. for divisions three, four and five respectively.

222

The 2008 N.G.U. Scratch League consists of five Divisions with almost every Club represented.

HOLLINGSWORTH TROPHY
1955-2008 MEN

The magnificent trophy was donated in the year I was born and when Bill Hollingsworth was Northants County Golf Union President. His father ran a carriage works in Abington Street Northampton and Bill was born at number 64 which was the Co-Operative premises. Bill took up golf when he retired from the motor trade in 1936.

My grandfather Walter Ruskin Faulkner ran a bakery shop at 90 Abington Avenue (Faulkners) and I remember as a teenager in the 1960s serving Mr Hollingsworth a "split top" which was still warm from the oven at the back of "granddad's house". The trophy was actually selected and purchased in London by Bill's daughter Mary Bird. Bill Hollingsworth made a significant contribution to the local golf scene and was twice N.G.U. President in 1955 and 1967 and Northampton Club President 1964-1982. After being elected Northampton's Club President in 1964 he presented two trophies to be competed for in fourball betterball format (The Presidents). In the sixties at Northampton, golfers played each other for Bill's Trophies on a Sunday morn-

Northampton G.C. Club President Bill Hollingsworth who was elected in 1962 and is the donor of the Hollingsworth Trophy, pictured here at Northampton G.C. in 1970.

ing at Kettering Road where play always started at eight o clock from the first, third, fifth, seventh, eighth, tenth, thirteenth and sixteenth tee. This format ensured that everyone completed their round at the same time and could be in the clubhouse together to hear the Captain's speech at 1 p.m. This tradition is still continued at the Club at Harlestone and accompanied by a draw for chocolates. The inaugural winners were hard working County stalwarts Tony Stevens and Tom (T.C.A.) Knight. To date no player from Northampton has held both trophies although my son A.J.Izzard once had a six foot birdie putt to achieve this in 2005.

In 1966 Bill attained a unique triple honour as an elected President of the Northants and Beds Alliance, President of Northampton G.C. and Vice President of the N.G.U. In 1976 Bill was made an Honorary Life Member of Northampton G.C.

Returning to the Hollingsworth Trophy, the format of five foursomes played to a result is very conducive to generating team spirit and a true test of nerves. Bill Hollingsworth had a great passion for the game and was even playing a few strokes at the age of 93. He was even taking lessons from Northampton Club Professional Alf Lovelady in his late eighties. One of his early victories was in the 1937 Christmas Day Stableford which attracted an entry of 33! In 1947 during my research for this book (reference 1 page 69) Bill won the N.G.U. Higgs

Bowl trophy, this has recently been added to the records.

Bill was always there to present the beautiful trophy. In his latter years when Bill was unable to present the trophy through ill health (ca 1980) Mary carried out this task until her last appearance at Kingsthorpe G.C. in 2001. Bill Hollingsworth died on the16th July 1981 at the age of ninety-four. His funeral was held at St Mary Blessed Virgin Church Great Houghton and attended by hundreds of county golfers and friends. A feeling for Bill's passion for the game can be felt from the letters he typed despite suffering with severe arthritis concerning the arrangements for the Final on letters returned to the N.G.U. by Club administrators. (the file is with N.G.U. Secretary in the archive). At Northampton G.C. there is a photograph of Bill proudly wearing his N.G.U. County Colours with the victorious 1978 Team.

Although this marvellous trophy has been dominated by the "bigger" golf clubs, the smaller clubs have also featured in the finals. Unfortunately for those of a romantic disposition those smaller clubs have not often managed to lift the trophy. Priors Hall is the only club to complete a hat trick of victories as a newly formed club between 1973-5. Rushden were narrowly defeated by Peterborough in the 1976 final, when one of their players, interrupted Bill Hollingsworth's lengthy speech as he became doubled-up in agony and fell under the dinner table, since he was "crossing his legs". Oundle and Priors Hall have twice finished runners up and Cold Ashby have reached the final once. Farthingstone reached their first final in 2003 narrowly losing to Northampton 3-2 in a well played and friendly final. Farthingstone member and N.G.U. Vice-President Mike Taylor was understandably emotional and remained philosophical!

Northampton were undoubtedly the team of 1980s when they played in five finals winning on three occasions. From 1988 onwards Kettering, Kingsthorpe and Northants County have dominated the trophy. Kettering were in the final a remarkable five times in succession between 1989-94, Kingsthorpe playing in eleven finals with Northants County reaching five finals. The 2002 final was notable since it was largely a battle of the "young lads" from Kingsthorpe against the "old boys" from Northants County, which saw the Northants County team win by 3-2.

Since 2003 the composition of the qualifying groups has been decided by a random draw. In recent semi-finals and finals as a result of developments in the N.G.U. a referee accompanies each of the five matches to answer any rules decisions and speed up play if necessary. At the post-final dinner the President of the N.G.U. traditionally delivers the grace given to us by Bill Hollingsworth. Bill's competition has evolved in to the best team event in Northamptonshire.

HOLLINGSWORTH GRACE

I shall pass through this world but once.
Any good thing therefore that I can do or any kindness
that I can show anyone, let me do it now.
Let me not neglect it, nor defer it.
For I shall not pass this way again.

At the start of the 2005 year I wrote "Perhaps we shall have a romantic winner in 2005 when the trophy is contested for the fiftieth time". This actually proved to be the case when Staverton Park beat Northampton 3-2 on a misty warm sunny autumn day (16 October) at Northants County.

The pressure on the final match was intense with about 100 people watching the last three holes of play. With the match poised at 2-2, it would have been special for the author, a nine times finalist in his 50th year during the 50th anniversary of the competition if his son A.J. Izzard (AJ – Nickname One Jab) had holed the winning putt on the eighteenth green for a birdie four. The previous day he had won another trophy donated by Bill Hollingsworth, Northampton's Presidents Trophy so unbeknown to him he was putting for a unique double. AJ's six foot birdie putt for victory somehow slithered just past the hole and Staverton went on to win on the 19th with a solid par four.

That's Golf for you. My disappointment lasted until the following day when AJ's sister Natalie put her arm around me and said "Oh come on Dad you all did your best, it just did not happen" Wise words from a sixteen year old non-golfer. It was a time to regroup and to remember Bernhard Langer's mental strength after the 1991 Ryder Cup at Kiawah Island USA when he had a similar length putt to retain the Ryder Cup. AJ was not outwardly upset by the experience and I suspect secretly enjoyed the limelight.

The result was good for the competition, Bill would have been proud of the players friendly though competitive spirit in all five matches played and it was appropriate that one of Staverton's stalwarts Simon Brown ("Browny" future Club Captain in 2007) was their hero as the team celebrated around the green on the 19th hole, Staverton's team captain, chirpy Tom Sawyer would probably argue a different scenario in his own inimitable fashion!

In 2006 Kingsthorpe G.C. overcame a spirited Whittlebury Park G.C. team by 3 matches to 2 at Northampton G.C. on a damp autumnal October afternoon. In fact for the last 5 years this has been the winning margin and testimony to five very tight matches. During the early stages of this match the higher handicapped team from Whittlebury Park held a slender advantage but the greater experience of the lower handicapped Kingsthorpe team over the closing holes brought them a record twelfth victory in the same manner as the 2004 final i.e. on the first extra hole.

Over the last two decades Kingsthorpe have dominated this magnificent trophy with 8 victories and 5 runners up places.

HOLLINGSWORTH CHRONOLOGY

1955 The beautiful trophy was donated by Bill Hollingsworth

1956 The trophy was first played for and won by Kingsthorpe G.C.

1959, 1960 There were two sections (Ten Teams), which consisted of

A	B
Northampton	Kingsthorpe
Northants County	Kettering
Wellingborough	Rushden
Daventry	Oundle
Castle Ashby	Peterborough Milton

Rule 2 "The home team in each instant being drawn by the President"

Rule 6 Matches shall be played between 1st April and 15th September, in evenings or on Saturday or Sunday afternoons ...."

Rule 7 of the conditions of entry states "Sheltering is permitted"

Rule 10 "each competing Club shall pay an entrance fee for the year of one pound five shillings"

1961 Castle Ashby withdrew due to course closure and the sections (Nine Teams) were redrawn as described below.

A	B
Kingsthorpe	Daventry
Northants County	Kettering
Peterborough Milton	Northampton
Rushden	Oundle
Wellingborough	

1962-6 Nine teams as described above played in two redrawn groups. Entrance fee still one pound five shillings (Rule 10).

1967 Corby joined, making ten teams in two divisions

A	B
Daventry	Kingsthorpe
Kettering	Northants County
Northampton	Oundle
Rushden	Peterborough Milton
Corby	Wellingborough

1968-1976 The same ten Clubs were playing as in 1967, entry fee now £1.25p (Rule 10) Corby now called Priors Hall. The composition of each group was determined bi-annually to provide variety. Priors Hall completed the first and only hat-trick of victories 1973-75. The reasons for their successes are lost in time and are unquantifiable. No club has to date emulated this unique achievement in a handicapped competition, although several clubs had achieved doubles. In 1976 Rushden reached their one and only final, narrowly losing to Peterborough Milton by 3-2. There is a photograph of the Rushden team on the wall in the clubhouse.

Kingsthorpe G.C. Hollingsworth Trophy Champions 2006.

1977 Peterborough Milton and Northampton tied at the head of Group A with the same number of matches won and the same goal difference. The play-off was held at Staverton Park G.C. on the 18th September and won by Peterborough Milton, Northants County won Group B.

1978 The first three cornered final was played between Daventry, Kettering and Northampton according to the Eastern Counties Foursomes format at Northants County on the 1st October and won by Northampton. The very detailed rules of play were circulated to the three Clubs several weeks prior to the final. At the Harlestone club-house a photograph taken that evening shows Bill Hollingsworth proudly wearing his County Colours with the victorious team gathered around the fireplace at the old ''Kettering Road'' clubhouse.

1979 The poor match result returns from some of the Clubs caused much confusion. It would appear that there were three groups. The finalists for the second and last three-cornered final were Kingsthorpe, Northants County and Peterborough Milton. The trophy was won by Peterborough Milton.

1979-88 Four Groups. During the 1987 final at the fine Peterborough Milton course on a glorious autumn day, Northampton won the trophy and this day was especially memorable since Europe won the Ryder Cup for the first time on American soil as the Hollingsworth finalists were enjoying the presentation meal. In fact the meal was temporarily suspended until Seve Ballesteros sank the winning putt on the seventeenth green against Curtis Strange. Captain Tony Jacklin's words, "This is the best day of my life", was being echoed miles across the Atlantic in the Milton clubhouse and latterly during the evening in a little wooden clubhouse on Kettering Road in Northampton. Northampton retained the trophy the following year against Peterborough Milton.

2001 Interestingly, Jim Howkins of Kingsthorpe G.C. who played in the first final was present at his home Club to watch the final between Peterborough Milton and Corby GCs, some forty-six years later, this time he was not wearing short trousers! The competition was moved to the start of the season instead of the end of the golf season "curtain closer" as a trial. This proved to be unpopular with the players and officials; normality was restored the following year.

2005 There was now for the first time, five groups of five teams representing 25 N.G.U. Clubs playing. A quarter final was introduced for the first time to determine the composition of the semi-finals. This featured Hellidon Lakes and Kingsthorpe G.C.s where the underdogs beat a heavily fancied Kingsthorpe team by 3-2 at Overstone Park G.C. and passage to their first ever Semi-Final against local rivals Staverton Park G.C. Staverton went on to become Champions.

2006 Kingsthorpe recorded a 12th victory to underline dominating this event for the past two decades.

2007 After two runners up places in 1999 & 2005 Collingtree Park G.C. finally got there hands on the trophy following a 4-1 victory against Priors Hall at Wellingborough G.C. This was Priors Hall's six appearance in the final.

The Ladies Cecil Leitch Trophy 1927-2007 including Joyce Wethered and the Sheringham "What Train" story

This trophy is one of the most prized trophies played for by the ladies. Cecil Leitch was a much-loved character in England & Northamptonshire and made a significant impact on the ladies golf scene both locally and nationally. The details of her life, the trophy and her rivalry with Joyce Wethered are described below.

During the middle of the nineteenth century although Britain was the home of golf, British women initially received little hospitality from male golf clubs. Women golfers at that time had no choice but to play golf separately and form their own organisations. One of the first to be formed was the Westward Ho and North Devon Ladies Club in 1868. By 1900,130 had been created in Britain. In some of the early tournaments several ladies distinguished themselves, most notable were Cecil Leitch and Joyce Wethered who won a record four British

Amateur titles each in 1914,1920,1921,1926 and 1922, 1924, 1925, 1929 respectively. Their records still stand today.

Cecil (Cecilia) Leitch (1891-1977) began playing golf at the age of nine on a thin strip of land at Silloth in 1900. In fact they were quite a golfing family as her four sisters Edith, May, Chris and Peggy all played golf. She played there on a short nine hole course that had been laid out by her father. Cecil Leitch describes her early links in her 1922 book "Golf Simplified" as follows " My father a Scottish doctor was the pioneer of golf at Silloth, laying out a 9-hole course on common land and playing there, with his sister, the first game of golf ever played on the shores of the Solway Firth. The natives of the place regarded them as a pair of lunatics. So there were hereditary reasons why I should not only play golf, but become 'mad' on the game. And I may say here than never once since I first took a club in my hand has there been any doubt about my love for golf; my love for it has never faltered; neither victory nor defeat has made any difference; I have just gone on growing fonder and fonder of the game. At the age of nine then, I began my golfing career, on a stretch of ground 200 yards wide and a quarter mile long; for this was all we made use of for our primitive 9-hole course. Our fairways were the paths made by pedestrians, our putting greens the good patches on these paths, our holes cut by ourselves and lined with treacle tins, and our 'trouble' the bents, sand holes and wiry grass common to seaside links.

"My first club was one of the old-fashioned cleeks, and my first ball - and only one for a long time - a guttie. This was my introduction to the game, and in its independence, it bears a close relationship to the rest of my golfing career. My golf has developed along independent lines; I am entirely self-taught, and I never had a lesson in my life. I watched others of course, and learnt from them. Then I have received many valuable tips from leading players - from Mr. Hilton, from the late Tom Ball, from Arnaud Massy. Watching his even, rhythmical swing, one soon finds oneself falling into his way of doing it. It is a sort of unconscious mimicry."

At the beginning of the book she describes her feelings about the Solway and her original course. "... there used to be a stretch of natural seaside ground remembered by Sillothians as 'The Banks' - 'used to be,' for gradually the encroaching waters of Solway Firth have eaten it away, until little remains of the bonnie 'Banks' of my childhood. Although I love the dear old Solway in all its moods, I can never forgive it for this act of destruction. In devouring 'The Banks' it destroyed the actual birthplace of my golf, the spot where I first hit a golf ball, disregarding the sanctity that always attaches to a birthplace." Throughout her career, Cecil Leitch never forgot her humble origin, on the banks of the Solway.

Miss Leitch known as the "young flapper" at the age of 17 in 1908 had "like a meteor, swept across the sky at St. Andrews" (golf writer Enid Wilson) when she reached the semi-final of the British Ladies Championship, striking the ball with a crispness and ferocity not previously seen from a woman. When Cecil Leitch's book was published in 1922, by this time the ladies were given more respect on the golf course. To highlight this cause, in 1910 Cecil Leitch played a match against one of the most famous male golfers, Harold Hilton, winner of the British Amateur and British Open. Now at 41 in 1910, Hilton was past his prime but still one of the best male amateurs of the day, evidenced by his victory in the U.S. Amateur in 1911. He faced Miss Leitch, still a teenager at 19, and at the beginning of her career. One of the purposes of the match was to promote women's golf since it was sponsored by The Ladies' Field magazine. People were also curious to see how a woman could hold up against one of the best male golfers. Miss Leitch was allowed nine strokes per 18 holes, according to Hilton's estimate of handicapping. She describes the match and all its excitement, "The 'test' in which Mr. Hilton and I met was one of 72 holes - 36 at Walton Heath, 36 at Sunningdale - on October 11 and 13, 1910. For weeks before, the match was widely discussed, opinions greatly differing as to the probable result. ... Perhaps I was given some confidence by the wise and encouraging advice of that wonderful judge of form, James Braid, who during a friendly round at Walton Health told me just to play my own game and I would come through. ... So unique a match was likely to attract a following, but I shall never forget my surprise when I arrived at the Clubhouse at Walton Heath to find a crowd of about 3,000 spectators, one of the biggest crowds ever seen on a Southern course.

At times it was hard to find room to swing a club, so eager was the crowd to see every stroke, and on one occasion Mr. Hilton was not allowed to finish his follow through! The chief thing that I recollect about the first half of the match is that I seldom saw my opponent play a shot through the green. It was only after the crowd had formed a circle around the green that I was given an opportunity to watch Mr. Hilton. We both struck a patch of somewhat indifferent play during the first 36 holes and both slipped a number of chances, but on the other hand we occasionally did something brilliant. The result of the first day's play was a lead of 1 hole for my opponent.

"The considerate organizers of the match allowed us a day's rest before commencing the second half of the match. At Walton Heath we had a perfect day; at Sunningdale the weather conditions could not have been worse - a gale of wind and drenching rain. I remember little about the third round except that we were soaked to the skin before we reached the first green, and that I was 4 down with 18 holes to play." Consider this scenario: a young woman in a man's game pitted against a seasoned veteran, in a driving rain, four down with one round left. How many people today could even walk 36 holes a day, let alone do it in a rainstorm? "In the afternoon a win in 4 at the 1st hole [not a stroke hole] slightly improved my position, but the next 2 holes went to my opponent, and I felt that any chance of success I had ever possessed had now finally vanished. Five down and 15 to play with 8 strokes to come! The only thing that now interested me was to try to make my defeat as light as possible. On the 4th green Mr. Hilton missed a comparatively short putt, which allowed me to win back a hole with the help of the stroke allowance.

In a 72-holes match the pendulum swings first one way and then the other, but little did I think as I took the honour on the fifth tee of the fourth round that the time had come for it to take a decided swing in my favour. From that point I lost only 1 hole, and eventually won on the 71st green by 2 up and 1 to play." She comments that the match "certainly increased the interest taken in ladies' golf by the amateurs [meaning the male players], and vice versa, and before long a Ladies v. Men Match became an annual event at Stoke Poges." The first of these matches took place in 1914 which included Cecil Leitch and Bernard Darwin, the match was described by Dr.A.MacKenzie in the magazine "Golfing" (price one old penny) as "The Sex Test Match". Writing this in piece in 2007 make one realise my how things have changed, men and woman even play together now!

Cecil Leitch holds the record for the biggest margin for a major title when she won the Canadian Ladies Open Championship in 1921 by - 17 up and 15 to play. It was at Royal St David's that Cecil Leitch won the last of her British Championships in 1926 and retired from competitive play. Cecil Leitch made a considerable impact on British golf where many counties have trophies played for in her honour and memory. For example in Lancashire the ladies play for The 5 Club Trophy which was donated by Cecil Leitch in 1963, Cumbria and Northumberland also hold events linked to Cecil Leitch. In her later years she played the odd society event or open meeting, one such an occasion in truly dreadful conditions she returned the winning score 76, this had the local golf correspondent reporting the headline "76 at 67".

In Northamptonshire, Cecil Leitch had a close relative in the County and played often at Church Brampton on her frequent visits. In fact a match between the two great rivals Cecil Leitch and Joyce Wethered was played at the course during the 1920s. In 1924 Miss Cecil Leitch played in the Brampton Ladies Open meeting off +2 handicap breaking the course record with a score of 81 and collected the scratch prize. She was the first lady to be given a plus handicap. In 1926 she gave the Cecil Leitch trophy to the Club to be played as an Inter Club event under handicap 12-36. The format was modelled on the Pearson Trophy a significant event which the London Clubs competed for. The ladies committee at Church Brampton was asked to draw up the original rules, which were approved by Cecil Leitch. Six clubs competed in the first year 1927 with Kingsthorpe becoming the winners on their home course. The organisation of the trophy passed to the County Association in 1934. When time allowed Cecil Leitch presented the trophy at the final and also provided a signed photograph to Church Brampton which hangs in the clubhouse. Such is the interest in the competition that in 1996 The County Ladies Association purchased a runner up shield for the competition. A complete list of winners is given in Appendix 1.

Cecil Leitch's arch rival was Joyce Wethered (1901 - 1997) Born Devon, England; Wethered is remembered

2007 Cecil Leitch Finalists:
Above: Elton Furze; and Below: Collingtree Park.

as probably the greatest lady golfer of all time. Her victories include 5 English Amateur and 4 British Ladies Amateur championships. Wethered grew up in a well to do family in southern England. As a child she often spent her summer holidays at her parent's summer home in Scotland. It was there that she and her brother, Roger, developed their skills as golfers. Roger went on to become a professional and gave Joyce the challenge she needed to develop a competitive game. However she always competed as an amateur.

In 1920, Wethered exploded onto the scene by beating the great Cecil Leitch to win the 1920 English Ladies Championship. Her career lasted only nine years and in that time she won 5 consecutive English Amateur titles and 4 British Ladies titles. Her forte was accuracy and power. Indeed her statistics show that she could have qualified for the men's Walker Cup at the time. Her talents were considered so superior, that even the legendary Bobby Jones reportedly called her "the greatest golfer of all time, man or woman". Henry Cotton and many others paid tribute to her abilities and her modesty earned her the affection of golf fans. Interestingly when she became president of the English LGU in 1954, the R&A re-instated her amateur status thus enabling her to legitimately hold the office. She later retired to Knightshayes Court (The house and gardens now belong to the National Trust) a few minutes from Tiverton Golf Club Devon where she died age 96.

Easily the most famous Joyce Wethered story of all concerns an incident in her first major victory, the final of the English Ladies' Championship at Sheringham on the Norfolk coast. The facts of the day are part of the history of golf. The Championship was played in June on a fast running course, which had been baked hard by the Norfolk sunshine. In the final Joyce Wethered faced Cecil Leitch and launched one of golf's great comebacks in the afternoon round. Wethered was four down at lunch, six down at the twenty-first and four down with nine to play. Some fine play on the back nine, which included several three hundred yard drives and a string of threes from the eleventh, reduced the deficit to one down. A fine third shot to the sixteenth hole put Miss Wethered ahead for the first time.

At the famous seventeenth played down the hill and up to a green adjacent to the railway line Miss Leitch attempted to find the green in two but instead found the cross bunkers. Miss Leitch continues the story "As Miss Wethered was preparing to putt for the win and the title of 1920 English champion, a long train suddenly rattled by, making the most horrible noise. She appeared quite unbothered by the train, in fact appeared almost in a trance, quite unconscious of any of her immediate surroundings." While the crowd winced, Wethered calmly stroked the putt into the hole for a 2 and 1 victory. Asked by reporters later why she didn't back away from the putt and wait for the train to go by, she replied, **"What Train"**.

Those two simple words are part of golfing history at Norfolk's magnificent seaside links, Sheringham G.C [21]. The seventeenth hole is named "What Train". In 1975 she was inducted into the PGA World Golf Hall of Fame, along with long-time rival Glenna Collett Vare. In 1994 The Daily Telegraph created the Joyce Wethered award, to be presented annually to an upstanding woman golfer under the age of 25. They were two remarkable lady golfers.

When playing the 17th at Sheringham G.C. recently my mind wandered because of the emotions of this lovely area and this beautiful poem came in to my mind. It captures the essence of seaside golf.

Seaside Golf

How straight it flew, how long it flew,
It clear'd the rutty track
And soaring, disappeared from view
Beyond the bunker's back -
A glorious, sailing, bounding drive
That made me glad I was alive.

Golf in Northamptonshire

And down the fairway, far along
It glowed a lonely white;
I played an iron sure and strong
And clipp'd it out of sight,
And spite of grassy banks between
I knew I'd find it on the green.

And so I did. It lay content
Two paces from the pin;
A steady putt and then it went
Oh, most assuredly in.
The very turf rejoiced to see
That quite unprecedented three.

Ah! Seaweed smells from sandy caves
And thyme and mist in whiffs,
In-coming tide, Atlantic waves
Slapping the sunny cliffs,
Lark song and sea sound in the air
And splendour, splendour, everywhere.

Sir John Betjeman 1906-1984, former Poet Laureate.

What Train - the famous 17th hole at Sheringham G. C.

Inspiration for the poem came after a rare birdie on the 13th hole at St. Enodoc G.C. Cornwall.

In the County the Cecil Leitch matches consist of teams of seven players who play each other off handicap, in 2007 there are currently four divisions. Like the men's Hollingsworth Trophy there are no halved matched which adds spice and excitement to the matches. The semi finals are played at a neutral course where the four teams establish who will compete in the final.

Northamptonshire Ladies Scratch League

The Scratch League Trophy was presented by Mrs Judy Ray Oundle G.C. in 1991. The teams consist of three players and in 2007, there were three leagues. The semi final consisting of the league's top Club and the best runner-up. The final is held on a neutral venue, Northampton & Northants County G.Cs have dominated the winner's rostrum.

"The older I get, the better I used to be."

Lee Trevino

N.G.U. Seniors Champions 2002 (Gross) Richard Cole (PMGC), left, and Graham Golding (Priors Hall) (Nett) at Stoke Albany G.C.

CHAPTER 7

THE NORTHAMPTONSHIRE PROFESSIONAL GOLFERS ASSOCIATION

"In golf your strengths and weaknesses will always be there. If you improve your weaknesses, you will improve your game. The irony is that people prefer to practise their strengths"

Harvey Penick

THE Professional Golfers Association (P.G.A.) of Great Britain owes a great deal in its formation to the five times Open Champion J.H.Taylor who was largely responsible for it's formation in 1901. In the early years of the twentieth century professional golfers were viewed as little more than club servants who were employed to carry out many menial tasks for a tiny wage. Each club decided the employment conditions. Typically they were responsible for the Clubhouse and it's safety, the management of the caddies, to assist the Greenkeeper for eight hours per week at such times as the Greenkeeper or Committee may require and other duties, which from time to time may arise. All of this for a salary of five shillings per week although they were allowed to take the profits from making and mending golf clubs and balls!

This pay level was virtually the same over the whole country such that the formation of the P.G.A. was thought to be one way to improve their pay and conditions at work. The date of when this was first proposed is lost in the history of time however the first record of the proposed formation is given in the April 12 1901 edition of *Golf Illustrated*. A letter from "A Professional in North Wales" who suggested that it was timely for them "to band together into an association to promote the general welfare of the professional and look after his interests". Many thought that the initiative was likely to fail without the support of The Great Triumvirate (James Braid, Harry Vardon and JH Taylor) and other prominent professionals (Sandy Herd, Jack White). These gentlemen were happy for this idea to go ahead such that the P.G.A. was formally launched on the 2 December 1901. J.H.Taylor was the elected Chairman, James Braid was elected as Captain. The organisation has grown into a multi-million pound business over the years and celebrated its Centenary in 2001.

History of the Northamptonshire P.G.A.

The names of Richard Kemp (Corby G.C.), John Freeman (Kingsthorpe G.C.), Stuart Murray (Northants County G.C.) and Alf Lovelady (Northampton G.C.) may not mean much to some of the current county amateur and professional golfers but they organised the first Pro-Am in the county in 1968[24]. It was played at Northants County Golf Club, consisted of nine teams of three and cost 27 shillings to enter. Although Northamptonshire Professionals have been playing for trophies since 1947, it was only in 1967 that the Association first started to be discussed. One of the earliest recorded matches took place between the Amateurs and Professionals on April 3rd 1955, the match sheet is shown below. The match consisted of two teams of sixteen; clearly, Bill Hollingsworth the organiser of the event had a fine sense of humour as the teams were nicknamed Kilsbiams and Proparkers after the respective Captains R.W. Kilsby and J.S. Parker. Foursomes and fourballs were played in the morning and afternoon respectively.

In 1988, Northamptonshire P.G.A became one of the first counties to be constitutionally set up. Tim Giles (Kingsthorpe G.C. was the driving force behind this, with the late Stuart Brown (Northants County G.C.) who became the first official chairman. George Mobbs (Northants County) became the secretary. Brian Mudge (then Staverton Park G.C.) became the first captain. His phone call to Les Cantrell's company Venture Business Forms to ask for sponsorship was the start of the nationally renowned Winter Series Pro-Am, which continued with Les Cantrell's sponsorship for ten years. During this time, his sponsorship amounted to over £50,000 and a significant amount went to local charities. N.G.U. President 2006-8 Les Cantrell now sponsors the prestigious Cantrell Cup played for annually by the county's professionals and leading amateurs.

In 1989, there were 10 events in the Pro-Am series – averaging 25 teams consisting of one professional

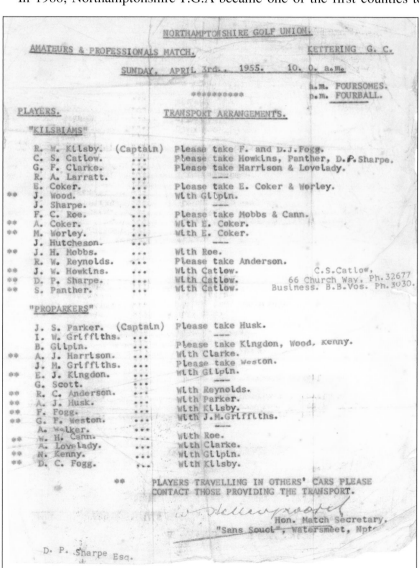

Match sheet sent from Hon. Match Secretary Bill Hollingsworth to Kingsthorpe's David Sharpe for the Amateurs vs Professionals match in 1955.

Alf Lovelady in his shop at Northampton G.C. 1970.

and four amateurs. In the 2001/02 series there were 18 events covering virtually all of the courses as well as the 12th Overseas Pro-Am. This was then the best supported Overseas Pro-Am in the country (30 Teams).

The association was fortunate to have the continued sponsorship of The Order of Merit from Barclaycard, Richard Underwood of Echo Plc and Ray Kingston of EBS mobile phones. The mantle of main sponsor then passed to Mike Abbotts of Cert'n'fase. The long term and extremely valued support of the Late Tom Hillery's Lionverge Company from 1990 for the young professionals in the county continued for 10 years and helped bring through many fine players, especially Shane Rose (Cold Ashby), Stuart Reynolds (Northants

N.P.G.A. Cantrell Cup 3rd May 2006 Winners: England International Gary Boyd and Jason Newman (Cherwell Edge G.C.) with Peterborough Milton G.C. Captain Tony Huggins (left) and Les Cantrell (President 2001-2005) (right).

County) and Simon Lilly (Kettering & Wellingborough). Dave Croxton (Cold Ashby), John Pulford (Autohaus), Tom Pearson (Nene Group plc), Colin Bishop (A&B Metalcraft) and Dave Mead (Weedon Motor Co) are also very long-term sponsors of the Northamptonshire P.G.A.

In 1991 Stuart Brown moved to the prestigious Slaley Hall in Northumberland to take up the position of Director of Golf. His chairmanship had passed the previous year to Brian Mudge (Overstone Park who held this position for 10 years, before passing it to Henry Bareham (Collingtree) in 2000.

As the county's first chairman, Stuart Brown's death in the mid 1990s came as an enormous shock, as he prepared to join the senior circuit. Many N.P.G.A. Professionals attended his funeral in his hometown of Edinburgh. In 1994 Sydney Cruickshank took over from George Mobbs as the secretary of the association. George was very experienced and former secretary of Northants County. Sid's style of administration and deep knowledge of golf was much loved by everyone he knew, and his death in April 2001 was met with great sadness throughout the County especially at Overstone Park G.C. where he was the Club starter. He had only been the Association's first President for a few months. His position as secretary was taken over by Kash Naidu. After a short stint in the hot seat, Greg Croxton (Cold Ashby) took over as Secretary and in 2004 Richard Lobb (Northants County) took up charge of the day to day running of the association. Since 1999 Malcolm Pounds (Northants County) has been the Treasurer of the N.P.G.A. and has worked alongside the various Secretaries to help the smooth running of each event.

The Northamptonshire P.G.A. has provided several Midland P.G.A. Captains. In a 12-year period Stuart Brown, Tim Rouse, Brian Mudge and Shane Rose were all afforded the honour.

In 1998 the then N.P.G.A. chairman organised the first Sponsors day event, held to say thank you to all the Northants P.G.A. tournament sponsors too numerous to mention. The following year Mudge oversaw the N.P.G.A.'s first charity event linked to Sponsors Day. The Northampton Association of Young Carers and Clubs for young people benefited from the N.P.G.A. organised golf events. Chairman Mudge commented that during his time as chairman, we have built up our profile and some financial security therefore it is great to give something back. On the golf course, our professionals have been successful as follows. Early success was achieved in the Midland Professional Foursomes in 1913, 1919, 20 and 1921 by G.V.Tuck (South Staffs) and Len Holland (Northants County) no further events were organised after 1933. Len Holland was a superb iron player and one of his famous exhibition shots at the Church Brampton course was from the left of the tenth tee through the railway arch on to the fifteenth green! In The Midland Professional Championship Kevin Dickens in 1991 and Shane Rose (Cold Ashby) in 1995 have featured on the winners rostrum, this event has been running since 1897 and is run by the Midland section of the P.G.A. Shane Rose also won the Midland Masters in 1991.

In 1977 Mike Gallagher from Farthingstone G.C. qualified for The Open Championship at Turnberry which became the classic Jack Nicklaus/Tom Watson Open unfortunately Mike did not make the last two rounds but really enjoyed the experience among the best in the world. In the same year he was a member of the P.G.A. Cup team vs USA played at Palm Springs where the match was halved. Mike has been a prolific winner locally and has won the County Match Play and Stroke play titles a record twelve times up to 1993. Continuing the P.G.A. Cup theme was Tim Giles who played in the1992 match at The K Club Ireland, he was followed by Kevin Dickens in 1998 who played in the matches at the Broadmoor Resort Colorado.

In 2003 Cold Ashby professional Andrew Hare was selected for the Great Britain and Ireland team for the P.G.A. Cup in Port St Lucie Florida, a tournament widely regarded as the Club Professionals Ryder Cup. Hare flew out to the United States to join up with the other nine team members, who have been selected based on their performances in the Glenmuir Professionals Championship over the last two years.

At the time P.G.A. spokesman, Ron Marshall saw the competition as something of a "mission impossible", with the British and Irish team without a victory since 1984. He stated at the time:

"The bookies won't give odds on us winning, speaking with my head and not my heart I have to say the Americans really are the top dogs at the moment. But we've got a good side, Andy Hare's a good player and you never know what will happen. The Cold Ashby pro admits he didn't know too much about the course at Port St Lucie in the Florida panhandle, but knows it will be tough, especially with the visiting team playing completely out of season. "I've never been on this course before but I've played my way into the team and I'm confident of getting a result," he said. "It's a very busy schedule, but I'm hoping to get in three or four practice rounds before we get going just to acclimatise to the weather and the playing conditions."

Andy Hare was looking for a distinctive double; having guided the British amateur team to victory over their American counterparts in the Walker Cup in Peachtree, Georgia in 1989.The competition consisted of four four-somes and four four-balls on Friday and Saturday, then 10 singles on the Sunday. The Cup was retained by the U.S.A. with a score of 19-7.

Andrew Hare is currently with Woodhall Spa G.C. at the home of English Golf.

P.G.A. Cup Representation from Northamptonshire's Professionals

Player	Year	Won	Lost	Halved
Kevin Dickens	1998	1	1	1
Mike Gallagher	1977	1	2	0
Tim Giles	1992	0	1	1
Andrew Hare	2003	1	4	0

1998 GB&I P.G.A. Cup Team. The Broadmoor Club, Colorado Springs.

Brian Rimmer Mike MaCara Russell Weir Stephen Bennett Paul Wesselingh Kevin Dickens
Andrew George Michael Jones Craig Defoy (C) John Greaves Paul Simpson

The 1998 G.B. & I. P.G.A. Cup Team which included Northamptonshire's Kevin Dickens (Back Right)

Coaching Successes

As well as success on the golf course, many of the Professionals have enjoyed some notable coaching achievements. Brian Mudge (then at Staverton Park) coached Gary Wolstenholme MBE during 1989-1992, culminating in his British Amateur Champion victory at Ganton in 1991. Gary has subsequently become England's most capped player and made a record 200th appearance for his country when he lined up for England against Spain in May 2007. This is a remarkable record for the Leicestershire-based 46 year old, who was awarded an MBE in the New Year Honours List, which marks him as the most successful England amateur of all time. Also at this time, Brian Mudge was also working with Kevin Dickens who had his most successful year as a Tournament Professional. Kevin's success which in no small part assisted by the tremendous sponsorship given by Steve Cass of SMC Engineering and included finishing second in the Belgium Open, securing his Tour Card by finishing in the top 100 in the European Order of Merit and winning the Midland Order of Merit all in 1991.

Tim Rouse, himself a competitor in the 1986 Open at Turnberry has most recently assisted Gary Boyd in his quest for Tournament stardom. Gary a plus 4 player nurtured by Cherwell Edge GC is probably the best Amateur player to emerge from Northamptonshire and move into the Pro ranks along with Simon Lilly, who also works under the eye of Tim Rouse. It must not be forgotten that Stuart Reynolds working as a Professional under the tutorage of Tim became a member of a very exclusive club in 2001. Stuart shot 59 in tournament play (see Chapter 11 for the details of this phenomenal achievement) David Duval; World number 1 in 2001 is also one of this elite group.

Shane Rose the Cold Ashby Professional oversees the County Ladies Team. Tim Rouse (Northants County) has been working for several years as the County First Team Coach. Brian Mudge (now Collingtree Park G.C.) was appointed as one of the first Golf Professional Managers to become a County Junior Team Manager. As of 2008, there are signs that this approach is working well with the juniors.

The Northants P.G.A. under the careful guidance of their Secretary Richard Lobb are now working with the Sport England Partnership who are providing much needed funding for Junior coaching. This is a Government led initiative to get more children into sport and Northamptonshire is at the forefront of this project. Talented youngsters below the age of 14 and as young as 9 are being identified by clubs and their Professionals to help bring them through as future County Under 14, Under 16 and Under 18 players. Ryan Rowe from Peterborough Milton, the talented 13 year old and World under 14 Championship competitor is one such player who has emerged.

Many of the County Professionals are also now working in local schools through the Golf Foundation Tri-Golf initiative. This is aimed at bringing more children into contact with golf as a sport and showing them the opening for membership of golf clubs.

The Northamptonshire Professional Golfers Association with all its work, is living up to its responsibility of upholders of the integrity and tradition of the game through its teaching, playing and introduction of people to this great game of golf.

Northants P.G.A. Professional Profiles 2008

At the time of writing there are 30 members of the Association[24], I have included here several examples of their personal profiles, which I thank them for supplying.

Ed Chapman
Ed was born in Northampton in 1986 and started playing golf as a 16 year old he turned professional 3 years later on the P.G.A. training programme with a handicap of 3.

Positions held: P.G.A. Assistant Professional at Overstone Park Hotel, Golf and Leisure Resort - 2004 - Feb

2007, P.G.A. Assistant Professional, Northamptonshire County Golf Club Feb 2007 – Present.

Notable Victories/Events: N.G.U. County Singles Matchplay Champion 2004, Junior Club Champion 2004 (amateur). Tied third N.P.G.A. Winter Series Pro-Am at Overstone Park 2005 & 2007, Kingsthorpe 2007. Regional Open Qualifying 2006 (professional). NPGA USA Overseas Pro-Am 2006 10th (Harbour Town Golf Links) and 2007 8th (TPC Sawgrass).

Ed's current passions include snowboarding, fitness/gym, foreign languages, cooking, reading and movies.

Rodney Holt

Rodney was born in Chiswick London in 1969; and is married with three children. He started playing golf aged 8 but didn't really take the game seriously until his mid to late teens when he had lessons with Peter Thompson in Aldershot (Formally at Kettering G.C.). Although Rodney's first choice as a career was as an Electronic Engineer, he changed career path in 1989 and joined Tom Gates at Buckingham Golf Club as an Assistant. Rodney is currently (2008) the Northamptonshire P.G.A. Captain.

Positions Held: Assistant Professional: Buckingham Golf Club 1989-1993, Assistant Professional: Silverstone Golf Club 1992-1994, Head Professional: Silverstone Golf Club 1994-Present.

Professional Victories: 1990 BBO PGA Berkshire Pro-Am, 2001 NPGA Wellingborough Pro-Am, 2003 NPGA Silverstone Pro-Am, 2004 NPGA Brampton Heath Pro-Am, 2006 NPGA Kingsthorpe Pro-Am

Course Record: 2003 Professional Silverstone 65
Other Notables: 1992 3rd BB&O Open
                          2006-2008 N.P.G.A. Captain
                          2002-Present N.P.G.A. Committee Member
Other Interests: Manchester United Football Club

Brian Mudge

Brian was born in New Milton in 1957 and represented his home county Hampshire as an amateur. After leaving the amateur ranks, Brian has been Head Professional at Staverton Park, Overstone Park and Collingtree Park golf clubs. He lists his notable victories as Sunningdale Foursomes Semi-finalist, National Assistant Professional Matchplay Quarter Finalist, and Northants Open Runner up with hopefully more victories to come!

Points of Interest – Brian was coach to Gary Wolstenholme MBE in his title-winning year when he became the English Amateur Champion. At the other end of the spectrum he coached a lady who started to play golf at 78 with no ball & socket joint in her left shoulder and within 18 months she had broke 100. Brian also gave Richard Branson's grandmother a golf lesson when she was 97 years old.

Brian lists his current passions as family, playing golf and coaching – especially children, football, personal health & fitness including food, all history and culture, world geography and animals.

Brian has made a major contribution to golf in Northamptonshire especially with juniors.

Shane Rose

Shane was born in Northampton in 1968 and turned Professional in November 1985; he is with Partner Karen and has two children Chelsea and Ben.

Positions held: Assistant to Tim Giles at Kingsthorpe GC Nov 1985-1 Dec 1987
Teaching assistant to Tim Giles at De Hoge Kliej GC (Holland) Dec1987-Jan 1989.
Assistant to Stuart Brown Northants County G.C. Jan 1989-Feb 1990.

Became a fully qualified P.G.A. member in Dec 1989.

Attached to Cold Ashby G.C. Playing full time under the sponsorship of Venture Business Forms Feb 1990-April 1993

Head Professional at Cold Ashby G.C. April 1993-Present.

Notable Achievements:

1991 Midland Masters Champion

1991 Midland P.G.A. Assistants Order of Merit Champion.

1991 Sixth in the European under 25s in France

1995 Midland Professionals Champion.

2006 Midland P.G.A. Carlsberg Tour Championship

Northamptonshire P.G.A. Strokeplay Winner 1995 and 2004

Northamptonshire Matchplay Winner 1991 and 1993

Northamptonshire Winter Order of Merit Champion 1992, 1993, 2002

Northamptonshire P.G.A. Captain 1994-1996

Northamptonshire P.G.A. Chairman 2003-Present

Midland P.G.A. Captain 1998 (The youngest ever regional Captain aged 29)

Course Records 67 Forest of Arden G.C., 63 Oundle G.C., 64 Ormond Fields G.C., Shane has recorded six holes in one.

Other Interests: Snooker, Chelsea FC, Speedway (Coventry Bee's),

Current Passions Shane enjoys Team Coaching and had some success with the Ladies County Team and Cold Ashby's Scratch Team.

Nick Soto

Nick was born in Northampton in 1976 and developed an interest in the game through caddying for his father Tony at Northampton's Kettering Road course. Nick's first appearance for Northamptonshire as an amateur was against Lincolnshire in September 1995 the weekend that Frank Bruno became World Champion by out pointing Oliver McCall over twelve rounds.

Positions Held: Assistant Professional Northampton G.C 2004-2006

Assistant Professional Northants County G.C. 2006 - Present

Victories: Amateur: 1999 & 2001 N.G.U. County Champion, 2001 N.G.U Open.

Professional: 2006 Northampton Pro Am, 2006 N.P.G.A Overseas

Pro Am - Hilton Head, 2007 N.P.G.A Kingsthorpe Pro Am, 2007 N.P.G.A Overseas Pro Am – Sawgrass.

In 2000, Nick reached the final stages of Open Qualifying at Lundin links and acquitted himself very well, whilst the likes of Mark Calcavecchia and Jack Nicklaus were casually walking the course. It was also a new experience for Nick to be signing autograph books at the back of the eighteenth green as the local lads and lasses assumed that he was someone famous; it must have been the haircut!

Nick is one of life's natural comedians and lists his interests as Manchester City Football Club and socialising.

Past Presidents

2006-Present	John Pulford	Northamptonshire County GC
2001-2005	Les Cantrell	Northamptonshire County GC
2000-2001	Sydney Cruickshank	Northamptonshire County GC

Past Captains

Date	Captain	Club
2004 & 2005	Stuart Reynolds	Northamptonshire County GC
2002-2003	Richard Hudson	Brampton Heath GC
2000-2001	Tim Rouse	Northamptonshire County GC
1998 & 1999	Henry Bareham	Collingtree Park GC
1996 & 1997	Richard Mudge	Staverton Park GC
1994 & 1995	Shane Rose	Cold Ashby GC
1992 & 1993	David Clifford	Wellingborough
1990 & 1991	Andy Jolly	Northamptonshire County GC
1988 & 1989	Brian Mudge	Staverton Park GC

Past Chairmen

Date	Chairman	Golf Club
2003-Present	Shane Rose	Cold Ashby GC
2000-2003	Henry Bareham	Collingtree Park GC
1990-2000	Brian Mudge	Staverton Park GC/Overstone Park GC
1988-1990	Stuart Brown	Northamptonshire County GC

Midland Professional Winners in recent times 1991-2008

Year	Stroke Play	Match Play	Year	Stroke Play	Match Play
1991	K.Dickens	B.Waites	2000	D.J.Russell	R.Rock
1992	J.Higgins	J.Higgins	2001	Tim Rouse	Jeremy Robinson
1993	P.Baker	C.Clark	2002	Robert Rock	Ian Lyner
1994	P.Baker	N.Turley	2003	Philip Edwards	–
1995	S.Rose	D.Eddiford	2004	Paul Streeter	–
1996	D.J.Russell	S.Bennett	2005	Adrian Carey	-
1997	J.Higgins	J.Higgins	2006	Paul Streeter	Cameron Clark
1998	S.Webster	J.Robinson	2007	Ian Lyner	–
1999	C.Hall	I.Ball	2008		–

Red = Northamptonshire winner

Once the P.G.A. was formed each of its three big sections, of which the Midlands became one, started to hold tournaments on an annual basis. The first body to hold regular regional tournaments was the Midlands Golf Association, beginning in 1897. The Stroke Play event is called the Midland Professionals Championship; it is the oldest professional championship in the world and is one of seven strokeplay championships played each year. The Matchplay event is not held every year now. A complete list of winners is given in Appendix 1.

Prior to the successes described previously Northamptonshire Professionals were victorious in 1964, 1967 & 1968 Stuart Murray Northants County, 1974 Mike Gallagher Woodlands (Farthingstone), 1986 Tony Skingle Cold Ashby.

CHAPTER 8

The Northamptonshire & Bedfordshire Golfers' Alliance

"The wind is the symbol of all that is free"
"My mission in performing is to communicate the joy in living"

John Denver 1943–1997

THE origins of the "Alliance" have been lost in time however; the first meeting with a known result was held in 1926 as a singles competition and won by A.Randall from Mid Beds G.C. In 2007/8, the Alliance held six events during their winter playing season; the first starting in October with monthly events thereafter, January is omitted due to weather considerations and festivities, three in each county. The events are played over 27 holes, 18 in the morning and 9 holes in the afternoon with the November & December meeting restricted to 18 holes in view of the available daylight. The December meeting is traditionally held at the Captain's golf club. During the April meeting the two "Gray" Trophies are competed for.

The meetings are well supported; however, it will be interesting to see how the two for one scheme, county cards & initiative such as golf central affects the turnout of players. The format is fourball betterball played off $3/4$ handicap, maximum 18. In 2007 the entry fee was £35 including meals. If a pair has "too frequent successes" an Alliance handicap will be enforced which will remain in place for the current season only. The meetings are open to all E.G.U. affiliated Clubs. In an old fashioned way Alliance Rule 10 states "Sheltering is permitted" although the current Rules of Golf state that play must be continuous. A dilemma for the committee. Junior members are allowed to play and compete for prizes.

The known results are given in Appendix 1. Unfortunately there are numerous omissions and some inconsistencies, the reasons for this are unknown. A notable treble of victories was recorded in 2003-2005 by S.Rodriguez and N. Mendel.

244

CHAPTER 9

The Northamptonshire Schools Golf Association

"Anyone who keeps developing stays young"

Henry Ford

WALTER Dunne head school teacher from Daventry in response to an initiative from the English Schools Golf Association started the association in 1984. Walter was a member at nearby Daventry G.C. and during his playing career was a member of the team which competed in the 1978 Hollingsworth final. Walter also became a N.G.U. County Selector in the late 1980s and helped me in my post as Hon. Match Secretary to determine which players should progress from Club to County level. Even in times when his body did not respond to the transmissions from his brain he remained cheerful, sadly we lost this nice kind man a few years later to motor neurone disease.

The golfing concept, which Walter applied in the County, was to give the young players an opportunity to play at a higher level and play at the Midland Championship with the possibility of being selected to represent the Midlands at the National Schools Championships in the summer.

Schools entered teams and played individually for the Walter Dunne Salver, with the top four boys and girls representing Northants at the Midland event. The Walter Dunne trophy has sadly been mislaid and replaced by individual trophies for boys and girls and the Champion School. In the last two years, there has been a National Schools Championship run by the E.G.U., E.L.G.A. and the E.S.G.A., with the winning school from the County event going forwards to represent Northants.

The County has twice hosted the Midlands Championships at Wellingborough and the prestigious National Championship at Northants County.

There have been individual successes at the higher levels. Within the girls ranks Kelly Hanwell (1996) and Roseann Youngman (2003) both won the Under 18 title and represented England Schools. In 2001 Roseann

Youngman won the Under 16 trophy at Blankney G.C. with scores of gross 73&70, a new course record, Roseann was given courtesy of the course as long as she holds the record. In 2002 Emma Parr from Northants County won the Under 16 English Schools Golf Championship. Emma, 15, triumphed in the junior girl's event following rounds of 76 and 79 to post a 155 aggregate. Having started the season with a seven handicap she has now seen it reduced to five. Emma was asked to play for England Schools in a match against Wales but had already been named as a first reserve for England in an under 16 clash against Spain at Pannal. In 2006, Alex Banham from Elton Furze G.C. represented the E.S.G.A. girl's team.

In the boys event Stuart Ashwood was named as Vice Captain for the Home International Schools matches after his good season in 2004 (see Chapter 3).

Golf has never been more popular with a wider audience now being reached. Tri Golf is being introduced at primary school level and Golf Xtreme at secondary through the wok of the Golf Foundation and Northamptonshire Golf Partnership. Both introductory activities featuring as a curriculum activity in a number of schools and as part of the after school programme. This widening of appeal to a younger section of the schools population can only bring new players in to the game at an early age. Two new trophies were introduced for the 2005 season for the Under 15 Champions.

Officers

Secretary:
Walter Dunne 1984-1990
Martin Baglee 1990-1995
Graham Hardinges 1996-2000
Stuart Pitcher 2000-2003
Richard Lobb 2004-present

President:
Trevor Scholey 1985-present

Roseann Youngman 2003 England Schools Champion (centre) with runner up Felicity Johnson (left) & 3rd Fiona Telfer-Brunton (Cornwall).

CHAPTER 10

The Society of Northamptonshire Golf Captains

"Enjoy present pleasures in such a way as not to injure future ones"

Senaca (4BC-65AD)

THIS organisation was founded on the 16th May, 1965 as a result of an initiative driven mainly by Peter Palmer from Northants County G.C. and currently has approximately 325 members. The list of Captains/ Presidents below, reads like a who's who of the county's administrators.

The 1968/9 Captain H.W. (Bert) Colton from Rushden G.C. and 1957 County President presented a beautiful pair of trophies in 1957 for the Union's annual Family Foursomes competition. It was lovely to see him present at Oundle in 1996 when he was able to describe the history of the trophies and present them in their fortieth anniversary to S.J. & L.J. Costello from Delapre G.C.

R.O. Baillon was President in 1975/6 and son of L.C.Baillon who was a founder member of Northants County Golf Club, Northampton Hockey Club and the Northampton Tennis Club and who captained the England Olympic hockey team to a winning gold medal in the 1908 Olympics at the White City Stadium. Richard Obie (Spriggs) was Northants County's Captain in 1969 some thirty-two years after his father Louis Charles (Turkey), who was Captain in 1937/8.

Another very well known local golfer and Captain in 1978/9 was Alex Good who conceptualised and introduced the *Chronicle & Echo* Foursomes trophy to Kingsthorpe G.C. which ran from 1962-1999. This tournament was extremely popular in the town and was well supported by organisations from around the County. Some were very long standing such as Old Wellingburians, NALGO (National Association of Local Government Officers) and Old Northamptonians. In fact the event was so popular it was extremely difficult for new teams to enter until a drop out occurred. The trophy was presented after a post match dinner by the Mayor of Northampton who was accompanied by Miss *Chronicle & Echo*.

President in 1995/6 Clive Blackburn was a successful selector of the N.G.U. winning Anglian League A team in 1990 which was Captained by his fellow Northants County Club member Richard (Dick) Biggin. Local golf legend Richard Aitken was President in 2004/5.

The society hold a dozen or so golf events throughout the playing season and have an annual fixture to support the N.G.U. Junior team which is their first event, played at the start of the golf season in March or April. The society has for the last twenty or so years made a significant financial contribution to the development of junior golf in the county through the N.G.U. which has been very much appreciated. Matches are played against neighbouring counties and against the ladies. The spring meeting is traditionally held at Northampton G.C., President's day is held in the summer and a well attended annual dinner is held in October followed by the A.G.M.

The President attends the annual N.G.U. County Dinner and displays the magnificent chain and badges around his neck. This colourful weighty chain fortunately does not appear to have a significant effect on the President's calorific intake and enjoyment. In fact many golfers at the dinner are quite attracted to its beauty and respectfully inquire about its history.

S.N.G.C. Vice President John Kelly (left) & President Bryan Barwick (Rushden) at the 2007 N.G.U. Dinner.

Captains/Presidents of the Society of Northamptonshire Golf Captains
1965-2007

Year	Officer	Year	Officer
1965/6	R.A. (Peter) Palmer NC	1986/7	T.J.H. (Jack) Vollmar R
1966/7	A.P. (Alex) Foulis PM	1987/8	J.S.(John) Mumford O
1967/8	C.S. (Charles) Catlow NC	1988/9	C.M. (Myers) Tennyson PM
1968/9	H.W. (Bert) Colton R	1989/90	R.D. (Roger) Jervis Kg
1969/70	W. (Bill) Hollingsworth N	1990/1	W. (Bill) Walls K
1970/71	W.G.C. Knowles Kg	1991/2	L. Wilkinson W
1971/2	N.H. (Norman) Brinton PM	1992/3	J.W. (John) Halliwell N
1972/3	P.H. (Peter) Meacock D	1993/4	F. (Frank) Higham D
1973/4	F.E. (Eric) Douglas NC	1994/5	D.G.L. (Don) Rigby O
1974/5	D. (Don) Bates K	1995/6	C.T. (Clive) Blackburn NC
1975/6	R.O. (Spriggs) Baillon NC	1996/7	D. (David) Jones R
1976/7	G.B. (Joe) Pyke N	1997/8	R. (Robert) Brown PM
1977/8	H.W. Ellis (Humphrey) R	1998/9	P.W.(Peter)Campbell SP
1978/9	A. Good (Alex) Good Kg	1999/00	J.F. (Jim) Edmonds DP
1979/80	S.G.(Sid) Thompson D	2000/1	A.J. (Alan) Gadsen Kg
1981/82	R.S. (Ron) Coltmann PM	2001/2	R.C.(Robert) Handley W
1982/3	F.M. (Frank) Moses N	2002/3	A.E.(Tony) Noone K
1983/4	C.H. (Jack)Walker W	2003/4	D.C.(David) Prior N
1984/5	K.C. (Ken) Hunter NC	2004/5	R.G. (Richard)Aitken NC
1985/6	M.G. (Mike) Anderson D	2005/6	J. (John) Bishton O
		2006/7	B.E. (Bryan) Barwick R

Secretary
? May1965 to Oct 1970
Joe Pyke N Oct 1970 to Oct 1976
Eric Douglas NC Oct 1976 to Oct 1989
Mike Anderson D Oct 1990 to Oct 1996
Jack Halliwell   NC Oct 1996 to Oct 2002
Tony Warren N Oct 2002 to present

Treasurer

Frank Moses N	to Oct 1984
Eric Douglas NC	Oct 1984 to Oct 1996
David Prior N	Oct 1996 to Oct 2001
David Bale K	Oct 2001 to Oct 2004
John Henderson Kg	Oct 2004 to present

Key to Golf Clubs

D Daventry	K Kettering	Kg Kingsthorpe
N Northampton	NC Northants County	O Oundle
PM Peterborough Milton	R Rushden	SP Staverton Park
W Wellingborough		

THE SOCIETY OF NORTHAMPTONSHIRE
GOLF CAPTAINS

FOUNDED 16th MAY, 1965

Captains/President

1965/6	R.A. PALMER	Northants County G.C.
1966/7	A.P. FOULIS	Peterborough Milton G.C.
1967/8	C.S. CATLOW	Northants County G.C.
1968/9	H.W. COLTON	Rushden G.C.
1969/70	W. HOLLINGSWORTH	Northampton G.C.
1970/1	W.G.C. KNOWLES	Kingsthorpe G.C.
1971/2	N.H. BRINTON	Peterborough Milton G.C.
1972/3	P.H. MEACOCK	Daventry G.C.
1973/4	F.E. DOUGLAS	Northants County G.C.
1974/5	D. BATES	Kettering G.C.
1975/6	R.O. BAILLON	Northants County G.C.
1976/7	G.B. PYKE	Northampton G.C.
1977/8	H.W. ELLIS	Rushden G.C.
1978/9	A. GOOD	Kingsthorpe G.C.
1979/80	S.G. THOMSON	Daventry G.C.
1980/1	P.S. JAMES	Wellingborough G.C.
1981/2	R.D. COLTMAN	Peterborough Milton G.C.
1982/3	F.W. MOSES	Northampton G.C.
1983/4	C.H. WALKER	Wellingborough G.C.
1984/5	K.C. HUNTER	Northants County G.C.
1985/6	M.G. ANDERSON	Daventry G.C.
1986/7	T.J.H. VOLLMAR	Rushden G.C.
1987/8	J.S. MUMFORD	Oundle G.C.
1988/9	C.M. TENNESON	Peterborough Milton G.C.
1989/90	R.D. JERVIS	Kingsthorpe G.C.
1990/1	W. WALLS	Kettering G.C.
1991/2	L. WILKINSON	Wellingborough G.C.
1992/93	J.W. HALLIWELL	Northampton G.C.
1993/94	F. HIGHAM	Daventry G.C.
1994/95	D.G.L. RIGBY	Oundle G.C.
1995/96	C. T. BLACKBURN	Northants County G.C.
1996/97	D. JONES	Rushden G.C.
1997/98	R. BROWN	Peterborough Milton G.C.
1998/99	P. W. CAMPBELL	Staverton Park G.C.
1999/00	J. F. EDMONDS	Delapre Park G.C.
2000/01	A. J. GADSDEN	Kingsthorpe G.C.
2001/02	R. C. HANDLEY	Wellingborough G.C.
2002/03	A. E. NOONE	Kettering G.C.

Hon. Secretary
| TONY WARREN | Northampton G.C. |

THE SOCIETY OF NORTHAMPTONSHIRE

GOLF CAPTAINS

37th
ANNUAL DINNER

at

KETTERING GOLF CLUB

on

FRIDAY, 10th OCTOBER, 2003

President:

TONY NOONE

PAST CAPTAIN OF

KETTERING GOLF CLUB

2003 Annual Dinner Menu Card.

CHAPTER 11

SUCCESS AT NATIONAL LEVEL, SHORT STROKES, CHARACTERS AND MISCELLANY

"The only real voyage of discovery consists not in seeking new landscapes but in having new eyes"

Marcel Proust

SUCCESS AT NATIONAL LEVEL

ca 1920 One Northampton lady, Mrs.G.J. Phillips, gained national fame by being selected for the English Ladies side against Scotland early in the twentieth century and won her match by 4 and 3.

1953 Richard Aitken reached the last eight of the British Boys Championship at Dunbar G.C. (age 15) the same year that his elder brother won the Scottish Boys Championship. Richard was beaten by Alec E. Shepperson from Coxmoor G.C. a future Walker Cup player (1957, 59) and in 2007 their Club President. In the 1959 match Shepperson played against Jack Nicklaus in the foursomes and Tommy Aaron in the singles.

1960 Having just graduated, Richard Aitken won the British Universities Championship at Dalmahoy representing Edinburgh University, the team tournament was retained, completing a treble of victories.

1972 Conrad Ceislewicz age 17 and playing off scratch became an England Boy International for the match against Scotland. He was successful in both foursomes and singles, which he won by 2 and 1. Prior to this in 1970 he was the youngest ever player to be selected for Northamptonshire's Anglian League team age 15. In 1973 he awakened the attention of the England selectors once more in the England Youth's match play when he defeated John Davies, a previous finalist of the event and a Walker Cup player. Conrad also secured one of two qualifying places for the 1973 Italian Amateur Open where he played in two of the four rounds.

Conrad was Northamptonshire County Champion five times including a hat trick between1978-80 and County Boys Champion in 1971&2. In Gil Sibley's Northampton Centenary book[4] he describes Conrad as "a slight scarcely seven stone schoolboy driving the ball well over two hundred yards from the teeing ground at our former fifth hole at Kettering Road, and with a long iron able to reach the upland green with an accurate second shot for a possible eagle or more certain birdie at this attractive par five hole".

- Kettering G.Cs. nineteen year old Robert Larratt a pupil from Uppingham School was selected for the E.G.U. Youths team for the Home Internationals at Glasgow Gailes August 8&9th, this is thought to be Northamptonshire's first youth's national representation.

1974 Carol Gibbs nee LeFeuvre represented Great Britain and Ireland in The Curtis Cup in San Francisco. Carol played in three matches.

1983 Richard Catlow and Richard Aitken won the Presidents and Guests Trophy with a total of 63 Stableford pts at the English Golf Union's County Presidents and Guests Tournament played at Thorpness Suffolk.

1990 Chris Lane became Golf Foundation's Weetabix Age Group Champion in the under 16 category at Patshull Park Shropshire. This addition to his "golf cv" probably assisted in him securing a golf scholarship in the USA.

1991 Angela Duck played for England in the Senior Ladies International against Europe in France. Angela is a native of Staffordshire, a countrywoman by upbringing and preference. She soon learnt to ride and remains a fine horsewoman. Her parents were both keen golfers at Beau Desert G.C. A pretty challenging heathland course located on Cannock Chase where Angela took up the game age 14. At the age of 19 her handicap was down to five and her form attracted the attention of the England selectors, and later that year she played for England in the girls home internationals at Wollaton Park. From this point her golfing career blossomed, she represented Staffordshire regularly, won both the county championship and the Midland championship twice and also the Spanish ladies open in 1969, and the Swiss championship in 1972. She was semi-finalist in the German championship in 1962 and 63 and a runner-up in 1964.

Angela moved to Northamptonshire in 1963, and played for Northamptonshire, she won the County championship in 1972, 1984, 1985, and 1988. At Northants County, she was lady's club champion between 1985 and 2001. Angela married Michael Duck in 1970 and their two sons Robert and Thomas have become very proficient players. Robert represented England as a full international and holds the course record at Northants County. Thomas also played at county level and was a member of the winning Anglian league team in 2002.

1995 Robert Duck became an England Boy International at Woodhall Spa in the European Boys Championship 12-16 July and also played in the Boys Home Internationals, Robert represented England as a full International in 1997. Around this time Luke Donald was also starting out on his golfing career and the two boys played together. Amusingly some wag had a sense of humour when constructing the foursome pairings, this was the first time a Disney character had appeared on the starting sheet in an International match i.e. Donald Duck!

Robert's first full International appearance was in the International European Amateur Golf Championship in Switzerland where he finished tied for second in a high class field. Robert had rounds of 70,72,71,68 for a seven under par total of 281 and played four times for his country in the Home Internationals. On his return to the county Northants County Club and County Captain Les Cantrell made a special surprise presentation to him on behalf of the members. Also in 1997 he won Bronze in the European Amateur Championship.

One of Robert's greatest victories occurred in 1994 at his home course Northants County where he won the English Golf Union's Carris Trophy. Robert scored a total of 280 for the four rounds including breaking the course record with a magnificent 65. He was also Northamptonshire's County Boys Champion in 1995 and County Open Champion in 1998. Robert comes from a family of locally famous golfers often referred to affectionately as the "Duck Dynasty".

E.G.U. Carris Trophy 1994
Robert Duck Amateur Course Record
Northants County G.C. 21/07/1994

Hole	1	2	3	4	5	6	7	8	9
Par	4	5	3	4	4	3	4	4	4
Score	5	4	2	4	3	2	3	4	3

Hole	10	11	12	13	14	15	16	17	18
Par	4	4	3	4	4	3	4	4	5
Score	5	4	3	5	3	3	5	4	3

30+35 =65

Robert Duck (right), Carris Trophy winner 1994 with Earl Spencer (left) and 1993 Northants County Golf Club Captain Peter Haddon (centre).

Robert moved to America to continue his studies where he was a student at Augusta State University for four years. We visited him at his house in 1998, which was at the back of Amen Corner just of Berckman's Road where we spent a good hour talking over what was going on at Club, County and National level "back home". The road is named after the Belgian horticulturist Prosper J.A.Berckman who set up the first commercial nursery in the south in 1861 on the land that was to become Augusta National Golf Club. A short walk on to The Masters course (name changed in 1939) followed this, where we watched the Tuesday practise round. Before the start of play Robert issued me with a challenge to find a weed on the course. We also visited Robert in 2001, by this time he had moved house so we had no idea where he was living and agreed to meet up on the right of the 10th Tee (Camellia Par 4) next to the putting green. This hole has an abundance of this colourful evergreen shrub Camellia japonica and sasanqua these actual plants being derived from stock that was originally imported by the Berckman's family from Europe and Japan. After we had watched the players practise and taken in the almost clinical beauty of the course we decided to walk back to Robert's house. We were completely astonished to find that we had actually parked the hire car right outside his new house and also after three days on the Masters course we had still not found a single weed! Such is their attention to detail at the Masters Tournament.

Robert was there on the course on the Sunday (together with Nick Soto County Champion 1999&2001 and Tony Soto (Robert's frequent caddie from Northants County) to witness Tiger Woods "Slam" of holding all four major titles at once. We were however back home "in front of the box" although emotionally still at Augusta.

In 2001 Robert was a member of the The National Collegiate Athletic Association Division I team from Augusta State that also included Oliver Wilson (Nottinghamshire) and Jamie Elson (Warwickshire) who won the Cleveland Golf/Augusta State Invitational following a play-off over the par 72, 6,875-yard Forest Hills Golf Club.

Robert turned professional during 2002 becoming an assistant at Forest Hills where the Augusta State University team is based. Whilst chatting to him at the 2004 Masters, he has decided to change careers and return to the amateur ranks, he now has a job in golf with Hambric Stellar Golf as a Player Manager. Robert's job involves working with such Open Championship legends Sandy Lyle and Justin Leonard and his friend the emerging European tour golfer Oliver Wilson. What a life, someone has to do it!

1995a Andrew (A.R.P.) Lynch became an Irish Boy International, in the Boys Home Internationals (1995-6) Andrew played ten matches winning five and halved one match to register 11 pts. In The European Amateur Boys Team Championship (1995-6) he played in 6 matches winning 3 and registered 6 pts. Andrew went up to Scotland to study at the fine Stirling University and strengthened their traditionally strong University team. In 2006 Andrew was back in Northampton and running his own business.

1995b Miss Suzanne Sharpe was chosen to train with the England Team in Spain at Las Brisas near Marbella and to represent the English Ladies in the Spanish Open Championship.

1996 Miss Kelly Hanwell captained the English Schools team against Scotland and Wales, both matches were won. Kelly Hanwell also won the Daily Telegraph Junior Championship at Hanbury Manor, which won her a trip to Lake Nona, USA for the finals.

1998 Gary Boyd literally burst on to the National scene at the age of 12 when he won the English Golf Union Gold Medal at the home of English Golf, Woodhall Spa Lincolnshire with scores of 32+40=72 points. He was Northamptonshire's qualifier for this event with a score of 59 nett off a handicap of twenty. At the tender age of 15. He became an English Boy International in 2002 and was capped at under-16 level against Italy, Spain and Scotland and in the Boys Home Internationals.

Gary was a member of the winning England Boys team, which triumphed, in the Home Internationals at Carnoustie. In 2003 and playing off one handicap Gary was selected for the England School of Excellence for the second successive season and may well impress the selectors in the under-18s bracket in a series of intense training sessions at Woodhall Spa. In 2003 Gary was selected for the four "man" English team to attempt to defend the World Junior Team Championships in Rosewood Golf Club in Hyogo Japan. In 2003 he also played in the winning England team who won the Boys Home Internationals for a record sixth time at Blairgowrie and was of member of the team in 2004 who once again defended the trophy at Portmarnock Dublin in 2004. He personally collected $4^1/_2$ points from 6 games of foursomes and singles.

Gary's fine season in 2004 also contained a third place in the English Golf Union's Carris Trophy where Gary scored 282 at Northumberland G.C. finishing six shots behind the talented Spanish golfer Pablo Martin. Locally he won the Midland Youth Championship at Stoke Rochford GC also with a total scores of 282 He also represented GB&I in the Jacques Leglise Trophy and the E.G.U. in the Chiberta Grand prix in France.

In 2005 Gary played well in the English Amateur Championship at Bromborough G.C. where he reached the quarter finals losing to the eventual runner-up Steven Capper from nearby Caldy G.C. he became a member of the E.G.U. A squad. Gary also retained the Midland Youth's title with the same total as the previous year, 282 also winning the Kymin Cup. In 2006 Gary was a member of the winning England team who retained the trophy in the Costa Ballena Quadrangular match in Spain and also reached the semi-finals of the Spanish Amateur Championship at Sherry Golf Jerez losing to the very talented Italian Edoardo Molinari. The Italian will line up with the world's leading professionals in The Open at Royal Liverpool Golf Club in July 2006 on an exemption as the reigning US Amateur Champion. In the 36 hole final he came back from three down after 18 holes single-putting 10 times in the final 15 holes. His exemptions will also allow him to play in the US Masters and US Open. Gary, one of Northamptonshire's stars gave him a good tussle in the semi-final. Molinari did not win the final and was beaten 7&6 by another rising star from Hampshire, 17 year old England Boy International Sam Hutsby a friend of Gary's also from the E.G.U. "stable".

Gary started his golfing life at the age of six with father "Chic" Boyd at Cherwell Edge G.C. but transferred to Northants County for 2003-5. I am certain that Chic's car must have travelled tens of thousands of miles as chief taxi driver and proud supporter of his talented son. Chic was honoured for his commitment to the game by becoming Cherwell Edge Captain in 2005.

In 2006 Gary migrated back to Cherwell Edge G.C. and assisted in setting a new record for the N.G.U. Scratch League. When the division 3 game was played in April against Northampton G.C. the combined handicap of the first pair was plus three. The past two times County Champion Glenn Keates (+1) was level par when beaten 6/4 by English Elite Squad member Gary (+2) who recorded seven birdies, things are on the up at Cherwell Edge! Gary became N.G.U. County Champion in June 2006 with scores of 69+66=135 at Peterborough Milton G.C. In August 2006 following a second quarter-final place in the English Amateur Championship and defeat by the eventual winner Ross McGowan, Gary received full International colours being selected to represent England in the Home Internationals at Pyle and Kenfig Golf Club, South Wales on the 6th - 8th September 2006 losing only one of five matches. This performance was Gary's and "Northamptonshire's" first international point. Following Robert Duck in 1997, Gary is only the second male golfer from Northamptonshire to have achieved this honour and position in the game. Back in 1998 Glenn Keates had much better luck when he tied for first place together with the author in the inaugural National Final of the Portugolfe foursomes competition played at Vila Sol. A weeks golf holiday in the sun for £22, was very good value for the Northampton G.C. pair.

Chatting to Gary as we walked the fairways during those Home Internationals, it emerged that his goals are firstly to make the Walker Cup team and then to join the paid ranks. In fact, Gary became first reserve. Greater success followed in November for our young England International when came from five shots back to win the inaugural Asia Pacific Open Amateur Championship at Mission Hills in China. A closing round of 71 over the 7,323 yard Mission Hills course in Shenzhen for a level par aggregate of 288 (72,76,69,71) left 20 year old Gary tied with Japan's Ryutaro Nagano. In the playoff on the par four tenth hole, both players had putts from around six feet but while the Japanese missed, Gary holed out for his first major international title.

1999 Following a kidney transplant, Alex Wray from Northampton G.C. became the British Transplant Games Golf Champion in 2000 when he led the field scoring 37 points at Westerhope, Newcastle-Upon-Tyne. This together with his swimming prowess took him to the World Games in Tokyo in 2000 where he collected a

Above: Gary Boyd (Cherwell Edge G.C.) in action.
photograph courtesy of Tom Ward
Right: Gary Boyd Cherwell Edge G.C. with the Asia Pacific
Open Amateur Championship trophy at Mission Hills
China, November 2006

monumental five gold and two bronze medals in the swimming, which is actually his stronger sport. He is Northampton Golf Club's first World Champion. Alex was unfortunately less successful in the golf tournament where he finished well down the result list.

– N.G.U. President David Croxton won the trophy for the best performance at the English Golf Union's County Presidents and Guests Tournament at Woodhall Spa G.C. with a score of 34 pts. This was the County's second success in this event after Richard Catlow and Richard Aitken's victory at Thorpness 1983.

2001 Kevin Aherne from Wellingborough and David Wells (Woburn) won the National Final of the Portugolfe competition at Vila Sol Portugal defeating the 1998 winners during the preliminary rounds.

– Roseann Youngman won the English Schools Under 16 Trophy at Blankney G.C. 73&70

2002 Roseann Youngman represented the winning England team in the Girls Home Internationals at The Heritage G.C. Dublin and was unbeaten in her matches. Roseann was also a member of the England team which played in the Under 18 European Team Championship at Esbjberg Denmark and a member of the England team

Dave Croxton, E.G.U. County President Tournament winner receiving the trophy from E.G.U. President John Flanders at the N.G.U. Annual Dinner in 2000.

which played in the Quadrangular Match in Rome. Roseann also represented England vs England Boys at Pleasington G.C.

Emma Parr won the Under 16 English Schools Golf Championship with rounds of 76, 79 which reduced the fifteen year old's handicap to 5.

2003 Roseann Youngman won the Under 18 E.S.G.A. title (gross 144) and represented England Schools. Represented England in the European Team Championship at Tourino G.C. Italy and played in the Italian Ladies Championship Milan. She was Team Captain in the England International Schools match against Wales at Ashburnham G.C. Dyfed.

2004 County Champion Stuart Ashwood (Northants County G.C.) became England School Boys Vice-Captain.

– Simon Williams Northampton G.C. reached the final of the Daily Telegraph Junior Golf Championship held at Sun Sity, South Africa after a 67 gross at his home club. After rounds of 75, 82, 71 Simon finished a creditable 6 shots behind British Boys Champion Scotland's Jordan Findlay.

2005A) Adam Myers (Northants County G.C.) won the English Boys under 16 Open Stroke Play Championship at Radcliffe-on-Trent G.C. The fourteen year old scored 72, 72, 72, and 70 =276 to land the McGregor Trophy by one stroke. Adam was subsequently selected to represent England against Spain for the annual under 16 international at Pannal G.C. Harrogate Yorkshire. In 2005 he also played against Scotland and the English Girls.

2005B) The N.G.U. Senior team qualified for the inaugural English County Seniors Team Championship by finishing the top county during the Midland region's qualifier held at Burghley Park G.C. Lincolnshire in August 2005. Peterborough Milton players Richard Cole and Geoff Dyson took a leading role as they scored 70 and 74 gross respectively, they were backed up by the rest of the six man team by David Dare and Captain Martin Harris (Northampton) and Rodney Haig and Brian O'Connell (Northants County). The team's total of 379 was eight strokes fewer than Warwickshire.

In the National final held at E.G.U. Past President Paul Fisher's home club Minchinhampton G.C. the county team were playing against much lower handicapped players. Possible the best player on show was English Seniors Captain Roy Smethurst from Cheshire the European and British Senior's Champion playing off +1 handicap. Cheshire, the winning team's highest handicap was 1! Our "lads" acquitted themselves very well and were

Adam Myers McGregor Trophy & Jean Case Salver winner 2005 at Radcliffe-on-Trent G.C.

described as the friendliest team by several of their opponents.

Despite finishing in fourth place all of the "senior lads" enjoyed the week and are hoping to qualify again for three more days of foursomes and singles against some friendly and a few feisty opponents. The results of the matches are given in Appendix 1.

2005C) The County Ladies team reached the English County Championship finals for the first time in the 53 –year history of the competition by winning the sub-division finals at Copt Heath G.C. Warwickshire. The previous year they won county week for the first time in 33 years and went on to the Midlands sub-divisional finals where they narrowly missed going through to County Finals by a single point.

In 2005 the team were on fine form and thrashed C a m b r i d g e s h i r e / H u n t i n g d o n s h i r e , Carnarvernshire/Anglesey and overcame the holders Warwickshire to qualify and raise the glasses on that memorable July day. The team consisted of Sarah Carter, Emma Parr, Kirstie Jennings, Kelly Hanwell (Northants County), Mary McLaren, Carol Gibbs and Roseann Youngman(Wellingborough), Lucinda Davies, Georgina Dunn (Peterborough Milton). The ecstatic non-playing Captain Heather Williams said when interviewed by the press "Carol and Kelly both won five points each which was superb. But this was a fantastic team effort-all the girls played well. It was a thrilling experience to watch such excellent golf and I'm so very proud of the team. We are now looking forward to the County Finals.

In the finals at Brancepeth Castle Durham 7-9 September 2005 our Ladies gave their best performances, though as usual Yorkshire were very strong and were victorious on games won after a points tie with Gloucester.

The Ladies team from Yorkshire all had plus handicaps with two players playing off plus three. Notable performances from Northamptonshire were from Kelly Hanwell on the first day who recorded a halved match against Yorkshire's Rachel Bell despite being four down after eight holes; she also won her match against Hampshire's Tracy Boyes 1up by winning the last four holes. Carol Gibbs and Georgina Dunn recorded a fine 4/3 win in the foursomes against Hampshire and a 6/5 win against Gloucestershire.

2005D) Nine-year-old Charley Hull from Kettering G.C. wrote her name in ladies golf history as a National Champion when she became the youngster ever winner of the Health Perception LGU Championship at Turnberry on the 26 September 2005. This national event had an entry of over 24,000 ladies from 1,270 Clubs in GB&I. Charley amassed a total of 28 Stableford points off a handicap of 26 around the Ailsa Championship course which was being battered by winds gusting up to 45 miles per hour. This put her in to a tie with 46 year old Janice Cloran from Alkrington Manchester and Charley won at the second play-off hole." I am so excited to win and can't believe it" Charley said after receiving her trophy from the managing director of sponsors Health Perception: the Olympic Gold Medallist David Wilkie.

Top left: Peterborough Milton's Geoff Dyson & John McCallum in action at the inaugural English Seniors County Championship held at Minchinhampton G.C. 2005.

Top right: Geoff Dyson punches the air in celebration of holing his bunker shot at the English Seniors County Championship.

Bottom left: Past N.G.U. County B Team Captain Rodney Haig demonstrates his unique putting grip during the English Seniors County Championship at Minchinhampton 2005.

Bottom right: The Northamptonshire Team for the English Seniors County Championship.

Game Points. Each individual game in each match. 1 point for a wi	
Northamptonshire	
Martin Harris **Northampton**	
Brian O'Connell **Northamptonshire County**	
Rodney Haig **Northamptonshire County**	
Geoff Dyson **Peterborough Milton**	
John MacCallum **Peterborough Milton**	
Mike Abbotts **Staverton Park**	
John Clarke **Northamptonshire**	
Team Captain **Martin Harris**	

259

The Northamptonshire Ladies Team and Officials at the National Finals in 2005.
Back Row: Sarah Carter, Kirstie Jennings, Kelly Hanwell, Roseann Youngman, Georgina Dunn, Mary McLlaren and Emma Parr.
Front Row: Lucinda Davies, Heather Williams, Pam Giles, Susan Hennigan, Carol Gibbs."

Perhaps we have a potential Michelle Wie in the County! Let us hope the National Lottery money assists the development of her game. Charley was put forward for the BBC East Midlands junior sports woman of the year award and attended the 2005 ceremony at De Montford Hall Leicester; the prize was picked up by another county athlete Sian Edwards for cross-country. The disappointment lasted a few minutes until Charley collected the Judges Special Achievement of the Year Award.

In August 2006 Charley was invited to play in the pro-am day at the Women's British Open at Lytham St.Annes. The 10-year-old starlet played along side 18 year old American prodigy Morgan Pressel, after the Pro-Am lunch she was introduced to some of the other stars of the women's game by the caring young American. I suspect Father Dave's camera was much in action to record this for the family scrapbook. What an amazing experience!

In June 2007 the 11-year-old made her US debut at The Texas Women's Open at Eastern Hills Country Club. Our four feet nine inch, handicap 7, 77 pound prodigy scored 82 in the first round, twelve over par from the men's tee and was the best player on the day "pound for pound". Charley was playing by special invitation as her father Dave has a cousin who is a member of the Club. Despite out driving her playing partners a couple of times a second round of 90 was recorded. I suspect she must have been quite tired since this was the sixth day in succession on the course; however this was a great experience and good preparation for the future.

As reported in the *Dallas Morning News* "her coach is not David Leadbetter but Kettering Pro Kevin Theovould, her hometown is Northamptonshire, England, somewhere between London & Birmingham"! We eagerly wait to see what scores Charley will record after the teenage growth spurt and whether Kevin Theobold will become as famous as David Leadbetter?

In July 2007 Charley became the Club's youngest ever Ladies Champion romping away with the title by 16 shots with scores of 82 &75. What a prospect she is and even has her own website.

2005E) A young Northamptonshire golfer called Tiger from Wellingborough is following in the footsteps of his famous namesake by competing in a top US tournament at the age of five. Tiger Adams, of Wellingborough, who is coached by Carl Sainsbury at Brampton Heath Golf Club, represented England in the under-six age group of the Junior World Golf Championships in San Diego in July 2005.

The golfing prodigy, who has been playing the sport since before he could walk, is also being provided with clothing and equipment by Nike, which also sponsors golf star Tiger Woods. Proud father Steve Adams said: "Golf runs in the family, hence the decision to call him Tiger, but it was a coincidence he turned out to be so good." He started swinging about with those kids' plastic golf clubs when he was about ten months old. I could see then he already had a virtually perfect swing. I used to have to hold him up while he took a shot."

The five-year-old has golf lessons three times a week and plays at Wellingborough G.C. and practises every day in the garden and on a purpose-built pitch and putt course in the garage. Tiger, who has just been given a handicap of 54, qualified for the world championships after winning a competition in Leicestershire. Brampton Heath G.C. arranged a deal to provide Nike equipment for him to take to America, where he competed against 50 other five and six-year-olds.

2006 Was a very eventful year for England Under 16 training squad member Adam Myers (Northants County). In July he represented the English Golf Union in the annual 54-hole European Young Masters tournament at Styrain Golf Club, Murhof, Austria. In August, he played for England against Spain in the annual one-day Under 16 International at Heswall Golf Club, Cheshire, on 22nd August.

2007 Gary Boyd (Cherwell Edge) & Adam Myers continued to fly the flag for Northamptonshire with the National teams as Elite & Under 16 Squad members respectively.

An interesting little cameo occurred at Rushden G.C. in October when they competed against each other in the annual N.G.U. Champion of Champions Tournament, Gary coming out as the winner, setting a new course record of 67 in the process.

Gary had an extremely busy year and the highlight was probably as a member of the England team that regained the Raymond Trophy as Home International Champions at County Louth G.C. Ireland. Gary played in every match and won four of his six games as follows:-

First Day England 7¹/₂ vs Wales 7¹/₂

Foursomes Gary Boyd & Daniel Willett lost to Craig Evans & Ryan Thomas 4/3

Andrew Lilly Kettering G.C. with English Internationals Adam Myers Northants County (centre) & Gary Boyd Cherwell Edge (right) on the 1st tee at Rushden G.C, Finals Day 2007.

Singles Gary Boyd beat Ryan Thomas 2/1

Second Day England 8$^1/_2$ vs Ireland 6$^1/_2$

Foursomes Gary Boyd & Dale Whitnell beat Cian McNamara & Neil O'Briain 5/4Singles Gary Boyd lost to Neil O'Briain 1 hole

Third Day England 9 vs Scotland 6

Foursomes Gary Boyd & Daniel Willett beat Glenn Campbell & Paul O'Hara 2/1

Singles Gary Boyd beat John Gallagher 5/4

Final Points Totals England 25, Ireland 24, Scotland 21$^1/_2$, Wales 19$^1/_2$.

In October 2007, Gary was a member of the England team that successfully defended the biannual Spirit International Championship held in the United States at Whispering Pines Texas. The two man + two women team score was 32 under par over 72 holes, Gary personally contributing 16 birdies.

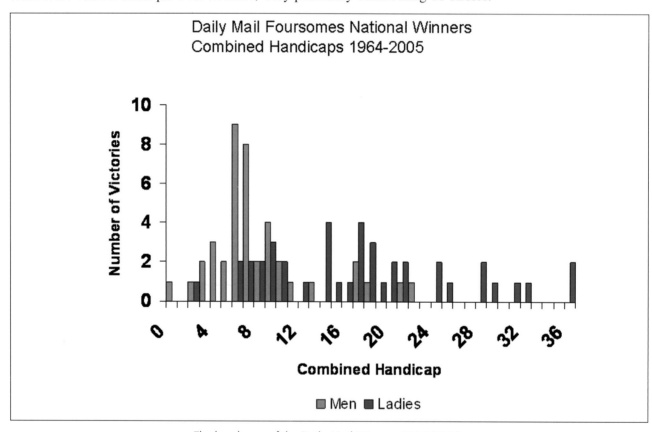

The handicaps of the Daily Mail Winners 1964-2005.

Daily Mail Amateur Foursomes, National Finalists, Northamptonshire

This popular competition has been running since 1964 and players initially qualify as their Club's foursomes Champions. There are approximately six local/regional rounds before the competitors battle it out on the national stage over three days of golf and entertainment.

In 2005 more than 2800 men and 3600 ladies qualified from the 210,000 who initially entered the competition at Club level. The closest Northamptonshire have come to winning the trophy was in 2005 when Sarah Carter and Kirsty Jennings from Northants County reached the final at Marriott St Pierre Chepstow narrowly losing on the last hole. It must have been very disappointing, since it looked as though they had taken control with three birdies in four holes from the ninth. The rocks on the seventeenth were to blame apparently; the pair have 5 county titles and over 30 years county experience between them.

The pairs that have qualified for the national finals (last 16) from Northamptonshire are given in Appendix 1.

Interestingly, despite the fact that to win the trophy a pair would need to play something in the region of twelve matches after qualifying at their club, the national trophy was actually retained in 1979 by a pair from Dirleton Castle Lothians.

The combined handicaps of the winners are shown on the previous page. It is interesting to note that for the men most winners have between 8-10 as their combined handicaps whereas the lady winners have a much greater range.

Kettering G .C. and MacGregor

Northamptonshire has a wonderful claim on a global scale since the world wide, multi million pound golf equipment company MacGregor, owes its origin directly to one of Kettering's members H.W. Mobbs. In 1898 Mr Mobbs (Kettering Captain 1908/9) paid a visit to the USA to messer's Crawford, MacGregor and Canby Co, Dayton Last Works, Dayton Ohio, to purchase last blocks for his company Mobbs and Lewis Ltd of Kettering.

Last blocks are usually made of Maple, and are rough turned in eight or nine sizes to cover the range of sizes of the finished article. On this occasion, they also offered me some blocks for making children's lasts, which they said were made out of persimmon wood. (Persimmon is similar to Maple but harder, the trees do not grow to any size and are a member of the ebony family). "I told them that this wood would be excellent for making golf clubs out of, to which they replied " Hell Mobbs what is this golf!" (they had not heard of the game of golf, as it was not generally known of in the USA at that time) I promised I would send them a model from which they could turn the golf heads, as these are turned on similar copying turning lathes as lasts.

Mobbs continues the story "On returning home I sent this model and in due course, they sent me a few samples, rough turned word from the model. On their arrival, I soon realised they had turned the heads the wrong way of the grain, so I wrote explaining this and asked them to turn and send me further samples the opposite way of the grain. On these reaching me, I asked Davey, the professional at Kettering Golf Club to make up a trial driver for Dr Allison, a Scotsman who introduced golf to Kettering and became the founder of the Club. Having tried out the club he declared it to be very good, better than those made of beech wood which was then in general use.

On my business trips to call on Scottish shoe manufacturers, I took my samples of those persimmon wood golf heads and showed them to Tom Morris and Forgan Taylor who also agreed on their superiority over beech. The two professionals provided me with models which I sent over to the USA to the copied in bulk, and steadily built up a very good trade with all the golf professionals in Great Britain. Golf heads were spliced in those days and bound on to the wooden shaft of the club by waxed thread. The balls used were gutty balls and they did not damage the face of the persimmon head.

As golf became more popular and began to be played in the USA Messes Crawford, MacGregor and Canby Company decided they would commence to manufacture golf clubs. They were desirous to give their clubs a brand-name and wrote to me if I could suggest one.   I promptly replied that they could not find a better name than MacGregor which they adopted fourth-with. I further promised to send them a specimen of the MacGregor tartan, and suggested they covered the grips of the clubs with a paper with this printed on. This they did, and in later years developed a considerable trade in this country for MacGregor clubs, as well as in the USA"

Thus a multi million pound company was born, the one minor discrepancy in this story is Mobbs recollection of the time he visited America as 1898 and the date on the MacGregor logo which states 1897, who worries about a year? As a scientist it still amazes me, how many different routes there are to inventions and innovations. Sometimes you just see it!

Golf in Northamptonshire

Record Scores, 59 Gross by a Northamptonian

Northampton golfer Stuart Reynolds from Church Brampton became the first British golfer ever to break the 60 barrier as he fired a stunning 12 under par 59 on the par 71 course to win the Midland PGA pro-am at Burton-on-Trent on the 3rd August 2001. Stuart joins a distinguished handful of golfers including Sam Snead (59 in the1959 Greenbrier Open), Jack Nicklaus (59 in an exhibition match in 1973 at Palm Beach), Al Geiberger (59 in the Danny Thomas Memphis Classic, Colonial Country Club 1977), Chip Beck (59 in the Las Vegas Invitational, 1991), David Duval (59 in the 1999 Bob Hope Chrysler Classic), Shigeki Maruyama (58 in qualifying for US Open 2000 at Woodmont Country Club), Jason Bohn(58 in the Bayer Championship Huron Oaks Ontario, 2001), Annika Sorenstam (59 in the Standard Register Ping Moon Valley Phoenix 2001) and Phil Mickelson (59 PGA Grand Slam of Golf Poipu Beach Hawaii) who have accomplished this feat in competitive play.

To achieve such a score the golfer must be in the "Zone". Annika Sorenstam certainly was in 2001 when she birdied the 12 of the first 13 holes. At the last hole when Sorenstam's playing partner gave her congratulatory pat on the back Annika said "Don't hit me too hard because I'll wake up" she was certainly in the zone. Stuart spread his birdies around more as his round consisted of two nines of six under par where Stuart started his round from the tenth tee.

Hole	1	2	3	4	5	6	7	8	9
Par	4	3	5	5	4	3	4	4	4
	359 yds	140 yds	548 yds	489 yds	454 yds	165 yds	384 yds	366 yds	379 yds
Score	4	2*	5	3**	3*	2*	3*	4	4

Hole	10	11	12	13	14	15	16	17	18
Par	3	4	3	5	4	4	4	4	4
	198 yds	318 yds	214 yds	514 yds	445 yds	349 yds	432 yds	446 yds	379 yds
Score	2*	3*	3	4*	3*	3*	3*	4	4

*Birdie ** Eagle

Stuart's putter was extremely hot, especially on the back nine, since he only required 25 putts. The longest one he holed was of twenty feet. In his own words," I did not really feel nervous at all until the last green when I realised that I had two putts from ten foot for a 59". In golfing terms he literally knocked the stick out and reaped the rewards!

Interestingly of all the players who have scored below sixty, none of them have broken seventy the next time they played. Stuart has decided to return to the amateur ranks in 2007 and could frighten many an opponent with this story, although as a gentle modest man I suspect he would not raise the story himself.

264

Northamptonshire Course Records at 2008

Club	Men	Ladies	Professional
Brampton Heath	Dan Wood 66	-	Shane Rose 67
Cherwell Edge	Gary Boyd 63	-	-
Cold Ashby	Frazer Carnihan 64	-	Paul Bagshaw 63
Collingtree Park	Brendan Moss 67	-	Darren Clark 63
Daventry and District	Adam Tarbox 62	-	
Delapre Park	Andy Duncan 65	-	Gary Casey 68
Elton Furze	No male members in the N.G.U. Ed Conduit 63	Coral McCullogh 68	-
Embankment	J.King 58 -	-	
Farthingstone	Darren Mathews 68	-	David Thorpe, Mike Gallagher, Kevin Dickens 66
Hellidon Lakes	Paul Craig 68	-	-
John White	Allan Bowman 53	-	
Kettering	Rod Handyside 63	-	Simon Lilly 63
Kingfisher	David Willis 71		
Kingsthorpe	Steve McDonald 63	-	Bob Larratt 64
Northampton	Lewis White 65	Kelly Hanwell 71	Robert Rock 63
Northants County	James Conteh, Robert Duck, Stuart Ashwood 65	-	Simon Lilly 63
Oundle	John O'Hagan 68	Roseann Youngman 73	Shane Rose 63
Overstone Park	Richard Dalton 67	-	Tim Rouse 67
Peterborough Milton	Gary Boyd 66	-	Stephen Bennett 69
Priors Hall	Ryan Evans 67	-	Dick Kemp 70
Pytchley Lodge	Stewart Philp 65	-	-
Rushden	Gary Boyd 67	-	-
Silverstone	Douglas Mitchell 65	-	Rodney Holt 65
St Andrews	Stuart Pitcher 67	-	-
Staverton Park	Paul Taylor 65	-	Matthew Stanford 64
Stoke Albany	Scott Marlow 65	-	-
Wellingborough	Jonathan Harris 65	-	Mike Gallagher 68
Whittlebury Park	Dave Wells 69	Roseann Youngman 71	-

Rules/Referees/Decisions

Almost 500 years ago when the game was first played on Scotland's east coast, golfers in each Club or society were free to set their own rules. It was only with the explosive expansion of the game in a 10-year period towards the end of the 19th century, when the number of Clubs in Britain rose from less than 200 to almost 1,000, that the need for a common set of rules and a governing body became obvious.

The R&A had issued a code of rules for St Andrews and the majority of Clubs loosely followed these, but any disputes were settled within the club where they arose.

The need for an overall rules authority was debated as early as 1888 and in November 1891 the editor of *Golf* magazine argued the case strongly. "Almost alone among high class sports," he wrote, "golf stands out as a conspicuous example of a difficult and intricate game played by thousands upon thousands of our educated classes absolutely without organisation, with no cohesion among the body of players, with no code of rules made by duly accredited representatives of golf as a whole."

Four years later the senior golf clubs in Britain asked the R&A to take control of the situation. In true democratic style the R&A proposed a committee of 14, with seven of its own members and seven representing the leading clubs. But so fierce was the in fighting between the other clubs that the exasperated members of the R&A took the decision on September 28, 1897, to form the Rules of Golf Committee from among their own ranks.

In that moment the R&A changed from being a well-respected figurehead into a firmly established governing authority with clearly defined powers. In the century that has followed those powers and responsibilities have grown enormously. By the end of the 19th century golf clubs throughout Britain looked naturally to St Andrews for guidance and the members of the R&A somewhat reluctantly agreed to take command of the rules of the game. This was to be the first step towards becoming golf's most powerful authority.

Every country where the game is played has affiliated to the R&A and accepts the club's authority over the Rules of Golf and the regulations on amateur status. The exceptions are the United States of America, where allegiance lies with the United States Golf Association, and Canada, which is self-governing but remains affiliated to the R&A.

A common world-wide code has been administered by the R&A and the USGA since 1952 following a four-day conference in a committee room at the House of Lords which thrashed out the differences in the rules that had arisen on opposite sides of the Atlantic. The two independent bodies now meet on a regular basis and have worked successfully since 1952 to create a common code.

The original rules were written in long hand on parchment in the same year as the rules of Cricket were written. In Cricket there were twenty-one rules, which have changed considerably over time, in golf seven of the original 13 articles and laws have remained unchanged for over 250 years.

The original set of Rules are given in Chapter 2.

Temporary Rules during World War 2 at Richmond Golf Club 1941

1. Players are asked to collect bomb and shrapnel splinters to save these causing damage to the mowing machines.
2. In competitions, during gunfire or while bombs are falling, players may take shelter without penalty for ceasing play.
3. The position of known delayed action bombs are marked by red flags at a reasonable, but not guaranteed, safe distance there from.
4. Shrapnel and/or bomb splinters on the fairways or in bunkers, within a club's length of a ball, may be moved without penalty, and no penalty shall be incurred if a ball is thereby caused to move accidentally.

5. A ball moved by enemy action may be replaced or, if lost or destroyed, a ball may be dropped not nearer the hole without penalty.

6. A ball lying in a crater may be lifted and dropped not nearer the hole, preserving the line to the hole, without penalty.

7. A player whose stroke is affected by the simultaneous explosion of a bomb may play another ball. Penalty one stroke.

For those who are specifically interested in the history of the rules see the excellent website[20].

Registered Golf Societies in Northamptonshire

This book describes the many Clubs and organisations, which are present in the county. There are also a considerable number of Northamptonshire golfers who are not members of clubs but still enjoy the game. In England, this number is estimated to be approximately 2,000,000 compared to the 700,000 who are Club members and pay affiliation fees to the Northamptonshire & English Golf Unions. The number of non club members in our county is unquantified to date. These players are very enthusiastic about the game and have e.g. pub teams, work teams and many groups of friends who benefit from two for one green fee systems and enjoy visiting local and national golf clubs. In these difficult recessionary times, the Clubs benefit from the income generated by the fees, bar and restaurant sales, nowadays.

In Northamptonshire, several organisations feel the need to be linked in with the local & national game and have registered with the E.G.U. as Associate & Registered Golf Societies. These are

Associate
Northamptonshire Irish Golf Society (4039)
Secretary Mr .D.Green Weston Favell Northampton NN3 3BZ

Registered
Chichele Golf Society (0139)
Secretary Mr.D.E. Steele Wellingborough NN8 5WS
Overstone Lakes Golf Society (6853)
Secretary Mr.D.King Sywell Northampton NN6 0BD

Miscellanea, Holes in One etc

– In 1939 at Northants County G.C. on the 16th July Hubert.S.Martin and George.E.Mobbs (Club Secretary 1966-81) halved the 160-yard par three third hole in one. Both players seeing the balls disappear on this clearly visible green.

This incredible piece of our golf history was confirmed by George in January 2008. Our telephone conversation lasted some five minutes and George clearly recalled the event from seventy years ago stating"It took place during a friendly game between myself and my next door neighbour who was a Clerk for the County Council, following the match Hubert went home not knowing whether or not this had been done before. The details were sent to Bernard Darwin at the Times who included it in his weekly column. In fact, this was the eighth time it had been achieved. Even though Hubert was disappointed he was not the first he was comforted by the fact that he was the first Clerk for any County Council to have achieved this".

I felt Northamptonshire's golf history oozing through me during that memorable five minutes, simply incredible. The odds of achieving this are calculated to be seventeen million to one.

– The Late Stuart Brown holed in one twice in one day with the same club and same ball at Tewksbury G.C.

Golf in Northamptonshire

This sequence of events was captured on television and is unique in the history of the game. He had 26 holes in one in his career. One of Stuart's holes in one had no value at all when he was competing in the 1980 Kenyan Open. At the second hole at Muthiaiga G.C. he hooked his tee shot into some bushes, and then following the right procedure announced that he was playing a provisional ball, which was despatched, straight into the hole. Unfortunately for him, his original ball was found by an enthusiastic spectator and eventually holed out for four. When play had been completed for the day Stuart found that he had missed the cut by a single stoke! 26 holes in one is a great achievement although still some way behind the global leader in this category Norman Manley from Long Beach California who has recorded 59! Stuart was the 1965 Sir Henry Cotton P.G.A. Rookie of the Year and professional at Northants County from 1982-91. He left Northants County in 1991 to become Golf Director at Slaley Hall Golf and Country Club Northumberland. Stuart sadly died at a relatively early age in 1995.

– In 1966 at Harborne G.C. The Late Ray (R.J.W.) Baldwin Secretary of the Midland Golf Union playing in the monthly medal chipped in to the hole for an eagle three on the par 5 4th green. The stroke cut up a thin layer of turf and revealed a metal object, which turned out to be an 1853 penny which was later valued at 30 shillings as a collectors item, a double stroke of luck.

– In 1973 at Peterborough Milton G.C. during an R.A.F. outing two holes in one were recorded with the same ball. In the morning singles Des Tuson holed in one at the 142 yards 11th hole, then in the afternoon foursomes competition his partner Keith Schofield who had gained possession of the ball at the previous hole, fired his tee shot in to the hole at the 174 yards par 3 second hole. The ball was carefully preserved.

The County Rose

From the earliest times, indeed throughout the history of civilization, people from around the world have held the rose close to their hearts. We know now that roses have existed much longer than any of us imagined. Even before human time roses flourished. 35 million year old fossilized rose flowers and hips have been found in Europe and petrified rose wreaths have been unearthed from ancient Egyptian tombs. A rose has long been the symbol of Northamptonshire having been used by the magistrates in Quarter session as far back as 1665.

Northamptonshire's Rose, which is strongly featured, on the badges of all the County's golfing bodies is derived from the Tudor Rose. For example, the current design of the men's badge is taken from The Arms of the Northamptonshire County Council which were granted in 1939 and contain the motto "Rosa Concordiae Signum" meaning "The Rose-The emblem of harmony". The emblems embodied in the design are suggested by the badges in use during the critical period of English history (1399-1485) which ended with the War of the Roses, the Red Rose being borne by the Lancastrians and the white Rose by the Yorkists. When the families of York and Lancaster were subsequently united following the Battle of Bosworth on the 22 August 1485 in neighbouring Leicestershire, the badge adopted by King Henry VII comprising a White Rose superimposed on a Red Rose (The Tudor Rose) became an emblem of unity and concord.

I shall never forget how proud I was and the warmth I felt from the loving look in my mother's eyes as I left the family house, wearing for the first time my brand new navy blazer complete with County Rose badge, grey slacks, blue shirt and County Rose tie to represent Northamptonshire in 1980. It was one of those timeless moments.

CHAPTER 12

2000 AND BEYOND AND THE GAME GOES ON

A Personal View of the Future – By David Croxton

"Universally it is clear that all we really have, beyond money, material possessions and breeding is the time that is given to us. Play good golf wisely, enjoy your time on the course, gently tempered with the traditions of the game and remember those great shots, good friends and memories forever"

The author 26/06/2003 for Colin Green sadly his last day with us and my 48th birthday.

ANY gaze into the future usually requires a reflection on the past and the past would show that Golf has gradually increased its profile and participation over the years and indeed, over the century. We now have more Golf Clubs, more competitions and more players than ever before. The Game, as well as being a forum for like-minded friends to enjoy each other's company in a sporting environment, now has its Showpiece Events and indeed Showpiece players. There is a National and International stage on which the game is played and there are international stars who play it. As such, there will be a desire from the young and the not so young to emulate the stars and to play on their stage.

Thus, the game has a two-fold appeal. The Glamour which this 'Stardom', if we could emulate it, would bring and also the sheer competitive enjoyment of the Saturday morning fourball with like-minded players who wish nothing more than to get as much as they can from their own perhaps limited skills.

The game will undoubtedly continue in this vein. Those involved with the Glamour will attempt to make the Glamour more Glamorous. Those involved in the local game will attempt to make it more enjoyable for those

Golf in Northamptonshire

who wish to play it. This philosophy probably reflects the fact that two factors now drive the game forward. The first is the desire to play it by individual golfers, whether at local or international level. This desire stems from the enjoyment derived from its competitive challenges. But the second motivating force is the business, or dare we use the word 'Profit' element which has driven the expansion of the game in the latter third of the 20th Century and now continues into the 21st. Once again, this is seen at both ends of the spectrum. The success of the Stars usually has a moneymaking connection to it both to the player and to the associated business. At local level, not only do the players compete with each other but also the Clubs are now more money driven and are competing vigorously to attract more play and more players to their Course.

Now to the crystal ball and lets take the different aspects of the Golfing structure in order:

1. The Golf Courses
2. The Equipment
3. The Players
4. The Game

1. The Golf Courses

It may well be that the expansion in the number of courses will not be so significant certainly in the early part of the 21st Century as it was in the latter part of the 20th. It is widely recognised that some consolidation is required to enable supply and demand to reach an equilibrium. We have moved from a position of under-supply of Golf facilities in the 1980's to what is now a probable over-supply.

However, it is likely that some development will take place. Northampton is forecast to expand in housing and population as will Daventry and Corby and it may be that a small number of speculative new Golf Course developments will evolve. In addition, where there is the potential for existing sites to expand then they will gradually do so. We are already seeing some existing courses endeavouring to make changes and extensions to their current layouts. As equipment technology improves, which it inevitably will, then the continuing consequence will be for courses to adapt to these improvements. Some nine hole Courses may acquire additional land in order to become 18 holes and inevitably facilities will be improved at all Clubs with the passing of time.

Cold Ashby Golf Club increased from 18 to 27 holes in the 1990's. Northamptonshire County Golf Club have added three extra holes and now have a total of 21 thus accommodating those players who wish to play a nine hole game and finish back at the Clubhouse. As we approach the end of the first ten years of the new Century, Rushden Golf Club has plans to expand from 9 holes to 18. This type of expansion will, no doubt, continue.

In addition, more subtle changes will be made to Courses with new tees being constructed, probably to create extra distance. New bunkers will appear and old ones will be phased out. Thus, the facilities will evolve and change as time goes on.

At the same time, some may close or re-locate. The geographical location of some Golf Courses may make them targets for an opportunist developer and in these instances, where money and profit, once again, become the driving force some clubs may be persuaded to allow their Course to be built on, thus resulting in closure.

For those that remain, the natural drive by Club Managers and Course Managers to 'Present' their Courses in a continually improving way will continue. There is far more technical information available to Golf Course Managers than ever before and they will react to this in a positive way seeking to present their Course in the best way possible. Techniques, currently unique to the management of greens, will be introduced on tees and even on fairways in order to improve these playing surfaces. The inevitable debate on 'pace' of greens will continue. Can they or should they be faster? If so, it will create a conflict between the competitive requirements of the player (for fast greens) and the desire by Course Managers to maintain the agronomic principles and thus grow healthy

270

and sustainable grasses.

The design and presentation of course furniture, such as tee signage and course markers, will continue to change but let us look even further ahead. There will undoubtedly be those who will wish to introduce variations to the game to make it more 'novel' and hence more marketable. The 'Texas Scramble' was an example of this and similar innovations can be expected. A version has already been introduced where two flags are present on the green and the player is given the option to choose which target (a difficult position or a less difficult position) to play to. Will we see more than one green (or target area!) on a hole?

Where land is limited but there is a requirement for golf, such as inner cities and built up areas, expect these innovations to continue but hopefully not at the expense of the 18 hole game on well designed and scenic Courses that we all know and love.

2. The Equipment

Development in club technology and ball technology cannot be resisted. It has been happening for over a century and will, no doubt, continue. This creates problems in that Courses designed for a certain standard of technology are perceived to be not suitable for the 'new' technology. This fact of life will not go away, but surely that is the challenge that we have to rise to. Indeed this is no more true now than it was 100 years ago, which illustrates that the one thing that does not change about golf is that developments in the game and its equipment bring about change itself. The benefit of improved technology is that it can improve the satisfaction and enjoyment of the player by providing the ability to 'improve' personal standards. This can be particularly true where a player is perhaps in later years and the improved technology helps to overcome a personal decline in physical ability.

We now have those who argue that courses cannot withstand even further developments in equipment technology or those who argue that golf has always had to deal with this and will continue to do so. Should any legislation be required to control this area then it is probably that which concerns the ball itself. It is possible to standardise the type of ball being used so that performance differences are purely down to the shot played.

In other areas, equipment technology will have a big influence on the way we play the game of golf as satellite communication and navigation systems take over our lives. Distance measurement will be at every player's fingertips. Remote control on buggies and electric trolleys will become the norm, as indeed it surely must in the longer term for green keeping equipment. The time must not be too far away before a mower can be programmed to navigate its way around a green without the requirement for someone to steer it. How soon before this technology extends to the golf ball itself so that it can be traced to its eventual destination?

3. The Player

During the 20th Century when someone took up the game of golf, it was the norm to join a Golf Club and to support the various activities of the chosen Club. Whilst that is still the norm for some in the 21st Century, there is, however, a different approach becoming commonplace. Many golfers now voluntarily choose not to join a club but to regularly play more than one Golf Course as a visitor. This transient approach can probably be attributed to changing lifestyle priorities, particularly among the 20 to 40 year olds.

I use this example to point out that 'golfers' are changing and hence those who administrate the Game should not be afraid to change also. Currently the Governing Bodies tend to confine their activities to the Golf Clubs and their members. However, the non-member golfing group is becoming a significant force and the time will come when their needs should be addressed. They are regular and keen golfers and they regularly and keenly use our golfing facilities. If the game is to continue to be strong and if the Governing Bodies wish to influence it in the right way then they should recognise this. This is true of the Northamptonshire bodies as well as the National ones. The answer to this is not new. We need to look no further than the home of golf, namely St. Andrews. For years and indeed centuries, the Courses of St. Andrews have been open to all to play on and this philosophy is important. Also in the St Andrews environment, there are a number of transient Golf Clubs who run their affairs independently of the Golf Course and will stage their events on more than one Course. These Golf Clubs are properly structured and properly administered within the guidelines laid down by the Governing Body. However, in some ways they resemble what we would call Golfing Societies in that their activities are not confined to one Golf Course.

This is the pointer for the future. The 'transient' players must be embraced by the game and we should start by forging stronger links between our Golf Clubs and our Golfing Societies.

4. The Game

In 2008, the R & A have published some changes to the Rules of Golf. Similarly the Handicapping System which is administered by the Council of National Golf Unions (CONGU) has also undergone some changes and been updated. These changes, albeit minor, to the way the game is played tend to occur every 4 or 5 years. Thus, the Game is regularly being subjected to minor fine-tuning.

This, we can assume will continue but we should also be aware of the influence of some of the pressures mentioned earlier. Changing lifestyles are leading to a move towards 'shortened' versions of the game, particularly 9 hole competitions. In common with other sports (notably 20/20 Cricket) we will see the 18 hole Strokeplay competitions challenged by alternative formats. These may or may not catch on.

There will almost certainly be a call for a 'uniform' golf ball to be used and this could provide the answer in the desire to protect the course layout and design from the effect of advancing technology. There could be a move to nominate the type of ball to be used in any given situation i.e. a low performance ball on one day, an average performance ball on another and a high performance ball on another. Or maybe different types of player could be allowed to play with different types of ball – another variation on handicapping.

Whatever happens we can be sure that Golf will evolve as we go through the next 100 years. Let us hope it maintains its ability to provide countless enjoyment to all types of player, male and female, the good and the not so good, the young and the not so young, the fit and the not so fit. More people play the game worldwide than ever before. The administrators have an enormous task to allow sensible progress whilst at the same time maintaining its traditions.

Northamptonshire sits well in regard to dealing with these challenges. Geographically it may be a small County but this makes it easier to react to changing circumstances. The establishment of the Northamptonshire Golf Partnership has shown how all its administrative bodies (Men's, Women's and Professionals') can and do work together. In addition, the history and traditions described in this book are great examples of the strength of the game in the County of Northamptonshire.

NORTHAMPTONSHIRE GOLF PARTNERSHIP

In 1999 the then President of the Northamptonshire Golf Union, David Croxton, and his counterpart as Captain of Northamptonshire Ladies County Golf Association Carol Gibbs, got together to form a Millennium Committee. Their aim was to arrange an Event to celebrate the start of a NEW CENTURY and also to create a Fund, which could be used to support development of Golf particularly at grass roots level in the county. Hence, the inaugural County Ball was held in January 2000. This proved to be a tremendously enjoyable social occasion resulting in the establishment of the Millennium Fund. Since then this fund has been used to help several young players along the way to improve their game and playing opportunities.

As the years moved on it became apparent that other opportunities were opening up. Grants and other financial support for Sports Development were available, but were not being accessed by the County's Golfing bodies. The requirement was for a united front in order to meet the necessary criteria. Consequently, a 'PARTNER-SHIP' of all the governing bodies – Northamptonshire Golf Union, Northamptonshire Ladies County Golf Association and Northamptonshire Professional Golf Association - was formed in 2004. Thus from small beginnings the Development of Golf in Northamptonshire was given a new impetus with the official formation of the Northamptonshire Golf Partnership. In tandem with the formation of the Partnership came the appointment of a County Development Officer on a part-time basis. The first person to occupy this post was Richard Lobb who had recently taken early retirement from a Head of Sport post in Education.

Northamptonshire should be justly proud of these groundbreaking moves. The County Golf Partnership and the Golf Development Officer were the first of their kind in England and as a result of their considerable achievements, many other County Golf Partnerships were subsequently formed. It was quickly seen that this 'joined up' approach brought new opportunities. Funding from local or national bodies, which hitherto would not have been available to an all male (the NGU) or an all female (NLCGA) body, was utilised to provide taster sessions to the young and the not so young.

Immediately an improvement was seen in the introduction of golf into schools where several School Club Links were forged. These Links have been strengthened and it is now evident that these taster sessions are giving youngsters the chance to try the game of golf where previously this opportunity was not present.
The Partnership has now put a County Coaching strategy in place for all levels of playing ability and this is all part of a strong structure to further develop the future of golf in Northamptonshire.

A programme has also been introduced to address the responsibilities of the Governing Bodies to ensure they avoid any form of discrimination and have correct Child Protection Procedures in place.

However, perhaps the biggest step forward has been the way in which the Northamptonshire Golf Partnership has provided a platform for the Male section (Northamptonshire Golf Union, the Female section (Northamptonshire Ladies County Golf Association) and the Professionals (Northamptonshire Professional Golfers Association) to act as one unit in moving golf development forward. This alliance has been mirrored at National level and also in other Counties and the additional benefit has been the establishment of strong links with County Sports Development Bodies. From this has come much-needed funding back up for the Golf Clubs of the County to tap into in the future.

For the PARTNERSHIP website, see **www.northamptonshiregolf.org.uk**

CHAPTER 13

CHRONOLOGY

"Golf is not a mere game, it is a disease; infectious and contagious. Once acquired it cannot be shaken off. Once a golfer always a golfer-there's no help for it"

L.Latchford 1890

1876-1895 Golf was played during this period "some time" at Great Harrowden Hall by young ladies of the Great Harrowden School for Daughters of Gentlemen in the grounds currently occupied by Wellingborough G.C.

1889 Scottish Doctor John Allinson M.D. (age 26) took up a post in Kettering and proposed golf in the County.

1891 Kettering G.C. formed on land owned by the Duke of Buccleuch, laid out by Old Tom Morris from St Andrews, Annual Subscription £1 11s 6d, Captain Dr John Allinson.

1893 Northampton, Oundle and Wellingborough G.C.s formed

– Earl Spencer (The Red Earl) President Northampton G.C.

1908 Kingsthorpe G.C. opened as a nine hole course.

– Rushden G.C. opened at Stanwick 6 holes.

– Daventry and District G.C. opened for play.

1910 Northants County (designed by Harry. S.Colt), opened by J.H.Taylor & T.Ball, first Captain Edward Algernon Fitzroy.

1912 Kingsthorpe G.C. moved to a new location and opened as 18-hole course.

1915 Northampton G.C. moved to a new location and opened as 18-hole course.

1919 Rushden G.C. moved to its current location on Kimbolton Rd.

1920 Len Holland Professional from Northants County G.C. finished in fifth place at The Open with scores of 80, 78, 71 and 79 at Deal G.C. He also finished 16th in 1921, 13th in 1922 and 6th in 1924.

1921 Northamptonshire Association of Golf Clubs formed (in 1929 it changed it's name to the Northamptonshire Golf Union)

1922 The 1st County Championship took place, the trophy (Presented by Frederick Bostock, President 1921-22) was won by his son Lancelot Bostock both members of Northamptonshire County Golf Club.

– Higgs Bowl (presented by T.Higgs, Esq) won by County Secretary (1921-26) G.A.T. (Tubby) Vials.

– Scratch League Division 1 trophy (Formerly the Inter-Club Challenge Cup Presented by W.P.Cross, Esq.) introduced and won by Northants County G.C.

1927 Cecil Leitch trophy presented by Miss C Leitch to the Northants County Golf Club

1928 Miss Grieg (Northamptonshire) & Miss Enid Wilson (Derbyshire) participated in the "Eves" Ladies Northern Foursomes at Woodhall Spa G.C. Lincolnshire.

1930 N.L.C.G.A. minutes of meetings started

1932 The future King of England (King George VI) the Duke of York elected Captain of Northants County G.C. handicap fourteen.

1934 Charles Catlow won the first of his record 11 N.G.U. County Championships.

1935 N.G.U. Men's Handicap Challenge Cup (Presented by F.F.Parsons President 1936-37) first won by W. D. Graham

1949 N.G.U. Braid's Driver (Presented by C.S.Catlow) first competed for and won by A.J.Harrison Northampton.

1950 Market Harborough G.C. left the Northamptonshire Union and joined the Leicester & Rutland Union.

1956 Hollingsworth Trophy introduced Presented by W (Bill).H.Hollingsworth, Esq. President 1955-56, 1967-68) first won by Kingsthorpe G.C.

1959 N.G.U. Men's Scratch Foursome's tournament introduced, The Catlow Salvers were presented by Past President Charles.S.Catlow Esq and won by J.Crawford & E.J.Kingston PMGC.

– Family Foursomes introduced (Presented by H.W.Colton Esq N.G.U. President 1957-58 and won by Mr & Mrs Peter H Meacock Daventry Golf Club).

1960 St Andrews Hospital Golf Club opened.

1961 N.G.U. Boys Trophy Presented by the Past President Mr D. Chamberlain.

– Girls Championship Introduced.

1962 *Chronicle & Echo* tournament launched by Alex Good at Kingsthorpe G.C.

– Richard Aitken won the first of his eight N.G.U. County Championships.

1963 Bobby Locke, The Open Champion (1949, 1950, 1952, and 1957) from South African visited Rushden. Having collected a new pair of shoes, which were manufactured, to his specification they were broken in on the course.

1965 Northampton's Men Walter Clarke & Brian Jones qualified for the finals of the Daily Mail Amateur Foursomes tournament at Hunstanton.

– Society of Northamptonshire Past Captains formed

1966 Northampton's Men A.F. (Tony) Stevens (President 1990-92) & L.A. (Laurie) Johnson qualified for the finals of the Daily Mail amateur foursomes tournament.

– The E.G.U. County Champions Tournament was held at Northants County on the 25th September 1966.

1967 Priors Hall G.C. officially opened with a celebrity fourball, which included Tony Jacklin.

– N.G.U. Men's team finish in their highest ever position as Runners-Up at the Eastern Counties Foursomes at Hunstanton G.C.

1968 First Northants Professional Golf Association event, a Pro-Am was held at Northants County.

1969 N.G.U. Men's Stableford Cup (Presented by T.Higgs, Esq) first played for and won by K.C.Hunter Northants County

1970 The N.G.U. consisted of ten clubs, 1800 Golfers in the Northampton area.

– W.H. (Sam) Abbott Secretary retired after 27 years service for the Union.

– Daventry G.C.s Men S.Rooney and D.Gill qualified for the National Finals of the *Daily Mail* amateur four-somes tournament.

– John White Golf Club opened

– Conrad Ceislewicz selected for England Boys vs Scotland, won his foursomes and singles 2/1.

1971 Northants County G.Cs. Men J.D. & Rodney.A.Haig qualified for the finals of the Daily Mail amateur foursomes tournament.

1972 Northamptonshire's Men won the Anglian League First team Shield for the first time

– N.G.U. Men's Senior Trophy Presented by A.J.Everard, Esq and won by T.H.Goode Kingsthorpe G.C.

– Kettering G.Cs. nineteen year old Robert Larratt selected by the E.G.U. for the Youth's Home Internationals at Glasgow Gailes August 8&9th, our first ever English representation.

1973 Farthingstone Golf Club opened

1974 Northants County G.Cs. Men, Richard Halliday & Tony Bishop qualified for the finals of the Daily Mail Amateur Foursomes Tournament.

– Leicestershire golfer and friend of the N.G.U., Bob Taylor (Leicestershire &Rutland G.U. President 1996/7) enters the Guinness Book of Records by recording three holes in one in three days at the sixteenth hole, during practise, and play using 1,6,6 irons during the Eastern Counties Foursomes Tournament at Hunstanton G.C.

– Cold Ashby G.C. opened.

– Carol Gibbs nee LeFeuvre represented Great Britain and Ireland in The Curtis Cup at San Francisco G.C.

1975 Tim Giles Northants County selected for England Youths vs Scotland

– Wellingborough G.C. opened it's new course at Great Harrowden.

– Embankment Golf Club opened

1976 A record dry summer brings a sprinkler ban at many courses,

– Past N.G.U. President Bill Hollingsworth made a Life Member of Northampton G.C.

– Delapre Park G.C. opened

1977 Staverton Park Golf Club opened

– Woodlands G.C. Professional Mike Gallagher played two rounds in The Open at Turnberry and became a member of the P.G.A. Cup team which drew with the U.S.A. at Mission Hills G.C. Palm Springs U.S.A.

1978 Future Wellingborough G.C. greenkeeper Ian Marshall played two rounds in The Open at Royal Birkdale G.C.

– The U.S.G.A. introduced the Stimpmeter to golf to provide a uniform way of measuring green speeds.

1979 Priors Hall G.C. Men N.Dean & P.Robinson qualified for the finals of the Daily Mail amateur foursomes tournament.

1980 N.G.U. Men's Team won the Anglian B League for the first time, Captain Barry Highfield Daventry G.C.

– N.G.U. Men's Scratch league Division 2 Trophy introduced and won by Northampton G.C.

– New holes at Rushden G.C. added (the current 5th and 14th), approved by former member and the 11-times County Champion Charles Catlow, hole named in his honour.

1981 Kingsthorpe G.C.s Ladies S.Tookey & P.Coles qualified for the finals of the Daily Mail amateur foursomes tournament.

– Cherwell Edge G.C. opened

– Woodlands G.C. Professional Mike Gallagher played two rounds in The Open at Royal St Georges scoring 75,78 (caddie Andy Poole ex Cobblers Goalkeeper)

1982 Men's Northamptonshire Open tournament introduced, trophy presented by Carlsberg and won by Professional Charles Ray on his home course, Staverton Park G.C.

1983 E.G.U. County President & Guest tournament won by R.B. (Richard) Catlow & R.G.(Richard)Aitken, Northants County 63pts at Thorpeness.

1984 Kettering G.C.s Ladies L.White & T.Rolf qualified for the finals of the Daily Mail amateur foursomes tournament

1987 N.G.U. Men's Match play Championship introduced and won by Duncan Ellson from Wellingborough G.C.

1988 Northamptonshire P.G.A. formally constituted

1989 N.G.U. Men's team finish runners-Up at the Eastern Counties Foursomes at Hunstanton G.C. with a total of $22\frac{1}{2}$ points, Captain Ian Marshall.

– Professional Kevin Dickens (attached to Cold Ashby G.C.) finished runner-up in the European Tour event the Belgian Open

1990 Northamptonshire's men won the Anglian League First team Shield for the second time.

– Collingtree Park G.C. opened.

– Northampton G.C. moved out of the town from Kettering Road to a new course at Harlestone.

– Hellidon Lakes G.C. opened

– Chris Lane became Golf Foundation's Weetabix Age Group Champion in the under 16 category at Patshull Park G.C. Shropshire.

1991 Silverstone and Whittlebury Park (West Park) Golf Clubs opened.

1993 Northants County and N.G.U. County Stalwart Jack Humphries (Captain 1968, President 1984, Chairman M.G.U. 1990-93) passed away on the 10 December.

– Elton Furze G.C. opened

– S Hennigan & P Cook represented the County in the L.G.U. Centenary Foursomes at St Andrews.

1994 Stoke Albany G.C. opened

– E.G.U. Carris trophy held at Northants County and won by home player Robert Duck (280) including breaking the amateur course record with a score of 65.

– Bill Hollingsworth died age 94

– Overstone Park G.C. opened

1995 European Tour P.G.A. event, the British Masters played at Collingtree Park G.C., with nine Ryder Cup players present including Seve Ballesteros and Colin Montgomerey who successfully recaptured the trophy at Oak Hill New York USA. Tournament won by Sam Torrance Scotland 67, 66, 68, 69 = 270.

– Kingfisher opened at Deanshanger.

– Death of the ever popular Kingsthorpe G.C. President and N.G.U. Past President Alex Good age 91.

– Pytchley Lodge and Brampton Heath Clubs established

– Miss Suzanne Sharpe was chosen to train with the England Team in Spain at Las Brisas near Marbella and to represent the English Ladies in the Spanish Open.

1996 European P.G.A. tour event the British Masters played at Collingtree Park, and won by Australian R.Allenby with a score of 284.

– N.G.U. Izzard Club Team Trophy Presented by M.J.Izzard, Esq. and won by Kingsthorpe G.C. at Northampton G.C.

– N.G.U. Club Champion of Champions tournament introduced and won by Paul Taylor of Staverton Park G.C.

– Northampton's Men M.J.Izzard & G.H.Keates qualified for the finals of the Daily Mail amateur foursomes tournament at Sandmore G.C. Leeds

– N.G.U. Scratch league Division 3&4 Trophies introduced and won by Staverton Park & Priors Hall G.C.s.

– N.G.U. Yearbook launched together with a new mobile competitions office.

– 75th anniversary of the N.G.U. celebrated at Wellingborough G.C.

1997 N.G.U. Inter Club Handicap League Trophy Presented by M.McMahon, Esq President 1992-94 and won by Collingtree Park G.C.

– Rob Duck (Northants County) received a full England International Cap, playing in four games during the Home Internationals at Burnham & Berrow G.C. Somerset

1998 Kevin Dickens (from Cold Ashby/Northampton G.C.s) represented Great Britain & Ireland in the P.G.A. Cup team at The Broadmoor Club, Colorado Springs U.S.A.

– 12 year-old Gary Boyd Cherwell Edge G.C. won the inaugural E.G.U. Gold Medal at Woodhall Spa with Stableford scores of 32+40=72.

1999 Five year old (Five year, seven months and nine days) Mathew Draper entered the Guinness Book of Records as the youngest player to record a hole in one, using a cut-down four wood on the 122 yard fourth hole at Cherwell EdgeG.C.

– Northamptonshire Millennium Committee formed consisting of the N.G.U., N.L.C.G.A. and N.P.G.A.

– E.G.U. County President's tournament won by Dave Croxton Cold Ashby G.C. with a score of 34 points

– Luke Hillier (Collingtree Park G.C.) selected for England Under18 team

2000 N.G.U. County Junior Match play Championship trophy kindly donated by John and Dorris Redden (Wellingborough G.C.) and won by Luke Hillier Collingtree Park.

– Miss Roseann Youngman (Oundle G.C.) qualified for the English Girls Championship at Sheringham G.C.

– Millennium Ball held at Wicksteed Park, Kettering, attended by all Clubs in the County.

2001 Northants County Professional Stuart Reynolds enters the World Record books by scoring 59 gross at Burton on Trent G.C.

– N.G.U. County Match Play Singles, Fourball, Foursomes Trophies introduced and won by T.Sheridan Priors Hall, I.Donald & S.Chalcroft Farthingstone and S.McDonald & P .Scott Kingsthorpe respectively.

– Kelly Hanwell (Northampton G.C.) won the Ladies Midland Championship beating L Day of Worcestershire.

2002 N.G.U. Men's Team won the Anglian B League for the second time Captain Richard Brown Wellingborough G.C.

– Roseann Youngman (Oundle G.C.) was a very sucesfull member of the winning England team in the Girls Home International Matches played at The Hermitage G.C. Dublin

2003 County Golfer Colin Green killed by lightening during a Scratch League match, a young witty gentleman sadly missed by all. Words barely touch the emotions of that very sad June day. Air ambulance funds raised by his friends in Colin's memory.

– Hollingsworth Trophy won by Northampton G.C. Their eighth success.

– Roseann Youngman (Oundle G.C.) won the National Schools Championship held at Trentham G.C.

2004 Former Amateur Boy and Men's County player from Priors Hall and Oundle G.C.s Neil Evans, now Professional at Greetham Valley G.C. played in The Open Championship at Royal Troon G.C.

– Gary Boyd (N.C.G.C.) won the Norman Russell Memorial Salver for the best performance at the E.G.U. Midland Counties Qualifyer at Woodhall Spa and the Midland Youths Championship at Stoke Rochford G.C. and represented England and G.B&I.

– Scratch League Division 5 trophy introduced by N.G.U. and won by Delapre Park G.C.

– New Clubhouse opened at Kingsthorpe G.C.

– Colin Green's 2003 Northants County Club Championship shared victory retained by his twin brother Roger.

– Stuart Ashwood (N.C.G.C.) age 16 became the first youngest player ever to win the gross, nett and Braid's driver trophies at the N.G.U. County Championship and later in the season the County Boys Championship.

– Northamptonshire Golf Partnership conceived and funded by Sport England, the first of the 34 English Counties.

2005 The N.G.U. Men's Senior Team qualified for the inaugural E.G.U. Seniors Championship and finish in fourth place behind Somerset, Kent and Winners Cheshire.

– The N.L.C.G.A. Ladies qualified for the National finals and finish in fourth place behind Hampshire, Gloucestershire and winners Yorkshire.

– Rushden G.C. floated plans to become an 18-hole course close to its current location on the B645.

– England Under 16 squad member Adam Myers (Northants County) age fourteen won the English Boys under 16 Open Stroke Play Championship (McGregor Trophy) and The Jean Case Salver.

– Nine year old Charley Hull from Kettering G.C. won the Grand Final of the Health perception L.G.U. Championship at Turnberry.

– On its 50th Anniversary the Hollingsworth Trophy was won by Staverton Park 3/2 against the donor's club Northampton G.C.

– Northants County's Sarah Carter and Kirstie Jennings reached the final of the Daily Mail Foursomes at St Pierre narrowly losing 2/1.

2006 Gary Boyd (Cherwell Edge G.C.) received a full England International Cap by playing in the Home Internationals at Pyle and Kenfig G.C. Wales collecting $1\frac{1}{2}$ foursomes points and $1\frac{1}{2}$ singles points in the England team that finished runners up to Scotland. Northamptonshire's first ever English International point was scored on 06/09/2006 when Gary Boyd and Paul Waring (Bromborough G.C.) defeated the Welsh pair 2/1 in the morning foursomes. A few weeks later, the 19 year old reduced his handicap to plus four following a 67 gross during the E.G.U. Champion of Champions Tournament at Woodhall Spa. This is the lowest recorded handicap from a Northamptonshire member since golf began in the county. Gary was promoted to the England Elite Squad in October. In November Gary won the inaugural Asia Pacific Open Amateur Championship at Mission Hills in China for his first international victory with a level par aggregate of 288 (72, 76, 69, 71).Gary claimed victory at the first play off hole. In the recently launched R&A world rankings, Gary Boyd was in 18th place out of 1150 World Amateurs.

Adam Myers (Northants County) played for England Boys in the European Young Masters, and was a winning member of the England Boys team in the annual match played against Spain at Pannal G.C. Harrogate. Adam was a member of the winning Nations Cup team at the McGregor Trophy at Worthing. Adam also represented England at the Dutch Junior Masters in September, against England Girls winning his foursomes (team lost 8-7) and against Scotland (team won $12\frac{1}{2}$-$2\frac{1}{2}$) in October. Adam is a valued member of the England under16 squad. We are justifiably very proud of our two young stars.

– Gary Boyd reached the later stages of The Amateur Championship.

– Kingsthorpe G.C. won the Hollingsworth Trophy for a record twelfth time in sudden death 3/2 over Whittlebury Park G.C.

– Cold Ashby G.C. won the Scratch League Division 1 trophy for the first time in their history.

– In September, the author won the Midland Golf Union's Flanders Trophy at the M.G.U. A.G.M.

– November, Gary Boyd was selected to prepare as a squad member for the 2007 Walker Cup.

2007 During the European Men's Team Championship held at Western Gailes, whilst representing England "our" 20-year-old Gary Boyd (Cherwell Edge G.C.) recorded his fifth hole in one at the seventh hole using a six iron, his first on a links course.

– Ryan Evans (Wellingborough G.C.) became the N.G.U. County Champion when the event was held at Oundle G.C. for the first time in June.

– Rebecca Gee (Wellingborough G.C.) qualified for the finals of the Daily Mail Junior Golf Championship following a score of level par over her home course. Gary Boyd (Cherwell Edge G.C.) lead the qualifying for The English Amateur with scores of 70+64=134, the 64 gross equalling the course record at Royal Cinque Ports G.C. In the match play stages of the Championship played over Royal St Georges G.C. Gary was unfortunately knocked out in the first Round at the 19th hole. That's golf for you!

– Gary Boyd (Cherwell Edge G.C.) was first reserve for the Walker Cup team for the biennial match against the U.S.A. at Royal County Down 7-9 September. Gary finished in 8th place in the Ping/E.G.U. Order of Merit with 563.27 points.

– Adam Myers (Northants County G.C.) had a busy season representing England. Some highlights of the season were: - Adam was a member of the team that beat Sweden $5\frac{1}{2}$-$3\frac{1}{2}$ at The Buckinghamshire Golf Club on the 10th April. Adam played in the Harder German Junior Masters Club in Heidelberg on 7th - 9th August. In

September Adam was a member of the team that completed another superb victory against Scotland 12-3 in the annual Under 16 International at Prestwick St Nicholas. In October Adam was a member of the England Boys team that defeated England Girls 12-3 at Ogbourne Downs in Wiltshire, in the afternoon all Midlands singles clash Adam beat another rising star Alex Peters from Nottinghamshire 1up.

  – Collingtree Park G.C. won the Hollingsworth Trophy for the first time in October after being runners up on two occasions

  – In November Gary Boyd (Cherwell Edge G.C.) played as an amateur in the Tour School Qualifier at San Roque G.C. This gruelling marathon over the new and old courses dictates who qualifies for the P.G.A. European Tour in 2008.There was 156 in the field, Gary played in all six rounds, having survived the cut after four rounds and scored 71, 71, 75, 71, 73, 79 = 440 19 strokes behind the winner and in 67th place. A superb effort from the talented young man. Fellow Club member ex county player Chris (El Tomahawk) Lowe caddied, a nice gesture. Gary therefore gained Category 14 status because of this marathon effort; he finished ahead of many famous names. As a result, Gary Boyd turned professional, we eagerly await his impact upon this new bigger challenging stage, and we wish him well. In fact, Gary started his professional career with a bang, which included a hole in one (his sixth) on the 11 January 2008 during the Johannesburg Open and also qualified for the 2008 Open Championship.

Addendum

DURING my research for this book, I noted with great interest that Claridge Druce travelled the county in the back of his chauffeur driven Daimler in order to complete the 1930 Flora of Northamptonshire, since he was getting on in years (see Introduction, page vii, for the significance of this addendum). The chauffeur was under strict instructions not to exceed 20 m.p.h since below that speed he was able to recognise the flowers in the fields and verges.

I now understand how he managed to cover such a large area in such a relatively short time. How would travelling at this speed be interpreted these days as people charge about everywhere without even seeing the fields and verges?

I can simply admire his patience and diligence; I trust readers of this book will agree that I have followed his lead from three quarters of a century ago in drawing this book together, having emotionally travelled the highways and byways of our great county.

APPENDIX 1

RESULTS

Chapter 3 NORTHAMPTONSHIRE GOLF UNION
N.G.U. COUNTY CHAMPION MEN 1922-2008

Year	Champion	Year	Champion	Year	Champion
1922	L.Bostock NC	1954	R.L.Mobbs NC	1980	C.R.Cieslewicz NC
1923	J.Allison Ke	1955	C.S.Catlow NC	1981	M.Haddon KG
1924	W.J.Thompson Ke	1956	C.S.Catlow NC	1982	S.McDonald KG
1925	H.Broomfield N#	1957	G.F.Clarke NC	1983	D.Warren 153 NC
1926	E.Speakman Kg	1958	C.S.Catlow NC	1984	M.Scott PH
1927	W.J.Thompson Ke	1959	R.G.Halliday NC	1985	M.McNally DP
1928	L.F.Brown NC	1960	C.S.Catlow NC	1986	M.Scott PH
1929	G.N.Somers N	1961	E.J.Kingdon PM	1987	D.K.Jones Kg
1930	L.Bostock NC	1962	R.G.Aitken 74,67 N	1988	D.K.Ellson 72,78 W
1931	F.C.Roe N	1963	R.G.Aitken N	1989	N.Goodman139 Kg
1932	R.W.Kilsby R	1964	R.G.Aitken N	1990	A.Print 72,72 NC
1933	R.W.Kilsby R	1965	J.E.Saxby 76,75 W	1991	S.McDonald Kg
1934	C.S.Catlow R	1966	R.G.Aitken 77,68 N	1992	A.J.Wilson74,72 NC
1935	R.W.Kilsby R	1967	J.M.Pettigrew 143 N	1993	R.McIlwain PH
1936	R.W.Kilsby R	1968	R.G.Aitken N	1994	A.Print 71,69 NC
1937	C.S.Catlow N	1969	R.G.Aitken 71,70 NC	1995	A.M.S.Lord* NC
1938	C.S.Catlow N	1970	R.G.Aitken 76,76 NC	1996	I.Dallas 139 C
1939	C.S.Catlow N	1971	R.P.Larratt 68,78 Ke	1997	P.Langrish-Smith 73,72 C
1946	M.Gear-Evans PM	1972	R.J.Gray PM	1998	G.H.Keates 74,70 N
1947	C.S.Catlow NC	1973	C.R.Cieslewicz NC	1999	N.Soto 69,71 NC
1948	C.S.Catlow NC	1974	J.C.Hodgson W	2000	A.Print 70,72 NC
1949	F.C.Roe NC	1975	C.R.Cieslewicz NC	2001	N.Soto 71,70 NC
1950	C.S.Catlow NC	1976	T.J.Giles NC	2002	M.Peacock71,71 PM
1951	A.J.Harrison N	1977	R.G.Aitken NC	2003	G.H.Keates 71,75 N
1952	F.C.Roe NC	1978	C.R.Cieslewicz NC	2004	S.Ashwood 74,71NC
1953	M.J.Worley NC	1979	C.R.Cieslewicz NC	2005	D.Wood* 71,69 BH
				2006	G.Boyd 69,66 CE
				2007	R.Evans 70,68 W
				2008	S.Ashwood 68,69 NC

Northampton G.C.s first County Champion was H.Broomfield, he was made the Club's first ever Life Member at Kettering Road and had the sixteenth hole named after him "Broomfield's", this was in 1924/5. Interestingly he was never Captain though teed off first and won for "Lancashire" as fellow Club members and leading players competed against Scotland to celebrate the formation of the Scottish Golf Association in 1925[4p29]. Mr Broomfield was later Northampton's Club Champion in 1927 with a score of 79 over the Kettering Road "Links".
 * After play-off

N.G.U. COUNTY CHAMPIONS BY CLUB 1922-2008

Brampton Heath (1)
D.Wood 2005

Collingtree Park (2)
I.Dallas 1996
P.Langrish-Smith 1997

Delapre Park (1)
M.McNally 1985

Cherwell Edge (1)
G.Boyd 2006

Kettering (4)
J.Allison 1923
R.P.Larratt 1971
W.J.Thompson 1924, 27

Kingsthorpe (6)
E.Speakman 1926
N.Goodman 1989
M.Haddon 1981
D.K.Jones 1987
S.McDonald 1982, 91

Northants County (34)
R.G.Aitken 1969, 70, 77
S.Ashwood 2004, 2008
L.Bostock 1922, 30
L.F.Brown 1928
C.S.Catlow 1947, 48, 50, 55, 56, 58, 60
C.R.Ceislewicz 1973, 75, 78, 79, 80
G.F.Clarke 1957
T.J.Giles 1976
R.G.Halliday 1959
A.M.S.Lord 1995
R.L.Mobbs 1954
A.Print 1990, 94, 2000
F.C.Roe 1949, 1952
N.Soto 1999, 2001
D.Warren 1983
J.Wilson 1992
M.J.Worley 1953

Northampton (15)
R.G.Aitken 1962, 63, 64, 66, 68
H.Broomfield 1925
C.S.Catlow 1937, 38, 39
A.J.Harrison 1951
G.H.Keates 1998, 2003
J.M.Pettigrew 1967
F.C.Roe 1931
G.N.Somers 1929

Priors Hall (2)
R.McIlwain 1993
M.Scott 1984, 86

Peterbo'h Milton (4)
M.Gear-Evans 1946
R.J.Gray 1972
E.J.Kingdon 1961
M.Peacock 2002

Rushden (5)
C.S.Catlow 1934
R.W.Kilsby 1932, 33, 35, 36

Wellingborough (4)
J.C.Hodgson 1974
J.E.Saxby 1965
D.K.Ellson 1988
R.Evans 2007

N.G.U. County Matchplay Champion

Year	Winner	Runner-Up	Year	Winner	Runner-Up
1987	D.K.Ellson 20th W	A. Lord NC	1998	J.Campbell 2Up Ke	R.Connolly CP
1988	M.S.Herson 1 up PM	C.Ceislewicz	1999	D.Matthews Wo	J.Evans Kg
1989	M.Scott 2/1 PH	D.J.Jessup N	2000	G.H.Keates 1Up N	M.Peacock PM
1990	A.I.Marshall 3/1 W	R.McIlwain PH	2001	N.West 3/1 NC	M.Scott SA
1991	M.Scott 38th PH	G.Shelton PM	2002	S.Hawkins 37th W	M.Scott SA
1992	A.Print NC		2003	K.Cullum 36th NC	B.Moss CP
1993	A.J.Wilson NC		2004	A.Firman 3/2 PM	N.Presto PM
1994	A.M.S.Lord 3/2 NC	A.J.Wilson NC	2005	I.Symonds 4/3 PM	A.Myers NC
1995	P.Langrish-Smith 2/1 CP	A.M.S.Lord NC	2006	G.Boyd 5/4 CE	R.Edwards PM
1996	S.Marlow 2/1 Ke	R.McIlwain PH	2007	R.Evans 3/2 W	J.Chamberlain CA
1997	S.Crowson 4/3 Ki	P.Langrish-Smith CP	2008		

Key

BH Brampton Heath	C Collingtree	CA Cold Ashby
CE Cherwell Edge	D Daventry	DP Delapre Park
F Farthingstone	Ke Kettering	Kg Kingsthorpe
N Northampton	NC Northants County	O Oundle
PH Priors Hall	PM Peterbo'h Milton	R Rushden
SP Staverton Park	S Silverstone	SA Stoke Albany
TW Thorpe Wood	W Wellingborough	WP Whittlebury Park

N.G.U. Club Champion of Champion

Year	Winner	Runner-Up	Year	Winner	Runner-Up
1996	P.Taylor SP	G.Keates N	2002	K.Cole 76 CE	A.Firman 78 PM
1997	D.Matthews F		2003	G.Keates 72 N	M.Peacock 72 PM / R.McIlwain 72 PH
1998	P.Taylor SP	M.Abbott R	2004	R.Connolly 73 CP	F.Carnihan 73 CA
1999	P.Taylor SP	S.Crowson Kg	2005	D.Wood 68 BH	A.M.S.Lord 69 NC
2000	P.Taylor SP	J.Ward OP	2006	R.Evans 68 SA	J.Chamberlain 69 CA
2001	J.Campbell 75 Ke	G.Keates 77 N	2007	G.Boyd 67 CE	P.Askew 68 CA

N.G.U. County Boys Champion

Year	Winner	Year	Winner
1938	A. Shaw 77	1979	N. Pyne 76 Wo
1939	J.H. Baxter 88	1980	J.M. Payne 72 Ke
-	E.J. Kingdon 76	1981	D. Scrowther 112 SP
-	E.J. Kingdon 73	1982	G. Norrie 154 W
-	S. Panther 81	1983	D. Scrowther 154 SP
-	J.D. Jackson 81	1984	G. Constable 158
-	J.W. Howkins 81 Kg	1985	D.K. Jones 151 Ki
-	R.W. Carpenter 83	1986	G.C. Wills 150 CE
-	J.E. Saxby 84 W	1987	A.D. Rudge 150 Ke
-	J.E. Saxby 81 W	1988	A. Print 153 NC
-	N. Roberts 84	1989	A. Print 140 NC
-	P.F. Braithwaite 88	1990	J. Newman* 151 CE
-	J.P. Baker 84	1991	I. Oliver 145 CA
-	M.R.T. Punch 79	1992	G.S. Lunn 144 BH
-	M.R.T. Punch 80	1993	A. Fletcher 147
-	J.N. Cheatle 80	1994	D. Spragg 150 CP
-	J.M. Pettigrew 77 N	1995	R. Duck 139 NC
-	J.M. Pettigrew 85 N	1996	A.R.P. Lynch 142 NC
-	K.J. Bowyer 76	1997	J. Wood 147 CP
-	D. Farrer 75	1998	J. O'Hagan 143 SP
-	C.E. Pickerill 78	1999	J. O'Hagan 146 SP
1970	S.A. Maxwell 77	2000	A.J. Izzard 147 N
1971	C.R. Ceislewicz 71 N	2001	J.J. Ward 144 OP
1972	C.R .Ceislewicz 70 N	2002	K. C. Cullum 148 NC
1973	T.J. Giles 70 NC	2003	G. Boyd* 139 CE
1974	D.K. Ellson 76 W	2004	S. Ashwood 72+35* NC
1975	S. McDonald 70 Kg	2005	S. Ashwood 143 NC
1976	S. McDonald 72 Kg	2006	S.Davis 144 W
1977	D.K. Ellson 75 W	2007	L.White*1 72 N
1978	M. Scott 74 PH	2008	

* After Play Off, *1 The event was restricted to 18 holes due to rain.

N.G.U.County Senior Champion 1972-2007

Year	Winner	Year	Winner
1972	T.H.Goode Ke	1990	A.Norrie W
1973	W.Griffith Ke	1991	J.Dalton 76 W*2
1974	P.S.James W	1992	G.C.Andrews NC
1975	-	1993	M.Pounds NC
1976	F.Overson O	1994	R.G.Aitken NC
1977	G.E.Mobbs NC	1995	M.Pounds NC
1978	G.E.Mobbs NC	1996	R.G.Aitken NC
1979	J.H. Humphries NC	1997	R.G.Aitken NC
1980	J.H. Humphries NC	1998	L.A.Johnson NC
1981	G.E.Collison O	1999	J.V.Smith 75,O
1982	H.E.Richards N	2000	R.G.Halliday73 NC
1983	F.Overson O	2001	M.Pounds 78*1 NC
1984	J.H. Humphries NC	2002	R.Cole 73 PM
1985	W.Sloan O	2003	R.G.Halliday 73 NC
1986	R.W.Coltman PM	2004	A.Lenaghan 72 SA
1987	J.T.Haddon 78* N	2005	B.O'Connell 72 NC
1988	J.Dalton W	2006	T.Carter 72 Kg
1989	J.J.Harwood N	2007	I.Marshall 74*3 W

* Play-off against Jim Dalton W.
*1 Sudden death play-off victory first extra hole over David Jenkins W.
*2 Sudden death play-off victory first extra hole over defending Champion Alex Norrie W
*3 Sudden death play-off victory 2 hole, over Jim Pagan

Northamptonshire Open Champion 1982-2007

Year	Winner	Year	Winner
1982	C.Ray P	1995	A.D.Hare P
1983	N.Grimmitt 77+72=149 A	1996	A.D.Hare P 68+70
1984	S.Brown P	1997	K.Dickens P 71+71
1985	S.Ward P	1998	R.Duck A 69+73=142
1986	G.Wills A	1999	N.Soto A 144
1987	T.Giles P 72+69=141	2000	T.Rouse P 67+68=135
1988	K.Dickens P 68+72=140	2001	A.D.Hare P 68+66 =134
1989	K.Dickens P	2002	A.D.Hare P 71+70=141
1990	S.Brown P 137	2003	C.Sainsbury P 70+67=137
1991	P.Smith P	2004	A.Print A 68+68=136
1992	T.Rouse P	2005	S.Lilly P 72+71=143
1993	J.Campbell 68+79 A	2006	S.Lilly P 67+63=130
1994	A.D.Hare P	2007	C.Sainsbury P 67+68=135

A Amateur P Professional

County Cup winner 1962-2007

Year	Winner	Year	Winner
1962	J.H.Mitchell 143	1985	J. Vaughan 145
1963	G. F. Clarke 151	1986	Not played for
1964	G. E.Mobbs 153	1987	P.N.Wharton 146
1965	Not played for	1988	A.S.King 143
1966	A.Forrester 147	1989	N.Williamson 141
1967	A Forrester 144	1990	P.N.Wharton 138
1968	J. M. Pettigrew 138	1991	S.J.Jarman 138
1969	R. A. Durrant 146	1992	G.Waller 140
1970	D. Butler 141	1993	W.A.Nicholson 141
1971	P.Elson 138	1994	J.Frankum 142
1972	G.A.L.Colman 140	1995	A.M.S. Lord 143
1973	R.G.Hiatt 142	1996	A.Print 134

1974	P.McEvoy 139	1997	R.M.Duck 135
1975	M.James 141	1998	N.J.West 136
1976	K.R.Waters 141	1999	O.Wilson 136
1977	P.M. Harris 144	2000	A.M.S. Lord 143
1978	T.Leigh 138	2001	S.Dunn 137
1979	P.Downes 138	2002	G.S. Boyd137
1980	I.Mackenzie 139	2003	G.P.Wolstenholme 137
1981	J.E.Ambridge 142	2004	P.Maddy 135
1982	N.L.Roche 143	2005	A.Myers 135
1983	G.R.Krause 145	2006	R.Brown 136
1984	Not played for	2007	B.Stafford 141

ANGLIAN COUNTIES RESULTS A & B Teams 1969-2007

Year	"A" Team Winners	Points	N.G.U. Points	"B" Team Winners	Points	N.G.U. Points
1969	Norfolk	9	1	-		
1970	Lincolnshire	8	6	-		
1971	Norfolk	7	2	-		
1972	Northamptonshire	10	10	-		
1973	Lincolnshire	7	3	-		
1974	Lincolnshire	10	2	-		
1975	Lincolnshire	6	2	-		
1976	Lincolnshire	10	2	-		
1977	Norfolk	8	2	Leicestershire	10	6
1978	Lincolnshire Suffolk	9	0	Norfolk	8	4
1979	Norfolk	7	4	Leicestershire	9	5
1980	Suffolk	8	6.	Northamptonshire	8	8
1981	Leicestershire	8	2	Suffolk	10	2
1982	Suffolk	8	6	Norfolk	9	5
1983	Leicestershire	8	3	Lincolnshire	9	2
1984	Suffolk	8	4	Suffolk	10	3
1985	Leicestershire	10	4	Lincolnshire	10	6
1986	Leicestershire	10	3	Lincolnshire	10	2
1987	Leicestershire	10	2	Lincolnshire	8	4
1988	Norfolk	9	3	Leicestershire	8	0
1989	Lincolnshire	8	0	Lincolnshire	8	6
1990	Northamptonshire	8	8	Lincolnshire	8	5
1991	Lincolnshire	6	3	Lincolnshire	10	4
1992	Leicestershire	8	3	Leicestershire	10	4
1993	Norfolk	9	3	Lincolnshire	8	6
1994	Norfolk Leicestershire	8	3	Leicestershire	8	4
1995	Leicestershire	8	3	Leicestershire	8	4
1996	Leicestershire	9	4	Leicestershire	10	5
1997	Lincolnshire	7	1	Lincolnshire	9	5
1998	Leicestershire	9	3	Suffolk	8	1
1999	Leicestershire	10	6	Lincolnshire	8	4
2000	Suffolk	8	3	Suffolk	7	6
2001	Cambridgeshire	9	0	Leicestershire	10	2
2002	Suffolk	8	6	Northamptonshire	8	8
2003	Leicestershire	8	4	Norfolk	8	5
2004	Lincolnshire	10	8	Lincolnshire	7	7
2005	Leicestershire	9	3	Lincolnshire	6	4
2006	Lincolnshire	8	2	Lincolnshire	9	5
2007	Lincolnshire	9	1	Lincolnshire	8	4

"A" Team Winners 1969-2007	"B" Team Winners 1977-2007
Leicestershire 13	Lincolnshire 14
Lincolnshire 12	Leicestershire 8
Norfolk 7	Suffolk 4
Suffolk 6	Norfolk 3
Northamptonshire 2	Northamptonshire 2
Cambridgeshire 1	Cambridgeshire 0

Total Shield Wins 1969-2007

Lincolnshire 26
Leicestershire 21
Suffolk 10
Norfolk 10
Northamptonshire 4
Cambridgeshire 1

Anglian League results 1969-2007 A Team

	NORTHANTS		LINCS		LEIC&R		NORF		SUFF		CAMBS	
	Pos	Pts	Pos	Pts	Pos	Pts	Pos	Pts	Pos	Pts	Pos	Pts
1969	6	1	4	4	(3)	7	1	9	(2)	7	5	2
1970	(4)	6	1	8	(2)	6	(2)	6	6	0	5	4
1971	(6)	2	(2)	7	4	5	(1)	7	(3)	7	(5)	2
1972	1	10	(4)	4	(4)	4	(5)	4	6	2	(2)	5
1973	6	3	1	7	(5)	4	(2)	6	(3)	6	(4)	4
1974	(6)	2	1	10	2	8	4	3	3	5	(5)	2
1975	6	2	(1)	6	(1)	6	(3)	6	(4)	5	(5)	5
1976	(5)	2	1	10	3	6	(4)	2	2	8	(5)	2
1977	6	2	2	6	(3)	5	1	8	(4)	5	5	4
1978	6	0	(1)	9	4	4	3	6	(1)	9	5	2
1979	(4)	4	(5)	4	2	6	1	7	3	5	5	4
1980	3	6	(4)	3	(2)	9	6	2	(1)	8	(5)	3
1981	6	2	(5)	4	1	8	(3)	6	(2)	6	(4)	4
1982	2	6	(4)	4	(5)	4	(3)	5	1	8	6	3
1983	(6)	3	4	4	1	8	(3)	6	(2)	6	(5)	3
1984	(3)	4	(5)	3	(2)	8	(5)	3	(1)	8	(4)	4
1985	(4)	4	(6)	2	1	10	(5)	2	2	8	(3)	4
1986	5	3	6	2	1	10	3	5	4	4	2	6
1987	(5)	2	4	4	1	10	(3)	6	(6)	2	(2)	6
1988	4	3	(6)	3	2	8	1	9	(5)	2	3	6
1989	6	0	(1)	8	(2)	8	(3)	5	(4)	5	5	4
1990	1	8	(5)	4	2	6	(3)	4	(4)	4	(6)	4
1991	6	3	(1)	6	(3)	6	5	4	(2)	6	4	5
1992	(5)	3	2	7	1	8	(6)	3	3	6	(4)	3
1993	(6)	3	(5)	3	2	7	1	9	(3)	4	(4)	4
1994	(4)	3	(1)	8	3	6	(1)	8	6	2	(5)	3
1995	(5)	3	6	2	(1)	8	3	6	(2)	8	(4)	3
1996	(5)	4	(2)	5	1	9	6	3	(4)	4	(3)	5
1997	6	1	1	7	(2)	6	(3)	6	5	4	(4)	6
1998	5	3	2	6	1	9	(4)	5	(3)	5	6	2
1999	3	6	6	1	1	10	(5)	3	(4)	3	2	7
2000	6	3	3	5	2	6	(4)	4	1	8	(5)	4
2001	6	0	5	3	2	8	4	4	3	6	1	9
2002	3	6	2	7	(4)	4	5	4	1	8	6	1
2003	5	4	2	6	1	8	4	5	6	2	(3)	5
2004	2	8	1	10	3	6	6	1	5	2	4	3

	Pos	Pts	Pos	Pts	Pos	Pts	Pos	Pts	Pos	Pts	Pos	Pts
2005	6	3	(5)	3	1	9	3	5	2	6	4	4
2006	5	2	1	8	3	6	4	5	2	7	6	2
2007	6	1	1	9	3	5	5	4	2	7	4	4
Points Total	131		211		271		196		208		153	
Lifetime Position	6th Northants		2nd Lincolns		1st Leic & R		4th Norfolk		3rd Suffolk		5th Cambs	

Bracketed positions calculated by count-back on match results, 1969-2007, 39 years at 30 points per season = 1170 total points.

Anglian League Results 1977-2007 B Team

	Pos	Pts	Pos	Pts	Pos	Pts	Pos	Pts	Pos	Pts	Pos	Pts
	NORTH		LINCS		LEIC		NORF		SUFF		CAMB	
1977	3	6	2	8	1	10	4	4	5	2	6	0
1978	(4)	4	(1)	8	3	6	(2)	8	5	4	6	0
1979	(4)	5	2	6	1	9	(3)	5	5	4	6	1
1980	1	8	(4)	4	(5)	4	6	2	3	5	2	7
1981	6	2	3	5	2	6	4	4	1	10	5	3
1982	3	5	6	2	(4)	4	1	9	2	6	(5)	4
1983	5	2	1	9	2	7	(3)	6	4	6	6	0
1984	5	3	(3)	4	2	8	(4)	4	1	10	6	1
1985	(2)	6	1	10	5	3	4	4	(3)	6	6	1
1986	(6)	2	1	10	(4)	5	2	6	(3)	3	(5)	2
1987	(5)	4	1	8	2	7	(4)	4	6	1	3	6
1988	6	0	3	7	(1)	8	4	5	5	2	(2)	8
1989	3	6	2	8	1	9	5	3	4	4	6	0
1990	(3)	5	(1)	8	5	4	(4)	5	6	0	(2)	8
1991	4	4	1	10	3	5	2	8	5	3	6	0
1992	(5)	4	(3)	4	1	10	(4)	4	6	2	2	6
1993	3	6	1	8	4	5	5	4	2	7	6	0
1994	4	4	(3)	7	1	8	6	1	(2)	7	5	3
1995	(6)	4	2	6	1	8	(4)	4	(4)	4	(3)	4
1996	3	5	(5)	2	1	10	2	8	4	3	(6)	2
1997	(4)	5	1	9	(5)	2	(6)	2	2	7	(3)	5
1998	6	1	(4)	3	3	7	(5)	3	(1)	8	(2)	8
1999	(5)	4	1	8	6	2	(4)	4	3	5	2	7
2000	(2)	6	4	5	(5)	3	(6)	3	1	7	(3)	6
2001	5	2	3	6	1	10	(6)	3	2	8	4	4
2002	1	8	4	5	3	6	6	0	2	7	4	4
2003	4	5	2	7	6	1	1	8	5	3	3	6
2004	(2)	7	1	7	3	6	(5)	3	6	3	4	4
2005	5	4	1	6	(2)	5	6	0	*		3	5
2006	4	5	1	9	2	6	6	0	3	6	5	4
2007	5	4	1	8	4	4	3	5	2	6	5	3
Points Total	136		207		188		133		148		108	
Lifetime Position	4th Northants		1st Lincolns		2nd Leic & R		5th Norfolk		3rd Suffolk		6th Cambs	

* In 2005 Suffolk failed to produce a team for a match which resulted in them being excluded from the league table. 31 years at 30 points per season = 930 points, this total actually becomes 920 points in view of this regrettable incident. Bracketed positions calculated by count-back on game results.

Anglian League Boys Winners 1980-2007

Year	Winner	Year	Winner
1979	Norfolk or Lincolnshire	1994	Lincolnshire
1980	Suffolk	1995	Suffolk
1981	Lincolnshire	1996	Norfolk
1982	Northamptonshire	1997	Lincolnshire
1983	Norfolk	1998	Suffolk
1984	Northamptonshire	1999	Suffolk
1985	Norfolk	2000	Suffolk
1986	Lincolnshire	2001	Suffolk
1987	Lincolnshire	2002	Leicestershire & Rutland
1988	Lincolnshire	2003	Norfolk
1989	Lincolnshire	2004	Suffolk
1990	Norfolk	2005	Lincolnshire
1991	Lincolnshire	2006	Lincolnshire
1992	Suffolk	2007	
1993	Lincolnshire	2008	

Totals
Cambridgeshire	0
Leicestershire & Rutland	1
Lincolnshire	12½
Norfolk	6½
Northamptonshire	2
Suffolk	7

Note: In 1979 Norfolk & Lincolnshire both reached the final, unfortunately the Champion County is unknown.

NORTHAMPTONSHIRE'S ANGLIAN LEAGUE RESULTS FOR THE 1972, 1980, 1990, & 2002 WINNING TEAMS.

1972 A League Winners Captain R.G. (Richard) Halliday
Match 1 vs Leicestershire & Rutland, Northampton G.C. 23 April 1972

Foursomes					
J.H.Humphries & R.Larratt		½	E.Hammond & P.Wood		½
R.G.Aitken & C.R.Ceislewicz		½	R.Christian & D.Kirkland		½
J. M.Pettigrew & M.Pounds	4/3	1	P.Taylor & P.Haddon		
R.G.Halliday & R.J.Gray		½	E.Blackadder & A.Harper		½
Foursomes Total 2½			Foursomes Total 1½		
Singles					
R.Larratt			E.Hammond	2/1	1
R.G.Aitken			P.Wood	1up	1
C.R.Ceislewicz	4/3	1	R.Christian		
J. M.Pettigrew	3/2	1	D.Kirkland		
R.J.Gray	2/1	1	P.Taylor		
R.G.Halliday	3/2	1	P.Haddon		
J.H.Humphries	1up	1	E.Blackadder		
M.Pounds		½	A.Harper		½
Singles Total 5½			Singles Total 2½		
Foursomes Total		2½	Foursomes Total		1½
Singles Total		5½	Singles Total		2½
GRAND TOTAL		**8**	**GRAND TOTAL**		**4**

Match 2 vs Cambridgeshire, Newmarket G.C. May 7th 1972

Foursomes					
R.G.Aitken & C.R.Ceislewicz	3/2	1	R.A.C.Blows & S.Bonham		
J. M.Pettigrew & M.Pounds	1up	1	R.Guy & P.Darton		
R.B.Catlow & R.J.Gray			B.Wheeler & A.Garner	5/4	1
R.G.Halliday & J.H.Humphries			S.Derbyshire & C.Maltman	3/2	1
Foursomes Total 2			Foursomes Total 2		
Singles					
R.B.Catlow		½	A.Garner		½
R.G.Aitken	2/1	1	S.Bonham		
C.R.Ceislewicz			S.Derbyshire	2/1	1
J. M.Pettigrew		½	B.Wheeler		½
R.J.Gray		½	R.Guy		½
R.G.Halliday	1 up	1	P.Darton		
J.H.Humphries			C.Maltman	1up	1
M.Pounds	5/4	1	R.A.C.Blows		
Singles Total 4½			Singles Total 3½		
Foursomes Total		2	Foursomes Total		2
Singles Total		4½	Singles Total		3½
GRAND TOTAL		**6½**	**GRAND TOTAL**		**5½**

Match 3 vs Suffolk, Peterborough Milton G.C. 1972

Foursomes					
J.H.Humphries & R.Larratt	2/1	1	A.Pearce & J.Broad		
R.G.Aitken & C.R.Ceislewicz	4/3	1	J.Cook & M.Ivor-Jones		
J. M.Pettigrew & M.Pounds		½	G.Gibbs & G.Adams		½
R.G.Halliday & R.J.Gray	5/4	1	R.Langdale & N.Reiss		
Foursomes Total 3½			Foursomes Total ½		
Singles					
R.J.Gray	5/4	1	N.Reiss		
R.Larratt	1up	1	J.Cook		
C.R.Ceislewicz	5/4	1	J.Broad		
R.G.Aitken	2/1	1	A.Pearce		
J. M.Pettigrew	2/1	1	G.Gibbs		
R.G.Halliday	3/2	1	M.Ivor-Jones		
J.H.Humphries	5/4	1	G.Adams		
M.Pounds	4/3	1	R.Langdale		
Singles Total 8			Singles Total 0		
Foursomes Total		3½	Foursomes Total		½
Singles Total		8	Singles Total		0
GRAND TOTAL		**11½**	**GRAND TOTAL**		**½**

Match 4 vs Norfolk, Northants County G.C. 1972

Foursomes					
R.G.Aitken & J.H.Humphries			R.Trower & J.Nudds	2/1	1
J. M.Pettigrew & M.Pounds	1up	1	R.Richardson & D.Rains		
R.G.Halliday & A.D.Bishop	3/2	1	B.Ashton & T.Emery		
R.B.Catlow & R.J.Gray	5/4	1	A.Watt & N.Lambert		
Foursomes Total 3			Foursomes Total 1		
Singles					
R.J.Gray			J.Nudds	3/2	1
R.G.Aitken	3/2	1	R.Trower		
R.B.Catlow		½	B.Ashton	1	½

J. M.Pettigrew	3/2	1	D.Rains		
R.G.Halliday	1up	1	R.Richardson		
J.H.Humphries	4/3	1	T.Emery		
M.Pounds		½	N.Lambert		½
A.D.Bishop	7/5	1	A.Watt		
Singles Total 6				Singles Total 2	
Foursomes Total		3	Foursomes Total		1
Singles Total		6	Singles Total		2
GRAND TOTAL		**9**	**GRAND TOTAL**		**3**

Match 5 vs Lincolnshire, Torksey G.C. 1972

Foursomes

R.Larratt & J.H.Humphries	5/3	1	R.J.Barrell & F.W.Wood		
R.G.Aitken & C.R. Ceislewicz	5/4	1	P.Taylor & S.B.Cartledge		
J. M.Pettigrew & M.Pounds	5/4	1	J.Bramley & R.Nix		
R.G.Halliday& R.J.Gray			M.G.Lee & J.Bacon	1up	1
Foursomes Total 3			Foursomes Total 1		

Singles

R.J.Gray		½	R.J.Barrell		½
R.Larratt	1up	1	J.Bramley		
C.R. Ceislewicz	5/3	1	S.B.Cartledge		
R.G.Aitken	2/1	1	F.W.Wood		
J. M.Pettigrew			R.Nix	2up	1
R.G.Halliday			M.G.Lee	2/1	1
J.H.Humphries			J.Bacon	3/2	1
M.Pounds			I.Stackhouse	6/4	1
Singles Total 3½			Singles Total 4½		
Foursomes Total		3	Foursomes Total		1
Singles Total		3½	Singles Total		4½
GRAND TOTAL		**6½**	**GRAND TOTAL**		**5½**

1972 A LEAGUE TABLE

	P	W	H	L	F	A	P
Northamptonshire	5	5	0	0	41 ½	18 ½	10
Cambridgeshire	5	2	1	2	31	29	5
Leicestershire &R	5	2	1	2	29 ½	30 ½	5
Lincolnshire	5	2	0	3	32	28	4
Norfolk	5	2	0	3	25 ½	34 ½	4
Suffolk	5	1	0	4	20 ½	39 ½	2

1980 B League Winners Captain N.B. (Barry) Highfield
Match 1 vs Leicestershire & Rutland, Scraptoft G.C. 27 April 1980

Foursomes

P.Scott & S.McDonald		½	D.Cannon & P.Howkins		½
I.Marshall & M.Scott			M.Nutt & D.Mayfield	2/1	1
N.B.Highfield & M.J.Izzard	6/5	1	R.Spence & S.Adams		
R.Haig & M.Haddon	1up	1	R.Taylor & P.Colclough		
Foursomes Total 2½			Foursomes Total 1½		

Singles

S.McDonald			D.Cannon	4/2	1
M.Haddon	3/2	1	M.Nutt		
P.Scott	1up	1	D.Mayfield		
M.J.Izzard	1up	1	P.Howkins		

I.Marshall			R.Spence	5/4	1	
R.Haig	3/1	1	R.Taylor			
N.B.Highfield	3/1	1	P.Colclough			
M.Scott			S.Adams	1up	1	
Singles Total 5			Singles Total 3			
Foursomes Total	2½		Foursomes Total		1½	
Singles Total	5		Singles Total		3	
GRAND TOTAL	**7½**		**GRAND TOTAL**		**4½**	

Match 2 vs Cambridgeshire Kettering G.C. 4 May 1980

Foursomes						
P.Scott & S.McDonald	5/4	1	M.Sievewright & A.Fitzjohn			
R.Haig & M.Haddon	2/1	1	M.Unsworth & D.Smith			
N.B.Highfield & M.J.Izzard			R.Seaton & G.Barnard	1up	1	
I.Marshall & R.Hall	5/4	1	M.Hamblin & A.Dodman			
Foursomes Total 3			Foursomes Total 1			

Singles						
M.Haddon	3/2	1	M.Sievewright			
S.McDonald			D.Smith	5/4	1	
M.J.Izzard	2/1	1	M.Unsworth			
R.Hall	6/5	1	R.Seaton			
R.Haig	6/5	1	G.Barnard			
P.Scott		½	A.Dodman		½	
N.B.Highfield		½	A.Fitzjohn		½	
I.Marshall	2up	1	M.Hamblin			
Singles Total 6			Singles Total 3			
Foursomes Total		3	Foursomes Total		1	
Singles Total		6	Singles Total		2	
GRAND TOTAL		**9**	**GRAND TOTAL**		**3**	

Match 3 vs Suffolk, Aldeburgh G.C. 29 June 1980

Foursomes						
D.Evans & S.McDonald			A.Savage & M.Hatton	2up	1	
M.J.Izzard & K.Newman		½	P.Ayres & K.Tredway		½	
R.Haig & R.Killip	1up	1	M.Turner & J.Symon			
N.B.Highfield & N.Grimmitt	4/3	1	M.Podd & R.Doddington			
Foursomes Total 2½			Foursomes Total 1½			

Singles						
N.Grimmitt			A.Savage	1up	1	
D.Evans	2up	1	M.Hatton			
S.McDonald			P.Ayres	6/5	1	
M.J.Izzard	5/4	1	M.Turner			
K.Newman			K.Tredway	2/1	1	
R.Haig	4/3	1	R.Doddington			
N.B.Highfield	5/4	1	M.Podd			
R.Killip		0	J.Symon	5/4	1	
Singles Total 4			Singles Total 4			
Foursomes Total		2½	Foursomes Total		1½	
Singles Total		4	Singles Total		4	
GRAND TOTAL		**6½**	**GRAND TOTAL**		**5½**	

Match 4 vs Norfolk Barnham Broom G.C. 20 July 1980

Foursomes					
D.Evans & S.McDonald	3/1	1	G.Cullum & R.Palmer		
M.J.Izzard & K.Newman	4/3	1	G.Morgans & C.Lamb		
J.Ellis & P.Scott			S.Amey & A.Barker	1up	1
N.B.Highfield & R.Haig	1up	1	I.Williamson & P.Allott		
Foursomes Total 3			Foursomes Total 1		
Singles					
D.Evans			G.Morgans	5/4	1
R.Haig			G.Cullum	2/1	1
S.McDonald	3/1	1	S.Amey		
M.J.Izzard	3/2	1	C.Lamb		
K.Newman			R.Palmer	1up	1
P.Scott	1up	1	I.Williamson		
N.B.Highfield			A.Barker	6/5	1
J.Ellis	3/2	1	P.Allott		
Singles Total 4			Singles Total 4		
Foursomes Total		3	Foursomes Total		1
Singles Total		4	Singles Total		4
GRAND TOTAL		**7**	**GRAND TOTAL**		**5**

Match 5 vs Lincolnshire Staverton Park G.C. 7 September 1980

Foursomes					
M.J.Izzard & K.Newman	2/1	1	J.Robinson & S.Wood		
P.Scott & D.Evans			D.Bell & S.Cranidge	1up	1
N.B.Highfield & R.Haig			C.Clarke & G.Robinson	4/3	1
J.Payne & A.Lord			A.Kennedy & J.Woodcock	4/3	1
Foursomes Total 1			Foursomes Total 3		
Singles					
M.J.Izzard			J.Woodcock	4/3	1
K.Newman			A.Kennedy	2/1	1
D.Evans	3/2	1	S.Cranidge		
P.Scott			C.Clarke	3/2	1
R.Haig			G.Robinson	2/1	1
J.Payne		½	J.Robinson		½
N.B.Highfield		½	D.Bell		½
A.Lord			S.Wood	3/2	1
Singles Total 2			Singles Total 6		
Foursomes Total		1	Foursomes Total		3
Singles Total		2	Singles Total		6
GRAND TOTAL		**3**	**GRAND TOTAL**		**9**

1980 B LEAGUE TABLE

	P	W	H	L	F	A	P
Northamptonshire	5	4	0	1	33	27	8

The result for the other five counties has unfortunately not been recorded.

1990 A League Winners Captain R.S. (Dick) Biggin (Non-Playing)
Match 1 vs Cambridgeshire Gog Magog G.C. 22 April 1990

Foursomes					
M.Lynch & J.Evans	3/2	1	R.W.Guy & M.T.Seaton		
J.Wilson & M.Herson	2/1	1	T.Ryan & D.Hayns		
R.Beekie & P.Flude			N.K.Hughes & A.Emery	6/5	1
I.Marshall & M.Pask	4/3	1	L.Yearn & R.Seaton		
Foursomes Total 3			Foursomes Total 1		
Singles					
M.Lynch	3/2	1	R.W.Guy		
J.Evans		½	L.Yearn		½
J.Wilson	2/1	1	M.T.Seaton		
I.Marshall	1up	1	A.Emery		
P.Flude		½	T.Ryan		½
M.Herson			D.Hayns	1up	1
M.Pask	2/1	1	R.Seaton		
R.Beekie			N.K.Hughes	1up	1
Singles Total 5			Singles Total 3		
Foursomes Total		3	Foursomes Total		1
Singles Total		5	Singles Total		3
GRAND TOTAL		**8**	**GRAND TOTAL**		**4**

Match 2 vs Leicestershire & Rutland Peterborough Milton G.C. 13 May 1990

Foursomes					
M.Lynch & G.Shelton	1up	1	D.Gibson & T.Stevens		
J.Wilson & M.Pask	1up	1	A.Martinez & I.Middleton		
J.Evans & P.Flude		½	J.Cayless & K.Mountford		½
I.Marshall & R.McIlwain	2/1	1	C.Harries & S.Williams		
Foursomes Total 3½			Foursomes Total ½		
Singles					
M.Lynch			D.Gibson	4/3	1
G.Shelton			T.Stevens	2/1	1
J.Wilson		½	A.Martinez		½
J.Evans	5/3	1	C.Harries		
P.Flude		½	I.Middleton		½
M.Pask		½	J.Cayless		½
R.McIlwain			S.Williams	3/1	1
I.Marshall		½	K.Mountford		½
Singles Total 3			Singles Total 5		
Foursomes Total		3½	Foursomes Total		½
Singles Total		3	Singles Total		5
GRAND TOTAL		**6½**	**GRAND TOTAL**		**5½**

Match 3 vs Suffolk Wellingborough G.C. 17 June 1990

Foursomes					
M.Lynch & G.Shelton	1up		J.Maddock & D.James		
M.Pask & D.Jones			N.Meadows & S.MacPhearson	2/1	1
I.Marshall & J.Wilson	2/1	1	P.Buckle & D.Tricker		
J.Evans & P.Flude	6/5	1	M.Youngs & R.Whisker		
Foursomes Total 3			Foursomes Total 1		
Singles					
M.Lynch	2/1	1	N.Meadows		
G.Shelton	2/1	1	D.James		

D.Jones	4/2	1	J.Maddock		
J.Evans	2/1	1	P.Buckle		
J.Wilson	6/4	1	S.MacPhearson		
M.Pask	3/2	1	R.Whisker		
P.Flude	1up	1	D.Tricker		
I.Marshall	4/3	1	M.Youngs		
Singles Total 8			Singles Total 0		
Foursomes Total		3	Foursomes Total		1
Singles Total		8	Singles Total		0
GRAND TOTAL		**11**	**GRAND TOTAL**		**1**

Match 4 vs Norfolk Northants County G.C. 15 July 1990

Foursomes					
M.Lynch & G.Shelton			P.Little & T.Hurrell	3/2	1
J.Wilson & A.Print	5/4	1	M & I. Sperrin		
J.Evans & P.Flude	6/5	1	M.Williamson & D.Edwards		
I.Marshall & D.Jones			C.Lamb & A.Brydon	5/4	1
Foursomes Total 2			Foursomes Total 1		
Singles					
M.Lynch			P.Little	4/3	1
G.Shelton			M. Sperrin	5/4	1
A.Print	3/1	1	C.Lamb		
J.Wilson	7/5	1	M.Williamson		
J.Evans	3/2	1	D.Edwards		
D.Jones	3/2	1	I. Sperrin		
P.Flude	½		T.Hurrell		½
I.Marshall			A.Brydon	3/2	1
Singles Total 4½			Singles Total 3½		
Foursomes Total		2	Foursomes Total		2
Singles Total		4½	Singles Total		3½
GRAND TOTAL		**6½**	**GRAND TOTAL**		**5½**

Match 5 vs Lincolnshire, Stoke Rochford G.C. 19 August 1990

Foursomes					
I.Marshall & M.Izzard			J.Payne & C.Wetherall	2/1	1
G.Shelton & D.Jones	4/2	1	J.Wilson & R.Milne		
J.Evans & P.Flude	5/3	1	A.Anderson & P.Britcliffe		
A.Print & I.Achurch			G.Hotson & G.Lee	2up	1
Foursomes Total 2			Foursomes Total 2		
Singles					
A.Print			J.Payne	4/3	1
G.Shelton	2/1	1	P.Britcliffe		
M.Izzard	4/3	1	G.Hotson		
J.Evans			G.Lee	1up	1
D.Jones	4/3	1	J.Wilson		
P.Flude			R.Milne	1up	1
I.Achurch			C.Wetherall	2up	1
I.Marshall			A.Anderson	2/1	1
Singles Total 3			Singles Total 5		
Foursomes Total		2	Foursomes Total		2
Singles Total		3	Singles Total		5
GRAND TOTAL		**5**	**GRAND TOTAL**		**7**

1990 A LEAGUE TABLE

	P	W	H	L	F	A	P
Northamptonshire	5	4	0	1	37	23	8
Leicestershire&R	5	3	0	2	30 ½	29½	6
Norfolk	5	2	0	3	30	30	4
Suffolk	5	2	0	3	28	32	4
Lincolnshire	5	2	0	3	28	32	4
Cambridgeshire	5	2	0	3	26½	33½	4

2002 B League Winners, Captain Richard Brown

Match 1 vs Norfolk, Royal Cromer G.C. 12th May 2002

Foursomes					
G.Croxton & S.Hawkins			A.Huskinson & J.Conway	1Up	1
I.Symonds& R.Green		½	G.Price& C.Waugh		½
D.Jessup & C.Green			M.Egglington & J.Ollington	4/3	1
R.Brown & M.Bearman			S.Peet & D.Wilson	3/2	1
Foursomes Total ½			Foursomes Total 3½		
Singles					
G.Croxton	2/1	1	J.Ollington		
I.Symonds	2Up	1	S.Peet		
S.Hawkins		½	J.Conway		½
D.Jessup			D.Wilson	3/1	1
M.Bearman	2/1	1	A.Huskinson		
C.Green			M.Egglington	3/1	1
R.Green	1Up	1	C.Waugh		
R.Brown		½	G.Price		½
Singles Total 5			Singles Total 3		
Foursomes Total		½	Foursomes Total		3½
Singles Total		5	Singles Total		3
GRAND TOTAL		**5½**	**GRAND TOTAL**		**6½**

Match 2 vs Lincolnshire Kettering G.C. 9th June 2002

Foursomes					
R.Brown & S.Young			S.Brattan & K. Blow	4/3	1
G.Condon & J.Ward			M.Underwood & J.Drake	4/3	1
M.Bearman & C.Green	1Up	1	P.Morrison & G.Waddington		
R.Green & D.Jessup	1Up	1	M.Lawes & S.Graves		
Foursomes Total 2			Foursomes Total 2		
Singles					
S.Young	3/1	1	J.Drake		
D.Jessup	3/2	1	M.Underwood		
G.Condon	2Up	1	G.Waddington		
R.Green			S.Brattan	4/3	1
J.Ward			K. Blow	2/1	1
C.Green	2Up	1	P.Morrison		
M.Bearman			M.Lawes	3/2	1
R.Brown	4/3	1	S.Graves		
Singles Total 5			Singles Total 3		
Foursomes Total		2	Foursomes Total		2
Singles Total		5	Singles Total		3
GRAND TOTAL		**7**	**GRAND TOTAL**		**5**

Match 3 vs Suffolk, Haverhill G.C. 14th July 2002

Foursomes					
G.Croxton & R.Green			S.Debenham & D.Fairweather	3/1	1
T.Duck & C.Green			R.Pudney & K.Day	3/1	1
M.Bearman & D.Jessup	1 Up	1	J.Philpot & N.Howe		
R.Brown & S.Young		½	A.Middle & J.Blackmore		½
Foursomes Total 1½			Foursomes Total 2½		
Singles					
G.Croxton			K.Day	1Up	1
T.Duck	2/1	1	S.Debenham		
D.Jessup	2/1	1	J.Blackmore		
R.Green	1Up	1	J.Philpot		
M.Bearman			N.Howe	1Up	1
C.Green	2/1	1	A.Middle		
S.Young	2Up	1	R.Pudney		
R.Brown			D.Fairweather	3/2	1
Singles Total 5			Singles Total 3		
Foursomes Total		1½	Foursomes Total		2½
Singles Total		5	Singles Total		3
GRAND TOTAL		**6½**	**GRAND TOTAL**		**5½**

Match 4 vs Cambridgeshire, Northampton G.C. 4th August 2002

Foursomes					
Foursomes Total			Foursomes Total		
Singles					
C.Green			D.Mallett		
G.Croxton			R.Mallett		
T.Duck			M.Dean		
A.Lilly			D.Webb		
M.Bearman			K.Diss		
S.Hawkins			A.Richardson		
S.Tootell			S.Burns		
R.Brown			?		
Singles Total			Singles Total		
Foursomes Total			Foursomes Total		
Singles Total			Singles Total		
GRAND TOTAL		**7½**	**GRAND TOTAL**		**4½**

The result sheet for the Cambridgeshire match cannot be located in either county!

Match 5 vs Leicestershire & Rutland, Willesley Park G.C. September 8th 2002

Foursomes					
I.Symonds & A.Firman	3/2	1	P.Frith & S.Marriott		0
G.Croxton & S.Tootell		0	M.Whelband & P.Meakin	1Up	1
D.Jessup & M.Bearman		½	K.Shaw & J.Amos		½
T.Duck & S.Young		½	J.Chechlacz & K.Thomas		½
Foursomes Total 2			Foursomes Total 2		
Singles					
A.Firman		½	P.Frith		½
I.Symonds			M.Whelband	3/2	1

G.Croxton		½	P.Meakin		½
S.Tootell	4/3	1	S.Marriott		
T.Duck	4/3	1	K.Shaw		
M.Bearman	3/2	1	J.Amos		
D.Jessup	8/7	1	J.Chechlacz		
S.Young	2/1	1	K.Thomas		
Singles Total		6	Singles Total		2
Foursomes Total		2	Foursomes Total		2
Singles Total		6	Singles Total		2
GRAND TOTAL		**8**	**GRAND TOTAL**		**4**

2002 B LEAGUE TABLE

	P	W	H	L	F	A	P
Northamptonshire	5	4	0	1	34½	25½	8
Norfolk	5	3	1	1	33½	26½	7
Leicestershire&R	5	3	0	2	32½	27½	6
Lincolnshire	5	2	1	2	32½	27½	5
Suffolk	5	2	0	3	25½	34½	4
Cambridgeshire	5	0	0	5	22.5	37.5	0

EASTERN INTER COUNTIES SHIELD

The nine counties that compete for this wonderful trophy are currently Bedfordshire, Cambridgeshire, Essex, Hertfordshire, Leicestershire & Rutland, Lincolnshire, Norfolk, Northamptonshire and Suffolk. Prior to this in 1990 Berks, Bucks and Oxon (BB&O) withdrew and Middlesex joined for a ten-year period before withdrawing in 2000 when Essex joined.

YEAR	VENUE	WINNERS & PTS	RUNNERS UP & PTS	WOODEN SPOON
1954	Hunstanton	Norfolk		
1955	Hunstanton	Leicestershire		
1956	Hunstanton	Norfolk		
1957	Hunstanton	Lincolnshire		
1958	Royal West Norfolk	Norfolk		Northamptonshire
1959	Royal West Norfolk	Norfolk		Cambridgeshire
1960	Hunstanton	Norfolk		Lincolnshire
1961	Hunstanton	Leicestershire		Suffolk
1962	Hunstanton	Norfolk		
1963	Hunstanton	Hertfordshire		
1964	Hunstanton	Hertfordshire		
1965	Hunstanton	Leicestershire		
1966	Hunstanton	Bedfordshire		Northamptonshire
1967	Hunstanton	Bedfordshire	Northamptonshire =2nd	Suffolk
1968	Hunstanton	BB&O		Lincolnshire
1969	Hunstanton	BB&O		Northamptonshire
1970	Hunstanton	Norfolk 27.5	BB&O 23	Suffolk 14
1971	Hunstanton	BB&O		Cambridgeshire
1972	Hunstanton	BB&O 28	Hertfordshire 27.5	Bedfordshire 11
1973	Hunstanton	Bedfordshire 27.5	Hertfordshire 23.5	Leicestershire 15
1974	Hunstanton	Hertfordshire 26.5	Leicestershire 24	Bedfordshire 14.5
1975	Hunstanton	Lincolnshire 27.5	Bedfordshire 25.5	Suffolk 14
1976	Hunstanton	BB&O 26.5	Lincolnshire 22.5	Cambridgeshire 15
1977	Hunstanton	BB&O 29.5	Lincolnshire 23.5	Northamptonshire 10*
1978	Hunstanton	Hertfordshire 25.5	Cambridgeshire 24	Lincolnshire 16.5
1979	Hunstanton	BB&O 31.5 *	Norfolk 30.5 *	Cambridgeshire 11
1980	Hunstanton	Hertfordshire 29.5	BB&O 23.5	Lincolnshire 13.5
1981	Hunstanton	BB&O 24	Bedfordshire 23	Lincolnshire 16
1982	Hunstanton	BB&O 28.5	Suffolk 26.5	Norfolk 13.5
1983	Hunstanton	Lincolnshire 24.5	BB&O 24	Hertfordshire Northamptonshire 15
1984	Hunstanton	Hertfordshire 26	BB&O 25.5	Lincolnshire 12.5
1985	Hunstanton	BB&O 23.5	Hertfordshire 22.5	Leicestershire 15
1986	Hunstanton	Cambridgeshire 26.5	BB&O 25.5	Hertfordshire 12.5
1987	Hunstanton	Hertfordshire 24	Suffolk 23	Northamptonshire 13.5
1988	Hunstanton	Hertfordshire 25	BB&O 24.5	Suffolk 14.5
1989	Hunstanton	Leicestershire 26.5	Northamptonshire 22.5	Hertfordshire 16
1990	Seacroft	Leicestershire 26	Bedfordshire Hertfordshire 25.5	Middlesex 13.5
1991	Seacroft	Hertfordshire 24	Bedfordshire Cambridgeshire 23.5	Suffolk 11
1992	Seacroft	Hertfordshire Lincolnshire 27.5	Bedfordshire 24.5	Middlesex 13
1993	Seacroft	Leicestershire 27	Lincolnshire 24.5	Northamptonshire 12
1994	Seacroft	Lincolnshire 23	Leicestershire 22.5	Middlesex Northamptonshire 17
1995	Seacroft	Leicestershire 28	Hertfordshire 26	Suffolk 11.5
1996	Seacroft	Hertfordshire 29.5	Bedfordshire 25.5	Middlesex 9.5
1997	Seacroft	Bedfordshire 25	Norfolk 22.5	Northamptonshire 14.5
1998	Seacroft	Norfolk 28.5	Hertfordshire 24.5	Middlesex 13.5
1999	Seacroft	Hertfordshire 25	Cambridgeshire Leicestershire 23.5	Middlesex 10.5

			Norfolk
2000	Seacroft	Bedfordshire 28.5	Norfolk 26.5	Suffolk 9.5
2001	Seacroft	Lincolnshire 25	Bedfordshire Leicestershire 23.5	Norfolk 14.5
2002	Seacroft	Leicestershire 27	Lincolnshire 26	Hertfordshire 15
2003	Seacroft	Lincolnshire 24.5	Essex 22	Northamptonshire 16.5 Suffolk
2004	Seacroft	Lincolnshire 29	Essex 24.5	Bedfordshire 13.5
2005	Seacroft	Lincolnshire 25	Norfolk Cambridgeshire 23.5	Suffolk 12.5
2006	Seacroft	Essex 24.5	Hertfordshire 24	Northamptonshire 13.5
2007	Seacroft	Cambridgeshire 26	Leicestershire 23.5	Hertfordshire 16.5
2008	Seacroft	Essex 23.5	Bedfordshire 23	Hertfordshire 16.5

* Highest, runners up and lowest points totals to 2008.

Northamptonshire's Charles Catlow donated the wooden spoon for ninth and last position (so we could win something!). Unfortunately, we hold the record for the most victories in this category and are the only county still competing not to have won this event. Let us hope for success in 2009.

WINNERS	RUNNERS UP	WOODEN SPOON
Hertfordshire 12	Bedfordshire 8	Northamptonshire 11
BB&O 10	Hertfordshire 7	Suffolk 10
Lincolnshire 9	BB&O 5	Middlesex 6
Leicestershire 8	Norfolk 5	Lincolnshire 6
Norfolk 8	Lincolnshire 4	Cambridgeshire 4
Bedfordshire 5	Leicestershire 4	Hertfordshire 5
Cambridgeshire 2	Cambridgeshire 4	Bedfordshire 3
Essex 2	Suffolk 2	Leicestershire 2
	Northamptonshire 2	Norfolk 2
		Essex 2

Northamptonshire at the Eastern Inter Counties Foursomes 1954-2008

Year	Points	Position	Year	Points	Position
2008	17	8th	1987	13½	9th
2007	18	6th	1986		
2006	13½	9th	1985		
2005	18	7th	1984		
2004	24	3rd	1983	15	=9th
2003	16½	=9th	1982		
2002	23½	3rd	1981		
2001	17		1980	22	4th
2000	16½	7th	1979		
1999			1978		
1998	20½	7th	1977	10	9th
1997	14½	9th	1972	25	3rd
1996			1971	19	6th
1995			1969		9th
1994	17	=9th	1967		=2nd
1993	12	9th	1966		9th
1992			1962	20½	3rd
1991	15½	8th	1961	3< the winners	3rd?
1990	21½	4th	1959		3rd
1989	22½	2nd	1958		9th
1988	18	7th	1954-7		?

Red colours indicate runners-up or wooden spoon winners.

Champion Club Northamptonshire & England 1984-2007

Year	N.G.U. Champion Club	Venue for E.G.U. Final	N.G.U. Team Score & Position	E.G.U. Winning Team, County & Score
1984	Northants County	Copt Heath	301 14th	Ealing Middlesex 291
1985	Wellingborough	Pleasington	317 30th	Porters Park Hertfordshire 299
1986	Priors Hall	Ashridge	308 26th	Ealing Middlesex 286
1987	Peterbo'h Milton	Coventry	321 29th	Swindon Wiltshire 292
1988	Peterbo'h Milton	Beaconsfield	309 30th	Brokenh'st Manor Hants IOW&C 280
1989	Peterbo'h Milton	Southport & Ainsdale	321 29th	Ealing Middlesex 289
1990	Northants County	Goring & Streatley	299 20th	Ealing Middlesex 278
1991	Kingsthorpe	Porters Park	315 29th	Trentham Staffordshire 279
1992	Northants County	South Staffs	308 16th	Bristol & Clifton Gloucestershire 294
1993	Northants County	Rotherham	297 20th	Worksop Nottinghamshire 276
1994	Northants County	Coxmoor	290 5th	Sandmoor Yorkshire 287
1995	Northants County	Purdis Heath	296 11th	Sandmoor Yorkshire 289
1996	Kingsthorpe	Frilford Heath	314 30th	Hartlepool Durham 287
1997	Northants County	Sandiway	301 25th	Royal Mid-Surrey Surrey 281
1998	Northampton	Northumberland	309 27th	Moor Park Hertfordshire 287
1999	Northampton*	Moor Park	302 21st	Royal Mid-Surrey Surrey 286
2000	Northants County	Berkhamstead	288 4th	Coxmoor Nottinghamshire 286
2001	Northants County	Minchinhampton	299 15th	St Mellion Cornwall 274
2002	Peterbo'h Milton	Northants County	300 20th	Woodcote Park Surrey 285
2003	Northants County	Kings Lynn	311 26th	Southern Valley Kent 287
2004	Northants County	Sandwell Park	288 6th	Tavistock Devon 282
2005	Northants County	Brancepeth Castle	455 5th	Rotherham Yorkshire 416
2006	Northants County	Stoke Park	466 31st	Kilworth Springs Leicestershire & Rutland 428
2007	Northants County	Hesketh	485 29th	Brokenhurst Manor Hants IOW& ChIslands 452

* Northampton represented Northamptonshire as the previous year's winners, since the qualifying event the County
Championship at Cold Ashby was postponed due to severe rain. Northants County were in fact the "true"
Champions in 1999 when the Championship was replayed later in the year

Chapter 4
NORTHAMPTONSHIRE LADIES COUNTY GOLF ASSOCIATION
N.C.L.G.A. County Champions 1932-2007

Year	Winner	Year	Winner
1932	Mrs R.T.Phipps NC	1973	Mrs J.G.Sugden NC
1933	Miss D.R.Wooding NC	1974	Miss V.J. Dicks NC
1934	Mrs C.Everard Ke	1975	Miss J Lee NC
1935	Mrs R.T. Phipps NC	1976	Miss J Lee NC
1936	Mrs G.E.Dazeley N	1977	Miss J Lee NC
1937	MrsW.T.Swannell N	1978	Miss V.J. Dicks NC
1938	Mrs R.T. Phipps NC	1979	Miss V.J. Dicks NC
1939	MrsW.T.Swannell NC	1980	Mrs M.Hutcheson Ke
1940-45	No Competition World War 2	1981	Miss V.J. Dicks NC
1946	MrsW.T.Swannell NC	1982	Mrs P.P. Coles NC
1947	MissA.M.Troup N	1983	Miss V.J. Dicks NC
1948	MrsW.T.Swannell NC	1984	Mrs M.D. Duck NC
1949	MissA.M.Troup N	1985	Mrs M.D. Duck NC
1950	Mrs J.W.Taylor N	1986	Mrs P.Levoir PM
1951	Mrs R.A.Larratt Ke	1987	Mrs J.D. Kendrick Km
1952	Mrs H.A.Lock Ke	1988	Mrs M.D.Duck NC
1953	Marchioness of Northampton N	1989	Mrs Carol Gibbs CA
1954	Marchioness of Northampton N	1990	Mrs Carol Gibbs CA
1955	Miss M.P.Spencer NC	1991	Mrs Carol Gibbs CA

1956	Marchioness of Northampton N	1992	Mrs Carol Gibbs CA
1957	Mrs L.V. Everard Ke	1993	Miss Suzanne.E.Sharpe PM
1958	MrsW.T.Swannell NC	1994	Miss Suzanne.E.Sharpe PM
1959	Mrs L.V. Everard Ke	1995	Miss Suzanne.E.Sharpe PM
1960	Mrs L.V. Everard Ke	1996	Miss Sarah.L.Carter N
1961	Mrs G.Hollingsworth N	1997	Miss Sarah.L.Carter N
1962	Mrs G.Hollingsworth N	1998	Mrs Carol Gibbs CA
1963	Mrs L.V. Everard Ke	1999	Miss Sue.C.Turbayne SP
1964	Mrs L.V. Everard Ke	2000	Mrs Carol Gibbs CA
1965	Mrs J.H.Paton N	2001	Miss Sarah.L.Carter N
1966	Mrs S.Stephenson PM	2002	Miss Kelly Hanwell N
1967	Mrs S.Stephenson PM	2003	Mrs Kirsty Jennings NC
1968	Mrs J.G.Sugden NC	2004	Mrs Carol Gibbs W
1969	Mrs S.Stephenson PM	2005	Miss Roseann Youngman W
1970	Mrs H.A.Lock Ke	2006	Miss Kelly Hanwell NC
1971	Mrs J.G.Blezard Ke	2007	Miss Kelly Hanwell NC
1972	Mrs A Duck NC	2008	

BH Brampton Heath	C Collingtree	CA Cold Ashby
CE Cherwell Edge	D Daventry	DP Delapre Park
EF Elton Furze	F Farthingstone	Ke Kettering
Kg Kingsthorpe	Km Kirby Muxloe	N Northampton
NC Northants County	O Oundle	PH Priors Hall
PM Peterbo'h Milton	R Rushden	SP Staverton Park
S Silverstone	SA Stoke Albany	TW Thorpe Wood
W Wellingborough	WP Whittlebury Park	

N.C.L.G.A. Girl County Champion 1961-2007

Year	Winner	Year	Winner
1961	Miss Heather Needham N	1994	Miss Kelly Hanwell N
1962	Miss Heather Needham N	1995	Miss Kelly Hanwell N
1963	Not known	1996	Miss Kelly Hanwell N
1964	Not known	1997	Miss Katie Brown W
1981	Miss Samantha Harris SP	1998	Miss Rachel Freshwater N
1982	Miss Samantha Harris SP	1999	Miss Roseann Youngman O
1983	Miss Jane Billson W	2000	Miss Roseann Youngman O
1986	Miss Emma Print SP	2001	Miss Roseann Youngman O
1987	Miss Emma Print SP	2002	Miss Lucinda Davies PM
1988	Miss Charlotte Jones R	2003	Miss Emma Parr NC
1989	Miss Suzanne Sharpe PM	2004	Miss Emma Parr NC
1990	Miss Heather Young F	2005	Miss Emma Parr NC
1991	Miss Heather Young N	2006	Miss Alex Banham EF 79
1992	Miss Paula Taylor W	2007	Miss Alex Banham EF
1993	Miss Kelly Hanwell N	2008	

Individual County Treble Winners

There have only been a couple of handfuls of trebles of victories recorded, which reflects the degree of difficulty involved.Those fortunate "trebles" are listed below :-

Years	Name	Title	Venue	Member Club
1937-39	Charles Catlow	County Champion		Northampton
1962-64	Richard Aitken	County Champion	Northampton Kingsthorpe Northampton	Northampton
1962-64	Richard Aitken	Braid's Driver	Northampton Kingsthorpe Northampton	Northampton

1968-70	Richard Aitken	County Champion		Northampton(1968) Northants County
1975-1977	Miss Jane Lee	Lady County Champion		Northants County
1978-1980	Conrad. Ceislewicz	County Champion	Wellingborough Northampton Peterborough Milton	Northants County
1983-1985	Anthony Lord	Braid's Driver	Northants County Kettering Peterborough Milton	Northants County
1989-1992*	Mrs Carol Gibbs	Lady County Champion		Cold Ashby
1993-95	Miss Suzanne Sharpe	Lady County Champion		Peterborough Milton
1993-1996*	Miss Kelly Hanwell	Girl County Champion		Northampton
1994-96	Andrew Hare	N.G.U. Open	Kingsthorpe Northampton Kettering	Professional
1998-2000	Paul Taylor	Champion of Champions	Cold Ashby Kettering Staverton Park	Staverton Park
1999-2001	Miss Roseann Youngman	Girl County Champion		Oundle
2003-5	Miss Emma Parr	Girl County Champion		Northants County

* Actually four victories in succession

CHAPTER 6
NORTHAMPTONSHIRE'S CLUBS
Chronicle & Echo Golf Trophy 1962-1999

Year	Winners	Year	Winners
1962	Scottish Association	1981	N.A.L.G.O.
1963	Old Wellingburians	1982	Old Wellingburians
1964	Boot and Shoe Trade	1983	Foilwraps G.S.
1965	Scottish Association	1984	Retail Trades
1966	Old Wellingburians	1985	Queens Park G.S.
1967	Old Wellingburians	1986	Greenkeepers
1968	County Hall	1987	Old Northamptonians
1969	Old Wellingburians	1988	Old Northamptonians
1970	R.A.F. Association	1989	Greenkeepers
1971	Old Northamptonians	1990	Scottish Association
1972	Saints H&C Club	1991	Scottish Association
1973	Daventry Conservatives	1992	Queens Park G.S.
1974	N.A.L.G.O.*	1993	Scottish Association
1975	N.A.L.G.O.	1994	Retail Trades
1976	N.A.L.G.O.	1995	Retail Trades
1977	Saints H&C Club	1996	Croxford Builders
1978	Old Wellingburians	1997	Jon-Par Builders
1979	N.A.L.G.O.	1998	The Builders
1980	Old Northamptonians	1999	The Builders

HAKKO Team/Camden Motor Group Foursomes

Year	Winners	Year	Winners
2000	Jon-Par Builders	2002	?
2001	White Lodge	2003	?

* N.A.L.G.O. National Association of Local Government Officers

N.G.U. Inter Club Challenge Cup (1922-1966) then Scratch League Division 1 (1980-2007) Presented by W.P.Cross, Esq.

Year	Winners	Year	Winners
1922	Northants County	1961	Peterbo'h Milton
1923	Kettering	1962	Northampton
1924	Northants County	1963	Northants County
1925	Northampton	1964	Northants County
1926	Northampton	1965	Peterbo'h Milton
1927	Kettering	1966	Northampton
1928	Northampton	1980	Wellingborough
1929	Northampton	1981	Peterbo'h Milton
1930	Northampton	1982	Northants County
1931	Northampton	1983	Northants County
1932	Rushden	1984	Wellingborough
1933	Northants County	1985	Priors Hall
1934	Northants County	1986	Peterbo'h Milton
1935	Rushden	1987	Peterbo'h Milton
1936	Rushden	1988	Peterbo'h Milton
1937	Northants County	1989	Northants County
1938	Northampton	1990	Northants County
1939	Northants County	1991	Kettering
1946	Northampton	1992	Kingsthorpe
1947	Northampton	1993	Northants County
1948	Northants County	1994	Northants County
1949	Northants County	1995	Kingsthorpe
1950	Northants County	1996	Northants County
1951	Northampton	1997	Northants County
1952	Northants County	1998	Northants County
1953	Northampton	1999	Northants County
1954	Northants County	2000	Northants County
1955	Northants County	2001	Peterbo'h Milton
1956	Northants County	2002	Northampton
1957	Northants County	2003	Peterbo'h Milton
1958	Northants County	2004	Peterbo'h Milton
1959	Northants County	2005	Collingtree Park
1960	Peterbo'h Milton	2006	Cold Ashby
		2007	Kingsthorpe

Victories

Northants County	29
Northampton	14
Peterbo'h Milton	10
Kettering	3
Rushden	3
Kingsthorpe	3
Wellingborough	2
Cold Ashby	1
Collingtree Park	1
Priors Hall	1

SCRATCH LEAGUE DIVISION 1 2005 PLAYERS PERFORMANCE

POSN	PLAYER	CLUB	HCP	IZZARD INDEX	P	W	H	L
1	F.CARNIHAN	CA	+1	12	8	5	2	1
2	M.SPENCE	OP	5	8.75	7	4	2	1
3	G.BOTT	CA	3	8	8	6	-	2
3	R.EDWARDS	PM	4	8	8	6	-	2
3	M.FRANKLIN	SP	+1	8	8	6	-	2
3	A.SHERLOCK	CP	4	8	8	6	-	2
7	S.BROWN	SP	1	7.3	8	5	1	2
8	A.LINDSEY	CP	5	5.8	7	5	-	2
9	A.CLARK	CA	3	5.24	7	4	1	2
10	N.PRESTO	PM	0	5	5	4	-	1
11	J.BARKER	OP	2	4.5	8	4	1	3
11	R.PAULEY	PM	4	4.5	3	3	-	-
11	P.TAYLOR	SP	+3	4.5	3	3	-	-
14	I.SYMONDS	PM	1	4.4	5	3	1	1
15	S.SMITH	CP	5	4.08	7	3	1	2
16	R.DAWBER	CA	4	4	6	4	-	2
17	E.CHAPMAN	OP	3	3.5	6	3	1	2
17	I.ROCHE	OP	4	3.5	7	4	-	3
17	R.FROST	OP	6	3.5	6	3	1	2
20	B.MOSS	CP	2	3.2	8	4	-	4
20	G.CROXTON	CA	2	3.2	8	4	-	4
22	L.HILLIER	CP	1	3	4	3	-	1
23	R.BROWN	SP	5	2.5	5	3	-	2
23	R.CLAYTON	CA	4	2.5	5	3	-	2
23	M.PEACOCK	PM	0	2.5	5	3	-	2
26	R.COLE	PM	2	2.4	8	2	2	4
27	A.FIRMAN	PM	+1	2.2	8	3	-	5
28	A.FREEMAN	OP	2	2.1	7	3	-	4
29	D.RALFS	PM	4	1.9	6	2	1	3
30	D.COULL	CP	6	1.87	6	2	1	3
31	D.MORRIS	CP	0	1.67	5	1	2	2
31	J.TRICKLEBANK	OP	5	1.67	5	2	1	2
33	G.DYSON	PM	1	1.5	6	1	2	3
34	C.WHITE	PM	5	1.33	4	2	-	2
35	S.BARNES	SP	4	1.25	5	2	-	3
36	R.DALTON	OP	1	1.17	7	2	-	5
37	L.FOSTER	SP	3	1.14	8	2	-	6
37	D.HAYLE	SP	4	1.14	8	2	-	6
39	S.GOODSEN	CP	4	1.13	3	1	1	1
40	T.SAWYER	SP	5	1.125	3	1	1	1
41	P.ASKEW	CA	4	1	4	1	1	2
41	R.SWANN	SP	6	1	4	1	1	2
43	P.SAUNDERS	CP	4	0.87	7	1	1	5
44	M.CONWAY	CA	2	0.58	7	-	2	5
45	I.DALLAS	CP	6	0.5	2	1	-	1
45	R.FREDRICKS	PM	5	0.5	3	1	-	2
45	L.DAVIES	CP	4	0.5	2	1	-	1
45	C.RAY	SP	0	0.5	4	1	-	3
49	L.ESSEX	SP	3	0.495	3	1	-	2
50	J.CHAMBERLAIN	CA	4	0.25	4	-	1	3
50	M.HERSON	PM	3	0.25	3	-	1	2
50	M.SPRAGG	CP	2	0.25	3	-	1	2
53	D.BURGESS	CA	4	0	3	-	-	3
53	A.TALLANTIRE	CA	4	0	3	-	-	3

53	R.HEMAS	SP	5	**0**	3	-	-	3
53	T.ANDERSON	OP	2	**0**	7	-	-	7
	L.WATSON	CA	4	-	1	-	-	1
	R.HOLDING	OP	5	-	1	1	-	-
	A.WOAN	OP	7	-	1	1	-	-
	J.GREESON	OP	7	-	1	-	-	1
	D.SYMONDS	PM	5	-	1	-	-	1
	A.BUTHEE	CP	5	-	1	-	-	1
	J.STEVENS	CP	8	-	1	1	-	-
	S.HARRIS	SP	2	-	1	-	-	1
	W.MARKS	SP	5	-	1	-	-	1

CA COLD ASHBY, OP OVERSTONE PARK, PM PETERBOROUGH MILTON, CP COLLINGTREE PARK, SP STAVERTON PARK.

A minimum of two matches is required to obtain an Izzard Index.

$$\text{IZZARD INDEX} = \frac{\% \text{ VICTORIES} \times \text{NUMBER OF APPEARANCES}^2}{2 \times (1 + \text{NUMBER OF LOSSES})}$$

100

N.G.U. Hollingsworth Trophy Winners & Runners up 1956-2007

YEAR	WINNER	*RUNNER-UP*	SCORE
1956	**KINGSTHORPE**	-	
1957	**DAVENTRY**	*OUNDLE*	3-2
1958	**KINGSTHORPE**	*NORTHAMPTON*	3-2
1959	**WELLINGBOROUGH**	-	
1960	**DAVENTRY**	*PETERBOROUGH MILTON*	3-2
1961	**KINGSTHORPE**	*KETTERING*	5-0
1962	**KINGSTHORPE**	*NORTHANTS COUNTY*	4-1
1963	**WELLINGBOROUGH**	*PETERBOROUGH MILTON*	3-2
1964	**NORTHAMPTON**	*NORTHANTS COUNTY*	3-2
1965	**NORTHAMPTON**	*KETTERING*	3-2
1966	**KETTERING**	*KINGSTHORPE*	3-2
1967	**KINGSTHORPE**	*KETTERING*	3-2
1968	**KETTERING**	*PRIORS HALL*	3-2
1969	**DAVENTRY**	*WELLINGBOROUGH*	3-2
1970	**PRIORS HALL**	-	
1971	**NORTHANTS COUNTY**	-	
1972	**NORTHANTS COUNTY**	*NORTHAMPTON*	
1973	**PRIORS HALL**	-	
1974	**PRIORS HALL**	-	
1975	**PRIORS HALL**	-	
1976	**PETERBOROUGH MILTON**	*RUSHDEN*	3-2
1977	**PETERBOROUGH MILTON**	*NORTHANTS COUNTY*	?
1978	**NORTHAMPTON**	*KETTERING* *DAVENTRY*	3-2 & 4-1 N7, K6, D2
1979	**PETERBOROUGH MILTON**	*KINGSTHORPE* *NORTHANTS COUNTY*	?
1980	**STAVERTON PARK**	*PETERBOROUGH MILTON*	3-2
1981	**PETERBOROUGH MILTON**	*NORTHAMPTON*	5-0
1982	**KETTERING**	*NORTHAMPTON*	3-2

1983	**NORTHAMPTON**	*PETERBOROUGH MILTON*	4-1
1984	**WELLINGBOROUGH**	*NORTHANTS COUNTY*	4-1
1985	**NORTHANTS COUNTY**	*OUNDLE*	3-2
1986	**PETERBOROUGH MILTON**	*KETTERING*	?
1987	**NORTHAMPTON**	*PRIORS HALL*	4-1
1988	**NORTHAMPTON**	*PETERBOROUGH MILTON*	3.5-1.5
1989	**KETTERING**	*KINGSTHORPE*	4-1
1990	**KETTERING**	*KINGSTHORPE*	3-2
1991	**KINGSTHORPE**	*KETTERING*	3-2
1992	**KETTERING**	*NORTHANTS COUNTY*	3-2
1993	**STAVERTON PARK**	*KETTERING*	3-2
1994	**NORTHANTS COUNTY**	*KINGSTHORPE*	4-1
1995	**KINGSTHORPE**	*COLD ASHBY*	4.5-0.5
1996	**NORTHAMPTON**	*PETERBOROUGH MILTON*	5-0
1997	**KINGSTHORPE**	*NORTHANTS COUNTY*	3-2
1998	**NORTHANTS COUNTY**	*KINGSTHORPE*	3-2
1999	**KINGSTHORPE**	*COLLINGTREE PARK*	3-2
2000	**KINGSTHORPE**	*WELLINGBOROUGH*	4-1
2001	**PETERBOROUGH MILTON**	*PRIORS HALL*	5-0
2002	**NORTHANTS COUNTY**	*KINGSTHORPE*	3-2
2003	**NORTHAMPTON**	*FARTHINGSTONE*	3-2
2004	**KINGSTHORPE**	*COLLINGTREE PARK*	3-2
2005	**STAVERTON PARK**	*NORTHAMPTON*	3-2
2006	**KINGSTHORPE**	*WHITTLEBURY PARK*	3-2
2007	**COLLINGTREE PARK**	*PRIORS HALL*	4-1

Multiple winners of the Hollingsworth trophy 1956-2007

TEAM	NUMBER	YEARS
KINGSTHORPE	12	1956, 58, 61, 62, 67, 91, 95, 97, 1999, 2000, 2004, 2006
NORTHAMPTON	8	1964, 65, 78, 83, 87, 88, 1996, 2003
KETTERING	6	1966, 68, 82, 89, 90, 1992
PETERBOROUGH MILTON	6	1976, 77,79, 81, 86, 2001
NORTHANTS COUNTY	6	1971, 72, 85, 94, 98, 2002
PRIORS HALL	4	1970, 73, 74, 75
DAVENTRY	3	1957, 60, 1969
WELLINGBOROUGH	3	1959, 63, 1984
STAVERTON PARK	3	1980, 1993, 2005
COLLINGTREE PARK	1	2007

N.C.L.G.A. Cecil Leitch Trophy Winners 1927-2007

YEAR	WINNER	YEAR	WINNER	YEAR	WINNER
1927	Kingsthorpe*	1958	Kettering	1983	Kettering
1928	Kingsthorpe	1959	Daventry	1984	Daventry
1929	Kettering	1960	Northampton	1985	Daventry
1930	Northants County	1961	Kettering	1986	Daventry
1931	Kettering	1962	Rushden	1987	Northants County
1932	Northants County	1963	Kettering	1988	Northants County
1933	Northampton	1964	Northants County	1989	Rushden

1934	Northampton	1965	Northampton	1990	Daventry
1935	Northampton	1966	Rushden	1991	Northants County
1936	Northampton	1967	Rushden	1992	Cherwell Edge
1937	Northampton	1968	Northampton	1993	Kettering
1938	Northants County	1969	Northants County	1994	Rushden
1939	Wellingborough	1970	Northants County	1995	Wellingborough
1940	Not played until	1971	Northants County	1996	Oundle
1947	Northampton	1972	Kingsthorpe	1997	Oundle
1948	Abandoned	1973	Wellingborough	1998	Elton Furze
1949	Abandoned	1974	Wellingborough	1999	Rushden
1950	Northampton	1975	Wellingborough	2000	Kettering
1951	Kettering	1976	Wellingborough	2001	Overstone Park
1952	Northampton	1977	Northants County	2002	Northampton
1953	Northants County	1978	Kettering	2003	Northants County
1954	Northants County	1979	Wellingborough	2004	Kettering
1955	Northants County	1980	Wellingborough	2005	Collingtree Park
1956	Kettering	1981	Wellingborough	2006	Elton Furze
1957	Northants County	1982	Kettering	2007	Elton Furze

Collingtree Park   1 Victory 2005
Cherwell Edge   1 Victory 1992
Daventry   5 Victories 1959, 1984,1985,1986,1990
Elton Furze   3 Victories 1998, 2006, 2007
Kingsthorpe   3 Victories 1927, 1928, 1972
Kettering   13 Victories 1929, 1931, 1951, 1956, 1958, 1961, 1963, 1978, 1982, 1983, 1993, 2000, 2004
Northampton   12 Victories 1933-37, 1947, 1950, 1952, 1960, 1965, 1968, 2002
Northants County   16 Victories 1930, 1932, 1938, 1953-55, 1957, 1964, 1969-1971, 1977, 1987-88, 1991, 2003
Oundle   2 Victories 1996, 1997
Rushden   6 Victories 1962, 1966, 1967, 1989, 1994, 1999
Wellingborough   9 Victories 1939, 1973-1976, 1979-1981, 1995

* Miss Leitch presented the trophy

N.L.C.G.A. Scratch League

Year	Winners	Runners -Up	Year	Winners	Runners-Up
1991	NORTHANTS COUNTY		2000	NORTHANTS COUNTY	
1992	NORTHAMPTON		2001	NORTHANTS COUNTY	
1993	NORTHANTS COUNTY		2002	NORTHAMPTON	
1994	NORTHAMPTON		2003	NORTHANTS COUNTY 2/1	*PETERBOROUGH MILTON*
1995	NORTHAMPTON		2004	NORTHANTS COUNTY 2/1	*WELLINGBOROUGH*
1996	NORTHAMPTON		2005	NORTHANTS COUNTY	
1997	NORTHAMPTON		2006	NORTHANTS COUNTY	*WELLINGBOROUGH*
1998	NORTHAMPTON		2007	NORTHANTS COUNTY	*STAVERTON PARK*
1999	NORTHANTS COUNTY		2008		

CHAPTER 7 N.P.G.A.

The Midland Professional Championship 1897-2008

Year	Winner	Year	Winner	Year	Winner
1897	T.Williamson	1938	H. R. Manton	1977	B. J. Waites
1898	T.Williamson	1939	W. J. Martin	1978	B. J. Waites
1899	A.Toogood	1946	W. Lees	1979	B. J. Waites
1900	T.Williamson	1947	K W C Adwick	1980	D. J. Vaughan
1901	J.G.Sherlock	1948	A. Lees	1981	D. A. Stewart
1903	J.G.Sherlock	1949	A. Lees	1982	P. A. Elson
1904	A.Lewis	1950	C. H. Ward	1983	A. R. Minshall
1906	J. Fulford	1951	J. R. Moses	1984	M. Mouland
1907	T.Williamson	1952	J. Hargreaves	1985	K. Hayward
1909	G. Coburn	1953	C. H. Ward	1986	A. Skingle
1910	E. Veness	1954	A. Cunningham	1987	M. Mouland
1911	T.Williamson	1955	C. H. Ward	1988	G. Farr
1912	G .R .Buckle	1956	R. L. Hastleow	1989	J. Higgins
1913	G. V. Tuvk	1957	D. Snell	1990	G. Stafford
1919	B. S. Weasteil	1958	J. H. Cawsey	1991	K Dickens
1920	T.Williamson	1959	G. A. Maisey	1992	J. Higgins
1921	W. Robertson	1960	J. Hargreaves	1993	P. Baker
1922	T.Williamson	1961	P. J. Butler	1994	P. Baker
1923	G .R .Buckle	1962	A. Rees	1995	S. Rose
1924	J. Bloxham	1963	C. H. Ward	1996	D. J. Russell
1925	G .R .Buckle	1964	S. W. T. Murray	1997	J. Higgins
1926	E. S. Douglas	1965	S. A. Hunt	1998	S. Webster
1927	T. Barber	1966	J. Anderson	1999	C. Hall
1928	P. F.Weston	1967	S. W. T. Murray	2000	D. J. Russell
1929	G .R .Buckle	1968	S. W. T. Murray	2001	T. Rouse
1930	T. Green	1969	T. R. Squires	2002	R. Rock
1931	T. Green	1970	D. J. Llewellyn	2003	P. Edwards
1932	T. Barber	1971	R. A. Beattie	2004	P. Streeter
1933	C. H. Ward	1972	B. J. Waites	2005	A. Carey
1934	C. H. Ward	1973	R. D. S. Livingston	2006	P. Streeter
1935	W. R. Firkins	1974	M. Gallagher	2007	I. Lyner
1936	W. J. Branch	1975	H. F. J. Boyle	2008	
1937	A. G. Beck	1976	P. R. Herbert	2009	

Plum colour denotes a Northamptonshire winner

CHAPTER 8
NORTHAMPTONSHIRE & BEDFORDSHIRE GOLF ALLIANCE
Challenge Cup (Gray Cup)

This trophy was presented by E.C.Gray Esq. President 1925-26. Originally a singles event, it is currently played for as a pair's event format fourball better ball concurrently with The Gray Cup.

1926	A.Randall (Mid Beds G.C.)	1927	Captain Banks (Leighton Buzzard G.C.)
1928	A.J.Lacey	1929	C.M.Snodin (Northampton G.C.)
1930	A.E.Thomas (Kingsthorpe G.C.)	1931	H.A.Lees (Kingsthorpe G.C.)
1932	W.G.Groves (Leighton Buzzard G.C.)	1937	N.J.Green (Kingsthorpe G.C.)
1938	D.Shackman (Dunstable Downs G.C.)	1954	O.R.Robinson (Kettering G.C.)
1955	E.G.Freeman (Kingsthorpe G.C.)	1956	O.Snape (Beds & County G.C.)
1957	O.Snape (Beds & County G.C.)	1958	B Buckle (Wellingborough G.C)
1960	N.A Havart (Northampton G.C)	1962	R.D Edwards (Dunstable Downs G.C)
1964	S.T Gaskin (Leighton Buzzard G.C)	1965	M.Duck & J.B.S.Harris
1966	J.P.Morgan & G.Hogger	1967	W.F.Kearney & D.Brown
1970	J.Stewart & J.Mathers	1971	J.P.Morgan & G.Hogger
1972	S.Bonham & B.Jones	1975	R.Beekie & A.Cruden
1976	B.Felce & M.Searle	1977	R.A.Day & F.J.Richmond
1978	W.E.Crosbie & J.Abraham	1979	P.J.Rowling & P.J.Brennan
1982	T.Arnold & M.Burke	1983	D.Eborall & K.Billingham
1987	A.A.Cooper & G.C.Green	1989	P.Smith & V.Jones
1990	B.Sullivan & R.Freeman	1991	B.Sullivan & R.Freeman
1992	C.Wells & S.Bradshaw	1993	R.L.Bingham & P.K.Gregory
1994	J.Lamond & S.Field	1995	M.Fulcher & A.S.Brown
1996	C.J.Freeman & P.Murphy	1997	I.Cole & R.Farman
1998	D.J.W.McCoy & I.Humphries	1999	A.R.G.Harrison & J.D.Sadler
2000	G.D.Walters & T.R.Francis	2001	D.J.Bennison & A.J.Gibbs
2002	I.Hutchins & M.Webster	2003	S.Rodriguez & N.Mendel
2004	S.Rodriguez & N.Mendel	2005	S.Rodriguez & N.Mendel
2006	P.Kirk & R.Freeman	2007	C.P.Hollins & N.J.Robinson

Challenge Cup, The Gray Cup
This trophy was first played for in 1965

1965	M.Duck & J.B.S.Harris	1992	C.Wells & S.Bradshaw
1966	J.P.Morgan & G.Hogger	1993	R.L.Bingham & P.K.Gregory
1968	J.L.McDougall & E.V.Corps	1994	M.Fulcher & A.S.Brown
1975	R.Beekie & A.Cruden	1996	C.J.Freeman & P.Murphy
1976	B.Felce & M.Searle	1997	I.Cole & R.Farman
1977	R.A.Day & F.J.Richmond	1998	D.J.W.McCoy & I.Humphries
1978	W.E.Crosbie & J.Abraham	1999	G.C.Major & I.G.Bradley
1979	P.J.Rowling & P.J.Brennan	2000	R.Crouch & M.Field
1981	K.P.D.Cooper & J.E.Perkins	2001	D.J.Bennison & A.J.Gibbs
1982	T.Arnold & M.Burke	2002	I.Hutchins & M.Webster
1983	D.Eborall & K.Billingham	2003	S.Rodriguez & N.Mendel
1987	A.A.Cooper & G.C.Green	2004	S.Rodriguez & N.Mendel
1989	P.Smith & V.Jones	2005	S.Rodriguez & N.Mendel
1990	B.Sullivan & R.Freeman	2006	P.Kirk & R.Freeman
1991	S.Fuller & T.Puddicombe	2007	C.P.Hollins & N.J.Robinson 41 pts

Northamptonshire Schools Golf Association
Under 18 Champions

Year	Boy Winner	Club	Girl Winner	Club
1996	Robert Harris	Collingtree Park	Kelly Hanwell	Northampton
1997	James Howett	Collingtree Park	Kelly Hanwell	Northampton
1998	Scott Marshall 77	Brampton Heath	Rachel Freshwater 95	Northampton
1999	Luke Hillier	Collingtree Park	Rose Ann Youngman	Oundle
2000	Matthew Bearman	Silverstone	Rose Ann Youngman	Oundle
2001	Elliot Gray	Staverton Park	Rose Ann Youngman	Oundle
2002	Giles Kellett	Wellingborough	Rose Ann Youngman	Oundle
2003	Gary Boyd	Cherwell Edge	Samantha Round	
2004	Gary Boyd	Cherwell Edge	Emma Parr	Northants County
2005	Andrew Myers	Northants County	Rebecca Gee	Wellingborough
2006	Cancelled due to rain	-	Cancelled due to rain	-
2007				

Winning School Team

Year	School	Year	School
1996	Wellingborough School	2002	Roade School
1997	Moulton School	2003	Roade School
1998	Weavers School	2004	Roade School
1999	Wollaston	2005	Moulton School
2000	Prince William School Oundle	2006	Cancelled due to rain
2001	Roade School	2007	

Under 15 Champions

Year	Boy Winner	Club	Girl Winner	Club
2005	Mathew Beaver	Brampton Heath	Megan Liddington	Staverton Park
2006	Cancelled due to rain	-	Cancelled due to rain	-
2007				

CHAPTER 11

SUCCESS AT NATIONAL LEVEL, SHORT STROKES, CHARACTERS AND MISCELLANY

2005 ENGLISH COUNTY SENIORS TEAM CHAMPIONSHIP, MINCHINHAMPTON G.C.

Kent			v			NORTHAMPTONSHIRE
Foursomes						**Foursomes**
	Score	Pts	Pts	Score		
Chris Reynolds			v			Geoff Dyson
Chris Buckley	3/1	1	0			Mike Abbotts
Tony Jones			v			Rodney Haig
Roger Salmon	3/1	1	0			Brian O'Connell
		2	**0**			
Singles						**Singles**
Name	Score	Pts	Pts	Score		Name
David Jamieson	6/5	1	v	0	0	John MacCallum
Ian Mason		0	v	1	3/1	Brian O'Connell
Chris Buckley		0	v	1	4/3	Martin Harris

Cheshire			v		NORTHAMPTONSHIRE	
Foursomes					**Foursomes**	
Name	Score	Pts		Pts	Score	Name
Roy Smethurst			v			Geoff Dyson
Philip Jones	4/2	1		0		Brian O'Connell
George Payne			v			Martin Harris
Rolfe Furmston		0		1	3/2	Rodney Haig
	Foursome Points	1		1	Foursome Points	
Singles					**Singles**	
Name	Score	Pts		Pts	Score	Name
Roy Smethurst	6/5	1	v	0		John MacCallum
Philip Jones	6/5	1	v	0		Mike Abbotts
Tom Dickinson		0	v	1	2/1	Brian O'Connell
Rolfe Furmston	6/4	1	v	0		Martin Harris
Bob Walker	1 Hole	1	v	0		Geoff Dyson
	Singles	4		1	Singles	
	Foursomes	1		1	Foursomes	
	Result	**5**		**2**	**Result**	

Somerset			v		NORTHAMPTONSHIRE	
Foursomes					**Foursomes**	
Name	Score	Pts		Pts	Score	Name
John Whitcutt			v			Rodney Haig
John Smith	4/3	1		0		John Clarke
David Meredith			v			John MacCallum
Alan Peates	3/2	1		0		Mike Abbotts
	Foursome Points	2		0	Foursome Points	
Singles					**Singles**	
Name	Score	Pts		Pts	Score	Name
John Whitcutt	5/4	1	v	0		Martin Harris
John Smith		0	v	1	1 Hole	Rodney Haig
David Meredith		0	v	1	5/4	Geoff Dyson
Alan Peates	5/4	1	v	0		Mike Abbotts
Jim Scott		0	v	1	1 Hole	John MacCallum
	Singles	2	0	3	Singles	
	Foursomes	2	0	0	Foursomes	
	Result	**4**		**3**	**Result**	

Final Positions	1st Cheshire
	2nd Kent
	3rd Somerset
	4th **Northamptonshire**

N.C.L.G.A. sub-division finals winners at Copt Heath G.C. Warwickshire 2005

<u>Northamptonshire 7 Cambridgeshire & Huntingdonshire 2</u>

		Foursomes		
K.Hanwell & K.Jennings	4/2	vs	J.Gregg & S.Greenhall	
C.Gibbs & G.Dunn	2Up		P.Parker & J.McGuigan	
R.Youngman & S.Carter	4/3		J.Walters & S.Attwood	
		3		
		Singles		
R.Youngman		3/2	J.Gregg	
K.Hanwell		2Up	J.McGuigan	
L.Davies			J.Walters	7/6
S.Carter	3/1		P.Ewing	
C.Gibbs	1Up		S.Attwood	
K.Jennings			S.Greenhall	5/4
		4		2

<u>Northamptonshire 7 Carnarvonshire & Anglesey 2</u>

		Foursomes		
S.Carter & R.Youngman			T.Davies & K.Boulden	2/1
K.Hanwell & K.Jennings	4/2		D.Jones & A.Lewis	
C.Gibbs & G.Dunn		4/3	H.Bouldern & S.Sweeting	
		2		1
		Singles		
R.Youngmann		3/1	T.Davies	
G.Dunn			H.Bouldern	5/4
K.Hanwell		2Up	D.Jones	
K.Jennings		2Up	A.Lewis	
E.Parr		3/2	H.Bouldern	
S.Carter		4/3	S.Sweeting	
		5		1

<u>Northamptonshire 5 ½ Warwickshire 3 ½</u>

		Foursomes			
K.Hanwell & K.Jennings			T.Atkin & C.Dowling	3/2	
S.Carter & R.Youngman			C.Howells & J. Manders	9/7	
C.Gibbs & G.Dunn		4/2	L.Barton & B.Belcher		
		1		2	
			Singles		
R.Youngman		3/2	T.Atkin		
E.Parr		AS	C.Dowling		AS
K.Hanwell		2/1	C.Howells		
K.Jennings			J. Manders		1Up
G.Dunn	5/4		H.Coles		
C.Gibbs	5/4		L.Barton		
		4 ½			1½

E.L.G.A County Finals Brancepeth Castle Durham 7-9 September 2005

Yorkshire v Northamptonshire 7 Sept 2005					
Foursomes					
Emma Duggleby Naomi Edwards	2&1	1	Kelly Hanwell Kirstie Jennings		0
Rachel Bell Kiran Matharu	2&1	1	Carol Gibbs Georgina Dunn		0
Michelle Smith Cheryl Smith	2&1	1	Sarah Carter Roseann Youngman		0
		3			0
Singles					
Rachel Bell	A/S	½	Kelly Hanwell	A/S	½
Emma Duggleby	5&4	1	Kirstie Jennings		0
Naomi Edwards	4&2	1	Emma Parr		0
Kiran Matharu	5&4	1	Georgina Dunn		0
Jodi Ewart	4&2	1	Roseann Youngman		0
Rachael Lomas	6&4	1	Sarah Carter		0
		5½			½
Result		**8½**			**½**
Northamptonshire v Hampshire 8 Sept 2005					
Foursomes					
Kelly Hanwell Kirstie Jennings		0	Kerry Smith Chris Quinn	6&5	1
Sarah Carter Roseann Youngman		0	Liz Bennett Tracey Boyes	3&2	1
Carol Gibbs Georgina Dunn	4&3	1	Helen Wheeler Kelly Travers		0
		1			2
Singles					
Roseann Youngman	1up	1	Liz Bennett		0
Sarah Carter		0	Kerry Smith	2up	1
Kelly Hanwell	1up	1	Tracey Boyes		0
Emma Parr		0	Katie Thompson	4&3	1
Lucinda Davies		0	Olivia Higgins	5&3	1
Georgina Dunn		0	Kelly Travers	2&1	1
		2			4
Result		3			6
Gloucestershire v Northamptonshire 9 Sept 2005					
Foursomes					
Jo Hodge Linda Carruthers		0	Carol Gibbs Georgina Dunn	6&5	1
Hannah Barwood Charlotte Ellis	4&3	1	Roseann Youngman Sarah Carter		0
Sharon Heeley Sian James	1up	1	Kelly Hanwell Kirstie Jennings		0
		2			1
Singles Play abandoned due to heavy rain					

Final Placings

COUNTY	P	W	H	L	PTS	GAMES
YORKSHIRE	3	2	1	0	2 ½	15
GLOUCESTERSHIRE	3	2	1	0	2 ½	12
HAMPSHIRE	3	1	0	2	1	10 ½
NORTHAMPTONSHIRE	3	0	0	0	0	4 ½

Daily Mail Amateur Foursomes, National Finalists, Northamptonshire

Year	Gender	Club & Players	Results
1965	Men	Northampton W.Clarke 5, B.Jones 5	Lost to Hazel Grove
1966	Men	Northampton A.F.Stevens 8, L.A.Johnson	Lost to Royal Epping Forest 4&3
1971	Men	Northants County J.D.Haig 10, R.A.Haig 6	Lost to Royal Worlington and Newmarket
1974	Men	Northants County R.G.Halliday 3, A.Bishop 4	Beat Purley Downs 4/3 Lost to Gerrards Cross 3/2
1979	Men	Priors Hall N.Dean 6, P.Robinson 14	Beat Ringway Lost to Scarborough South Cliff
1981	Women	Kingsthorpe Mrs.S.Tookey 12, Mrs P.Coles 13	Lost to North Wales
1984	Women	Kettering L.White 7, T.Rolfe 15	Lost to Fulford
1990	Men	Daventry and District S.Rooney 7, D.Gill 5	Lost to Falkirk
1996	Men	Northampton G.H.Keates 1, M.J.Izzard 5	Beat Little Chalfont 2/1 Lost to Weston-super-Mare (1996 Winners) 2/1
2005	Women	Northants County S.Carter 3 K.Jennings 5	Beat The Lambourne 6/5 Beat Crondon Park 3/1 Beat Oxley Park Lost to Cowdray Park (2005 Winners) 1 Down

REFERENCES USED, KNOWN LITERATURE AND LINKS TO NORTHAMPTONSHIRE GOLF

1. Northampton Golf Club, The Competitive Scene at Kettering Road and Harlestone 1969-2002 M.J.Izzard ISBN 0-9520291-1-1.

2. The Flora of Northamptonshire by G.Claridge Druce, D.Sc., L.L.D., F.R.S. Arbroath T.Buncle & Co. August 1930. Ex Libris M.J.Izzard or the reference section of the Northampton Library on Abington Street.

3. Wellingborough Golf Club 1893-1993 by Ralph Grey-Jones, Stanley L Hunt (Printers) Rushden.

4. Northampton Golf Club "A Centenary history 1893-1993" by G.Sibley 1993 ISBN 0 9520291 0 3 Woolnough Bookbindings Ltd Irthlingborough Northamptonshire.

5. Northants County Golf Club 1910-1995 by Neil Soutar, Woolnough book binding ISBN 0952245558.

6. www.randa.org

7. The Northamptonshire Golf Union Yearbook Ed B.Barron, D.Croxton, G.Croxton, M.J.Izzard and J.Prentice 1996,1997,1998,1999, 2000 Falcon Press, 2001-2006 Charter Print Group.

8. www.northantsgolfunion.co.uk

9. Leicestershire & Rutland Golf Union website www.lrgu.co.uk.

10. Woodhall Spa A Celebration of Golf The Hotchkin Course 1905-2005, Longmore, Reiners & Bale WAYZ-GOOSE Print 2005 No ISBN.

11. The History of The English Golf Union, Diamond Jubilee 1924-1984 A Celebration in Words & Pictures.

12. English Ladies Golf Union www.englishladiesgolf.org

13. Golf in the Midlands 1895-1998 by the late Ray Baldwin, Chantry Cottage, Friar Street, Droitwich, Worcs WR9 8EQ. Single copy privately produced by the author.

14. Club websites
   Brampton Heath Golf Centre www.bhgc.co.uk
   Cherwell Edge www.cegc.co.uk
   Cold Ashby Golf Club www.coldashbygolfclub.com
   Collingtree Park Golf Club www.collingtreepark.com
   Delapre Golf Club www.delapregolf.co.uk
   Elton Furze www.eltonfurzegolfclub.co.uk
   Farthingstone Hotel and Golf Course www.farthingstone.co.uk
   Hellidon Lakes hellidon@marstonhotels.com
   Kettering Golf Club www.kettering-golf.co.uk

Kingfisher www.kingfisher-hotelandgolf.co.uk/
Kingsthorpe Golf Club www.kingsthorpe-golf.co.uk
Northampton Golf Club www.northamptongolfclub.co.uk
Northamptonshire Golf Union www.ngu.org.uk
Oundle Golf Club www.oundlegolfclub.com
Overstone Park Golf Club www.overstonepark.co.uk
Pytchley Golf Lodge www.pythchleygolflodgekettering.co.uk
Peterbo'h Milton www.peterboroughmilton.co.uk
Rushden www.rushdengolfclub.org
Stoke Albany www.stokealbanygolfclub.co.uk
Thorpe Wood www.thorpewoodgolfcourse.co.uk
Wellingborough Golf Club www.wellingboroughgolfclub.org
Whittlebury Park (West Park) www.whittlebury.com

15. Ref A Century of Warwickshire County Golf 1906-2006 John F.Moreton Grant Books Droitwich UK ISBN 0 907186 62 9.

16. Brian Reynolds: The Times and Life of the Northamptonshire Sportsman Diametric press Kettering by Ian Addis, Mick Dean & Brian Slough Diametric Publications (13 Nov 2000) ISBN-10: 0953348261, ISBN-13: 978-0953348268

17. Market Harborough Golf Club The First 100 Years by B.Barron. See also the Harborough Historian, published by the Market Harborough Historic Society and the Harborough Museum J Morgan Researching the History of the Market Harborough Golf Club 1999 16 3.

18 A History of Northamptonshire R.L.Greenhall Phillimore & Co West Sussex ISBN 1 86077 147 5.

19 A History of Oundle Golf Club 1962-1987 Major Guy Richardson, single copy only available from Club Secretary.

20 www.ruleshistory.com

21 Sheringham Golf Club A Centenary History 1891-1991 by J.K.Coleridge Published by S.G.C.Witley Press Hunstanton ISBN 0-9517947-0-1.

22. A Grand Man and a Golfer, The Novelist George Whyte Melville P.N.Lewis & A.D.Meadows ISBN 0907583105 Printed by West Port Print & Design, St Andrews.

23. www.northamptonshiregolf.org.uk

24. www.northamptonshirepga.co.uk

25. Northampton Golf Club Centenary Diary 1893-1993

26. www.1golfplace.com/

Other sources of information used

The Golfers Guide December 1 1893 p371.

The Northamptonshire Village Book Countryside Books, Newbury Berks ISBN 1853060550

Google Earth Northampton England.

Nisbet's Golf Year Book 1912

SUBSCRIBERS

Name	Title
Richard Aitken	N.G.U. Past President
Graham Alsop	Captain Northampton G.C. 2005
Scott Bailey	N.G.C. Hollingsworth Trophy Winner 1996
Bobby Bason	Green Course Record Holder Northampton G.C.
Alan Benson	Past President Nottinghamshire, Chairman M.G.U. Junior Golf
Andrew Blows	M.G.U. Championship Committee Chairman
Andrew Boyd	Worcestershire County Secretary
Ian Brooks	Bill Bailey, alias Pinkie
Simon SJ Bunn	Smooth Balls
John Bunyan	Past Captain Wellingborough G.C.
Bob Burrows	Big Bad Bob
Roy Case	E.G.U. President 2009
Arthur Coales	Arthur Coales
Dave Croxton	N.G.U. Past President
John Harris	John Harris (Kingsthorpe Golf Club)
Harvey Harrison	Hon Sec, L.U.G.C., Runners Up E.G.U. Presidents/ Guests, Woodhall Spa 2007
Melvyn Hazell	Melvyn Hazell
Chris Hollins	Gray Cup Winner 2007
Jim Howkins	Jim Howkins
Alex Izzard	N.G.U.Boys Champion 2000
Tony Lord	N.G.U. Past County Captain
Jon Lloyd	Northampton G.C. Junior Organiser 2000-2008
Angus McLeod	Angus and Dorothy McLeod
George Phillpott	George Phillpott
David Price	Past President L.U.G.C.
Nigel Robinson	Gray Cup Winner 2007
Robin Seabrook	Robin and Anne Seabrook
David Sharpe	David Sharpe
Jeremy Smith	JEZ Head Greenkeeper Rushden Golf Club
Adam Stevens	Tony's son
Shirley Suter	Sister of the author
Mike Taylor	N.G.U. Past President
Martin Thatcher	Martin of Duston Soutar Cup winner 1983
John Tickell	W.U.G.C Past President
Sam Wade	Sam Wade
Lewis White	N.G.C. Club Champion 2007 & 2008

Northamptonshire
Golf Courses in 2008

Pri

Pytchley Lodge

R.Wel

Stoke Albany

Cold Ashby

Overstone Park

R.Avon

Northants County
Northampton

Daventry

Daventry

Staverton Park

R.Nene

Northampton

Hellidon Lakes

R.Tove

Farthingstone

R.Cherwell

Toucester

Cherwell Edge

R.

Banbury

R.Ouse

R.Cherwell

Brackley

V

Silverstone

Brampton Heath